THE TRUTH
SHOWS UP

THE TRUTH
SHOWS UP

a reporter's fifteen-year odyssey
tracking down the truth about Mulroney,
Schreiber and the Airbus scandal

HARVEY CASHORE

KEY PORTER BOOKS

Library and Archives Canada Cataloguing in Publication

Cashore, Harvey
The truth shows up : a reporter's fifteen-year odyssey tracking down the truth about Mulroney, Schreiber and the Airbus scandal / Harvey Cashore.

ISBN 978-1-55470-192-6

1. Cashore, Harvey. 2. Mulroney, Brian, 1939-. 3. Schreiber, Karlheinz.
4. Investigative reporting--Canada. 5. Corruption investigation--Canada.
6. Political corruption--Canada. 7. Airbus aircraft. I. Title.

FC630.C395 2010   971.064'7   C2009-905837-5

ONTARIO ARTS COUNCIL
CONSEIL DES ARTS DE L'ONTARIO

The publisher gratefully acknowledges the support of the Canada Council for the Arts and the Ontario Arts Council for its publishing program. We acknowledge the support of the Government of Ontario through the Ontario Media Development Corporation's Ontario Book Initiative.

We acknowledge the financial support of the Government of Canada through the Book Publishing Industry Development Program (BPIDP) for our publishing activities.

Key Porter Books Limited
Six Adelaide Street East, Tenth Floor
Toronto, Ontario
Canada M5C 1H6

www.keyporter.com

Text design and electronic formatting: Marijke Friesen

Printed and bound in Canada

10 11 12 13 14 5 4 3 2 1

For my children
Massey, Jeremiah and Madison

CONTENTS

PART III
RUPTURE

PART IV
THE TRUTH SHOWS UP

Note to Readers

Up until 1998 German law allowed businessmen to pay "greasemoney" to foreigners to help facilitate the sale of products to other countries. The tax authorities called those payments *schmiergelder* which could lawfully be claimed as tax deductions. Yet as legal as those payments were in Germany, they were not necessarily legal in foreign countries. As a result, middlemen like Karlheinz Schreiber would set up secret offshore bank accounts in order to hide the money trail. This way, they believed, every payment would remain anonymous. No one would ever know who received the money. At least that was the idea. This is a story about one of those secret money trails.

"Sooner or later the truth shows up,
whether you like it or not, you have just to wait."
—Karlheinz Schreiber, 2005

Prologue

It is the winter of 2005 and I am in old Montreal about to meet Luc Lavoie, Brian Mulroney's friend and public spokesperson, at his elite men's club, known only by its address, 357C. We haven't seen each other for several years, but I have some new information linking the former prime minister to secret-commission accounts in Switzerland. I've also heard that Mulroney filed incomplete tax returns and that he may have sought some kind of a statement from Schreiber in advance of possible legal proceedings.

A concierge escorts me into a small but elegant room with plush, high-backed chairs. Lavoie is already seated, smoking a cigarette. A couple sits at the next table; otherwise, the room is empty. Lavoie will try to find out what I know; I am trying to find out what Mulroney knows.

"Hi, Harvey, long time no see," he says. "Sit down. Have a drink."

Lavoie's hair is perfectly combed, parted on the left, greyer than I remember. He is considerably smaller than his boss but his voice is nearly as deep. He's now the VP of Quebecor, the Canadian media giant, and I get the sense this is going to be a long evening. He needs to unburden himself, and I think I know why.

Six years before, he told me that he believed Schreiber was the "biggest fucking liar the world has ever seen." We broadcast that clip on *the fifth estate* back in the fall of 1999 and it changed everything. It was the beginning of the disintegration of the friendship between Mulroney and Karlheinz Schreiber: their secrets, once a sacred trust, weren't so sacred anymore.

And so now, despite the decorum of the club, the Scotch and the intimate atmosphere, Luc Lavoie spoke his mind.

Well known by all for his salty language, he bluntly let me know that he was unhappy with our broadcast. He called the airing of that quote the worst day of his life. I could understand why, but wasn't entirely clear why it was my fault.

"I'm from Rimouski," he cracked. "In Rimouski we don't settle disputes like this," he said. "We settle them in the back alley." Then he said something about wishing we lived years ago when there weren't any laws about beating people up.

I laughed. A moment passed. He told me he knew about my brother and my father. "What's your point, Luc?" I asked.

I would find out soon enough.

PART I
INVESTIGATION

CHAPTER ONE
GREASEMONEY

I was long overdue for a good story.

By the late summer of 1994 I had been an associate producer at CBC's premier investigative program, *the fifth estate*, for nearly three years. And yet for the past twelve months I had had a string of bad luck. Few of my story ideas had panned out. For example, I had spent months researching allegations about a Toronto-area man, Ahmed Said Khadr, who may have been involved in terrorist activities while working for a Canadian charity in Peshawar, a city in Pakistan at the edge of the Khyber Pass near the Afghan border. I made dozens of calls, typed up hundreds of pages of notes, but failed to get enough evidence to state conclusively what the real story was. I had to move on. My next research project was an investigation into how some American mothers were giving up their babies for adoption in Canada without the children's fathers' permission. That story, too, dead-ended.

I had wasted months of work with nothing to show for it. In the mid-1990s, the CBC did not really offer any new employees full-time staff positions; most of us at *the fifth estate* were on year-to-year contracts. I doubted my contract was going to be renewed, and I could see why: What's the point of an associate producer who hardly ever got anything to air?

Then, perhaps wondering what to do with me, my bosses asked me to help out on another story, already well under way. The story was about the sale of Canadian-made Dash 8 airplanes to the Bahamas. The rest of the team had flown to Nassau to interview government officials there about questionable side payments to relatives of cabinet ministers. I had the pleasure of making phone calls from my office.

My job was straightforward.

Seattle-based Boeing Company owned the Canadian subsidiary that produced the Dash 8s and I needed to find out if the giant American aircraft manufacturer paid bribes in the Bahamas in order to secure the sale. I knew that Boeing beat out other manufacturers when it won the Bahamasair contract, so I figured a good place to start would be with the losing bidders. If Boeing was asked to pay bribes, maybe they were also asked. And maybe they would talk about it, given that they had lost business. At least that was my thinking.

My hunch paid off, and in ways that I would never have predicted.

On September 14, 1994, I made a phone call that helped confirm the Bahamasair bribe allegations, but more significantly, steered me towards another story that would occupy me, in one way or another, for the next fifteen years. Without knowing it, I was making my first phone call on the Airbus story.

The phone call was actually to a sales agent for the Dutch aircraft manufacture Fokker. The agent had tried to sell Fokker aircraft to the Bahamas and admitted to me that, yes, government officials there had told him "in a subtle way" that bribes might be "required" if they hoped to win the contract. Perhaps it was a sign of my naïveté at the time that I was more surprised about what the sales agent said next. Fokker had not refused to pay the bribes because of any legal concerns. It was business, pure and simple. They would not have made any money on the transaction once they had factored in the cost of the kickbacks. "Once we came close to their price," he told me, "to subtract out of there any kickbacks, we would be left with a net loss on each airplane delivered. So we couldn't do that kind of thing."

Still, the Fokker sales agent wondered why I was interested in such a bush-league bribe story. He told me about a far bigger story he had recently heard involving Air Canada and Airbus Industrie, the European aircraft manufacturer challenging Boeing for supremacy in the worldwide market. He had heard Airbus had paid secret commissions in order to secure the sale of thirty-four A320 jets to the Canadian Crown corporation back in 1988. In fact, he told me that he heard the story directly from a former Airbus employee.

It was "accepted practice," he said, sounding angry, "that aircraft manufacturers paid kickbacks in certain parts of the world." But never in North America. At least that's how he explained it.

"It was kept hush-hush" he told me. "It was kind of a little game outside of North America. Had to be kept to a minimum obviously and of course away from the public's eye. But in some cases you just don't win orders unless you do that."

A little game outside of North America. That was the unwritten code: all airline manufacturers paid bribes, they had to, but North America was off limits. Everyone agreed to play by the rules. Until, he told me, Airbus Industrie came along and threw out the rulebook.

Or at least that was the allegation.

He went on to say, "I was told by a disgruntled ex–Airbus employee that it is certainly not beneath Airbus, even at carriers like Air Canada, to make things happen."

I affected a casual tone, in response to his comments, but I was giddy over the story's potential. Nonchalantly, I asked for the name of the ex–Airbus employee. The sales agent said he would think about it and call me back.

I hung up the phone. Now what? This is what one sales agent had alleged, anyway, I mused. I still had a lot of work to do to verify if it was true or not.

I walked down the hall to senior producer Susan Teskey's office. I told her about the conversation with the source at Fokker, and what he had said about Airbus and Air Canada.

"Close the door," she said. "You and Jock are onto the same story."

Jock was Jock Ferguson, the seasoned investigative reporter from the *Globe and Mail* who had recently become a freelancer, having brought the Dash 8 story to *the fifth estate.*

In fact, that same day Jock Ferguson had received a fax from Mathias Müller von Blumencron, a reporter for *Der Spiegel* in Hamburg, Germany;

von Blumencron was a rising star at the magazine. Legendary German journalist Hans Leyendecker, von Blumencron's colleague, had given him Jock Ferguson's name. *Spiegel* had received documents about a shady businessman named Karlheinz Schreiber who had had dealings in both Germany and Canada. They wanted to work with Ferguson to advance the story. "We have documents," wrote Blumencron, "that a certain Mr. Karlheinz Schreiber got high commissions from Airbus Industrie, the German helicopter producer Messerschmitt-Bolkow-Blohm (MBB) and Thyssen Industrie to push some deals with Canadian companies and the Canadian government. Our source told us that a big part of the commission was paid to 'political friends.'" Blumencron emphasized the need to be careful for now. "I take your word that you keep the full content of this letter confidential."

The next day, Ferguson had updated Teskey on the status of his investigative projects. On his way out, he mentioned the Airbus story, but said it would probably be a better print story, and that he was on his way to one of the Toronto newspapers to make the pitch.

It was like a bell went off. Teskey raised her eyebrows at him. "Come back here." The six-foot-two-inch Ferguson towered over Teskey, but size didn't matter. Her growl could frighten off a grizzly. She grabbed him by the shoulder and hauled him back into her office.

The fifth estate got the Airbus story.

Jock Ferguson filled me in on his conversations with *Der Spiegel*. They claimed they had documents that showed that Airbus Industrie had signed a secret agreement with a shell company in the Principality of Liechtenstein after Air Canada purchased thirty-four Airbus A320s in 1988. There was more: an accountant in southern Switzerland, Giorgio Pelossi, claimed to have all kinds of evidence. Pelossi had worked with Schreiber on Canadian business deals and alleged that Schreiber might have paid "useful expenses," also known as "greasemoney," to Canadian "decision-makers" in order to secure sales of European products. Pelossi also said Schreiber had worked with former Newfoundland premier Frank Moores. Why was Pelossi talking? It seemed he'd had some kind of falling-out with Schreiber and now wanted to talk to the media, albeit in secret.

I was suddenly embarrassed about my little scoop—my source knew *someone*, whose name I did not know, who *might* know *something, maybe*. Giorgio Pelossi, however, was a *real* name.

It wasn't long before Jock and I were on the phone to Germany, speaking with *Der Spiegel* reporter Mathias Müller von Blumencron. Von Blumencron was a thirty-four-year-old lawyer by profession who'd discovered somewhere along the way that he preferred journalism to law. Jock and I immediately liked him. The three of us agreed that we would work co-operatively, compare notes and try to advance the story as far as we could. I would work on the story full-time, Jock would work part-time as a free-lancer and Mathias would work full-time for *Der Spiegel*. From *the fifth estate*'s point of view, investigative stories like this one had two basic components: the research phase, in which we determine if there *is* a story; and the production phase, in which we produce the documentary. Producing a documentary meant bringing on board a host who would tell the story to the viewers, a producer who would direct the shoot and structure the story, a cameraperson and sound recordist who would film and record the interviews and the scenes for the documentary, and then an editor who would sit with the producer in a dark edit suite for days on end and assemble all the footage. But all that was a long way off. As the associate producer assigned to the story, I'd have to convince executive producer David Studer that this was a story worth telling. And at this point, I wasn't sure.

Von Blumencron told us that, so far, he had only spoken with Pelossi on the phone, but would soon be on his way to Lugano, Switzerland, where he lived, to meet him in person. We wanted to know more about Pelossi; it still seemed incredible to all of us that a Swiss accountant, whose job it was to hide other people's money, would want to speak openly about a former business partner.

For the time being I still had to finish my work on the Boeing bribery story. I interviewed dozens of people and realized later on that this was the perfect warm-up story to the Airbus investigation. I learned a lot about the airline industry in general and how it worked. Our Bahamasair story— "The Deal that Couldn't Fly Straight"—was broadcast in mid-October. Now I had time to explore the Airbus allegations. I called back the Fokker agent and convinced him to give me the name of that disgruntled ex–Airbus employee. He did.

A few days later I flew to Washington, D.C., and drove to nearby Herndon, Virginia, the headquarters of Airbus Industrie. Former Airbus employee Gary Kincaid wanted to meet me in person. Kincaid was an American who had spent twenty years working for aerospace manufacturer McDonnell Douglas, first as an engineer, then in sales and marketing. Kincaid had joined the Airbus Industrie sales team in North America in 1987. He was one of dozens of Americans who had gone to work for Airbus after it launched an aggressive campaign in the eighties to sell planes in North America. Airbus—owned by the British, French, German and Spanish governments—had been having a hard time competing with aircraft manufacturing giant Boeing. Dozens of planes sat unsold on Airbus tarmac at its headquarters in Toulouse, France, while Boeing kept on winning order after order in North America. Kincaid explained that Airbus chairman Franz Josef Strauss had had enough; the future of the aircraft manufacturer was at stake. Accordingly, Airbus put in place a strategy to tackle the North American market.

The company's plan involved beefing up operations in North America, hiring a new staff, moving Airbus's North American offices from New York City to Herndon, a closer commute to the power centres in the Capitol.

Kincaid's job was selling planes to the now-defunct Canadian Airlines in western Canada. He was successful. But shortly thereafter Canadian Airline officials complained about "hidden costs" in the purchase agreement. Confused, Kincaid blamed the snafu on his bosses; his Airbus bosses blamed Kincaid. As a result, Kincaid left the company under a cloud in the early nineties.

Kincaid had some interesting insight into the Airbus sales campaign that few were supposed to know about. And possibly with an axe to grind, he was ready and willing to talk. "Much was different about the Air Canada sale as opposed to the normal business that we did in the United States," he said. "There was an awful lot of involvement from Toulouse." (Airbus employees routinely referred to their French headquarters and manufacturing hub as "Toulouse.") Kincaid told me that in the spring of 1988 rumours began to surface that "Toulouse" had paid secret commissions. He went on to say that rumours indicated that a "bagman" had been hired by Airbus to make secret payments to anonymous Canadians, but no one knew what to do about it. If the rumours were true, Toulouse was keeping Herndon in the dark. The US Foreign Corrupt Practices Act banned secret commissions. Kincaid said people at Airbus were beginning to panic. Anxious to source the rumours, Kincaid agreed to give me the name of a former executive to call.

By now I had forgotten about last season's dismal string of failures.

The Airbus story was exactly the reason that I went into journalism. It was a story squarely in the public interest as it involved a Crown corporation, taxpayer money, and more than a billion-dollar contract with a mysterious side agreement. I was convinced I could crack the story, separate fact from fiction, and find out what was really behind all those rumours. For the first time in a long time, I couldn't wait to come to work in the morning.

CHAPTER TWO
ALL THE PRIME MINISTER'S MEN

I first heard about the Airbus controversy while studying journalism at Carleton University back in the 1980s. In fact, one had only to read the newspapers to hear allegations, albeit vague and unsubstantiated, that Airbus was being overly aggressive in its efforts to sell planes to Air Canada. Most of the rumours circled around Frank Moores, the man credited with the behind-the-scenes campaign to bring Mulroney to power. Having followed Mulroney to Ottawa, Moores set up shop across the street from Parliament Hill as a lobbyist. He soon came under fire, however, for allegedly trading on his public sector connections.

"Frank is running an 'escort service,'" one competitor told the *Globe and Mail*. "He packs the client's bag, carries it through the right door, and then makes his case for him. Frankly, he's marketing his connections, and if it doesn't stop, this whole profession is going to be under a cloud."

In the House of Commons, rookie Newfoundland MP Brian Tobin had put it bluntly: "It's not what you know but who you know and how much you're prepared to pay that gets results," he charged.

Moores took the criticism all in stride. "I've never had so much fun in my life as in the consulting business," he told reporters.

It was a great time to be an aspiring investigative reporter. Being a journalism student in Ottawa meant I could pop down to Parliament Hill whenever I wanted. A small group of Opposition Liberals, including freshmen MPs Sheila Copps, Don Boudria and Brian Tobin, would become known as the Rat Pack for their relentless assault on Mulroney's new government and his numerous patronage appointments to party faithful. I would sometimes watch those heated exchanges from the public gallery and feel like I was watching the greatest sporting event on earth. I couldn't get enough.

Mulroney's most controversial patronage appointments came in March 1985 when his government fired the entire board of directors of Air Canada and replaced them with Tory loyalists. The list of Conservative appointees included a few of Mulroney's personal friends, like Fernand Roberge, the manager of the Ritz-Carlton Hotel in Montreal, and David Angus, a Montreal lawyer who was also chairman of the PC party's fundraising arm. Frank Moores was also on the list. A few months later, Moores was forced to quit amid rumours, which he strenuously denied, that as an Air Canada director he was working on behalf of Airbus.

Frank Moores was the highest-profile member of the lobbying firm Government Consultants International (GCI), but there were others on the team with equally impressive Tory credentials; for example, Gerald Doucet, a Nova Scotia lawyer and brother of Fred Doucet, Mulroney's chief of staff; and Gary Ouellet, a key Quebec organizer who had briefly been chief of staff to the junior transport minister, Benoît Bouchard. Ouellet had also worked on Mulroney's 1983 leadership campaign. In 1984, Mulroney's government gave Ouellet a coveted Queen's Counsel designation, which meant he could put the initials QC after his name.

Gerry Doucet and Gary Ouellet—like Moores—vehemently denied they had ever lobbied for Airbus.

Still, the rumours persisted, once even engulfing the Prime Minister's Office (PMO).

In July 1985, *Globe and Mail* reporter Michael Harris quoted a former Liberal lobbyist alleging that the PMO itself had directed the Quebec-based company Bombardier to hire Moores's firm, Government Consultants

International. "Executives of [Bombardier] told me they were advised by the PMO to fire me and hire GCI," Don Mitchell told the newspaper. It was also alleged that Bombardier might have a reason to want Airbus to win the Air Canada contract—it stood to win tens of millions of dollars in sub-contracts from the European aircraft manufacturer as a quid pro quo. While the fired lobbyist Don Mitchell clearly had his own agenda, he would continue to speak out, later fingering Fred Doucet as the PMO official who told Bombardier to hire GCI.

Watching the political controversies play out in Ottawa was an eye-opener. It seemed as if a new scandal erupted every month.

At the time I was involved in an investigative journalism class taught by John Sawatsky. Formerly the *Vancouver Sun*'s Ottawa correspondent, he had become famous for his investigative books on the RCMP Security Service. He too had noticed the controversy surrounding the lobbying industry in Ottawa, and decided to pursue the topic for his next book. After I left Carleton in 1986, I joined Sawatsky as his researcher, first helping finish the book on lobbyists then assisting on his next ambitious project: a biography of Brian Mulroney's rise to power.

While working for Sawatsky, the Airbus scandal erupted again on the floor of the House of Commons. By spring 1988, everyone knew that Air Canada was close to making its decision—whether to choose the Boeing 727s or the Airbus A320s—and once again rumours surfaced that Moores and his firm, GCI, were involved in manipulating the decision behind the scenes.

Brian Tobin, the fiery Rat Pack MP, led the charge. On March 14, he issued a challenge to fellow Newfoundlander John Crosbie, the Conservative transport minister: "Is the minister prepared to make available to the House a list of all contacts and representations that have been made to the minister or to any official of Transport Canada by GCI owned by his good friend Frank Moores who he claims to know nothing about?"

"And I have to ask my honourable friend, is there no smear too low?" Crosbie shot back.

"This is a $1.5 billion contract we are talking about and the people of Canada have a right to have questions asked and answers given by a Minister without bluster or false outrage!" Tobin answered.

The next day, Tobin demanded to know why Air Canada had *suddenly* decided to keep its older DC-9s. Instead—and inexplicably, he suggested—it had opted in its wisdom to replace its newer 727s. Was it a coincidence, he wanted to know, that this was precisely the model for which Airbus had a suitable replacement?

"What kind of machinations are going on behind the scenes?" Tobin bellowed.

Crosbie had heard enough. "I would like to know whether the honourable member is making a charge against Air Canada's management with respect to its competency or its honesty or whatever. The honourable member is insinuating he is trying to set an innuendo—as he did yesterday—and he is being thoroughly unscrupulous in his approach."

Again, GCI denied all. "We don't act for Airbus, we have not been retained by Airbus, we have not lobbied for Airbus," Gary Ouellet told *Toronto Star* reporter Linda Diebel. "There is no dire plot to lobby anyone." Diebel later reported that James Baker, the US Treasury secretary, had personally raised the Airbus allegations with Mulroney. Crosbie had looked into the concerns, but having contacted Air Canada about the allegations, stated that he'd found nothing untoward.

The controversy seemed to go away. The election of summer 1988 was coming up and Canadians turned their attention to the proposed North America Free Trade Agreement (NAFTA). The Liberals and the New Democratic Party (NDP) were against it; Mulroney's Conservatives were for it. On election night, November 21, the Conservatives received 43 per cent of the popular vote to the Liberals' 32 per cent and the NDP's 20 per cent. Mulroney won another majority government.

I was relieved that Mulroney had returned to power. Sawatsky and I had already spent a year working on his (unauthorized) biography. We knew the story would be more interesting if Mulroney was still prime minister. A book about a defeated, one-term leader would sell less than one about a prime minister who had won two historic majorities. In the next few years I continued to work with Sawatsky, interviewing Mulroney's old friends from university, law and business. I helped Sawatsky piece together a chronology of Mulroney's life as he rose from the best debater at St. Francis Xavier University in Antigonish, Nova Scotia, to law school graduate in Quebec City, to up-and-coming labour lawyer in Montreal, to president of the Iron Ore Company of Canada, and eventually to his successful bid to become leader of the Progressive Conservative Party.

The two most significant things I learned about Mulroney were: a) his remarkable networking skills helped propel his rise to the top in business and politics; and b) he was so concerned about the mistakes or failures in his life, even minor ones, that he was not above fudging facts in order to make himself look better. A case in point: Mulroney had told his official biographer that, as a young law student, he had transferred from Dalhousie Law School to the University of Laval's law school. When I went through the chronology of those years, I realized that Mulroney had spent one more year studying law than most students. I did some more digging and ended up obtaining Mulroney's first-year marks at Dalhousie. It turned out he didn't "transfer" to Laval at all; he failed his first year of law school. (He received a 65 in Criminal Law, a 60 in Contracts, a 42 in Torts and as for the rest, Property I, Procedure I and Research and Writing, they were all incomplete.) What Mulroney had not understood, I think, is that had he told the truth about failing his first year, no one would have faulted him for it. In fact, people may have admired his ability to come back from such a setback.

In the meantime, as Sawatsky and I continued to research the Mulroney biography, the Airbus story simmered on the backburner. Once in a while reporters would dig around the lobby industry, in particular, *Ottawa Citizen* reporter Stevie Cameron. In 1989, she introduced readers to a man named Karlheinz Schreiber. She described him as being behind a controversial plan to set up a tank-producing facility in Cape Breton, Nova Scotia, in conjunction with German arms manufacturer Thyssen Industrie. The project, Cameron wrote in the *Citizen*, had been of concern to the Jewish community for years. They worried that the equipment might end up in the Middle East. "Mr. Schreiber has extensive business interests in Alberta and Germany, and in 1980 he set up an investment company in Alberta for the late premier of Bavaria, Franz Josef Strauss," Cameron wrote. "Sources say Mr. Schreiber has also been a business colleague of Mr. Moores."

In early 1991, Sawatsky's biography, *Mulroney: The Politics of Ambition*, was finally published. I had spent nearly four years on the project and had loved every minute. I had gained valuable experience about how to conduct investigative research. My work on the project had finished in mid-1990, which meant I was out of a job. I tried to get hired as a newspaper reporter but every major daily in the country turned me down. One managing editor told me I needed more experience. (I had mistakenly believed that my work for Sawatsky would have given me the experience they wanted.) Depressed about my future and not sure what to do, I applied to Carleton University to do a master's in Journalism. They too turned me down. Then, in the summer of 1991, I got a letter from the Canadian Broadcasting Corporation. They wanted me to apply for a summer job at *The Journal*, Canada's then most popular weekly newsmagazine. I got the job and then, later that year, *the fifth estate* hired me as a researcher.

I was happy to leave Mulroney behind. I had spent years looking at his life and told myself it was time to move on. And I did. In my first year at CBC, I researched a story about how the RCMP had accused the wrong man of being a KGB mole, another story about ambulance wars in Cape Breton, and another about all the Tories who landed jobs in the civil service after they lost power.

Then in early 1994, the Airbus allegations were making a bit of a comeback.

In the spring, journalist Paul Palango, in *Above the Law*, his book about the RCMP, alleged that Frank Moores's firm GCI had received $5 million in commissions on the Airbus sale. In the fall of 1994, Stevie Cameron's *On The Take* repeated allegations that GCI had received millions on the sale. Again, Moores denied it. "I read that stuff and I wish it were true," he told her.[1] Cameron wrote more about Karlheinz Schreiber, detailing his friendships with Frank Moores, Fred Doucet and the Bavarian premier and chairman of Airbus, Franz Josef Strauss.

So when I spoke to the Fokker agent in late summer 1994, his allegations did not come out of the blue. By providing me the name of the Airbus salesman, he took the allegations a step further. The biggest

1   See page 387, *On The Take*, Stevie Cameron.

development, however, was the revelation that Schreiber's accountant, Giorgio Pelossi, was willing to talk.

In early September 1994, Pelossi agreed to give his first-ever media interview, to *Der Spiegel*'s reporter, Mathias Müller von Blumencron.

CHAPTER THREE
THE PELOSSI PROBLEM

Giorgio Pelossi was nothing like what von Blumencron expected. He wore large glasses, had greying hair, and when he spoke never raised his voice, sounding oddly like Kermit the Frog. He would always cheerfully answer his phone "Pronto" and didn't look or act like a man who was betraying a former friend or someone making criminal allegations about politicians, bureaucrats and businessman in both Germany and Canada. He looked harmless. He was impossible to dislike and, it seemed, impossible to offend, no matter how tough the questions. A colleague of mine would later remark, "If you spat in his face he would call it rain."

Even the setting seemed incongruous. Lugano, one of the most expensive cities in Europe, was dubbed "the Monte Carlo of Switzerland." Tucked cosily in the Swiss Alps, on the edge of a stunning lake in the Ticino district, it was 50 kilometres north of Milan.

As an accountant in Switzerland, his real job was to hide money, set up shell companies[1] in offshore havens, in order to prevent outsiders from knowing where money was coming from and where it was going. In short,

---

1 A "shell company" is a business or corporation set up on paper but without any purpose other than to transfer money from one place to another. It has no products and no employees, other than a trustee and possibly a secretary.

29

if you needed to keep the authorities away from your secret stash of money, Pelossi was your guy. You would want to be careful to avoid a confrontation with him, however, as his partner, Karlheinz Schreiber, was about to find out.

Blumencron was a little wary; Pelossi had made it clear from the outset that he did not have access to Schreiber's Swiss banking corporation records: the final depository of the millions of dollars in secret commissions from Airbus Industrie and two other German companies, MBB Helicopter and Thyssen Industrie. It had been Pelossi's job to oversee the transfer of money from the three companies as it went into the shell company International Aircraft Leasing (IAL) in Liechtenstein, then to another shell company called Kensington Anstalt, and from there transfer it yet again to 18679 IAL, Schreiber's account in Zurich, Switzerland.

Pelossi had told Blumencron stories about cash payments to German officials and, on the Canadian side, said he had personally helped Frank Moores set up two accounts in Zurich to hold the proceeds of the Canadian funds for "Canadian friends." Jock Ferguson and I made plans to interview Pelossi in greater depth about the Canadian side of the story. In the meantime, Blumencron promised to send us dozens of pages of documents that Pelossi had given him during his meeting in Lugano.

The documents included secret contracts and agreements between the three companies (Airbus, MBB and Thyssen) and IAL, dozens of bank drafts, records of Liechtenstein numbered bank accounts, complete with the transfers in and out, as well as correspondence between Pelossi and executives at the three companies. One piece of correspondence noted that there would be only one signed copy of the Airbus contract and that it was to be held at a law firm in Zurich, Homburger, Ackermann, Müller und Heini, represented by a Mr. Kurer. The documents noted that a Denis Viard signed on behalf of Airbus. Giorgio Pelossi signed for International Aircraft Leasing. Still, with the only signed copy kept safely at the law office, Airbus apparently felt protected. This way, Pelossi had told Blumencron, if any copies ever did leak out, Airbus would simply ask if the document was signed. It wouldn't have been, and the allegations would vanish.

Without a doubt the Holy Grail of contracts was the one between Airbus Industrie and International Aircraft Leasing, dated March 13, 1985, exactly five days after the Mulroney government appointed Frank Moores to the board of Air Canada. The contract stated the deal would be terminated "automatically" if there was a major political change in Canada. In other words, if Mulroney was no longer in power, the agreement was null and void. The contract contained specific conditions. International Aircraft Leasing would only be paid if it was responsible for making the sale happen. Pelossi's file also contained numerous pieces of correspondence between Schreiber, IAL and a man named Stuart Iddles, the then vice-president of Airbus.

One document, dated June 28, 1989, confirmed that Airbus had made a down payment of $5 million to IAL but only after Air Canada itself made its first "predelivery" payment to Airbus in 1988. The thirty-four Airbus planes were manufactured in stages, so the remainder of the secret commissions would also come in stages *after* Air Canada paid for the planes as they arrived in Montreal from Europe. What this meant was that every time Air Canada wrote a cheque to Airbus to pay for another A320 delivery, Airbus took some of that money, about $500,000 per plane, and sent it to the shell company, IAL in Liechtenstein.

It was Jock Ferguson's turn to visit Giorgio Pelossi. He flew to Zurich from Toronto on October 30, 1994, then boarded a train that snaked its way south through the Swiss Alps. Three and a half hours later he arrived at the Lugano train station, perched high above the town, just north of the Italian border. Jock saw Pelossi, smiling broadly, as if greeting a tourist.

They drove zigzagging down the mountain, then through the city's busy streets, cars honking, scooters whizzing by, going as far south as they could to the lake, passing by a boardwalk and a park where children ate ice cream and seniors played chess, the pawns as big as garden gnomes, on the sidewalk. They chatted informally over dinner (Pelossi's mother tongue is Italian; he also speaks German and English) then met the next day at Giorgio Pelossi's office.

Pelossi was still insisting that he could not be named as a source. There were strict rules in Switzerland that prevented accountants from talking about their clients' business. We began referring to Pelossi as "Mr. P," which, we realized, sounded comically close to Mr. T, the bling-clad TV star from the eighties. Jock spoke into his tape recorder: "Monday, October thirty-first in Lugano, Switzerland, in the offices of Mr. P, as he will be known on this tape, and we are going to start our discussion about Karlheinz Schreiber." Ferguson wanted to get straight to the point—what did Pelossi know about all those secret commissions—but first he'd need some context. You just don't suddenly end up as the Swiss accountant for a German-Canadian businessman who hides more than $20 million in greasemoney, or *schmiergelder*. There's always a story, and we wanted to know his.

The conversation jumped from topic to topic, first a bit about Alberta, then about Franz Josef Strauss, then about Airbus, then back to Alberta, then back to Schreiber himself. Pelossi tended to speak in one-sentence answers. He came across as being careful, clearly outlining the difference between what he knew and what he had heard.

When Pelossi told Ferguson the story of how he and Schreiber first met, a quarter of a century before, it was as if, for a brief moment, he seemed to forget they were now bitter enemies. According to Pelossi, their introduction happened like this: It was back in 1969 and Schreiber, an aspiring businessman from Germany, was involved in a road-marking company called Unilite. Unilite happened to have a subsidiary in Lugano, where Pelossi worked as an aspiring Swiss accountant. At one point Unilite's Lugano subsidiary sustained some losses. Schreiber's associates in Germany didn't believe the losses actually occurred, and accused Schreiber and/or some Lugano investors of siphoning money from the company. Those allegations led one of the Lugano investors to ask Giorgio Pelossi for a neutral review the company's books. Pelossi obliged. His report concluded there was no malfeasance, and the Lugano associates and Karlheinz Schreiber breathed a sigh of relief.

"He was happy with my work," Pelossi said, "and since that moment, I worked for him on all his foreign companies and foreign investment."

Schreiber, who started his business career as a carpet salesman, with no formal education, would soon become an international wheeler-dealer. Pelossi, his accountant, was frequently at his side. Their activities took them to Central America where, in Costa Rica, Schreiber, surprisingly, obtained a diplomatic passport from President Alberto Monge. From there they travelled to Panama, setting up shell companies to hide more of their business dealings, and then on to Nicaragua where they tried to set up a deal to sell coffee. Schreiber would also fly to Thailand, where he would be involved in another secret side deal to sell Airbus to state-owned Thai Airways.

Pelossi seemed happiest talking about their Canadian adventures. He described how he and Schreiber first arrived in Canada in November 1974 with a delegation from Schreiber's road-marking company. Ten days, four cities: Toronto, Regina, Calgary and Edmonton. They liked Alberta the most, where they became friendly with provincial cabinet minister Horst Schmidt, who, like Schreiber, was from Bavaria. Pelossi and Schreiber would return to Alberta several times. They rented a motorhome and laughed around the campfire as Schreiber played his accordion. Sometimes Max Strauss, Franz Joseph Strauss's youngest son, tagged along on the visits. Schreiber was happy to take Max under his wing and taught him the ropes of doing business in Canada and other countries.

Eventually Schreiber and Pelossi set up a road-marking business in Alberta, Maple Leaf Enterprises (MLE). The Canadian MLE was patterned after Schreiber's German company, Bitumen, which owed its success in large part to Schreiber's political connections, none better than Bavarian premier Franz Josef Strauss. Schreiber didn't see why they couldn't use the same business model in Alberta. That meant getting to know the bureaucrats and politicians.

Pelossi told Ferguson how Schreiber had arranged a $150,000 loan for a sitting Alberta cabinet minister, Dr. Hugh Horner, which was never paid back. "I think [Schreiber] hoped to get some help from his road marking," said Pelossi. Road marking was just one of their Canadian ventures. In 1977 they tried, but failed, to sell Airbus planes in western Canada. They also got into real estate speculation in Alberta, along with the Strauss family and wealthy Europeans like Daimler-Benz heiress Barbara Flick. Still, the real estate ventures failed miserably during the 1982 recession as land values plummeted. Everyone lost money.

When Mulroney came to power in 1984, explained Pelossi, their fortunes turned around.

Pelossi told Ferguson that Schreiber and he were involved in three principal deals in Canada: the sale of Airbus jets to Air Canada, the sale of MBB helicopters to the Canadian Coast Guard, and efforts to establish a light armoured vehicle (LAV) factory in Cape Breton, known as the Bear Head project.

Pelossi's involvement in those deals was completely in the background. His job was to set up the infrastructure in which large sums of money could flow secretly into accounts in Europe and eventually make their way into the hands of various "anonymous" recipients. More than anything, Pelossi had to make sure that the money was untraceable.

The task had seven basic steps:

Step One. Set up a shell company in Liechtenstein.

Pelossi needed to create a paper company with which European manufacturers could do business. He decided to use an "off-the-shelf" company he had already set up called International Aircraft Leasing. The Canadian deals had nothing to do with leasing aircraft at all; the name had come from a previous attempt to lease helicopters to the Mexican government. When that venture failed, Pelossi simply used the same shell company for the Canadian deals.

Step Two. Establish agreements between the shell company and European manufacturers.

Two of the European companies, MBB and Airbus, would sign agreements with IAL, and its only named executive, Giorgio Pelossi. Airbus executive Denis Viard signed the Airbus agreement with IAL on March 7, 1985, and MBB Helicopter vice-president Kurt Pfleiderer signed their agreement with IAL on March 28, 1985. The agreements called for IAL to receive a percentage of the amount that the Canadian government would spend on the products. The Thyssen Industrie agreement was a little different, since there were no products for which Schreiber would receive commissions. On October 21, 1985, Winfried Haastert, a Thyssen executive, wrote Schreiber a letter directly mentioning its agreement with IAL Liechtenstein and agreeing to pay a "one-time fee" of $4 million Canadian if certain conditions were met.

Step Three: Set up bank accounts for Liechtenstein shell companies.

Pelossi set up bank accounts in Liechtenstein at the VPB Bank in Vaduz,

Liechtenstein, which, at the designated time, would receive the secret commissions. Liechtenstein has strict bank secrecy laws, even stricter than those in Switzerland, and there would be very little chance of other countries getting access to them if there were ever any questions.

Step Four: For good measure, send funds to a second *shell company in Liechtenstein.*

Pelossi said they decided to build another layer of secrecy into the transactions. They used yet another domicile company in Liechtenstein called Kensington Anstalt, which Schreiber had set up in the 1970s to be used in various business projects (Pelossi took over as Kensington's trustee in 1976). Once IAL received the secret commissions he would then transfer the money to Kensington. This way, if any outside authority ever got permission to look at IAL's bank accounts, which would probably never happen anyway, they would have to start all over again after realizing the money had been transferred to yet another company's bank account in Liechtenstein. The process would take years.

Step Five: Send the secret commissions from the second shell company in Liechtenstein to Switzerland.

Once the secret commissions passed through two shell companies in Liechtenstein, Pelossi would transfer the money to the Swiss Bank Corporation in Zurich where Schreiber had set up an account, "18679 IAL." By this time the money would have dodged in and out of two shell companies, three countries and four bank accounts. The money trail would be virtually impossible to trace.

Step Six: Have a middleman disperse the money.

Pelossi would not actually be the one to disperse the secret commissions. That responsibility would rest with Karlheinz Schreiber, who would set up a myriad of sub-accounts at the Swiss Bank Corporation to organize the funds. From there many (but not all) of the withdrawals would be made in cash. All of this meant that only two people in a particular transaction would know who got money: Schreiber, of course, and the recipient. Even Pelossi did not know the final resting place of the money, meaning the recipient could feel secure knowing that only one person— Schreiber—would know who had received the money.

Step Seven: Help the Canadians set up Swiss bank accounts.

Schreiber and Pelossi knew that it would be better for the Canadians if they also opened up Swiss accounts to hold their share of the secret commissions; this way, the Canadians would not have to bring the money back to Canada where the taxman might find it. It was this last step that Pelossi described in great detail for Jock Ferguson.

Pelossi said that Schreiber asked him to travel to Zurich on Tuesday, February 4, 1986. He met Schreiber that morning. Schreiber told him that they were going to meet Frank Moores, the Ottawa lobbyist, and help him set up two Swiss accounts. Pelossi claimed that's when Schreiber told him exactly who was supposed to receive the greasemoney.

Half of the commissions would go to Europeans, to be divided up between Schreiber and others, and the other half were for "Canadian friends."

"What he told me, he has to pay 50 per cent to the Canadian friends," Pelossi said to Ferguson.

And that day they would help Moores open not just one, but two, "Canadian" accounts.

"What Schreiber told me is that one was for Moores and one for Brian," Pelossi said.

"Brian who?" Ferguson asked.

"Mulroney."

Later that morning, according to Pelossi, the three of them (Pelossi, Schreiber and Moores) entered the Swiss Bank Corporation. They were promptly ushered into a private office where they met a senior banking officer, Paul Schnyder. As Pelossi and Schreiber looked on, Moores set up two accounts, 34107 and 34117. In order to distinguish between the accounts, Moores added the name "Devon" next to the latter account. The entire process took less than half an hour.

After setting up the accounts, Pelossi said that he, Moores and Schreiber went to dinner. Moores told Pelossi all about the bad publicity in Ottawa over his Air Canada directorship, explaining he had to resign the position after word got out he was representing Airbus. Still, for Moores that was a fading memory. The evening was pleasant. Pelossi, Schreiber and Moores had carefully laid the groundwork for the secret commissions to begin to flow into the accounts. Moores flew back to Canada, Schreiber went back to Germany, and Pelossi returned to Lugano. All they had to do now was wait.

Later that year all the planning paid off. The Canadian Coast Guard signed a deal to purchase helicopters from MBB, and MBB, in turn, sent a percentage commission of the sale to Liechtenstein. On July 22, 1986, MBB Helicopter's vice-president, Kurt Pfleiderer, made it official. He wrote a letter to IAL in Liechtenstein confirming that the money from the Canadian Coast Guard deal was on its way, explaining that the total amount they would pay IAL would be $1,122,072 Canadian.

But then something happened, something so bizarre and so out of the blue that neither Schreiber nor Pelossi had planned for it: on September 11, 1986, Pelossi was arrested. The arrest had nothing to do with his "accounting" work for Schreiber. Too late they realized they had overlooked an obvious detail: What if something happened to *Pelossi*? Who would transfer the secret commissions from Liechtenstein to Schreiber's account in Zurich?[2]

They devised a simple, if somewhat unsatisfactory, solution: bypass the Liechtenstein diversion and, instead, request that MBB send the funds directly to Schreiber's Zurich account. On October 7, 1986, Schreiber's Zurich account received $641,283 in Canadian funds directly from MBB's accounts in Germany, exactly as had MBB had promised.

The transaction was risky. It meant that if anyone ever got access to Schreiber's accounts, one could see a direct link between MBB's *schmiergelder* and Schreiber. When Pelossi exited jail on March 11, 1987, the money route through Liechtenstein was reinstated. On December 28, 1987, Thyssen Industrie, the German arms manufacturer, sent $1.9 million Canadian to IAL. On October 5, 1988, IAL received its first payment of $5 million USD ($6,037,000 CAD) from Airbus Industrie. Twenty days later IAL received an additional $2 million from Thyssen Industrie for more "useful expenses." In 1990, the rest of the Airbus commissions starting coming in on the Air Canada deal, coinciding with the deliveries of individual Airbus planes to

---

2 Pelossi told us that he was suspected of working with a bank manager who had illegally moved some funds from one account to another. The impropriety had been discovered but only after the bank manager died. In Switzerland you can be jailed merely on "suspicion" and investigators believed Pelossi was involved. After six months Pelossi was released without ever being charged.

Air Canada. On February 2, 1990, for example, Airbus sent $366,000 USD ($435,027 CAD) to the IAL account in Liechtenstein; February 28, an additional $385,000 USD ($442,711 CAD); March 26, $387,000 USD ($448,803 CAD); December 7, 1990, $540,000 USD ($625,860 CAD). On and on it went. Pelossi produced records that proved IAL had received more than $10 million in *schmiergelder*. These were not suppositions or guesses, or vague allegations; these were carefully documented transactions for which he had credible and substantial proof. The money was rolling in and had far exceeded anything that Schreiber and Pelossi had ever been involved in before. And that was where it all began to go wrong.

After Ferguson returned to Toronto, we transcribed the audiotapes of his interviews with Pelossi. I sat down at my desk and read every word, paying close attention to Pelossi's description of his falling-out with Schreiber. The two men were now bitter enemies; that much was clear. Pelossi told Ferguson that he began to resent Schreiber after the millions of dollars from Airbus began flowing through the accounts; Pelossi believed Schreiber was not giving him a big enough percentage of the cut. He claimed Schreiber paid him only 100,000 Swiss francs for his part in the deals.

"He thought he [would] make me happy with one hundred thousand," Pelossi said. "He was dreaming." Pelossi eventually decided to take more of the Airbus, MBB and Thyssen money without telling Schreiber. Pelossi explained he simply arranged to transfer funds out of IAL and into another Liechtenstein shell company, Erfel Anstalt. He even drew up a contract stating that Erfel had performed services on the Airbus, Thyssen and MBB deals in Canada. Between August 1990 and May 1991, IAL made payments to Erfel Anstalt in the amount of $826,640 USD.

There was an obvious flaw in Pelossi's plan. Eventually Schreiber would realize that not all the secret commission money was coming into his Zurich account. Then the inevitable happened. In May 1991, Schreiber discovered that Pelossi was siphoning off Airbus money. Schreiber was so angry, Pelossi explained, that he immediately threatened to lay criminal charges. Pelossi insisted he was owed the money, relying on an old piece of scrap paper Schreiber had given to him years before, back when they were the best of friends and setting up their companies in Canada. On stationery from Western International Hotels, Schreiber had sketched a series of boxes with company names inside each. At the top of the chart was written "Kensington"—one of those Liechtenstein shell companies—and on the right, towards the bottom, Schreiber had added: "Giorgio becomes a millionaire for he gets 20% from everything." Schreiber dated it: "27. Nov. 1976, 14:40 EST." Amid more scribbles was a phrase that read, "Flight Calgary AC Toronto."

The sparring between the former friends and colleagues came to a head in December 1992 at a meeting in Giorgio Pelossi's lawyer's office in Zurich. On Schreiber's side of the table sat Harald Giebner, a Zurich lawyer, and Robert Hladun, his Canadian lawyer from Edmonton. Representing Pelossi was Hans Kopp. Pelossi would be demanding an additional $2 million, he announced. Otherwise, Kopp said, his client would be forced to sue Schreiber. Meaning all their dealings—all the secret contracts—would become public. Still, Schreiber refused to pay Pelossi a cent. "He was an idiot," Pelossi said. "An idiot. He had enough chances."

Two years dragged by, however, without resolution. Pelossi said he finally decided to go to the media and the police after Schreiber laid criminal charges against him in Liechtenstein. Worried about going to jail, Pelossi felt backed into a corner. Going public with accusations against Schreiber seemed to be his only way out.

Ferguson's interview had consumed almost three hours of cassette tape. The allegations were explosive and damning. Ferguson told Pelossi that if what he said was accurate, his former friend could end up in jail.

"For a long time," agreed Pelossi.

CHAPTER FOUR
SECRET SOURCES

If genuine, Giorgio Pelossi's documents proved that Airbus had entered into a clandestine arrangement with a shell company in Liechtenstein to sell Airbus aircraft in Canada. He had in his possession evidence of criminal activity, carefully laid out and meticulously documented. By the fall of 1994, the story had moved from the eighties-era realm of rumours to newsworthy story. How could Airbus deny the obvious? How could Frank Moores continue to deny it all? I could not help but think this was the kind of information that might lead to a public inquiry. I threw myself headlong into the story only to realize there had *already* been a public inquiry involving Schreiber in Canada.

Our librarian at *the fifth estate*, Diana Redegeld, made the discovery after I asked what she could find on Schreiber. To my surprise, she uncovered *Edmonton Journal* articles about some mysterious land flips in and around Edmonton. The Brennan Inquiry ended up ruling that there was no evidence that anyone used insider information, but added that the activities of one of Schreiber's companies—ABS Investments—was "suspicious."

Redegeld went further, getting me a transcript of Schreiber's testimony. As I read the transcript it seemed to me as if Schreiber almost enjoyed the experience. When asked by the commission's chief counsel about his connection to Alberta politicians, Schreiber readily admitted that Franz Josef

Strauss, premier of Bavaria, was supporting him in his efforts to do business in Canada. He made no apologies for hiring ex–cabinet ministers.

"We will have some more cabinet ministers in the near future from other provinces in Canada to where we have some other big financing projects," Schreiber said, in broken English. "And who should know—from the standpoint of investors, who should know better the law, how to handle governments, how to represent companies and investors over here than these people?

"I am straight conservative," he continued. "You can see the communists and the socialists doing a job I don't like too much. And as I choose Alberta as my future homeland, I have to do something about it and I will . . . These people [ex–cabinet ministers] should have a job. What should they do when they retire? Four years in cabinet and then hang around as peddlers?"

I was puzzled. How did Schreiber go from being a target of all that negative public attention in Alberta, to being a successful middleman in Ottawa during the Mulroney years? Didn't anyone in Ottawa know about the controversy Schreiber had left behind in Alberta? Wouldn't that have sent out a clear message to beware of the wheeler-dealer from Bavaria?

A short while later, I learned that *the fifth estate* had already looked into the Airbus story (though nothing had ever made it to air). Eric Malling, the legendary *fifth estate* host from the 1980s, who was now at our competition, CTV's *W5*, and Kit Melamed, an associate producer, had spent weeks in the fall of 1988 tracking down rumours that $75 million was paid out in Airbus kickbacks on the Air Canada sale. And even though they had left CBC to join our competitor, Melamed had left behind her Airbus files with CBC archives. When I opened the dusty box, I was tempted to call her, to thank her for the incredible groundwork on the story and to tell her that, given Pelossi's allegations, she *really* was onto something.

Melamed's files revealed that she had spoken to Airbus employees in Montreal who confirmed they'd discussed with Moores the prospect of selling planes to Air Canada. The files also contained notes of interviews with US diplomats deeply concerned about the allegations.

Eric Malling had typed up notes of an interview with Charley MacMillan, a former adviser to Mulroney in the Prime Minister's Office and later a director of Boeing Canada. "GCI [Government Consultants International] works on behalf of Airbus . . . Is there any doubt?" Malling quoted MacMillan. "There was a lot of lobbying in transport and [the] PMO [the Prime Minister's Office]. I heard things that were said. I heard that Gerry [Doucet] and Frank [Moores] were pushing pretty hard. I heard the odd cabinet minister mention it, it was the buzz around town . . ." Malling noted that MacMillan "seems legitimately perplexed that there should be any doubt about Moores' role."

There were notes of a conversation between Kit Melamed and Stuart Iddles, the Airbus vice-president: "He said that neither Moores nor CGI are under contract to Airbus; that they were not hired to represent Airbus."

In one of their memos, Melamed and Malling described a meeting with staffers from the Prime Minister's Office over "the fear" that Air Canada might choose Boeing. "In attendance . . . Moores . . . Lucien Bouchard, then Canadian ambassador in France and now secretary of state; Bernard Roy, then Mulroney's principal secretary, Fred Doucet, also from the PMO."

The fifth estate never gave the green light to the story back in 1988. Perhaps by beginning their research in 1988, Melamed and Malling had actually started too soon. The bulk of the secret commissions in the sale of Airbus aircraft to Air Canada had not begun to flow until after their research had ended. But one thing was certain: Kit Melamed and Eric Malling had given me a huge head start on my research.

At the same time I was poring over the fifth estate files, Maclean's magazine published a story by Stevie Cameron, timed to coincide with the release of her book On the Take: Crime, Corruption and Greed in the Mulroney Years, which had come out that fall. In the Maclean's article, Cameron claimed that Fred Doucet, Mulroney's former senior adviser, provided Mulroney's wife, Mila, with envelopes containing thousand-dollar bills, for expenses. "Cash came in like it was falling from the sky," Cameron quoted former chef François Martin saying. I had no idea what to make of that story. Pelossi had not mentioned Fred Doucet as the source of funds to Mulroney. He had insisted that Schreiber told him Moores would be giving the money to Mulroney. Doucet's name never came up in this context.

As for the thousand-dollar bills, it was the first time any journalist had ever mentioned such a thing.

Having read all the old research notes and the Schreiber clippings, I decided it was time to start making my own phone calls. I divided the names into three categories: European contacts, Canadian contacts and American contacts. I discovered early, however, that few people wanted to speak to me. I wasn't being picky. I called airline executives in Canada and Europe, former and current Air Canada officials, former political staff, former politicians. If you were remotely involved in the airline industry I'd call you too. Ditto if you'd once worked for a Tory cabinet minister. If you'd once worked for Airbus, you were on my list. I kept dialing, typing notes, dialing, typing notes again. But my notes were pretty sparse. After the initial excitement of the Pelossi revelations, I was becoming increasingly frustrated. I switched gears. It had long been my practice to allow people to speak to me "for background," meaning I would agree not to identify them as having spoken to me. On that condition, some people agreed to talk. When I began to learn the reasons, I could understand their reluctance. Anyone seen publicly helping an investigative journalist by speaking out about the business of selling airplanes risked friendships, reputation and perhaps even career.

On November 11, 1994, Jock Ferguson and I were seated in a restaurant on the Danforth in Toronto's east end speaking to an Air Canada source who refused to be publicly identified. He was a former consultant who had been involved in the decision-making process that had led to the $1.8 billion Airbus sale. He explained there were three teams at Air Canada evaluating Boeing versus Airbus (McDonnell Douglas was also in the bidding but no one really expected them to win): there was a financial team, to decide which aircraft manufacturer was offering the best financial package; a technical team, which decided which airplane was the best in terms of fuel efficiency, and so on; and, a marketing team, which looked at issues like passenger comfort. Our source was on the marketing team and told us that, in his opinion, the entire process was ethical and above board. "Everyone wanted the Airbus," he said. He described a clash between Pierre Jeanniot, Air Canada's president, and Claude Taylor, the company's chairman, but added that it had nothing to do with the purchase of the aircraft. Then he told us that one of the people on the finance team asked him to artificially inflate his scores in favour of Airbus over Boeing. He said he was asked to do this to make the Airbus choice look even better. He didn't think the request was anything nefarious, but after the interview Jock and I wondered aloud: If Airbus was going to win the assessment over Boeing anyway, why would someone want scores to be inflated? We couldn't figure it out.

I spent much of October and November working on another project. The producer of the Dash-8 story, Morris Karp, had asked me to help him research another one about the high number of suicides among teenagers in Pikangikum, an Aboriginal reserve in northern Ontario near the Manitoba border.

When I returned to my Airbus research in December, I decided to call some old contacts from my Mulroney-biography days. I made a cold call, based on a hunch, to an old friend of the former prime minister, who insisted on anonymity but agreed to talk.

The friend filled me in on Mulroney's time out of office. It had been eighteen months since he had stepped down as prime minister. According to the friend, Mulroney had been travelling "too much," but that was good, in a way, because it kept Mulroney from wanting to get involved in public life. "If he had too little to do, it [life after politics] would have been a whole lot worse."

Mulroney's friend was also familiar with Karlheinz Schreiber. He even knew about the controversy in Alberta. "I remember there was a kerfuffle over a change in zoning or something," he said, referring to the Brennan Inquiry. (I wondered if outraged Albertans had thought of the situation as a "kerfuffle.")

He explained that Schreiber was close to the Strauss family (which owned a shopping mall in Montreal). Of course, the Strauss family not only held real estate in Canada, the patriarch was Franz Josef Strauss, the premier of Bavaria and chairman of Airbus Industrie.

"I had the impression that he [Schreiber] was sort of their ear to the ground in Canada," said the friend.

"Karlheinz was an active busy little guy. Rotund. Busy, busy. Forever going here there and everywhere. And very very much to the right," he said, adding that Frank Moores would joke that in Schreiber's philosophy, "Anybody who didn't own a car should probably end up in jail."

"In those days [Schreiber] also had a lady friend called Renata. He wasn't married [to her], but they appeared to be very much in love, and it was 'Renata this' and 'Renata that' and she was travelling with him and then all of a sudden, I don't know what happened. There was no longer Renata.

"For a while he was hanging around Montreal a fair amount. I must say that in those days Karlheinz had a great deal of interest in the Tory leadership. He was interested to see what was going on. He wanted to get into the right club or team or group, I guess. So he was courting very much the Mulroney campaign."

Schreiber was courting the Mulroney campaign? I mused. If true, it meant Schreiber might have known Mulroney at a crucial time in the history of the Progressive Conservative Party, which had been at war with itself in the early 1980s over its leadership. The current leader of the party, Joe Clark, was unpopular with the right wing of the party, and faced a leadership-review vote at an upcoming convention in 1983. The outcome of that internal struggle not only changed the future of the party, it changed the future of the country.

I asked more about exactly how Schreiber might have been involved. The friend explained that Schreiber had become close to Michel Cogger, one of Mulroney's classmates from Laval University law school. Cogger helped Schreiber get introductions to all the other players in the so-called "dump-Clark movement."

The first introduction was to Walter Wolf, an Austrian who, like Schreiber, was trying to develop business projects in Canada and who was friendly with Strauss. Wolf had been hugely successful in the oil and construction business, but was also a bit of a playboy known for his Formula 1 race car. Wolf himself was close to Mulroney's best friend, Fred Doucet. Wolf, Doucet and his brother Gerry had set up an oil exploration company in Nova Scotia called East Coast Energy. Wolf, like Schreiber, had become intensely interested in Canadian politics and could also see the benefits of helping the dump-Clarkers take over the party and install Mulroney as leader. During this period Schreiber invited Michel Cogger and

Walter Wolf to his house in Kaufering, Germany, just outside Munich, where Schreiber had six Mercedes-Benz in the garage and a bowling alley in the basement.

The friend added that Cogger and Wolf had introduced Schreiber to the chief dump-Clarker himself, former Newfoundland premier Frank Moores. Cogger, Wolf, Moores and Schreiber spent a lot of time together in the early 1980s, hanging out, talking about the dump-Clark movement and dreaming of what might happen if Mulroney became prime minister. At the same time, Schreiber got into business with a few of the dump-Clarkers. In 1981, Cogger helped Schreiber set up a company called NBM Land Investments, which purchased land in and around Shearstown, Newfoundland, hoping to take advantage of an economic boom surrounding the offshore oil project Hibernia. NBM, in turn, was partly owned by the Strauss family. In fact, Max Strauss, Franz Josef's son, made a trip to Newfoundland with Schreiber and Cogger to check out their new investment. Schreiber also got into a road-marking business with Cogger in Montreal, though nothing much came of the venture. In 1982, Schreiber became a Canadian citizen.

How close, I asked the friend, were Brian Mulroney and Karlheinz Schreiber? He said he believed Michel Cogger made the introductions back when Mulroney was the president of the Iron Ore Company of Canada. "I don't know that it went much beyond that. That was about [it for] the relationship. One knew of the existence of the other, period. As best I know."

As the interview wound down, he told me Cogger had seen less and less of Schreiber after Mulroney came to power in 1984. Cogger was the one who had introduced Schreiber to Frank Moores, but he would observe from a distance that those two had formed a kind of partnership of their own in Ottawa. As the years went on, the dump-Clark conspirators went their separate ways. Gary Ouellet, who was also involved in the dump-Clark movement (and later a lobbyist with Frank Moores) had left Ottawa to become a magician in L.A. (This did not come as a complete surprise to me since I remembered that Gary had come to my fourth-year journalism class in 1986 to speak about lobbying, but instead spent a considerable amount of time doing magic tricks.)

As for Moores, he too appeared to have checked out of Canadian politics and business. He had a place in Jupiter, Florida, and seemed to be enjoying life playing golf and staying out of the headlines.

"That's all I know," said the friend. "He is taking it easy."

I got off the phone still curious about Schreiber and how he first came to meet Mulroney. It happened right in the middle of the dump-Clark movement and yet, according to Mulroney's friend, he didn't think the two men knew each other that well.

Still, the dump-Clark angle got me thinking. Giorgio Pelossi had come to us with allegations that secret commissions were being funnelled to Canadian politicians. Now the story was even more intriguing. If Schreiber was involved in the dump-Clark movement, what did that mean? Everyone knew that Joe Clark called a leadership convention because he'd failed to get enough support at the leadership-review convention in Winnipeg in 1983. The question that nagged me was: Had foreign money and foreign interests helped change the course of Canadian history?

Research leads were coming at me from all directions. I wanted to get back to the original story and convinced my bosses that I needed to take another trip to Washington, D.C., where many former Airbus employees still lived.

In mid-December 1994, I flew to the U.S. capital. I met one nervous Airbus employee at a local restaurant, and he insisted we move to the back where no one would see us. Former Airbus employees I spoke to all told me similar stories. They mentioned an Airbus salesman named Anthony Lawler. Lawler had the Air Canada file and one day he came back from a business trip to Montreal not his usual cheerful self. "We have a problem," they recalled him saying.

The sources told me that by all accounts Anthony Lawler loved his job and was good at it. He had grown up in Rhodesia. His poor vision prevented him from fulfilling his childhood dream of becoming a pilot, so he got into airplane sales instead. He joined Airbus in 1985 during its hiring frenzy in North America. Lawler's job was simple: convince Air Canada to purchase Airbus aircraft. Around 1986 Lawler met Karlheinz Schreiber in Calgary, but came back to the office in the United States admonishing everyone "not to touch Schreiber with a barge pole." Lawler, according to the former employees, had assumed his warnings had been heeded.

By the spring of 1988 it was clear something was going on; Lawler was in a foul mood. He had heard rumours that a "bagman" named Frank Moores had spread money around to get the deal done. Soon the whole office was talking about it.

"If you can find that guy, that is your story," one of my sources told me. Obviously the source was unaware that "that guy" was actually a former premier of Newfoundland.

"I just heard that $34 million went through his hands," the executive continued. "This [amount] allegedly went directly from Toulouse—so it never came from North America. . . . Maybe Toulouse were handling the case as if it were another campaign to Thailand or India or Africa or something. And I must admit it ticked me off just to hear it. It upset me just to hear it." He added that he heard that "government people" were involved as well as Air Canada officials. Airbus sources told me that Anthony Lawler's freak-out back at the Airbus office in Herndon had reached the ears of their boss, Tom Ronnell, who was also in the dark about the secret side deal. Ronnell took the concerns to *his* bosses but was apparently told to "mind your own business." When I reached a senior Airbus executive on the phone, he told me that he, too, would have been kept in the dark about the secret agreement with IAL in Liechtenstein.

"I would not hear about it. And you understand why? I am the guy most exposed. Because I am a resident in the United States, the only part of the world where such an agreement would be totally illegal."

Back in 1988 it seemed as if Airbus employees in Herndon, Virginia, believed the story might soon break wide open, and that the media in the United States and Canada would be all over it. One employee summed up the prevailing mood: "Bury yourself in a bunker, let the others take the fall." But much to their surprise, nothing happened. Some even seemed surprised that the story was resurfacing, six years later, at least as far as a reporter from CBC Television was poking around and asking questions. As for Anthony Lawler, he was still working at Airbus. When I asked to talk with him, he seemed willing, until head of public relations David Venz intervened to lecture me at great length about how there was no story.

"Frank Moores didn't work for us," said Venz. "Schreiber means nothing to Airbus . . . Airbus believes that all this is based upon innuendo and back alley gossip." And forget about an on-camera interview with Airbus, he stated. "I have watched television before, I have dealt with television producers for many, many years, I know how the system works."

The person I most wanted to talk to was no longer with the company. Stuart Iddles, my sources told me, had left his job as VP of marketing at Airbus but was still living in France near Toulouse. Iddles, they believed, was the ringleader of the kickback scheme.

"Stuart Iddles," a source confided, "was alleged to have been the one who organized everything."

In Washington, I made a call from my hotel room to Keith Miller, a former airline economist wintering in Florida. I knew him from another story as the former president of Eastern Provincial Airways in the Maritimes. I wondered if he had heard anything about Air Canada's decision to purchase Airbus.

"Yes, I have," he said. Miller was blunt and no-nonsense, though he insisted on anonymity.[1]

He had first met Karlheinz Schreiber after the German-Canadian businessman moved to Ottawa and hooked up with Frank Moores and Gary Ouellet and their firm, Government Consultants International. Schreiber liked to brag, Miller told me. Schreiber boasted that he was Franz Josef Strauss's "right-hand man" in Germany and that he had been made a Canadian citizen through an "Act of Parliament."[2] And Miller said Schreiber was so keen on the Bear Head project that he would pull out a brochure and hand it to the unsuspecting.

Miller said it was no secret that Frank Moores and Gary Ouellet had worked closely with Schreiber on the Airbus deal, as well as with Stuart Iddles. Miller indicated that Moores and Schreiber weren't exactly secretive

---

1 Miller later agreed to be identified.
2 One report had Michel Cogger helping Schreiber arrange his citizenship, but there was certainly no "Act of Parliament."

about their lobbying when he met them, in 1986. The two men were actively trying to find people to work with them. Since Miller was an airplane economist, they sought his expertise. In fact, Miller said that both Boeing and Airbus were courting him for their respective teams. That's what led Frank Moores to introduce Miller to Schreiber at the GCI offices in Ottawa. "If you're okay with Frank, you're okay with me," Schreiber had told Miller. Moores wanted Miller to fly down to an airport hotel in Toronto to meet Iddles, who was visiting Canada on business. They wanted Miller's help on the "technical" side. Moores would handle the "political" side. "I got [the] feeling he felt [Moores] could handle the Ottawa end, but [I was] not so sure [about] the Air Canada end," Miller told me.

The meeting ended with Iddles simply advising Miller to write up a proposed consultancy contract. Then Iddles left that meeting for another with Max Ward of Wardair.

Ward had already decided to purchase Boeing jets. Wardair had even provided the Seattle-based company with a $1 million deposit. None of that stopped Stuart Iddles and Airbus. They came up with a generous financing package and a rock-bottom price. Airbus made Ward an offer he couldn't refuse. In January 1987, he announced that Wardair had purchased twelve Airbus A310-300 aircraft for US$675 million. (The Canadian government would also give Wardair landing rights in Paris, which meant Max Ward had access to a potentially lucrative route from Canada to Europe.) Keith Miller told me he eventually decided against joining the Airbus lobbying team; instead, he signed up with Boeing. He worked alongside Merv Cronie, a Boeing consultant, and another former Conservative member of Parliament, John Lundrigan, who had also set up shop in Ottawa as a lobbyist.

Miller had also heard a story that put the Frank Moores lobbying effort straight into Air Canada's offices in Montreal. Miller said that Air Canada chairman Claude Taylor told him he saw Moores and Gary Ouellet walking down the hall to a meeting with Pierre Jeanniot, the president of Air Canada. Taylor was not impressed. He was upset that Moores and Ouellet did not bother to come and see him. The meeting took place after Moores left the Air Canada board, but the purpose was not in doubt: "They [Moores and Ouellet] were there to discuss Airbus with Jeanniot."

That night in my hotel room, I wrote up my notes. I made a list of all the leads I had to follow. I believed I had clear evidence that Moores and Schreiber were involved in the sale of Airbus in Canada. It wasn't just Pelossi alleging it anymore.

Still, I was nervous at how complicated the story had become. It didn't just involve Airbus and Air Canada; it included Airbus, Wardair and Air Canada. And not only Toulouse-based Airbus, but a company called Thyssen in Germany and a Canadian company called Bear Head that wanted to set up a light armoured vehicle factory in Cape Breton. There was also MBB, which sold helicopters to the Canadian Coast Guard in 1986. Then there were all the people involved in the dump-Clark movement, some of whom would turn up later as lobbyists in Ottawa. Schreiber had a personal relationship with the Bavarian premier Franz Josef Strauss, and also with many of Mulroney's friends. Somehow it seemed connected, but how? My list of contacts to call had grown to an impossible number. Not only was the task impossibly complicated, it was utterly daunting. My notebook was a mess of scribbled notes and unanswered questions.

Then came a tantalizing moment of clarity. On one level, I realized that, in fact, the story really wasn't that complicated. More than $25 million in greasemoney had disappeared into a shell company in Liechtenstein. European companies had deposited the money so they could do business with the Canadian government. The money had disappeared into a black hole. I wrote down a question on my notepad. I underlined it, then circled it, then traced over the letters again and again. It would be the question that guided me for the next fourteen years:

"Where did the money go?"

CHAPTER FIVE
DENY, DENY, DENY

My old boss, John Sawatsky, used to tell me that an investigative journalist should take notes of everything, since you never know until later what facts are important. Sooner or later the truth will emerge, and more often than not from a tiny, half-forgotten detail. And with the satisfaction of knowing that I had a simple focus, I dived back into the complicated details of the research.

If the truth was going to emerge, however, it wasn't going to happen by itself. The clock was ticking on the project, for a couple of reasons. Our broadcast season at *the fifth estate* ended in March, which meant if I did not have a solid proposal to present the bosses soon, the story might not move beyond the research phase, and risked being shuffled to the back-burner *possibly* for the next season, or not at all. I also knew that *Der Spiegel* would not wait until the fall of 1995 before publishing. It was entirely possible that all my hard work would end up in the filing cabinets in my office.

I was so preoccupied with the story in December that I never found time to get to the Greyhound bus station to pick up the Christmas parcel my wife's parents had shipped from Edmonton. Instead, I drove to my office at the CBC to keep on making phone calls.

"Where are the Christmas presents?" my wife, Alisa, asked when I came home late that night.

"I forgot."

On Christmas morning the package from Edmonton sat, unopened, at the Greyhound bus terminal.

I continued to work between Christmas and New Year's. One day I got lucky, making three phone calls that left me believing I was making progress on the story.

The first call was to a retired airline consultant. I had heard that he used to be fond of talking with the media back in 1988 when the Airbus story first caused concern. But now he was keeping to himself. Six years had gone by since he had tried to expose the story and his protestations had got him nowhere.

"First of all, how did you find me here?" he said. "This is my security blanket; this is where I hide." He eventually agreed to talk on the condition that "you never heard of me."

"I knew there were big bucks going around, but I never could follow any money trail," he said. Then he told me what so many people had said before; I should look into the Wardair deal as well as the Air Canada purchase. "All of them were entwined." He insisted we talk to Don Mazankowski, the former minister of transport, deputy prime minister and minister of privatization. Earlier in his career Mazankowski had been Frank Moores's roommate. Mazankowski, the source claimed, had been instrumental in the Wardair deal, helping to clear up any regulatory problems.

My second call that day was to Frank Oberle, a junior minister in Mulroney's cabinet and the first-ever German-born cabinet minister. In 1985, Mulroney appointed Oberle minister of state for science and technology. I figured that Schreiber, being who he was, and Oberle, being who he was, must have connected at some point in Ottawa.

I was right. Oberle knew Schreiber well.

I asked about Airbus.

Oberle had heard Schreiber was working with Airbus to create jobs in Quebec—but only if Air Canada bought Airbus jets. Schreiber, he said, "may" have convinced politicians in Ottawa that this was a good idea. If what Oberle was saying was true, it meant that Schreiber really had lobbied Canadian politicians on the Airbus deal. The thought did not seem so far-fetched. The *Globe and Mail* had already reported a similar story, about how Quebec-based Bombardier might get those jobs. At the time, the Mulroney government had vehemently denied any connection to Air Canada's decision and potential offsets in Quebec. A side deal like that could have contravened the General Agreement on Tariffs and Trade (GATT). The government also insisted it would let Air Canada make up its own mind, without input from their political masters in Ottawa.

Soon, Oberle brought Mulroney's name into the story.

"I would speculate that Karlheinz would have suggested to whomever he had access in cabinet, perhaps the prime minister, saying, 'Look, why don't you guys get into the Airbus deal and get some real industrial spinoffs?'" Oberle said the real negotiations took place between countries. "The actual negotiations and deals were discussed at a much higher level than even cabinet," Oberle told me.

I pressed Oberle on Schreiber's exact role. "Well, with the knowledge he had of the European scene, and European culture, and his intimate relationship with Strauss who was the father of Airbus, as he liked to see himself, [Schreiber] knew what was available and the kind of business we were doing and who might get a share of it. And he got opportunities to encourage people who were in a position to make the decision."

Added Oberle, "Well, I think he had access to the prime minister on a couple of occasions."

My third phone call that day was to Gary Ouellet.

Apart from Frank Moores, Ouellet was the key player at Government Consultants International. And by now I had heard about the meeting at Air Canada he had attended with Frank Moores and Pierre Jeanniot.

I reached Ouellet at his home just outside Quebec City and right away I sensed he sounded different from when I last saw him in John Sawatsky's fourth-year investigative journalism class. Then he seemed confident, carefree. Now he sounded uneasy.

Ouellet denied having any involvement with Airbus, and said he could hardly remember the helicopter deal with the Canadian Coast Guard.

"We did not act for Airbus" he said. "People thought we did, but in fact we were acting for—Christ—I can't remember . . . it's so long—a helicopter manufacturer."

I asked if he remembered Schreiber.

"Yeah, I know, I know the man," Ouellet said. "Because he had a relationship with a company called Thyssen, who had Bear Head Industry who we also acted for, for, a while. Geez, I haven't seen him in years. I don't know where he is or what he's doing." As for the Airbus rumours, according to Ouellet, they had come from disgruntled Boeing lobbyists in Ottawa.

"If I remember that story, Air Canada did all these tests or something, this competition. I don't even know what aircrafts were involved or anything, but they did this competition and from what I heard, some of the losers of the Canadian operations were trying to explain why to their head office, why they didn't get it." And then came the spin Ouellet and Moores had been making for years. "I don't even know what the story is, even if we had represented them, what was the story, Harvey? I am missing something here. I mean, every time anybody asked me, my official quote was, 'I wish it were true and I wish I could claim credit for having done this. I can't.'"

I told Ouellet that I agreed with his observation that there would have been nothing wrong with Moores representing Airbus. What I couldn't figure out was why Moores had denied working on the file, when it was obvious he had.

"No, you see, you have to . . ." Ouellet paused. He didn't finish the sentence.

"Sorry?"

Ouellet tried again. "There was a lot of, there were sisters involved here. There was like—we were acting for MBB. It was owned by the same company. And—I don't know about—was it Karlheinz worked for Airbus?"

Ouellet must have realized how ridiculous it sounded, *him* asking *me* if Schreiber worked for Airbus. "Yeah, he did," I said.

"I mean, every discussion I ever had with him was on this Bear Head matter," Ouellet insisted.

Ouellet preferred talking about his new career in magic, telling me how he ran David Copperfield's organization, and had produced a magic show on NBC with "fifteen magicians."

When I asked what he knew about Schreiber's relationship to Franz Josef Strauss, Ouellet drew a complete blank at first.

"I don't know, you mean the premier of Bavaria?"

"Yeah."

"Don't know."

If Ouellet did not know that Schreiber and Strauss were close, he'd be about the only person who ever met Schreiber to be in the dark on that one. "'Cause I think they were friends too," I suggested.

"Could be, yeah, I mean, he, yeah . . . I know, what did I know? I think he went to his [Strauss's] funeral, but I mean, I don't know."

Ouellet didn't know that Schreiber and Strauss were friends but nevertheless knew Schreiber went to Strauss's funeral? Exasperated, I asked again about Air Canada.

"Jesus, I don't know what to tell you. I mean, Air Canada would surely tell you that we didn't lobby them. I mean, I had that discussion with Air Canada at one point."

For now I didn't tell Ouellet that one of my sources put him in a meeting at Air Canada with Frank Moores and Air Canada's president, Pierre Jeanniot. "You know, let me put it this way, you want to know the truth, Harvey?"

Finally, the truth! Yes, I wanted to know the truth.

Ouellet began: "The concept that one person, Frank Moores, or anybody, would call up somebody else and say, 'Hey, buy our jumbo-jet aircrafts, would you, as a favour?' 'Oh, okay, sure, let's order twenty' is the most ridiculous notion . . . I mean if you ask me why they [Airbus] won, I read in the papers that it was a financial deal. They had the best financial package for Air Canada at the time."

Next, Ouellet talked about his exit from political life. He said his last day as a political insider was at the 1993 Tory convention that elected Kim Campbell as leader. "I actually was convention chairman of the Charest campaign." But now he was out of public life and refused an on-camera interview. "I don't talk to media. I'm talking to you 'cause it's Christmas . . . The only place you're going to see my name is in rolling the credits 'Produced by.'" I could call him again, he said, but he might be hard to reach.

"You know how it is. I sort of disappear."

Early in the New Year I called an old source of mine who worked for the PC party. He suggested I call Karen Mosher, an assistant deputy minister with Citizenship and Immigration, who, in the 1980s, worked for Transport Minister John Crosbie as his air policy adviser. When I spoke to her, Mosher appeared to be in the dark about Schreiber's role with Airbus. She also appeared to be in the dark about Air Canada's decision to purchase Airbus. "I don't remember having any direct contact with anybody at Airbus. Or anybody representing them," she insisted.

"What about a guy named Karlheinz Schreiber?"

"Yeah, but he wasn't Airbus, was he? I thought he was connected with Thyssen." Mosher said she met Schreiber a couple of times, but "it wasn't anything to do with Airbus, as far as I recall." Perhaps it might have seemed odd that Schreiber had met the transport minister's air policy adviser and discussed Thyssen light armoured vehicles instead of Airbus planes. Odd, but not impossible. I let it go.

We decided that *Der Spiegel*'s Blumencron should call Mosher's former boss, Transport Minister John Crosbie. Crosbie told him that everyone had heard complaints by the US embassy about Airbus and that he personally called Air Canada's chairman, Claude Taylor, to ask if there was anything to the allegations. "It's the same old bullshit started by Boeing," Crosbie said. "They start thousands of rumours, it's a constant battle." Still, he told Blumencron that Airbus did lobby people in his office, but he didn't provide more details. It remained a big mystery who exactly Airbus had lobbied on his staff, and who from Airbus had done the lobbying.

Next, I called Pierre Jeanniot, president of Air Canada at the time of the Airbus acquisition. By early 1995, he was in Geneva, where he was the president of IATA, the International Air Transport Association. Jeanniot repeated what Jock Ferguson and I had heard before—that each one of the three internal selection teams picked Airbus over Boeing. Politics had played no role in the decision, he insisted. Transport Minister John Crosbie had stayed out of it. "John was extremely relaxed on this one. He really didn't want to get involved." Jeanniot said that while he talked with Deputy Prime Minister Don Mazankowski about the sale, he did not speak with the Prime Minister's Office. "I basically met with the deputy prime minister."

On the Airbus side, he said "Stu" [Stuart Iddles] was the head of marketing and certainly had been involved, as had Jean Pierson, the president of Airbus. I knew by now that Stuart Iddles and Schreiber had worked closely together on the deal, but Jeanniot said he'd never heard of Schreiber.

I moved on to questions about Frank Moores. "What was your sense of his role?"

"Nothing that I am aware of. He was briefly on the board and left. And of course he was involved in that consulting. The only thing I know about him is what I have read."

"And what have you read?"

"That his firm was supposedly involved in consulting in this area [on behalf of Airbus]. But I think if that's the case, I suspect that the manufacturers paid good money for nothing . . . But I was never approached, nor am I aware that any of my team at the time was approached by a lobbyist of any kind to try to persuade them to look at one or the other type of airplane more favourably."

Jeanniot couldn't recall why Frank Moores was forced to resign from the Air Canada board. "There was a potential conflict of interest of some kind. I can't even remember the details of that."

Stuart Iddles was next on my call list.

I had high hopes for the interview. Pierre Jeanniot knew him well enough to refer to him as "Stu." Schreiber had known Iddles for years. Iddles might be the bridge between the legitimate lobbying campaign to sell Airbus aircraft to Air Canada and allegations of a clandestine greasemoney campaign.

I reached him at his home just outside Toulouse, France. When he realized I was from the CBC and looking into the Air Canada purchase, he declined to talk. Airbus had made him sign a confidentiality agreement, he said. "So I am afraid I won't be able to make any comment at all."

I reminded Iddles that he spoke to *the fifth estate* back in 1988, that he specifically told Kit Melamed that Frank Moores had not been involved in lobbying for Airbus, nor had Schreiber.

"I have absolutely nothing to be concerned about in terms of my name or my reputation," he said. "I [did] the job for Airbus Industrie for a very good number of years. I have nothing whatsoever to be reproached about in that regard. I don't know what you're up to in that game. Whatever you're up to you have to do what you want to do."

"But you won't explain why you said something to us in 1988 that—"

"I have told you that I have no comment to make. And if you were calling me about any other business of Airbus Industrie you would get exactly the same reply. I am not at liberty to discuss Airbus Industrie. I can't help you. . . . The confidentiality agreement emanates from the president's office. I suggest you talk to the president." Iddles referred me to Jean Pierson.

"Would he know about the secret campaign?" I asked.

"You have to ask him," replied Iddles, adding quickly, "I don't know what you are talking about, so you ask him." Then he repeated the sentence. I got off the phone. Then I got to thinking: Iddles claimed an Airbus confidentiality agreement prevented him from speaking about Frank Moores. But Frank Moores had denied being involved in Airbus. Therefore, using Iddles's logic, wouldn't it be okay if Iddles talked about Frank Moores, since he apparently had nothing to do with Airbus. I got Iddles on the phone one more time.

"Can I ask you about people you met? Is that something we can talk about?"

"No, I really cannot discuss anything to do with Airbus business at all."

"What about meeting people like Frank Moores?"

"No, I am sorry. I cannot discuss any of the Airbus business. Sorry, can't help you, but thanks for the call."

"But the thing is, Frank Moores says he didn't work for Airbus. So if he didn't do any work for Airbus, why couldn't you talk about meeting Frank Moores?"

There was a rather long pause at the other end of the telephone.

"It has nothing to do whether it's Frank Moores or anybody else, I cannot discuss Airbus business."

"Right. But you see, Frank Moores says he didn't work for Airbus. So why couldn't you talk about meeting Frank Moores?"

"Look, you talk to Frank Moores or whoever you like, but I am telling you I can't discuss Airbus business. I don't want to keep getting telephone calls like this, because they are a nuisance."

In an odd way, I felt like I was making progress. My interview with former GCI lobbyist Gary Ouellet was a study in tortured non-sequiturs. The conversation with former Air Canada president Pierre Jeanniot seemed to raise more questions than it answered. There was no doubt that the former Airbus vice-president, Stuart Iddles, was hiding something (though inadvertently confirming he had worked with Moores on Airbus). But all those denials, inconsistencies and leaps of logic inspired me. There had to be a reason people were skittish. I was more determined than ever to find out why.

CHAPTER SIX
THE SMELL TEST

If you went to Liechtenstein in the 1990s looking for International Aircraft Leasing, you would take the Feldkirch exit off the highway and head towards Vaduz, its capital, nestled at the foot of a cliff where, if you looked up, you'd see the castle of the royal family. The prince and his relatives are esteemed in Liechtenstein, mostly by its bankers, since the tiny principality has created a secretive banking system that attracts investors from all over the globe who want to shelter their fortunes. Take the one-way street into Vaduz and immediately you would see the VPB Bank on the right-hand side, where IAL had its secret accounts. Just in front of the bank is the General Trust building, where IAL had its post-office box. Fifty metres down from the bank you would see the building that housed IAL's office, though to get to its parking lot you have to loop around and come back on the other one-way street going out of town. If you looked closely as you approached the entrance, you would see a small brass plate that said "I.A.L. International Aircraft Leasing" just to the left of the door. IAL had rented a small office from the Bernard Insurance Company.

Other than Giorgio Pelossi, the only man with any knowledge of IAL accounts was Karlheinz Schreiber. On January 24, 1995, *Der Spiegel*'s Mathias Blumencron called me about a conversation he'd just had with Schreiber about IAL. He said Schreiber had insisted he was not IAL's owner.

"Stop it with IAL," he said. "I cannot accept it that you presume that I own a company, which is not mine. There is no contract between Airbus and I, and IAL does not belong to me. I also do not know whether contracts existed between IAL and Airbus." According to Blumencron, Schreiber admitted he knew *something* about Airbus and IAL. He confirmed that IAL had paid *nützliche Abgaben* or NAS (translation: "necessary expenses") on the Airbus deal. Schreiber had described these expenses as proper business deductions in Germany for foreign business expenses. This admission that IAL had paid "necessary expenses" was significant. But Schreiber refused to provide specifics. To whom did IAL pay the necessary expenses? Schreiber refused to say.

The next day I had a meeting with a source who had been involved in both the Progressive Conservative Party and the airline industry. Because he worked in a skyscraper in Toronto I dubbed him "Tower."

"You cannot tape this conversation," he said as I came into his office with my tape recorder. He handed me a piece of paper with German phone numbers. "Those are Schreiber's numbers," he said. "Schreiber is bright, aggressive, well off and powerful in Europe." He was a businessman with "broad interests" who had extremely close dealings with Franz Josef Strauss.

I scribbled madly. Tower continued. Strauss had wanted Schreiber to lay the groundwork for expanded German business in Canada. "He tried footholds with certain industry. Armoured cars were always his pet project."

But if armoured cars were his pet project, Airbus airplanes were his cash cow. Tower told me what I'd heard before: that it was critical that Airbus make inroads in North America and that Strauss hired Schreiber to do it.

"Schreiber was dying to get a foothold in Canada for Airbus. Dying," he reiterated. Schreiber had "played a background role," he explained. "Using a front man like Moores was always his style. He will hire someone to do his work on his behalf." Part of Schreiber's plan involved convincing the smaller Canadian airline, Wardair, to purchase Airbus aircraft before

Air Canada made its decision. In the case of Wardair, there was really only one person they had to convince: Max Ward.

"It was easier to sell aircraft to a small board," Tower said. "Air Canada had a big board, and a huge technical committee. Every bolt is studied. But once the aircraft is acceptable, then it becomes easier to make the switch. 'Look who got one,' they figured Air Canada would say, 'Max [Ward] has never been wrong.'"

The information confirmed what I'd heard from Keith Miller: Airbus and Schreiber had stepped in at the last minute to help convince Max Ward to change his mind. Ward had always been a Boeing man, but the offer had been too attractive to turn down.

"Boeing was very pissed off that Ward changed his mind," said Tower.

He confirmed that Frank Moores, Gary Ouellet and GCI were deeply involved. "It is no secret on the street that GCI—through Frank Moores and Gary Ouellet—were in bed with Schreiber and his organization. . . . Frank Moores sat with Wardair executives and attended meetings. Max Ward was always intrigued at Frank's involvement. Frank was fronting for Karlheinz Schreiber and Airbus. I know this personally."

Tower insisted he had no personal knowledge of specific kickbacks, but added, "It would fit. If there were any payoffs here—rumours were rampant and it would not surprise me—Ward would not have been involved at all. That is foreign to his style."

I told Tower that Frank Moores had repeatedly denied that he had ever lobbied for Airbus, that he insisted he had lobbied only for MBB Helicopter and the Bear Head project to build Thyssen tanks in Cape Breton.

"Let's put it this way," said Tower. "When Frank Moores was dealing with Wardair he was not selling helicopters or armoured cars." He said the engineering people at Air Canada did not want the Airbus A320, preferring instead to stick with Boeing, with whom they had a long history. "That's no secret," he said.

Before I left, Tower had a question for me.

"Does the Airbus deal pass the smell test?"

"What?"

"It doesn't pass the smell test. It stinks."

The following day, January 26, 1995, I walked into my office and saw the red voice-mail light flickering on my telephone. The message was from Inspector Carl Gallant, Royal Canadian Mounted Police. He left me a number to call. I took a day to think about it. I had planned to call the RCMP—to see what they knew about the case. But now I was concerned that they might want information from me. When I called the inspector back, Gallant told me he had spoken with author and journalist Stevie Cameron, who had told him that I had "scooped" her on the Airbus story. He had also had a call from the FBI, stating they had received a call from a journalist named Harvey Cashore. (So they *were* interested, I thought.) "I'd like to meet if we feel there is anything of benefit to us."

I asked Gallant about their previous Airbus investigation in 1988. He corrected me. There was no "formal" RCMP investigation. He said he had to go to a meeting but that he would call next week. I wrote a note about the conversation. "I will of course refuse to say anything about what anybody said to me or give him any information, but maybe it's worth it to touch base."

It was time to call Karlheinz Schreiber. He answered the phone. "Hello?"

"Mr. Schreiber?"

"Yes?"

"Hi, my name is Harvey Cashore. I am calling from the Canadian Broadcasting Corporation in Toronto."

"Fine."

I stammered a little. I told him I hoped we could meet. But it was hard to pin him down. We talked about the story, sort of. It was clear very early on that Schreiber was guiding the conversation, not me. He knew that Pelossi had been speaking to us, and dismissed the allegations. "This other crap that is running around, it is just a waste of time."

"What other crap?"

Schreiber explained. Pelossi and his lawyer "are morally bankrupt and face criminal charges."

"We are just really confused about a lot of things," I said.

Schreiber laughed. "Look, this comment speaks for you, when you say you are confused with it. I can agree on that. Because I am confused too. Because I tell you this bugger down there thinks he knows something. And is mixing things. The only thing he is after is to survive and make some bucks out of a blackmail story, you know what I mean. It is just ridiculous. And this guy invented this whole thing by himself. It's an amazing stuff."

The rumours had been going on for years, he said.

"The whole damn thing started really as far as I could notice it, started really when this Airbus stuff was on. And I don't know how much you know about the efforts Boeing did all over the world to try to keep the Airbus people from what they think is their business field."

He mentioned that somebody from Calgary had wanted his money, too, but he had consulted his files and had "the biggest laugh" because the company he was talking about was founded three years later. Next the conversation turned to MBB and Boeing, then to a story about Fort McMurray, Alberta, and how Airbus could have helped Pacific Western with its cargo routes.

Schreiber name-dropped. He knew Rhys Eyton, the former head of Canadian Pacific Airlines; Bill Dickie, the former minister of mines and minerals in Alberta; Hugh Horner, who had served as both the deputy premier in Alberta and the minister of transport. Schreiber saw economic potential in Alberta—he had lobbied for Airbus to use Alberta as its base in North America, he said.

"This could really have gone to Alberta," he said.

"What year are we talking about here?"

"I have no idea."

On we went, back and forth in time and across continents; business deals here and there and politicians he knew. Canada was "the most beautiful country in the world," he said. "Show me where you can find more volunteers and humble human beings . . . everything the Lord could have given to people in this world was given to Canadians. And when you look at what the economic situation is, being really on the level of a third world country, it is pain, isn't it? It is pain. And I will tell you, there is a story, when you look at the system here. If Canadians are not going to change the system, this country will never come on the right track, I guarantee you this. I really tried to work my ass off, you know. I should get a monument for all the money I brought to Canada." He laughed at the notion, then repeated, "I should get a monument."

We arrived at the topic of Bavarian premier and Airbus chairman Franz Josef Strauss. "Without Franz Josef Strauss there would be no Airbus Industrie at all. Every child knows this. So it was really the man who worked his ass off to get that industry done."

We lost that thread pretty quickly as we turned towards a discussion of Elmer MacKay, the former federal minister in Mulroney's cabinet who had, along with Schreiber, lobbied tirelessly for the ill-fated Bear Head project. Schreiber had great admiration and affection for MacKay.

One day, he said, he and MacKay were walking down the street when they spotted a man walking on his hands because he had no legs. "And will you believe that Elmer MacKay went there and grabbed him, put him on his arms, and carried him to his car, called his driver and said, 'Now, sir, where do you want to go?' I tell you, there are wonderful people around the world. And I can really say there are a couple of Canadians, I don't want to mention more names now. But I am just delighted of the quality of human beings I found in Canada." I wondered if Schreiber had tears in his eyes.

"What is your first name?"

"Harvey."

"Harvey, the problem in my opinion is two things." Canada had too many lawyers and too many bureaucrats, he said. They were "the cancer of the country." He told me a story that he would repeat dozens of times in the future: a senior bureaucrat once told him that civil servants made decisions in Ottawa, not politicians. "We don't care what shitty ministers whisper to your ear and cannot deliver. We are the government," the bureaucrat told Schreiber. To which Schreiber says he responded: "Look, do me a favour. Would you say that Canada has two governments? One elected by the people and one which is just formed by yourself, being the bureaucrats? You must be kidding."

We talked about the Atlantic Canada Opportunities Agency ("Harvey, with grants you cannot buy success"); we talked about Elmer MacKay's son, Peter, coming to work in Germany for Thyssen Industrie, and how

Schreiber had fights with former defence minister Perrin Beatty over the state of Canada's submarines.

He was sixty, he said. He had a son, born in 1962, and a daughter, born in 1960. He had three grandchildren. "Yes, I have sort of become an old man, my friend." In the Chinese horoscope he was born in the year of the dog. I told him I had a child, Massey, who had just turned one. I asked him what his relationship was with Airbus.

"My friendship to the chairman. And wherever I went, if I could support something I did. And so the Airbus people in those days, Jesus Christ, was a struggle. No business and Boeing fighting them like hell."

He said he worked with two men at Airbus, Roger Bailly and Roger Beteille, one of the founding fathers of the company. "He was just a wonderful man. A small, very slim man, but really a very impressive person."

I don't know how long we'd been on the phone, but finally it seemed we were getting somewhere. Then, perhaps sensing where we were heading, Schreiber suggested we talk another time. It was getting late in Europe.

Before hanging up, Schreiber had some final thoughts to share with me. "Whenever you have a government you have good guys, you have bad guys, and many things are done in the name of the big boss. And the big boss might never know . . . And you have always people running around telling you, 'Oh, I am his friend, I have the right connection, you deal with me, you get everything. It is very normal.' So one has to be clear. When I look at Brian Mulroney, look, I know him from the days he used to be with Iron Ore. And when I look at Brian Mulroney, I don't know how many times I told him, 'What the hell are you doing?'"

Schreiber was referring to the Meech Lake Accord, which Mulroney had championed as an agreement to bring Quebec back into the constitutional family. Schreiber dismissed it.

"I said [to Mulroney], 'Look, you come home from your job. You open the door and your wife looks with frightened eyes at you, saying, how are you, honey, what is going on today, did you bring some money? Because I cannot pay for the groceries, we have problems to buy a pair of shoes for the kids, yesterday they took off the telephone.' And you say, 'Look, honey, forget this for a moment, let's sit down and talk about Meech Lake and the constitution.' What is your wife going to say? She is going to say, 'Harvey, you have to see the mental clinic first thing in the morning, you are out of your mind, you have a hole in your head.'"

I laughed.

We agreed to talk again, and he hung up.

CHAPTER SEVEN
"THIS IS NOT A GAME"

In early January I wrote an enthusiastic memo to senior producer of *the fifth estate*, Susan Teskey.[1] I suggested that in order to do the story, we would have to fly to Airbus Industrie headquarters in France; to Germany, where Schreiber lived; to Switzerland, home of the IAL bank accounts to the United States; to Herndon, Virginia, headquarters of Airbus North America; and to Florida, where Frank Moores lived. Possibly, I suggested, we should go to Ottawa, where Schreiber had a second home, and to Montreal, where Air Canada had its headquarters. Brian Mulroney, of course, also lived in Montreal.

It was an ambitious proposal. The first thing Teskey wanted to know was who we had to appear on-camera. Giorgio Pelossi had agreed to speak "in shadow." We had agreed to disguise his voice and show only a black silhouette as we filmed the interview. But who would talk publicly? I called back as many people as I could. Only one other person agreed to talk in front of the camera: Gary Kincaid.

Kincaid was not a central player, but he was the first person I had spoken to at Airbus. He had given us a road map for how the company worked

---

1 As senior producer, Teskey handled day-to-day tasks. Her boss, David Studer, ultimately made the decisions on what stories to broadcast and where to allocate resources.

and who the key players were in North America and Europe. I wanted to film a story that would take us all over North America and Europe, and yet I could find only one person to talk about it? Teskey agreed, for now, that we should at least interview Gary Kincaid before he changed his mind about going public. And that's when the first Airbus team began to take shape. Teskey assigned *fifth estate* host Trish Wood, with whom I had worked on the earlier story of bribes to the Bahamas, and producer David Kaufman, to whom I would report.

We flew to Washington with cameraman Colin Alison and sound recordist Alister Bell, then drove to nearby Virginia, rolling up to Kincaid's residence early in the evening. Kincaid was still working in the aviation business and, by going public, risked being alienated by colleagues who believed it was best to keep quiet about these kinds of stories.[2] We filmed the interview in his living room.

It was a good interview. "If you ask me," Kincaid said, "do I think that Airbus Industrie paid money to certain people in order to influence the A320 sale to Air Canada, I will tell you I think it happened." Unfortunately, it was the only interview.

On February 7, I received a letter from Superintendent Carl Gallant of the RCMP. "Further to our telephone conversation on January 27, 1995, I understand that you have information concerning possible criminal activity in relation to the purchase of aircraft from Airbus Industrie by Air Canada. I would like to meet with you at your earliest convenience to discuss this information to determine if a criminal investigation by the RCMP is warranted." I filed the letter and did not return the call. Journalists are taught not to hand over documents to the RCMP, as it could compromise their independence. Aside from the fact I did not want to help the RCMP, I had more important problems. My own investigation was fizzling. If I didn't get more results, there would be no story on *the fifth estate*.

As a kind of consolation prize, the bosses decided that rather than kill the story they would give me one last chance to resurrect it. And that's how I ended up at the Holiday Inn on Boulevard de Grenelle in Paris. The hotel was less than a kilometre from the Eiffel Tower and right next to the

---

2 Kincaid now drives a school bus to supplement his retirement income.

Bir-Hakeim metro stop in the Fifteenth Arrondissement, a location made famous as a backdrop for the film *Last Tango in Paris*. If I didn't make any more progress on the story, this might be my last tango on the Airbus file. Still, I remember feeling optimistic the first morning I arrived, sipping a latte and eating a *pain au chocolat* at a sidewalk café planning who I would try to meet, and desperately hoping one of them would agree to speak on-camera. My French was okay, but I was not close to being bilingual, so we hired a Canadian journalist living in Paris, Judi Rever, to act as both researcher and translator. I briefed her on the story and who, in theory, I wanted to speak with in France: Benoît Bouchard, the former Quebec minister in the Mulroney government was now ambassador to Paris; Pierre Pailleret, the former vice-president of marketing for Airbus was in Paris too. In Toulouse, we hoped to interview Denis Viard and Roger Bailly, the two executives who were still working at Airbus and who had arranged the IAL contract with Giorgio Pelossi. Stuart Iddles lived in Toulouse as well. Perhaps he would have a change of heart and sit down for a chat. Finally, I hoped to get an interview with Bernard Lathière, former president of Airbus Industrie. Lathière and I had already spoken and he had agreed to meet. I also left a message for Schreiber; I was in Paris. I hoped it might arouse his curiosity enough to call me at my hotel.

That Saturday night Judi Rever and her husband invited me to dinner at their apartment on rue Perignon near the Eiffel Tower. Judi's husband, John Huc, knew Charles MacMillan, the former senior adviser in Mulroney's PMO. MacMillan taught at York University, and Huc had become his protege. As we talked over dinner that night, I told Huc all about the Airbus research and how MacMillan was one of the first people who told *the fifth estate* about the lobbying on Airbus back in 1988.

Huc knew we were onto the Airbus story. MacMillan had recently called Huc to tell him about a call from my colleague, Jock Ferguson. What's more, MacMillan had told Huc about how GCI's Gary Ouellet had lobbied him on Airbus. It was a simple story. Ouellet had the Boeing proposal in one hand and the Airbus proposal in the other, and made the case to MacMillan that the Airbus proposal was far better than Boeing's.

But Ouellet had denied any involvement.

I could hardly wait to call Gary Ouellet again. I called him from my hotel in Paris, reaching him at his home in Sillery, Quebec. Now I had two unrelated sources suggesting Ouellet lobbied on Airbus. Keith Miller had put Ouellet and Frank Moores in a meeting with Pierre Jeanniot, president of Air Canada. This latest story put Ouellet in a meeting with a former senior adviser to Brian Mulroney. Could both anecdotes—originating from completely different sources—be wrong? It would have been a hell of a coincidence.

I asked Ouellet how he remembered first meeting Pierre Jeanniot.

"I don't know. I may, I mean, I hardly know Pierre Jeanniot. I don't even know what he is doing. I may have met him once or twice at a reception. Even then I can't be sure. I never knew Pierre Jeanniot very well."

I told him about the meeting I had heard about between him, Moores and Jeanniot.

"Somebody is giving you misinformation on that one."

The story had come from a credible source with a clear memory, I said. A pause. "You know, I can't remember much more than I told you the other day," Ouellet said. "If somebody is suspecting wrongdoing here I am telling you there was none. What would be the wrongdoing?"

I told Ouellet I was not suggesting wrongdoing. I just wanted to resolve the contradictory answers.

"I told you, you are speaking to the wrong guy here," Ouellet responded.

I repeated that a source told us there was a meeting with him, Moores and Pierre Jeanniot at Air Canada's offices in Montreal.

"You say the meeting was over Airbus?" Yes, I said. "I mean if you are asking me if at a meeting—I think I discussed this with you once before—if at a meeting Frank may have said, 'By the way I can give Airbus a ring,' that may have happened. If you are telling me there was a meeting that I went over Airbus, purposely meeting on Airbus?"

"Yeah."

"I . . ." Another pause. "I just can't. I just can't. . . . I can't tell you that is the truth. I mean I never worked on an Airbus file. I know I met Jeanniot. I really can't remember where I met him."

I asked about the story that he had approached Charley MacMillan in the PMO to talk about Airbus. Ouellet told me had not talked to MacMillan since he left the PMO in 1987, and that he had never ever lobbied MacMillan on anything.

"How is that for clarity?" Ouellet asked. But then he said, "God, the Boeing proposal, I never even saw that!" If Ouellet had never "even" seen the Boeing proposal, would it have meant he had at least seen the Airbus proposal? He corrected himself. "I never saw either one."

I went around the mulberry bush a few more times, asking about Giorgio Pelossi and IAL, but he denied knowing anything. He told me I was lucky to catch him on a Sunday and that he was just heading out of town.

"I will probably miss all of this when it comes out." He corrected himself again, "If there is a story here."

Monday morning I prepared for my meeting with Bernard Lathière, the former Airbus president. We had arranged to meet at 12:30 p.m. at a restaurant called Le Cercle on rue de Bercy, an upscale restaurant for senior civil servants in Paris.

When I reached the restaurant, the maître d' promptly escorted me to a table. Lathière was already seated. He had a round, pleasant face and wore a suit and tie. We talked for three hours about the origins of Airbus and how the Europeans wanted to build an aircraft manufacturer to compete with Boeing. He served as Airbus Industrie president from 1975 to 1985, and criticized Boeing for thinking that Airbus was "a flash in the pan." He had proved them wrong. Lathière also discussed his son, who had died in a car accident. We veered off into a discussion about how he was coping. After some time we were back to shop talk.

He was proud of his decade of work and seemed to regret how he was "eased out" of the presidency in 1985—the same year Airbus began negotiating the secret agreement with IAL. Lathière had left the company by the time the agreement was signed, but I knew he was present during the early negotiations. I showed him a copy of the Airbus/IAL contract. Lathière studied it. He flipped the pages back and forth. I asked him if the contract number "AI/CC-L-573-3/85" meant anything. He confirmed it was a unique numbering system used by Airbus. He told me that all contracts started with the initials AI, for Airbus Industrie.

Lathière expressed some annoyance at our having copies. They were supposed to have been kept confidential; it would be better if we did not talk about it, he said. "It will look like bribes were paid." In some "Middle Eastern" countries, he said, paying commissions is a "fact of life." There is no way to sell a plane without hiring someone close to the government, he said. But he swore on his son's grave that no bribes were paid in Canada. "It can be very dangerous, if you just say these people were consultants for Air Canada. Everybody will think, the listeners of the TV, that they were bribing, which is not true."

I pulled out a document from my briefcase: Amendment No. 3. This was an updated contract between IAL and Airbus dated 1988—just before Air Canada announced its agreement to purchase the Airbus aircraft. It contained specific details on the number of planes to be sold, along with detailed mathematical calculations explaining how IAL stood to receive more than 2 per cent of the cost of the plane, money it would receive once Air Canada began paying Airbus for the planes. Lathière's tone turned less friendly. "I stop talking with you if you go further that way," he said. I directed him to the section detailing the deal with IAL being null and void if there was a change in political leadership in Canada. He countered, "This money is going to the consultant, it does not say anywhere that the money is going to the airline."

I backed off. I sensed that I was going too far. I turned the conversation away from the IAL agreement and eventually away from Airbus altogether. We talked about Paris, what he liked about the city, and where I might go if I had time to sightsee. As the conversation ended, I asked Lathière if he would appear on-camera. He said he would think about it. Then I walked back to my hotel in order to prepare for the following day. Judi Rever and I were taking the train to Toulouse. At the very least we thought we could get a tour of the massive Airbus production facilities. At best, maybe someone at Airbus would agree to talk to us.

The phone rang early that morning. The hotel room was pitch-black and I fumbled around before I located the telephone. Perhaps my confusion was caused by jet lag, but for a moment I forgot where I was or what I was doing. Then I remembered the train ride to Toulouse. It must be Judi Rever calling from the lobby. I had obviously slept in.

"Hello?" I mumbled.

"Hello, Harvey. It's Karlheinz Schreiber."

I fumbled around for my notepad and the light switch. My hands patted the dark walls. Nothing. And how did those blinds open? Could I reach that far with the phone? Where was my tape recorder? I had a little suction-cup gizmo that allowed me to tape telephone calls, but I couldn't locate that either.

Schreiber was on his way to Moscow and was at the airport but would send me a fax outlining "legal" concerns he might have about our upcoming broadcast. If I thought Schreiber was friendly in our last phone call, I would have to rethink that impression: his manner had turned decidedly aggressive. The story was not just about Gary Ouellet, Gerry Doucet and Frank Moores, he said. I found the tape recorder. I put the suction cup on the back of the phone and pressed Record. "I have to caution you, this is not a game." Airbus, he said, was a "giant" company. "You can imagine where my position is. I am not going to do anything, you know, to upset them. This is my business, this is my job . . . My point, this is not a game with a little Moores or a little Ouellet or a Doucet or whatever . . . If you touch a huge, rich and powerful international company, you should have a good case. I can only say 'do what you want.' But be careful . . . as far as I can see, this company, they don't care about these people."

"What company doesn't care about what people?"

"The companies involved. Jesus Christ, Mr. Cashore, you are touching business interests of companies. You see what I mean? When you look at Moores or Doucet or Ouellet or whoever, where is the power there? Even when you look at me? You know, where is the power there? The power is—and their interests you have to watch—and the problems you may create when you come out with stories, which are not true, you touch directly the companies involved."

Then the old Schreiber returned—the one who had tried to make a personal connection when we spoke the last time. "When I see a young man, thirty years old . . . I think you are a pretty nice man . . . And you try to do your job and you have a family and a baby. So I try, I think, I try to be fair." I understood why he had called me. "Yesterday I learned I don't know whether you—or whoever—touched Gary Ouellet. It is you or somebody else?"

Schreiber had heard about my phone call to Ouellet. That, in itself, was interesting. They really were concerned. Schreiber had heard about the Charley MacMillan/Gary Ouellet anecdote and was now attempting to dismiss it.

"Would you ever invite Charley MacMillan to participate in important business? If you would do something like that?" He laughed. "You can't underestimate me completely, my friend."

I asked him how he had heard that I had called Ouellet. "You know exactly that these people worked for me. And you know exactly how many people I know. You can imagine that they contact one of my friends and say, 'Look, what is going on?' Gary Ouellet called and the story is this."

I asked about his meeting with Frank Moores and others at the lobby firm GCI and about a discussion about Airbus.

Frank Moores did some work for Daimler-Benz, he said. Daimler-Benz in turn was involved with MBB, the German aeronautics company, which owned a part of Airbus, but that was as far as it went. Pretty much the party line. "I was in Canada every day in the [GCI] office," he said. "I cannot see how this would have anything to do with Airbus. Because, Frank Moores, what the hell could he do? What the hell could he do on that?"

Schreiber then proposed that we make an agreement not to lie to each other. "If you don't want to talk about something just say simply I don't want to talk about it, and I will do the same. But why the hell should we lie and think the other one is a fool?"

In the middle of the call, Judi Rever knocked on the door. I was late for our train and we had to hurry. I ushered her into the room and quietly whispered I was talking with Schreiber.

"This goes back to, what can I say, it's ground to the roots of interest in the country in Switzerland," Schreiber continued. "So you can imagine they are not taking this as a little bluff. It is vital interest in their policy, when you do certain things with them . . . has to be done properly and has to be confidential. Because you and I, we cannot change the world. All this happened long before we were born, and they will happen when we pass away. It's life . . . So therefore, I tell you again, the only thing I can tell you, being not your enemy, check everything carefully you are using, because it is not the story of Frank Moores, Doucet, or whatever. You are touching the interests of these companies." Mulroney was never involved, he said. "That is just plain nonsense." Schreiber told me he had to leave to catch his plane. But I needed to get him on the record about his own involvement.

"What I still don't understand," I blurted, "is why you can't tell me what role you and Moores played on the Air Canada sale for Airbus."

"I have told you already. I played no role at all. I played no role at all on the Airbus." He then reminded me he had to catch his plane. "Okay, I wish you a pleasant stay in Paris," he said. "And stay away from the girls, you know, AIDS, all over the place."

I hung up. I must have looked shaken. Judi asked if Schreiber had threatened me.

"Is it that obvious?" I answered.

Then we raced to catch the train for Toulouse.

CHAPTER EIGHT
CLEVER PEOPLE

I figured our trip to Toulouse was a long shot. I told Judi I had already had that pessimistic conversation with David Venz, the Airbus PR rep back in Herndon, Virginia. He'd refused to let me speak to salesman Anthony Lawler, or anyone else with the company. Still, I hoped that by showing up in Toulouse, Airbus might give us someone to talk to. We checked into a hotel called the Grand Hotel de l'Opéra, just off the main square, la place du Capitole, where ubiquitous red bricks used in construction in the 1700s gave Toulouse the sobriquet *la ville rose*. It turned out that Airbus could not have cared less if we had travelled the globe to get there. On the phone from my hotel room, I spoke to someone in the president's office, who again refused to let us speak to Jean Pierson. We called John Leahy's office, the vice-president of sales. His office declined as well. Airbus also refused to let us speak with Roger Bailly and Denis Viard, the two Airbus officials who had actually met with Pelossi to set up the IAL agreement.

We rented a car and drove around the enormous Airbus facilities outside Toulouse in a suburb called Blagnac. It was a spectacular scene: from beyond the perimeter we could look past the wire fences and see the planes, half built, workers scurrying around. I wondered how many of those planes would come attached with a secret side agreement to pay

78

"necessary expenses" once they were sold to airlines around the world. Then we drove by Stuart Iddles's house, a modest, one-storey bungalow on the outskirts of Toulouse.

We returned to Paris without having accomplished much, but were pleased when the Canadian ambassador, Benoît Bouchard, agreed to speak with us. We had an appointment to meet him at his residence at 135, rue du Faubourg Saint-Honoré. I noticed a grand piano in the large but empty room where we waited and played the only thing I knew, the opening chords to the Beatles' "Let It Be."

Bouchard had been minster of state for transport from 1984 to 1985 and minister of transport from April 1988 to 1990. Mulroney had transferred Crosbie out of that position, and installed Bouchard, just a day after the Air Canada board had met in private to approve the Airbus purchase. This switch meant that Bouchard was the minister to shepherd the final approval through the government. We also knew Gary Ouellet had worked for Minister Bouchard briefly in 1984 before joining GCI as a lobbyist. Bouchard, it turned out, was not that helpful. He repeatedly suggested we speak to the other Bouchard—Lucien—who was ambassador to Paris in 1988 when Air Canada purchased Airbus aircraft.

Back in Toronto, we had a breakthrough.

Pierre Jeanniot had agreed to be interviewed on-camera. Jeanniot had faced a lot of questions over the years concerning what, if anything, he knew about Frank Moores's lobbying efforts, or the rumours that Airbus had paid GCI millions to make the deal happen. Now that we had Pelossi's documents, we knew that a lot of people got rich once Jeanniot made the decision to purchase the Airbus jets. Was it possible, we wondered, that a company might try to influence Jeanniot?

No, said Jeanniot. It never happened.

We arranged for an on-camera interview from Montreal with *fifth estate* host Trish Wood. Jeanniot admitted that Moores had been forced to resign his Air Canada directorship because of his connection to Airbus; he insisted, however, that Moores never lobbied him—even after he stepped down from his position at Air Canada.

"When you heard that Mr. Moores was lobbying for Airbus," asked Wood, "did you smell a rat? Did it make you nervous that this guy, who's a friend of the prime minister, who's lobbying for a foreign company that you're going to be negotiating with, is on your board? I mean, did you . . . were you uncomfortable with this?"

"I was not uncomfortable because he was no longer on my board, because he can't influence the decision of the company at that point; he's no longer on the board."

Had he ever wondered why Airbus would even hire Frank Moores? Wood asked.

"If companies want to waste their money, that's their business."

When Jeanniot denied that Moores had ever lobbied him, Wood asked, "He never phoned you up?"

"No," replied Jeanniot. "I think he knew he didn't have to, or he wouldn't, he shouldn't either."

"What do you mean?" asked Wood.

"Well, I think he knows me."

"And knows what?"

"Knows that there is no point in calling me to influence me on a decision on a manufacturer." Further, Jeanniot insisted that Airbus's vice-president, Stuart Iddles, whom he knew, never told him he had been working with Moores. Jeanniot said he was eager to defend himself against rumours that had dogged him after the decision was made.

"If your conscience is clear," he said, "it'll go away. So I never paid too much attention to it. I mean, of course it was not pleasant to have allegations made, the fact that you may have been assumed to be dishonest."

The way Jeanniot saw it, since the rumours about him were not true, the rumours about others were probably not true either. "And since there wasn't anything true about me, why should I believe anything about anybody else?"

Wood asked if he had investigated any of the rumours. "Did you go on the warpath around here [at Air Canada] and phone up everybody and say, did anybody take a buck from these people?"

"No." Wood asked why not. "Well, because I was meeting regularly with my deputies and you know at some of our meetings we talked about some of those rumours perhaps. But there was reassurance that nobody had, you know, was involved as far as we could see."

"Did you call Airbus in France and say, 'What the heck is going on?'"

"No, because I would have had to call Boeing. I mean, both were actively lobbying in all kinds of directions, from what I could see."

Why would Jeanniot have to call Boeing about the Airbus rumours? I wondered.

"I guess what I am getting at, though," Wood continued, "is at this time when the rumours are flying about, they're serious charges, involving a Crown corporation. It seems incredible that there wouldn't have been more hue and cry within this corporation to get to the bottom of it."

"Well, it's like fighting a shadow," Jeanniot replied. "I mean, what, what is it? In fact, you give more credibility by starting to do all kinds of things about it. I mean, if there are any serious allegations then please let them come up with some proof."

I thought I understood what Jeanniot was saying. If he had begun an internal investigation it might have sent a signal that there was something to the rumours, which would only add to the rumours. But was there not also an argument that a thorough investigation would put to rest the rumours, if there was no truth to them? On the other hand, an internal investigation may have discovered that Airbus had indeed signed that secret side agreement on the sale, that Moores and Iddles and Schreiber were all involved, and secretly earning millions on the sale. For whatever reason, Air Canada decided not to pursue the allegations.

It was time to bring out the secret Airbus contracts. We directed Jeanniot to the page that described how the shell company IAL received 2.5 per cent of the amount that Air Canada paid for each Airbus airplane, up to the first twenty planes. Then it went down to 2 per cent for the deliveries from twenty-one to thirty-four. That was about $20 million, Wood told Jeanniot.

Jeanniot whistled. "That's a lot of money."

"Why were they paying a company in Liechtenstein commission on planes that you guys bought?"

"I have no idea," he said. "That's absurd, these people are crazy."

"But what does it say to you, what does this document say to you, Mr. Jeanniot?"

"There are some clever people that made some money."

Some clever people made some money? That was one way of putting it, I supposed. Another way was to ask whether or not Air Canada paid too much for the planes. Shouldn't Airbus have charged Air Canada $20 million less instead of paying those "clever" people? Didn't all this mean that the Canadian taxpayer, and later the shareholders, paid too much for the planes?

Then we asked for Jeanniot's help. Since Airbus had refused to speak with us, we were hoping he would call them. Perhaps he could call Stuart Iddles, whom he knew personally, and ask him about the secret commissions. Jeanniot declined.

"I've helped to the extent that I can. I have an international association [IATA] and I'm not going to start diving into some specific issues that is really of concern between the morality of the Canadian public and a company."

Then Jeanniot barked at his assistant, who was also sitting in the corner, away from the cameras.

"Are we going to get some tapes of this so we know what the hell we've said?"

The next day I got a phone call from his assistant, who refused to be publicly quoted. She wanted to clear up a few things. "Jeanniot had nothing to do with asking Moores to leave the Air Canada board," she told me. "Claude Taylor did." Jeanniot did not really know why Moores left the Air Canada board, she said.

We talked about the secret IAL contract Airbus had signed with IAL. She sounded pessimistic. "The thing is, I don't think you're ever going to find a way [to get to the bottom of the story]. I don't think anybody has ever broken those [secret accounts]. They really are a system that is set up—the money goes in, but does anybody know who it ever goes out to?"

I tried to convince her to enlist Jeanniot's help to make calls to people like Stuart Iddles at Airbus. She told me that since Jeanniot was now president of IATA, he was in a real bind, given that he now had to answer to the entire airline industry for his actions. "He is caught," she told me. "The problem being that this is not something out of the blue for Airbus. I mean, this type of behaviour goes on in the airline business. So you are going to have several of his IATA membership that will have paid this kind of money . . . So he [Jeanniot] can't come out as going after them because right now he is representing those airlines that would have benefited from a system like this. That is the thing. Here in Canada it isn't a way of doing business, or shouldn't be a way of doing business, and Jeanniot is perfectly correct. Everything that Air Canada did to get this order was documented . . . that particular aircraft was what they wanted. Therefore it was like money being paid, if it was paid, for nothing. But [paying secret commissions] is standard practice in other parts of the world. So if Jeanniot is seen saying, 'Mr. Iddles, could you please come out and whatever,' he cannot, in his present position."

I was not sure I completely understood the reasoning. She seemed to be saying that Jeanniot had to decline to help us with our story because he now worked for airlines that had "benefited" from similar kinds of payments. But if there was corruption in the airline industry, wouldn't he want to try to clean it up? Either I was confused, or just very naïve.

I was puzzled about the relationship between the key players. Jeanniot said he knew Moores and Iddles but not Schreiber. But Jeanniot never talked to Moores about Airbus business, ever. Iddles knew Jeanniot and Moores and Schreiber. Yet Iddles never talked to Jeanniot about Moores or Schreiber. And Iddles wouldn't talk about Moores or Schreiber because it was all part of confidential Airbus business.

The relationship between Pierre Jeanniot and Frank Moores was a mystery. Did they really never talk about Airbus, as Jeanniot claimed? Or did they meet and discuss Airbus, as Keith Miller was told? Moores stood to earn millions if the Airbus deal went ahead with Air Canada.

I worried I was working too fast, trying to beat the clock before our season ended at *the fifth estate*. I couldn't complain about the time my bosses had given me, a few months, in fact, but I knew the story might not go ahead without more evidence. I had made hundreds of calls, but hadn't taken the usual steps of immediately typing up all my notes and making proper lists of questions for follow-up. I stared at my desktop. It was buried in audiocassettes not yet transcribed, books I had taken out of the library, scraps of paper, a photo of my son, Massey, now fourteen months old. Above my desk was a bulletin board that I never used anymore because it was harpooned with reports, buttons, photos, who knew what. Everything was a mess.

I noticed the cassette of my interview with a former senior vice-president of Air Canada, who had been deeply involved in the A320 decision. He had worked closely with Jeanniot. Hadn't he mentioned something about Frank Moores? I popped the cassette into my tape recorder and fast-forwarded until we got to the part about the controversial lobbyist.

He had never met Moores, the executive said, which I believed. Nevertheless, he *had heard* something quite remarkable from someone at Air Canada who had talked to Moores.

"I have no idea what his involvement was and how exactly it worked out with Airbus or whether he ever got paid anything or not. I don't think he ever got anything, I think that's why he was pissed off."

Moores was "pissed off" because he did not get paid? And Air Canada knew it? This was a new wrinkle. I had asked "how" he was pissed off. "Well, typical of Frank Moores, he wanted a piece off the top because it was his territory."

According to the former executive, everyone at Air Canada was on high alert when it came to the Frank Moores stories. "I know when the Frank Moores story was running around, we were all concerned about what the hell was going on . . . As I said, Frank Moores, he was making waves because he was mad at Airbus. But he wasn't mad at us [Air Canada], I don't think. It wasn't an Air Canada thing; he had nothing to do with Air Canada. But it was a delicate, delicate time."

I clicked off the recorder and sat back to think. Why would Moores tell someone at Air Canada that he was "pissed off" about not receiving commissions he was supposed to be getting from Airbus? Someone at Air Canada knew about Frank Moores lobbying for Airbus. But who?

It was time to call Frank Moores. I had a number for Moores at his Florida condominium, and left a message. Moores called me back the same day and denied everything.

He denied that he had ever had anything whatsoever to do with Airbus, denied meeting or even knowing Stuart Iddles, denied leaving the board of Air Canada because of Airbus, denied lobbying Wardair on behalf of Airbus, denied talking to Schreiber about Airbus, and denied knowing anything about IAL in Liechtenstein.

I was so excited, I could have done cartwheels.

The next day the bosses at *the fifth estate* called a meeting. David Studer wanted to hear our arguments for why we they should give the story the green light. We made the pitch, me, producer David Kaufman and host Trish Wood.

I had prepared careful notes, which began with Frank Moores's taped denials. But Iddles had said he could not talk about Frank Moores because it involved Airbus business; Lathière, meanwhile, had confirmed the authenticity of the IAL documents; Pelossi had agreed to talk on-camera—in shadow at least; and we had hopes that another one of my insiders would agree to speak, if only in shadow. I steered clear of making a single mention of Brian Mulroney or the allegation that he took money from Schreiber. That allegation was single sourced. We had no idea if it was true or not. I argued that the story's merits should be based on the strength of the revelations about the secret-commission contract with Airbus. The meeting concluded with no decision to approve anything.

That night I called Moores, to ask if he would appear on-camera.

"Really, Jesus, the last thing in the world I want to do, Harvey, is go on-camera, honest to God . . . Let me think about it, will you? Certainly I don't want everyone to come down here and interview Frank Moores in Florida. Jesus, that's about the last goddamn thing I need. Because there is an innuendo in that in itself, if you know what I mean." I asked him to elaborate. "You know what I mean, well, it depends on what twist is put on it."

His Florida condo was actually owned by one of Pelossi's Liechtenstein companies, Ticinella Anstalt. Was that the "twist" that spooked him? I didn't ask. Moores called back later and declined the interview.

Mathias Blumencron at *Der Spiegel* had recently called to tell us that Robert Hladun, Schreiber's Edmonton lawyer, might have been involved with IAL, the Liechtenstein company.

Blumencron had been speaking again with both Giorgio Pelossi and Schreiber, trying to figure out who really was the owner of International Aircraft Leasing. Pelossi insisted that Schreiber was the real owner; he controlled the company. Schreiber strenuously insisted he was not the owner; someone else was—someone he refused to name. It was an important detail. How could we do a story about IAL and where all the money went without knowing who the actual owner was?

Pelossi knew we wanted more proof about who actually controlled IAL and called Blumencron with some interesting news: IAL was launching civil and criminal proceedings against him [Pelossi] in Liechtenstein. To Pelossi this was a positive development because he believed he could now prove that Schreiber was the "beneficial owner" of IAL. Since Schreiber had already threatened legal action against him, Pelossi figured this proved Schreiber was behind IAL. Blumencron got off the phone with Pelossi and jumped back on the phone to Schreiber. Schreiber told Blumencron that *he* was not suing Pelossi—the "recent" owner of IAL was suing Pelossi and had even made criminal allegations against him in Liechtenstein.

"And who is the recent owner?" Blumencron asked.

"I can't tell you that," Schreiber responded.

Schreiber did tell Blumencron about a crucial meeting in Zurich in 1992 when Pelossi and Schreiber met one last time to try to resolve their differences. Schreiber identified those present as Pelossi, Hans Kopp, Pelossi's Zurich lawyer, Schreiber and his Munich lawyer, Harald Giebner, and a fifth person, whom he described as the "recent owner of IAL."

"Who was that person?" Blumencron asked.

"I won't tell you," said Schreiber.

But Schreiber had blundered. If Pelossi was present he would also know the identity of the fifth person. I got on the phone to Giorgio Pelossi. He told me the other person at the meeting was Schreiber's Edmonton lawyer, Robert Hladun. It turned out that Mulroney's justice minister, Kim Campbell, had appointed Hladun a QC, Queen's Counsel, on January 1, 1993. QC was an honour bestowed by the federal justice department to lawyers for their exemplary work in law, or as had been common, as a political thank-you for support to the party in power. The press release honouring Hladun stated that "the honorary title allows recipients to use the letters QC after their name in recognition of their dedication to the law and its advancement in our society."

I contacted Hladun at his office, but he didn't want to talk. As Schreiber's lawyer, he could not speak about his client, even if he wanted to.

"But I understood that you were not only his lawyer but that you are also now the president of IAL?"

"Well, as I say, I was there in a capacity that I felt—as a lawyer."

"Can I ask you, are you the president of IAL?"

"Whether I am or whether I am not, I was there as a lawyer. So anything that was discussed at that particular meeting, or in the context of what was discussed—or whatever office I held—I was there as a lawyer."

"So the questions that I have for Mr. Schreiber, and for you, would be: How do we describe the relationship between Airbus and IAL? How do we describe the relationship between IAL and Mr. Schreiber? How do we describe the relationship between IAL and yourself."

"Yeah, that would be interesting," he said.

I told Hladun that we had copies of the agreements between IAL and Airbus.

"I don't think you'll see my name anywhere there," Hladun said. He had a question for me. "What is your information as far as what kind of a company . . . ? I mean, where this company is incorporated and all of that?"

"It's a Liechtenstein company," I said.

"Yeah," he responded.

I took him through more of what we knew, that the Airbus/IAL contract was signed in 1985, that there were several amendments to it, and that the first payment came through in August 1988, a lump sum of $5 million.

"Yeah," he replied.

I told him that the commission payments started arriving once again after the first airplane arrived in Canada in 1990. "The questions for us," I said, "are: When did you become president [of IAL] and why, and when did you start to deal with IAL? And that's important to our understanding of the chronology and how we tell the story."

"Yeah, okay," he said.

Hladun emphasized that he had acted for Schreiber for many companies over a period of time, and that "quite often" lawyers can perform "specific tasks" as officers of companies, but only in their professional capacity as a lawyer. "And that takes you in all kinds of places and all kinds of situations," he said.

"I am not sure I understand," I said.

"Well, I mean I am being a little vague because it is that kind of an area, and as I say, those things are covered by, I feel, a professional responsibility.[1] So, anyway, I am talking more than what I think I'd like to at this point."

"I am just not even sure what you're saying to me," I admitted. "I am very confused."

We both laughed.

"Okay, good. No, I am just kidding you. I am just kidding."

The meeting ended with Hladun promising to get back to me. I hung up the phone and realized I had forgotten to ask about how he got his QC.

I was beginning to fidget. I figured we had enough to begin full-scale filming of the documentary. Why no green light? I understand now that the bosses at *the fifth estate* were simply being responsible. They were thinking about the implications and weighing the evidence. I certainly could not complain about the time they had given me to poke around. And there was another practical reason the story had not yet been officially approved. We still had very few sources who had agreed to appear on-camera. Maybe it was just a print story after all.

I turned my focus back to Bernard Lathière. I had kept in touch, had sent the former president of Airbus a couple more faxes and letters, and had even sent him the IAL documents. Then one day I got him on the phone. And just like that, he agreed to do the on-camera interview. I got off the phone and ran to Susan Teskey's office.

"Lathière has agreed to come on-camera."

For the rest of the day I made sure not to answer my phone. I didn't want him to call back to say he had changed his mind. The story, finally, had the green light.

The next day a *fifth estate* crew and I were on a flight to Paris.

---

1 A reference, I presumed, to a solicitor's confidential relationship with his or her client.

CHAPTER NINE
THE BOSS IS PROTECTED

What I remember about the flight to Paris is how quickly the sun came up over the Atlantic, bright and cheerful. My eyes only half-open, I felt a tap on my shoulder. A flight attendant was offering me a fresh cup of coffee. What time was it back in Toronto? I wondered. Two in the morning? I felt both jet-lagged and exhilarated. We would have to start work almost immediately. When I first started working at *the fifth estate* I did not really understand why the team preferred not to sit together on the airplane, but I soon realized it made sense. Over the next ten days we were going to see a lot of one another, and the plane was a rare chance for some quiet time. This was particularly important for the hosts and the camera crew who were travelling practically the entire season. Scattered around the airplane were host Trish Wood, producer David Kaufman, cameraman John Griffin and soundman Alister Bell. A friend of mine at the CBC once joked that filming a documentary "was like being in high school with money" and there was, for sure, some truth to that. Imagine going to Paris and not paying for the trip, then renting a van and driving wherever you needed to go, getting a per diem for your meals, telling jokes as you planned your next interview.

That was the upside. But there were downsides too. For starters, the camera crew was being paid by the hour. The meter was ticking and the producers and researchers were responsible for making sure the documentary was on time and on budget. We were constantly rushing from one location to another and always making the mistake of thinking we could get more done in a day than humanly possible. The logistics were always a nightmare. A documentary crew travels with about twenty cases of equipment, all of which must fit into the rental van, as well as the four or five passengers. Travelling to Paris sounded great on the one hand, but in reality there was never any time for sightseeing or idle conversation along the Seine. It wouldn't matter if you were in Toulouse or Toledo; you were simply too busy getting from one location to another, too worried about the budget, the schedule and the story. By far, the worst part was unspoken: you were away from your home for days or weeks at a time. Those with young families would always return inevitably having missed important milestones. And good luck to you if you were single and hoping to meet someone. Between the months of October and April, when *the fifth estate* was on the air, you were hostage to the work schedule, routinely having to cancel personal commitments in order to make a deadline for the airdate. As a result you sometimes spent far more time with colleagues at work than you did with friends and family. Some of your travelling colleagues would, over time, cross into the "genuine friend" category, some not; it might take you several years to understand the difference.

We landed at Orly Airport, groggy and tired, located our luggage and passed through customs, a process which seemed far less complicated than crossing into the United States. Not a single question. We managed to cram everyone into the van, and the equipment too, then drove to our hotel to get ready for our afternoon interview. This was before any Global Positioning System devices to show us the way, but it didn't matter. Johnny Griffin lived northeast of Toronto, on a farm near Fenelon Falls, but he was a veteran CBC cameraman who knew the streets of Paris like his hometown. Griffin wore his trademark blue beret, steering the van in and out of traffic, making our way towards the Seventeenth Arrondissement and our appointment with Bernard Lathière.

We lugged the equipment into the elevator, the kind with the gates on the outside that you have to close before you can open the doors on the inside. We emerged on the fourth floor and straight into Lathière's living room. We could have been in a palace: high ceilings, picture-length mirrors, antique furniture from around the globe and then Lathière, looking so much like the senior finance official that he was, in a blue suit, confident and relaxed. Griffin and Bell set up the camera and lights in Lathière's living room, we drank some coffee and made small talk. I just hoped that Lathière would not cancel the on-camera interview at the last minute and order us back down that elevator shaft.

Lathière had been pushed out of Airbus in 1985, after a new team led by the current president, Jean Pierson, took over. But he was still the boss at the time the IAL contract was negotiated. He could tell us about the business culture at Airbus. Was it really as corrupt as everyone was telling us? Trish Wood began the interview by asking what it was like to sell planes in the early days of the company.

"It was rough," Lathière acknowledged. "We went twice 'through the desert,' as we say in French. Sometimes we had fourteen [planes] on the tarmac, waiting." Airbus had better planes than Boeing, he said, but they were "nothing" at the time because Boeing had 99 per cent of the market. He told us that the Airbus consortium was formed in 1970 by Aerospatiale of France, Messerschmitt in Germany and British Aerospace in England, all partly owned by their respective governments. The Spanish owned a 4 per cent share. Lathière told us that as president he was the "ambassador" for the company, always trying to "sell, sell, sell."

He denied any impropriety on the part of the airline. He admitted that, of course, they used third-party consultants. "This has nothing to do with bribing, baksheesh [greasemoney], or that kind of thing. These are contracts, which are commercial but almost public. If there were any baksheesh, I don't think we'd be stupid enough to sign it."

Wood handed him a copy of the IAL contract. "This looks rather normal," he maintained. "I see nothing strange in that document." He pointed to the bottom of the back page. He smiled shrewdly. "I see no signature by the way. Why isn't it signed?" The implication being, of course: no signature; no proof that the agreement ever happened.

But certainly wouldn't someone in his position have known details about such a contract? Wood wondered. "They ended up paying this company tens of millions of dollars. Wouldn't you have known about a contract for so much money?"

He scoffed and turned almost dismissive. "The average contract was $800 million, so a contract about 2 per cent on a sale is nothing compared to that." The contract, in other words, was small potatoes and not something for him to be bothered about. "To the president," he reminded Woods, "important things came."

This contract was *not* important.

Had he himself ever paid bribes? she asked.

"Never. For what reasons?" he said. But then he said something odd, which put his denial in a strange new light. "Any country, or any kind of business in which it is done, the boss is protected."

Wood pounced. "What do you mean, 'the boss is protected'?"

Lathière seemed surprised at her naïveté. "I won't take a dollar and give it to somebody, if we ever did that. Somebody else will do it."

Somebody else will do it.

That's exactly what Pelossi had told us: Airbus had hired IAL so somebody else could do it.

Finally, two people who seemed to agree.

We had an ambitious shooting schedule. Later that day we drove to the Banque Française du Commerce Extérieur where we filmed Trish Wood talking to the camera, explaining how Airbus had used that bank to send anonymous cheques to Liechtenstein. The next day we flew to Zurich and went to the Paradeplatz, the heart of the banking district. At the north side of the square sat the Savoy Hotel, at the south end the Swiss Bank Corporation, where Schreiber maintained his personal account: 18679 IAL. I lingered in front of the building. How badly I wanted to be able to walk in and ask to see Schreiber's banking records. Wood did another stand-up in front of the Zurich bank, which we had to redo about a dozen times until, finally, the trams were quiet and there was no background noise.

We knew that Frank Moores had also set up two accounts here in 1986, numbered 34107 and 34117, the latter code-named "Devon." I thought it would be interesting if Trish Wood called Frank Moores from Zurich to ask him about his Swiss account, since I had deliberately left that question out of my previous conversations with him. Our sound recordist, Alister Bell, hooked up the telephone so he could tape the conversation. John Griffin filmed Wood as she dialed the number. Moores answered the phone himself. Trish got right to the point. We had evidence he had set up two secret Swiss bank accounts. Moores denied it all. He said he had never opened any account in Switzerland.

"You are absolutely full of it," he said. "Whoever told you that is right up to their ears in it."

Trish suggested maybe he had simply forgotten he had set up the account.

"Would I remember if I had an account? Of course. Now, what do you think?"

I wondered again how someone could lie so convincingly, and with such apparent contempt for the questioner. Moores seemed not the slightest bit embarrassed. We were convinced there had to be a reason he was denying even the mere existence of his Swiss accounts. More than ever, we wanted to find out why.

The next day we travelled from Zurich south, through the Swiss Alps, to Lugano, where I met Giorgio Pelossi for the first time. I felt like I had met him already. I had listened to his conversation with Jock Ferguson many times over, picking out the factual details to add to our expanding database of information. Pelossi was as unassuming as Ferguson told us, friendly and soft-spoken. If he was in turmoil he did a good job of masking it. We had to film him in shadow because, for now, he was not able to appear in public, concerned that he would be in trouble himself for exposing Schreiber's secrets. So he came to our hotel, where we lit the wall behind him; only his silhouette was visible. He repeated what he had told Jock in the fall: Schreiber had told him that Moores, Mulroney and "Canadian friends" were going to receive 50 per cent of the secret-commission money. He talked about how Schreiber told him all about the plans just before they set up the Frank Moores bank accounts in 1986.

"Schreiber said, before our meeting with the bank officer, he told me you have to go there and open two accounts, one for Moores and one for Mulroney."

"Schreiber told you that?" Wood asked.

"Yes."

"And that didn't surprise you?" Wood said.

"It is normal all over the world in such business. It didn't surprise me."

Pelossi said he suspected that if money went into those accounts, which he could not confirm, it would probably never return to Canada. "If you get untaxed money and you show it, that's dangerous. They can ask you from where do you have this money?"

Pelossi was concerned about how far he was going—not about the allegations he was making—rather, that if he was too specific, certain people might identify him as the source of the information. After all, there were some things that only he would know.

From our perspective we had a different problem, which none of us knew how to solve. We were trying hard to get a quote from Pelossi that would not mention Brian Mulroney because, as of now, we had no evidence to support the allegations. And yet how could Pelossi describe what he was told without actually naming the former prime minister?

Producer David Kaufman suggested we refer to him simply as "a very important political friend" of Moores.

"That's weird," Trish said, because any viewer at home would wonder why she wouldn't follow up and ask who this friend was. "It doesn't make sense," she said.

We knew we didn't want to name Mulroney without rock-solid evidence, but we didn't want to rule anything out for now. Perhaps we would get more evidence later. And so we went back and forth, worried that the quotes might somehow incriminate Mulroney, which we did not want to do.

"We're skirting a very dangerous area," said Kaufman.

"It's not dangerous, we're just trying to sort it out," said Wood.

She was right. Whatever Pelossi said on tape, we could choose what quotes to use later on, in the edit suite. For now, we decided we'd get one quote from Pelossi, leaving out Mulroney's name, and one mentioning him, just in case more evidence came along. In any event, we'd figure it out back in Toronto.

Then came a new revelation. Pelossi had already told us that one of the accounts that he'd helped Moores set up had been code-named, "Devon." We wanted to know how he knew it was called Devon.

"Because they told me," he said. "I wrote it down on my paper."

He wrote it down on his paper? This was new, at least to us.

"What paper?" asked Wood.

Pelossi explained that he wrote details about the accounts on the bank manager's business card.

"And I put down Mr. Moores's and Mr. Mulroney's, with my handwriting."

"Where is that [paper] right now?" Wood asked.

"Mathias [Blumencron] has a copy."

I made a mental note to get the copy from our *Der Spiegel* colleague. Then we asked Pelossi if he could get us a copy of the original.

"I don't know. I have it in the safe [of] the lawyer."

The next morning we were back in the van, driving north towards Liechtenstein. Two hours later we were in Vaduz, the town where Pelossi had set up the shell company IAL. The crew hopped out and put the camera in front of Wood. She talked to the camera about how this tiny principality of less than 30,000 people was where aviation giant Airbus Industrie sent millions of dollars to a shell corporation in order to hide a secret money trail from Paris to Liechtenstein, and later on to Zurich. We found the plate on the side of the building that read "I.A.L." and filmed Trish pointing at it, explaining its significance. We got back on the highway and headed north to Kaufering, Germany, just west of Munich, where Schreiber lived in his "compound" at Raiffeisenstrasse 27.

Schreiber had not agreed to an interview. Our once-cordial relationship had deteriorated. I had sent him a fax in early March that read: "Mr. Schreiber, you will forgive me for wondering if you will ever find a moment to speak with me." What Schreiber probably did not understand was that I needed to get a clear answer from him, one way or the other, about whether or not he would agree to an interview. I made the point rather forcefully: "You have promised me that you will speak to me in detail about my research, but so far that seems like an empty promise." Schreiber had not been amused. *The fifth estate*'s office manager, Suzanna Mayer, had left a message at my Lugano hotel room to call her back immediately. A fax had come from Schreiber. She read it to me over the phone:

> Dear Mr. Cashore. I confirm receipt of your fax dated March 6, 1995. In my opinion this fax shows an obvious lack of culture and intelligence. You seem to have a short memory or do you get carried away with your fantasy? For a short while I believed in your integrity—unfortunately I failed. It looks to me that you can't stop making a fool out of yourself. Future developments will prove the reality. I am convinced you will remember my last fax for a long time. In closing this fax I confirm that I do not want any further contact with you.
>
> Yours truly,
>
> Karlheinz Schreiber

"Well, I guess that's pretty clear," I told Suzanna. Had I blown a potential journalist/source relationship over a poorly worded fax?

"Sounds like this guy doesn't like you, Harvey," Suzanna said glibly.

We decided to approach him anyway, with our cameras rolling. In casual conversation we call this a "jump" and CBC policy dictates that we must seek approval. After a thorough review of the reasons why we wanted to "jump" Schreiber, CBC management gave us permission.

That's how I ended up walking north along Raiffeisenstrasse, casually stopping in front of a tall gate at number 27. I noticed security cameras strategically placed along the perimeter. Schreiber owned a sprawling property. Looking to the south I could see the top of the building that housed his Bavarian road-marking company. Straight ahead was the main residence, set back from the street about 30 metres. I knew from my earlier interviews that Schreiber had a bowling alley in the basement where he used to entertain his German and Canadian friends. To the right was the single-storey garage where he kept his fleet of luxury vehicles: a Porsche Carrera 4 Cabriolet, a 300GE Mercedes with four-wheel drive, a 300CE Mercedes Cabriolet for his wife, Bärbel, a 600 SEL Mercedes limousine, a fully restored 1945 M38 US Jeep[1] and a 500SL Mercedes Roadster Cabriolet.

I walked north to an empty lot where we had parked a small Fiat. Sitting in the driver's seat was the German translator we had hired for the day. And there we sat, waiting for Karlheinz Schreiber. Schreiber travelled most of the year; had residences all over the world and yet here we were, sitting in a rented Fiat, not knowing if he was inside his compound or thousands of miles away. Next to us, in a rented van, were Griffin, Bell, Kaufman and Wood. The plan was for Wood and Griffin to jump out of the van if they spotted Schreiber. Bell would stay in the van and monitor the sound levels on any conversation between Wood and Griffin.

Two hours later we were bored and hungry. This presented a problem: Who would go for food? We would never forgive ourselves if the cameraman wasn't around when Schreiber appeared. Trish could not leave since she was the host. Kaufman was the producer. I didn't need to ask. The translator and I drove off, got some food and returned. Nothing had changed. More time passed. Everyone needed to go to the washroom. We waited, uncomfortable, bored and restless.

Then we saw the garage door slowly open.

"That's him."

Schreiber was wearing a brown leather bomber jacket and dark sunglasses. A woman I presumed was his wife was next to him. They were about to get into their Mercedes roadster. We had been lucky: Schreiber chose to walk out of the garage and into the sunlight, as if to catch some fresh air. That meant Wood and Griffin could approach him on the sidewalk. I stayed in the Fiat and studied Schreiber from a distance. He was short but he carried himself in such a way that he seemed taller.

Wood and Griffin hustled towards him; he looked puzzled then turned for shelter back to the garage. Trish and Griffin hurried after him. Wood followed Schreiber into the garage. Then I noticed the garage door coming

1 Schreiber would later explain that he bought the vintage jeep after the memory of American soldiers who came to his village in the Harz Mountains at the end of the Second World War. He recalls seeing a black man for the first time, at first believing the Nazi propaganda that this was a cannibal who would eat him alive. Instead, the soldier handed eleven-year-old Karlheinz a piece of Wrigley's chewing gum, who still needed to be convinced it was not poison. The soldier tore off half the stick of gum and chewed it himself, convincing Schreiber he could do the same.

down. Griffin was filming from outside. The door had come all the way down. Holy shit, I thought. Now what? Moments later the garage door shuddered open. Schreiber and his wife were in the Mercedes roadster; Wood stood awkwardly beside the car.

The car moved away. As our sound recordist monitored the scene from the rental van, the German translator and I took off in the Fiat, following the Mercedes onto the autobahn. To our surprise we almost caught up. I swear I saw Schreiber smile at me. The 500SL Mercedes convertible can reach speeds of up to 300 kilometres an hour. The engines roared and the car disappeared so quickly that I had the feeling we were going backwards. We returned to the others to report the bad news. But no one was talking. In the panic to get Schreiber on-camera, Griffin had accidentally pressed the Record button twice, meaning he'd actually turned the camera off.

We had missed almost everything: Schreiber on the sidewalk, the conversation between Wood and Schreiber, the door closing and the door reopening. By the time Griffin realized his mistake, Schreiber and Bärbel were already driving away.

We returned to the Zurich airport in the rental van, travelling silently through the spring countryside, passing from Germany into Switzerland, on the south side of Lake Constance. The enormity of our disaster in Kaufering had started to sink in. We arrived at the airport and unhappily lugged the equipment to the check-in counter. Then we caught a flight to Toulouse.

The next day we woke up early and drove immediately to Colomiers, where Stuart Iddles lived. We waited, again, bored, again, hoping that he too would be at home and not in some faraway country. I worried Schreiber had tipped off Iddles to be on the lookout for a crazy camera crew from Canada.

Iddles emerged from his house wearing a track suit with "Ireland" stitched on the back. He walked down the path to a small, hip-high gate, which he opened and closed before he looked up to find Trish Wood.

"Mr. Iddles, I'm Trish Wood from CBC Television." He stopped, momentarily at least. "Did you not receive my fax?"

Iddles began his morning jog. Wood decided to join him. The cameraman ran ahead and then jogged backwards, in order to film Iddles and

Wood jogging together. Wood tried to get him to explain, again, why he couldn't talk about his friendships with Schreiber and Moores. "I'm just wondering, Mr. Iddles, if Schreiber and Moores and IAL didn't work for Airbus, how can that be Airbus business?" No answer. "Canadian people paid a billion dollars, over a billion dollars for those planes. Don't they have a right to some explanation of what went on?" Wood asked.

"Go to Airbus," huffed Iddles.

"Airbus won't talk to us." Iddles speeded up and disappeared down the street, leaving Wood and Griffin breathless. We decided to wait. He'd have to come back eventually, wouldn't he? Twenty minutes later a sweaty Iddles returned.

Trish had the IAL documents in her hand, plus copies of telexes Iddles had personally sent to Pelossi and Schreiber.

"Why can't you talk about them?" Wood asked him. "Don't you want to just see these? Some of them have your signature on them. Even this one that you see was written with a copy sent to Mr. Schreiber."

Iddles opened the gate and disappeared into his house.

As far as anyone could recall, it was the first time we ever "jumped" anyone while jogging.

We were giddy. All the way back to the town square in Toulouse we joked about the "jump and jog" with Iddles. We had forgotten all about the horror of the camera not working on the Schreiber jump; after all, we did get him driving away, so all was not lost. We realized that we had set out what we had hoped to accomplish. We had come across the Atlantic, interviewed Lathière in Paris and Pelossi in Lugano, captured both Schreiber and Iddles on videotape and filmed a series of stand-ups from Paris to Liechtenstein to Zurich. The stress had begun to dissipate. We ate dinner at a restaurant off the town square that billed itself as a centuries-old cave, and stayed the evening. Griffin and Bell regaled us with stories from other documentaries they had shot around the world. This was the upside of travel, being able to take an evening to unwind with colleagues, in a foreign city, after a job well done.

From that day on, everything seemed to go our way. We flew back to Toronto to join David Kaufman, who had left the European shoot a day early in order to begin editing. Kaufman worked alongside Gary Akenhead, one of *the fifth estate*'s most experienced and talented editors.

While Kaufman and Akenhead edited, I continued to work the phones. I called back Keith Miller, the airline executive once courted by Schreiber and Moores to join the Airbus lobbying team. I urged him to come on-camera, even if it was just in shadow.[2] After some careful thought, he agreed. Trish Wood and I flew to Florida for the interview.

"I know for a fact personally that Mr. Moores met with the vice-president of marketing [Stuart Iddles] and I know for a fact that he met with another gentleman by the name of Mr. Schreiber," Miller said.

"And what was the nature of the encounter between Mr. Moores and Mr. Iddles?" asked Wood.

"The nature of the encounter of which I have knowledge was the discussion of the sale of aircraft to Wardair and Air Canada."

"So this was the sale of Airbus aircraft to these two Canadian airlines?"

"That is correct."

"And Mr. Moores, you say, also met with Mr. Schreiber. What can you tell us about the nature of what happened at that meeting?"

"The meeting was about the sale of Airbus aircraft in Canada." Miller continued, "I don't understand at all why it's being denied. I've been told that Mr. Moores visited the Air Canada executives with respect to Airbus. I'm sure it wasn't social. I believe it was [about] selling aircraft."

Miller's interview, on its own, was a slam dunk that sunk Moores's denials that he had no involvement on the Airbus file. Which brought us to one piece of unfinished business. We had jumped Schreiber and Iddles; now it was Frank Moores's turn. We knew he was living in Jupiter, Florida, in a condominium owned by that Lugano company, Ticinella Anstalt. So we drove to Moores's gated community at 1000 NUS Highway, just fifteen miles north of West Palm Beach.

Because he was living in a gated community, we would have to walk in on foot. That was problematic; surely if we loitered too long we would be noticed and told to leave. I came up with an idea. I guessed that if Frank Moores was retired and living in Florida, he probably also enjoyed playing

2 Miller would later agree to be identified.

golf. Over dinner that night I asked our waiter for a list of all the golf clubs in the area. There were, unfortunately, dozens. Back in my hotel room I consulted the Yellow Pages and found even more names. I set the alarm for 5 a.m. When I woke up the next morning, I began calling the golf clubs, in alphabetical order.

"Pardon me," I said when I called the first pro shop, "but what time is Frank Moores's tee-off time?" I called more than a dozen courses. None had a tee-off time for Moores. Eventually I called the exclusive Loxahatchee golf club, a private course designed by Jack Nicklaus. They had a tee-off time for a Frank Moores at nine-thirty. We went to Moores's condo soon after nine and waited. Moores emerged from his condo wearing khaki slacks, a red-and-blue-striped golf shirt and sunglasses. I stayed behind the cameraman in the background. Trish Wood went up to greet him.

"Hi, Mr. Moores, I'm Trish Wood from the CBC's *the fifth estate*."

"Hello, Trish."

"I really have to ask a couple of questions on-camera."

"Well, you are not asking me anything this morning, Trish."

"Can you just tell me why sources have told us that you discussed the sale of Airbus with Mr. Schreiber, the sale of Airbus to Air Canada?"

"That is absolutely untrue and there is no verification for any of these rumours. I am not going to just be here talking to you when there is no truth to it . . . I think this is the most colossal waste of taxpayers' money I have ever seen. And I just think your time is wasted here, that is all."

Moores got into his blue sedan Mercedes and drove off to the Loxahatchee Club. We were thrilled. Now we had the final video we needed to complete our documentary. We flew back to Toronto.

Frank Moores hired a Bay Street lawyer, the respected Edgar Sexton, from the law firm Osler, Hoskin & Harcourt. On March 17, Sexton wrote a letter to the Canadian Broadcasting Corporation. Sexton said that he had understood that *the fifth estate* would allege that "Moores represented Airbus Industrie in its bid to sell Airbus aircraft to Air Canada and other airlines; that Mr. Moores earned substantial income as a consequence of sales of Airbus aircraft; and that Mr. Karl-Heinz [sic] Schreiber purchased a Florida condominium for Mr. Moores."

This is to advise you that it is our client's position that the foregoing allegations are completely false and seriously defamatory of his personal and professional reputation, and that, in particular: (i) although Mr. Moores acted in an unrelated transaction for Messerschmitt-Bolkow-Blohm [MMB], a partner of Airbus Industrie, he did not at any time act for Airbus Industrie, and he had no involvement whatsoever in any airline's purchase of Airbus aircraft; (ii) he earned no income as a consequence of any airline's purchase of Airbus aircraft; and (iii) he has never received a Florida condominium from Mr. Schreiber or anyone else. In fact, Mr. Moores has since April 30, 1990 rented a Florida condominium for which he has paid rent at full market value.

If any of the above "false and defamatory allegations" were broadcast, Sexton would recommend that Moores "immediately" commence an action in libel against CBC "seeking very substantial general, aggravated and punitive damages."

Whenever a letter arrives at *the fifth estate* threatening legal action we take it seriously. The evidence that Frank Moores was involved with Airbus was overwhelming and conclusive. Even so, we carefully reviewed Sexton's points carefully with Daniel Henry, the CBC's lawyer. Henry told me he was impressed with the evidence we had collected. If Moores thought that he could circumvent the public's right to know by hiring an expensive Bay Street lawyer, he was sadly mistaken. At least that's what I thought.

We had one final decision to make: whether or not to broadcast the allegation that Brian Mulroney received money from Schreiber. Everyone on the production team assembled in David Studer's office, including Daniel Henry. There are two kinds of media lawyers: those who want to help you find a way to broadcast a story in the public interest without getting into legal trouble, and those who are so worried, that they never want to report anything that has lawsuit potential. Daniel Henry belonged to the former category. We went over all the evidence that Pelossi had provided to us, including the key allegation about what Schreiber told him: money from the Moores account—code-named "Devon"—was to go to Mulroney. Trish Wood had figured out earlier that Devon was also the name of the street where Mulroney and his wife lived in the 1970s. Frank Moores was close to

Mulroney in the 1970s and would have visited the Mulroneys in their Devon Avenue home. It was an interesting and intriguing detail and certainly could have explained how Moores came up with the name.

Still, the meeting did not last very long. We had no proof Mulroney had received a penny from Schreiber, so why make libellous allegations without evidence? Just because Frank Moores had lied about certain details did not mean that he had lied about giving any money to Mulroney. But then we came to a decision I simply did not understand. The consensus was that we should not even call Mulroney; a phone call to Mulroney might in itself give the wrong signal. (We were not going to connect him to the money, but we were planning to mention him as the prime minister in power when Frank Moores and Schreiber were busy lobbying in Ottawa.) Still, I didn't see the logic. Shouldn't we at least call Mulroney and try to find out what he knew about Schreiber and Moores? Shouldn't we at least tell him about the allegations and monitor his response? What would be wrong with that? Today I understand the caution. Dan Henry knew we were entering a political minefield where every step could be our last. And so we retreated to a safe spot, or so we thought. We would not name Mulroney; nor would we even seek to speak with him.

On Tuesday, March 28, 1995, the day our documentary was to be broadcast, *the fifth estate* received a fax at exactly 11:46 a.m. from Schreiber's German lawyer, Stefan von Moers. "We will follow this report with interest and will prosecute each and every inaccuracy regarding the portrayal of our client and will proceed without indulgence." The lawyer explained that Schreiber was not pleased with our attempts to interview him at his home in Kaufering. "Your staff had no scruples whatsoever to trespass on our client's land or property, a fact which—according to German law—might be considered the legal element of a violation of the privacy of a person . . ."

That evening at 8 p.m. nearly one million Canadians tuned in to watch "Sealed in Silence."

"An Airbus A320 lands at Pearson International Airport in Toronto." Trish Wood's voice is heard over a breathtakingly beautiful shot of one of Air Canada's A320 Airbus jets. "It's another landing for the workhorse of the fleet. The A320 seats 180—perfect for domestic routes. It can carry cargo as well as passengers. And it's extremely fuel efficient—it can fly nonstop from

Montreal to Vancouver. In 1988, Air Canada ordered thirty-four of these planes at a cost of $1.8 billion—the biggest purchase ever by a Canadian airline. Ever since, there have been rumours circulating in Ottawa suggesting that the deal was tainted, that someone made financial payments to ensure that Air Canada bought the planes from Airbus instead of the competition."

In studio, Trish Wood summarized what we had learned. "*The fifth estate* has been investigating these rumours for five months. Although we found no evidence that anyone with decision-making power in the deal received payments, we have discovered that some of the rumours have a basis in fact. We have learned that it was Airbus Industrie itself that paid secret commissions to a mysterious company in Liechtenstein to help it win the contract with Air Canada. We have also learned that the principal figure behind this company is a German entrepreneur who has powerful friends at home and in Canada."

And with that we introduced Canadians to Karlheinz Schreiber and Giorgio Pelossi, the latter seen simply in shadow and described only as one of Schreiber's associates. We explained Schreiber's connection to Franz Josef Strauss, the Bavarian premier and chairman of Airbus, his connection to politicians in Alberta and his friendship with former Newfoundland premier Frank Moores who, we explained, had helped engineer the dump-Clark movement and supported Brian Mulroney. Gary Kincaid, the Airbus salesman, was quoted explaining how the European company had set up offices in North America to try to win business here. Kincaid said he knew nothing of Frank Moores's involvement, except to say there were rumours he was involved in a secret campaign.

"If you ask me do I think that Airbus Industrie paid money to influence the A320 sale to Air Canada, I will tell you I think it happened."

"You think it happened?" Wood asked.

"Yes, I think it happened," Kincaid said.

As for the most controversial part of our story, the Frank Moores bank accounts, we stepped lightly. We made not a single mention of Mulroney. Instead, we outlined what we actually knew compared to what others were claiming.

Wood explained: "About a year after Airbus signed its contract with IAL, Frank Moores came here to Zurich. He met with Karlheinz Schreiber and the two men went into this branch of the Swiss Bank Corporation. Schreiber already did his banking here and that day Moores opened two accounts. *The fifth estate* has learned that Frank Moores's bank account was number 34107. The second bank account was number 34117 with the additional code name: Devon."

We quoted Pelossi, in shadow: "I know that two accounts were opened in a Swiss bank for the Canadian friends of Mr. Schreiber. One of them was for a Canadian politician and one of them was for Frank Moores."

"And the purpose of those accounts was what?"

"To receive commissions, commissions on the Airbus business and on other business in Germany."

"And why were the accounts opened in Switzerland?"

"Because of bank secrecy."

And then we made it clear to viewers that we did not know why the accounts were opened, or whether they ever received any money.

"Whatever the reason for opening the accounts, *the fifth estate* has no evidence that any commissions were actually paid into them."

We ended the documentary making the point that it was possible Air Canada—hence the Canadian taxpayer—paid too much for the airplanes. Had the secret commissions not been paid, the price could have been that much less. "In the end, Air Canada's customers and shareholders, and Canadian taxpayers, paid for the aircraft. And if the bill for the aircraft included the commissions, then every one of these thirty-four A320s was overpriced by half a million American dollars."

When most documentaries at *the fifth estate* get broadcast, producers and researchers move on to another topic. While I knew that this story was different, I could never have predicted how long it would last, the toll it would take, and the consequences it would have on so many, both professionally and personally. It would leave me wondering on many occasions whether it had all been worth it. But those questions were far into the future. As the credits rolled at the end of our documentary in March 1995, I knew I had some unfinished business. I still wanted to find out where all that money had gone. And I knew I worked for a public broadcaster that wanted me to do just that. That night I felt like the luckiest journalist in the country.

CHAPTER TEN
AN UNNAMED POLITICIAN

To my surprise, that first Airbus story never got the kind of attention I had hoped for. The Canadian Press wrote a story about our program, which the *Ottawa Citizen* placed on page A4: "A European aircraft manufacturer paid secret commissions to smooth the sale of planes to Air Canada in 1988, says CBC-TV's The Fifth Estate [*sic*]." At the Montreal *Gazette*, Jeff Heinrich was, as far as I could tell, the only reporter to follow up. Heinrich wrote articles both about *Der Spiegel*'s Airbus story in Germany as well as our story, the headline quoting our interview with the former president of Air Canada: "Airbus 'crazy' to pay Tory lobbyists: Jeanniot." The only other news organization to cover our story in any significant way was *Der Spiegel*, a foreign publication. Certainly there were no calls for a public inquiry and, on Parliament Hill, not a peep. Author Paul Palango, who had seen our program, wrote an op-ed piece in the Montreal *Gazette* and questioned the lack of coverage. "I don't get it," he wrote. "One would have thought that after the CBC broadcast its program, there would be an uproar in Parliament and the media. But no, this is Canada. The world of politics and journalism doesn't work quite that way here any more. Politicians yawned and said the story was old news. The Canadian media, almost without exception, labeled *the fifth estate* story as old news or whatever excuse was needed to conveniently pass on it. The story disappeared from sight faster than a bombed airplane in the middle of the Atlantic Ocean."

Palango saw the lack of response to our story as part of a larger trend. "In virtually every other Western democracy in recent years, serious and successful investigations have been mounted against former government and business leaders for corruption. Only in Canada has such judicial scrutiny failed to materialize." If Palango was hoping his words would get other media to finally start to report on our story, he was wrong. I was thankful for his opinions, but they, too, seemed to drop from the sky and into the ocean.

Inside the CBC, however, the response was different. The day after the show went to air we all got a letter in our in-box from David Studer, reporting that he had had a call from Bob Culbert, the executive director of news at CBC. "He went on to offer that a program like last night's is as good an argument as could ever exist for the continued healthy existence of the CBC. You should be as proud as he and I are."

Meanwhile, I continued my research. Foremost in my mind: the banker's business card on which Pelossi had made the handwritten notations about the Swiss accounts. We asked our colleagues at *Der Spiegel* to fax us a copy. Pelossi had written "F. Moore" above account "34107" and "B.M." above account "34117." None of this proved Mulroney *got* the money. What it could have suggested is that Pelossi was *told* the second account was for Mulroney. Otherwise, why would he write it down?

I hoped banker Paul Schnyder would talk to me. Perhaps he would remember that day in 1986 when Schreiber, Moores and Pelossi asked him to set up the accounts. I tracked him down to a new bank location outside Zurich. Schnyder told me he left the downtown branch in 1990, confirming, in a small way, Pelossi's story, since the business card Schnyder had given to Pelossi in 1986 listed his old business address, not the new one. Schnyder said he was no longer in charge of those accounts and suggested I speak with Andre Strobl, Schreiber's personal banker. I called him too; he never called back.

The next week we heard from Airbus.

On April 4, 1995, the multinational wrote a letter to the president of the CBC, who happened to be the newly appointed former Mulroney cabinet minister Perrin Beatty. (The previous president, Anthony Manera, had resigned in protest after Jean Chrétien's government announced a series of future cutbacks at the Mother Corp.) The Airbus letter filtered down from Beatty's office to the vice-president of English television, Jim Byrd, then on to the head of news, Bob Culbert, then to *the fifth estate*'s executive producer, David Studer, and finally to my desk, the end of the chain of responsibility. I noticed that someone had written in the margins of the letter: "URGENT" for "Bob (Culbert) and David Studer."

David Venz, the same public relations person from Airbus's US office with whom I had spoken back in January, had signed the letter. In it he challenged the authenticity of Pelossi's documents, implying that they had been forged. Venz wrote that the "so called contract" that we had obtained was "unsigned" and "could have been produced on any computer by anyone." He repeated what others had said, that the decision that Air Canada made was legitimate and not influenced by any third parties or commissions. Venz concluded his letter with a rhetorical remark. "Perhaps the more interesting question *the fifth estate* did not ask was: 'Who is so interested in keeping this feeble fire stoked?'"

I wrote up a lengthy response to the Airbus letter. I questioned why Airbus refused to let us speak to anyone at the corporation. I outlined how a former Airbus president [Bernard Lathière] had actually confirmed that the contract number on the documents belonged to Airbus. I explained that we had proof Airbus had sent millions to the Liechtenstein company IAL. I suggested that Airbus drop the gag order on its employees and allow us to talk to them. David Studer, my boss, then wrote a formal letter of response to our bosses. Once again, David Studer told us that CBC management was impressed with the depth of our research. "Bob Culbert left me a voice-mail message to say that he'd read our Airbus letter and liked it. He went on to ask that I let you know how comforting it is to see just how well-researched and ready we are to rebut these attacks."

I had not come close to achieving my goal of finding out where the Airbus money had gone, and now that the documentary had been broadcast, I figured I could slow down a little but still poke around the edges of the story, and make some of the calls I'd never had time to make.

There was also something else on my mind, which I had yet to resolve: that call I had received from the RCMP in January. I had deliberately decided not to call them back, having all but concluded there was no point. I was never going to hand over any documents to our national police force. Still, I also knew that it would be a matter of time before the Mounties got their hands on them. Pelossi's objective, after all, was to go to the media and the authorities in order to punish Schreiber and protect himself. In fact, Pelossi had already told us he had made contact with authorities in Germany.

It was clear, however, that the Mounties were not going to wait. *Der Spiegel's* Mathias Blumencron had told me they would soon be flying to Hamburg to meet him. Blumencron wondered why I was being so stubborn. "We meet with all kinds of sources, why not the police?" he asked me.

He had a point. On Friday, March 31, 1995, I called Carl Gallant at the RCMP in Ottawa and told him I would be willing to meet him and Sergeant Fraser Fiegenwald.

Just to be careful, I decided to protect the Airbus documents. I was worried that the RCMP might obtain a search warrant and seize the materials, so I made sure that the documents were not anywhere near the building. I had reason to be concerned. My former boss, John Sawatsky, had told me of the day the RCMP knocked on his door in the 1980s, armed with a search warrant permitting them to seize his notes. Sawatsky had done nothing wrong. The RCMP were pursuing criminal charges against a former member of its security service and figured he had information to help them in their investigation. I considered Sawatsky's experience a journalistic violation. The Mounties went through all his personal records looking for information. Still, they hunted in vain. That's because Sawatsky, having anticipated the search warrant, had already moved his materials to a secret location. I decided to do the same thing. On a Saturday afternoon in early April I collected all of CBC's documents pertaining to the Airbus story and stuffed them into two bankers boxes. Then I drove to my aunt Jessie Ann Orme's house in Scarborough, Ontario. She was thrilled to play a part in my efforts to keep the documents safe from the RCMP. I placed the boxes in a musty storage room next to her basement rec room. Then we had coffee in her kitchen and speculated about what might happen next.

Blumencron told me that he had had a rather uneventful meeting with RCMP sergeant Fraser Fiegenwald on April 6 at the Canadian consulate in Hamburg. He refused to provide the Mounties with the identity of his source [Giorgio Pelossi] nor would he turn over any of his documents. The only thing he would do, he told me, was agree to take Fiegenwald's business card and send it to his source. That was all.

The more I thought about it, the more I realized I really did not want to meet with the Mounties after all. I called Gallant back and told him I'd had second thoughts, that I was simply unwilling to give them any information of any kind. Gallant suggested we meet anyway. He and Fiegenwald were going to be in Toronto on another matter and so why didn't we just get together for coffee? I agreed, as long as they understood they were not getting any information from me.

We met on May 4, 1995, at the Delta Hotel on Gerrard Street. I was a little paranoid and wondered, but did not ask, if they had secret cameras filming our discussion. Fiegenwald wanted me to know he already knew the identity of the Canadian politician in our documentary. "We understand why you are unwilling to share your documents or information," they said. They offered a compromise. Could I at least call my sources and ask them to contact the RCMP? I had no intention of doing any such thing, but remained noncommittal.

Then I left.

I kept in touch with Mathias Blumencron. That summer he told me Schreiber was under investigation in Germany for tax evasion. Then, on July 31, he called to tell me that Pelossi had met with Sergeant Fiegenwald somewhere in Switzerland. Pelossi did not contact the RCMP; they had called him first. Somehow the Mounties got his name. But from whom? Neither of us knew.

Pelossi let Sergeant Fiegenwald take a look at all the Airbus documents. He told Blumencron that the Mounties seemed interested. They indicated that the next step would be to begin the "difficult" legal procedure of getting information out of the Swiss Bank Corporation in Zurich. Fiegenwald cautioned Pelossi that it could be until September before any results came back from the bank, as they would have to request the information through diplomatic channels between the two countries.

I sat down at my computer and composed a note to David Studer.

Today I learned the RCMP have interviewed our source on the Airbus story. Apparently our source gave the RCMP all of his documents and the RCMP believes they now have enough information to apply to the normal channels in Switzerland to get access to the Devon bank account. I don't know how the RCMP have worded their request—which would have been made through External Affairs I believe—but they're likely to have mentioned the name of the "Canadian politician" in their diplomatic telexes.

We had been careful not to mention Mulroney in our original story, but we still had to consider what would happen if our competitors got their hands on the letter the Mounties wrote to Switzerland. I called a police contact in Switzerland who told me that he had seen a draft of the Letter of Request from Canada to Switzerland. Yes, it had named Mulroney. We held a team meeting in Studer's office. We had confirmed that Mulroney's name was in the draft Letter of Request for Assistance. But we also knew that nothing had changed about the facts of the story. Just because the RCMP was interested in the Pelossi allegations did not, in itself, advance anything. We chose not to name Mulroney in March because we had no evidence he received money, so why would we name him now? We decided not to broadcast the information. If other organizations were going to scoop us and mention Mulroney, so be it. We had showed restraint in March and we weren't going to do anything different now.

For most of the summer I had other stories on my mind: one about two Canadian brothers from a prominent Toronto family who had financially defrauded American clients, another a research project into the defence industry and its allegedly "cozy" relationship with the Department of National Defence (DND). But the story that got the green light was one that our Paris freelancer, Judi Rever, brought to our attention. It was about a Canadian man and spiritualist, Norman William, who had run a cult in Europe called Ecoovie, the members of which lived nomadically in teepees. She uncovered unsettling allegations of pedophilia and other abuse, yet for years William had been able to escape controversy. It's the story I was working on that fall when I learned Airbus was back in the news. On Sunday, November 12, 1995, I was working in the edit suite when a story was breaking in Europe about the RCMP's Letter of Request. On Monday morning I was so preoccupied with the Ecoovie documentary that I had not even bothered to read the morning *Globe and Mail*. I walked by Susan Teskey's office.

"Harvey, come back here!"

Someone had given Teskey a whip as a joke once, and she'd proudly hung it on her wall behind her desk, which is what I was staring at when she told me about the CP wire story in that morning's *Globe and Mail*. "RCMP probes Airbus deal," screamed the front-page headline, with the additional subhead "Alleged bribery, Swiss bank accounts for Tory politicians focus of investigation."

The story explained how the authorities in Canada and Switzerland were investigating the Airbus allegations. An RCMP spokesperson was quoted as saying they were assessing "certain allegations" concerning the Air Canada purchase of A320s. A Swiss television program *10 vor 10* got the story first, broadcasting an investigative report the previous Friday, complete with an interview with a highly placed confidential source who spoke in shadow. (I asked Georgio Pelossi if he was the source. He was.) The CP wire story accurately reported how careful *the fifth estate* had been in its original reporting. "CBC said it could not prove that any money was paid into either of [Moores's] Swiss accounts and that it had no evidence to suggest the involvement of anyone in a position to influence Air Canada's choice of Airbus planes."

All hell was breaking loose at the CBC and, as I would later realize, in newsrooms across the country. No one was talking about much else. On *The National* that evening, Peter Mansbridge introduced a Brian Stewart news item stating that a "major scandal" was about to "break open." The story showed scenes of Bern, the capital of Switzerland, which is where the RCMP's Letter of Request had ended up.

The *Toronto Star*, the *Globe and Mail*, the *Financial Post*, the *Toronto Sun*, CTV News and CBC News all began assigning teams to cover the story. And yet I couldn't help but wonder what had changed. Aside from the Montreal *Gazette*, the media had all but ignored our original story in March. Nothing more had happened since then, other than the fact that the RCMP seemed to be interested in the same story. It didn't seem to make sense to me that back in March the media ignored the story and now it equally didn't make sense that the media were about to trip all over themselves to report essentially the same story.

That evening I had a phone call at my home.

"Hi, Harvey. It's Phil Mathias."

I knew Mathias well. He worked at the *Financial Post* as a veteran investigative journalist. In late 1993 and early 1994, we had worked together on a story about allegations of sexual assault against former Nova Scotia premier Gerald Regan. Mathias had actually worked for *the fifth estate* in the early 1980s, and had pursued the same topic back when Regan had become a cabinet minister in Pierre Trudeau's government. Still, the story never got broadcast. There were suggestions that CBC president Al Johnson had killed the story. In December 1993, my then boss, Kelly Crichton, assigned me to work with Phil to see if we could resurrect the story. We did. "An Open Secret" was broadcast on *the fifth estate* in the spring of 1994, produced by Claude Vickery and hosted by Hana Gartner, detailing stories of how the former premier had sexually harassed dozens of young women in Nova Scotia.[1]

I had not talked to Phil for a while. He wanted to know if I was involved in *the fifth estate*'s Airbus story back in the spring. Then he wanted to know who the unnamed politician was. I refused to name Mulroney. I emphasized that whoever it was, it did not mean the politician actually got the money. Still, since we had worked well together on the Regan story, I saw an opportunity.

"We should work together on this, Phil," I said.

"We'll see," he replied.

The next day the *Financial Post* ran a story stating that "a one-time senior adviser to Prime Minister Brian Mulroney claimed yesterday to have

---

1 Gerald Regan was charged with sexual offences in March 1995. His lawyer, Edward Greenspan, successfully defended him.

knowledge that millions of dollars was laundered through bank accounts in Bermuda, the Cayman Islands, Liechtenstein and Jersey in Britain's Channel Islands. 'There is a paper trail of accounts all over the f—ing world,' said the Tory insider, who asked not be identified." The *Post* story also quoted Air Canada spokesperson Nicole Couture-Simard. "There were no bribes paid to Air Canada, absolutely not," she said, adding there was no third party involved in the transaction. It seemed like a strange denial. If there were bribes paid, surely the recipients would not have informed Air Canada's public relations office.[2] I was most intrigued by the quote from the senior adviser who knew about the "paper trail." It was clear to me that the *Financial Post* had an excellent source close to Brian Mulroney and, while I was envious, I looked forward to hearing more from them about this particular angle. I never would. The *Financial Post* never returned to this part of the story.

In the next few days, Airbus-related stories filled all the newspapers. There were revelations about how John Crosbie had investigated the allegations in 1988 and declared the deal clean; another about how US ambassador Tom Niles had raised concerns with the Conservative government. The RCMP told the *Toronto Star* that the investigation was in its infancy. The RCMP is "simply evaluating what is available as evidence to determine whether we get into it fully or not," Fiegenwald was quoted. "RCMP mum on whether politicians named in probe," echoed a *Globe and Mail* headline.

Globe reporter Paul Koring interviewed an Airbus spokesperson in Toulouse. "Airbus spokeswoman Sandy Smith said the consortium 'had never done any business with Schreiber.' She also said that 'all along we have denied the allegations' of irregularities and bribes . . . We are comfortable that everything we have done is legitimate . . . and we are not going to continue to feed the media grist mill."

That Monday and Tuesday were a blur. Everyone seemed to be calling me from within the CBC building, and many others from outside too. As I fielded calls and questions from my colleagues in the building, I was try-

---

2   A few weeks later the Montreal *Gazette* quoted Denis Biro, Air Canada's manager of investor relations, saying that the Airbus A320 was the best available option. "The A320 was bought because, all things considered, we thought we were better off," Biro said.

ing to advance the story as much as I could, making every possible call I could think to make. I called all my old sources in Canada and the United States and placed dozens of calls to Europe—to journalists, to the police, to the Office of Public Prosecutions, to PR people who ran the Justice Department and to the Swiss Bank Corporation itself. Mathias Blumencron sent me a fax with some names to call: a Mr. Lehmann, the spokesperson for the Swiss chief prosecutor, Carla Del Ponte; Beat Bieri, the producer of the Swiss TV program that broke the story about the RCMP's Letter of Request. Mathias told me that someone named Jörg Hillinger was leading the German investigation. He was in Augsburg, near Kaufering, and worked closely with another man named Reinhard Nemetz. The PR person for the Swiss Bank Corporation told me the bank was co-operating with Swiss authorities. Meanwhile, I was trying to get a copy of the official Letter of Request itself, but was having no luck. Folco Galli, the head of PR for the Swiss police, refused to give it to me. I even put in a phone call to Schreiber, hoping he might call back and give me an exclusive interview. I was working at a frantic pace, putting new names into my computer database every few minutes. We were entering a new phase in the research where I was now competing with other journalists.

The fifth estate host Trish Wood made some calls as well. RCMP sergeant Fiegenwald refused to name the Canadian politician identified in the Letter of Request. She called Frank Moores in Florida. His wife, Beth, told Wood she knew nothing about any Swiss accounts set up by her husband.

I got to work on Wednesday morning planning to work the phones from my office. Above all, I hoped Giorgio Pelossi would agree to speak out in public. Not only was I convinced it was a good idea, I also worried someone else would name him anyway. I stopped by Susan Teskey's office to explain my concerns. I believed that Canadians should understand who Pelossi was by name, his exact relationship with Schreiber and what exactly he knew and what exactly he did not know. Pelossi had not even agreed to do the interview, but Teskey told me it was time to get on a plane to Switzerland.

"When?"

"Now."

We walked over to the desk of Deborah Carter, CBC travel coordinator. There was a flight leaving that evening. Five minutes later I was a confirmed passenger. I had to call my wife with the news. Alisa was in her first year of teaching high school. Her job was as demanding as mine. I explained that she would have to pick up our son from day care and that I would be gone on an overseas business trip.

Despite the urgency to get to the airport, I had one interview that afternoon I could not cancel. The meeting was with Tower, the source who had helped me out back in January, the one who inspired me to keep digging with the reminder that the Airbus deal did not pass the "smell test." Had he heard anything new? On my way out to meet Tower, I had another call from Phil Mathias. I was still hoping he would agree to work with us on the story. I told him I was heading off to Zurich that evening. I had no idea that that casual remark would set off a chain of events that would lead to a dramatic development in the story.

Tower's office was close enough to the CBC that taking a cab did not make a lot of sense. I found myself jogging through the streets of Toronto, then running, realizing every minute mattered if I was to make the flight to Zurich that evening.

I arrived at Tower's office, exhausted, dishevelled and sweaty.

"Sorry, I have to catch a plane in a few hours," I tried to explain.

We spoke quickly. Yes, he had more to tell me.

"Key link is Greg Alford," Tower said.

I knew who Greg Alford was. I had tried several times to speak with him, unsuccessfully. Alford was from a place called Chaffey's Locks, in eastern Ontario, where Frank Moores had a family cottage. Alford worked in Ottawa for GCI then later became vice-president of Bear Head Industries.

Tower spoke in bullet points.

"The only reason for overseas accounts is to either avoid paying taxes or for subterfuge."

Don Mazankowski was squeaky clean.

Moores's involvement with Air Canada upset Mazankowski.

Mazankowski dealt with the principals in Europe to facilitate the aircraft deal. Maz made a phone call: Fish or cut bait.

I was unclear what Tower meant by this. Did he mean Mazankowski made a call to Airbus to help sell planes in Canada?

"Ramsey knew about the Airbus shit. Pursue him."

Ramsey was Ramsey Withers, former deputy minister of transport, who moved to Moores's lobby firm GCI in April 1988, the same month Air Canada approved the Airbus deal.

Tower told me that many of the key players would always meet over the same dining room table at Hy's Steakhouse in Ottawa. There they talked about the Airbus deal and the commissions that would flow to certain Canadians. "It was no secret. The only secret was who and how much. Frank would say this at Hy's. He was proud of his empire. Gary Ouellet should be tested. Speak to him in detail about a multitude of clients with European implications. Thyssen could be the vehicle through which money could be channelled.

"It was a massive campaign.

"Thyssen angle should be probed deeply.

"Do not concentrate only on Airbus. Broader on GCI. Gary Ouellet.

"There was a meeting between Ramsey Withers and Karlheinz Schreiber when Ramsey was deputy minister. Meetings have to be Airbus meetings. No other reason why.

"Gary Ouellet was close to the prime minister.

"Moores and Mulroney had a falling-out. Serious. Beth used to talk with Mila. Somebody shut the tap."

This was a new development. I had never heard about a falling-out between Mulroney and Moores before. From everything I had heard, Moores and Mulroney were best buddies. Moores had introduced Mulroney when Mulroney gave his speech at his failed attempt in 1976 to become leader of the PC Party. And Moores moved to Montreal in the early 1980s to organize the dump-Clark movement, where he frequently met with Mulroney. And Moores had, of course, set up shop in Ottawa as a lobbyist because of his good relations with Mulroney. I figured that if there was a falling-out it must have happened recently.

Tower must have seen the confusion on my face.

He said that after Moores had his falling-out with the prime minister, the contact between Mulroney and Schreiber was "through Gary," as in Gary Ouellet.

I left Tower's office, and then grabbed a taxi to the airport, making a pit stop at my house to pack.

I was back in the hunt for the Airbus millions.

PART II
COVER-UP

CHAPTER ELEVEN
A FISHING EXPEDITION

Despite the fact that *the fifth estate* is the CBC's premier investigative program, it does not mean we have limitless resources to do whatever we want. Sometimes, you have to be clever. I learned one particular technique from Trish Wood. Here's what you do: before you book yourself into the discount hotel, you take the paperwork into another, far nicer hotel. You tell the concierge that you are hoping to stay at their hotel, but only for the same rate quoted in your travel paperwork.

And that's how I ended up in the lobby of the Hotel Zum Storchen on Thursday morning after my flight had landed. The Zum Storchen, a six-storey hotel nestled in the centre of the city, sits on the edge of the Limmat River, not far from Lake Zurich. On the second floor was a smokey bar with someone playing the accordion. A stone's throw away the Rathaus Bridge connected pedestrians to the shops and cafés on the east side of the canal. In the other direction, a five-minute walk put you at the heart of the Paradeplatz, where Schreiber and Moores had opened up their Swiss accounts. The hotel rooms were tiny but elegant.

I started to make calls from my hotel room. I tried Schreiber again. I left his secretary a message for him to call me at the hotel. I also called Max Strauss, the son of the now-deceased Franz Josef Strauss. I called Giorgio Pelossi and spoke to his son, Mike. I pleaded with him to convince his father to come out of the shadows. He said they would think about it. I called the Swiss police, who told me that the package from the RCMP included a videotape of our original broadcast on March 26. I asked the Swiss police to appear on-camera and they, too, told me they would get back to me. Then I called Paul Schnyder, the banker who set up the secret accounts for Frank Moores in 1986. From my conversation with him in March I knew that he was at another location outside the city. Still, I asked him if he would meet with me to discuss the bank accounts. To my surprise, he said he would. He gave me his new address and told me to meet him the next morning.

I was so excited I called Trish Wood in Toronto.

"I can't believe it! Paul Schnyder has agreed to meet me."

Schnyder was in Aarau, a town about an hour from Zurich. We arranged to meet the next day, Friday, at 10:30 a.m. I still could not believe my good luck when I walked into his office that morning, and there he was, waiting for me. We shook hands. I enthusiastically promised Schnyder I would not mention him as a source. This interview would be for information purposes only, I assured him. A quizzical look came onto his face. I asked him, what did he remember about that day back in 1986 when Frank Moores set up those accounts with Karlheinz Schreiber and Giorgio Pelossi?

"I don't understand what you are saying," he said.

"The accounts. What do you remember about the accounts?"

I handed him a copy of his old business card with the notations that Pelossi had made. He seemed genuinely confused.

"Don't you want to set up a Swiss account?" he asked.

"Me?"

"Yes, you. You wanted to set up a Swiss account?"

"I don't want to set up a Swiss account."

"But that's why you're here," he said.

I realized there had been a colossal misunderstanding. Either he misunderstood, or I had been unclear, but he had obviously not realized I was a reporter. I confessed that I had no interest in setting up a Swiss bank account. He seemed as dejected as me.

"My secretary will show you the door," he said tersely.

On the train back to Zurich I tried, but failed, to think of a way to explain my stupidity to the office in Toronto, unaware that Phil Mathias at the *Financial Post* was busy putting the finishing touches on an explosive story. I went back to my hotel, exhausted, and started making calls again. I took a break and went for a walk. I noticed a small wooden toy truck in a store window. I bought it for my son who would be turning two in a couple of weeks.

I woke up Saturday morning knowing that since it was a weekend I couldn't call anyone at work. I searched my computer database for anyone with a home number. I came across the name Walter Wolf, remembering I had all but forgotten about one interesting angle in the story: that foreign interests had helped topple Joe Clark, the Progressive Conservative leader, in favour of Brian Mulroney. The dump-Clark angle seemed a little off topic now; it didn't seem to have much to do with finding out where the Airbus millions ended up, but I decided to call Wolf anyway.

Wolf was a flamboyant Austrian businessman who had developed a passion for Grand Prix racing and who, in the 1970s, began working with Montreal lawyer Michel Cogger on various Canadian projects. Cogger and Wolf would become involved in the dump-Clark movement, along with Karlheinz Schreiber. I also knew that Wolf had been close to Fred Doucet. In the early 1980s, Fred Doucet was a principal in that oil exploration company, East Coast Energy, in which Wolf had invested $500,000 on the advice of Michel Cogger. The company went bankrupt. Everyone lost money. Wolf was so upset he launched a lawsuit against Fred Doucet after Mulroney was elected prime minister. Walter Wolf was therefore on the outs with Brian Mulroney. But that might mean Wolf would be in a mood to talk. He was.

Wolf was clearly disillusioned with his time in Canada, and the financial losses he had endured, blaming both Fred Doucet and his brother, Gerry. Wolf had a soft spot for Michel Cogger. Wolf blamed Mulroney for hanging Cogger "out to dry." He said Cogger was "a fool" for continuing to admire Mulroney. "I pay him [Cogger] $100,000 a year. I still talk to him. I feel sorry for him."

Wolf told me he first met Schreiber in Calgary during the dump-Clark movement, when they realized they were both good friends with Franz Josef Strauss. In fact, both had befriended Max Strauss. Schreiber took Max on business trips around the world; Wolf took him to Grand Prix races.

Wolf also learned that Schreiber was lobbying to sell Airbus jets in Canada. "He was the agent. He was promoting Airbus."

Wolf said he had introduced Schreiber to Frank Moores, which more or less confirmed the version I had heard earlier; that Michel Cogger had made the introductions. Cogger was Wolf's lawyer, so I figured they had probably made the introduction together.

Wolf said he contributed to the dump-Clark campaign by purchasing a fishing camp that he had never seen on the Salmon River near Main Brook in Newfoundland for $50,000. Was he inclined to purchase real estate sight unseen? He laughed and shook his head at such a preposterous notion. "That cannot happen." Wolf told me the deal was simply a conduit for channelling money to Frank Moores. Wolf told me that Schreiber contributed as well: "I knew that Schreiber, he paid cash for the leadership for Mulroney. I do not know [how much]. Could be $25,000 to $50,000."[1] Of all the people who worked on the dump-Clark movement, Moores did the most, Wolf told me.

Wolf added that as far as what he knew of the Schreiber/Mulroney relationship, Frank Moores or Fred Doucet were "always in between." Wolf believed Mulroney had met Schreiber once or twice in the early eighties, though he did not know more than that, having left the Canadian political scene shortly after Mulroney became prime minister. Wolf said he continued to keep in touch with Cogger and Charley MacMillan, the former senior adviser in the PMO. MacMillan knew about Airbus, Wolf said. "I am close to Charley. He had concerns. Charley is not stupid. He did not want to go down."

Then Wolf told me something that seemed to link the dump-Clark movement with the future creation of the lobby firm GCI, which he called the "PR firm" for Schreiber. Wolf alleged that the idea to create the lobby firm actually came from Brian Mulroney. It was "Mulroney's brainchild," he told me.

Mulroney's brainchild.

---

1 Schreiber himself says he never actually paid for Mulroney's leadership campaign in 1983, but rather the dumping of Joe Clark, which happened at a convention in January 1983. Wolf probably did not distinguish between giving money to the dumping of Joe Clark versus the actual Mulroney leadership campaign.

I discounted the comment at the time as fanciful, one that would be impossible to prove, or probably not even true. In any event, almost immediately after my conversation with Walter Wolf the phone rang in my hotel room. Susan Teskey was on the line.

"Are you sitting down?"

"Why?"

"Mulroney's been named."

Teskey told me that our friend Phil Mathias had broken the story in the *Financial Post*, identifying Mulroney as the unnamed Canadian politician in the Letter of Request. Incredibly, a secret source had given Mathias a copy of the letter from the Canadian Justice Department to the Swiss.

Teskey faxed me a copy of the story.

"In letters rogatory[2] sent to Switzerland on Sept. 29, Justice Department senior counsel Kimberly Prost indicates Brian Mulroney received secret commissions from European manufacturers that did business with the government while he was in office," Mathias wrote. The article outlined the allegations that Airbus and the German arms manufacturer Thyssen had paid secret commissions, and that there was a "persisting plot/conspiracy by Mr. Mulroney [and others] . . . who defrauded the Canadian government in the amount of millions of dollars."

Mathias also reported that lawyers for Mulroney and others named in the document (in other words, Schreiber and Moores) had "met in Toronto to consider strategies." He did not elaborate. And he wrote that the letter contained "inaccuracies." "In one instance," wrote Mathias, "it indicates Mulroney received a secret commission for a Thyssen tank-manufacturing project in Cape Breton Island. That project didn't go ahead." I was not sure I understood. Even if the Thyssen project ultimately did not go ahead, why did that necessarily rule out secret payments? Pelossi had already proved to us Thyssen paid IAL $4 million in 1987 and 1988 towards the Bear Head project—payments partly triggered by an official Memorandum of Understanding between Schreiber and three Mulroney cabinet ministers.

Mathias reported that the letter "seemed" to rely "almost entirely" on information from *the fifth estate*, then quoted a lawyer for "one of the

2 A formal letter from a legal or judicial authority to a foreign country for a request for assistance.

people accused" as saying that the letter was a "fishing expedition—based on a bluff."

Mathias wrote that published media reports "are largely based on putative documents and claims coming from a disgruntled employee of one of the many European companies allegedly involved in the secret commissions . . . This informant is heavily in debt, according to court documents. He is also involved in litigation with his former employer over large sums of money."

The headline over Mathias's story in the *Toronto Sun* (the *Financial Post*'s sister newspaper) called the RCMP investigation "A fishing expedition."

According to Mathias's story, the "alleged Airbus–IAL agreement" was "unsigned." He quoted an Airbus spokesman who denied its existence. Schreiber was quoted denying any connection to IAL.

Mathias pointed out that the CBC had not named Mulroney. "The Justice Department says incorrectly: 'The CBC report made a connection between Mr. Mulroney and these [alleged Airbus] payments.' In fact, the CBC didn't identify Mulroney." *The fifth estate* stated it had found "no evidence that anybody with decision-making power received payments." Mathias had obtained what looked like a blanket denial from Mulroney's representatives. "Mr. Mulroney states unequivocally that he did not in any way influence or try to influence Air Canada's decision to purchase aircraft made by Airbus, a fact which has been repeatedly and publicly confirmed by Air Canada senior officers. Nor was he ever a party to any agreement to influence this decision or to receive any consideration directly or indirectly for so doing. Mr. Mulroney states categorically that he does not now have, nor did he ever have directly or indirectly a bank account in any foreign country. Furthermore no one now has, nor did anyone ever have, such an account on his behalf."

When I called Teskey back to discuss Mathias's story, she had even more news.

"Mulroney's lawyers are holding a press conference later today in Montreal." Revelations were not just happening by the day, they were happening by the hour. And I was stuck in Zurich with nothing to show for my work. I picked up the phone and called Pelossi again. I figured I could use the events that were occurring in Canada to make a final argument.

Now that Mulroney had been named he simply *had* to appear on-camera. Canadians needed to meet the source of the allegations, to hear what the evidence was—and what the evidence was not.

Phil Mathias was wrong to call the Airbus documents "putative," but we still did not know where the money actually ended up, and neither did Pelossi. More important, I was becoming less and less comfortable with the idea of not mentioning Pelossi by name. We knew he had spoken to the German authorities, we knew he had spoken to the RCMP, and we knew he had spoken to the media in Germany and in Canada. Whether or not Pelossi would agree to appear on-camera, we would have to report these facts. I made all the above arguments to Pelossi, who listened politely. Then he agreed. It was time to speak in public.

A flurry of phone calls followed.

Trish Wood was booked on the flight to Zurich that evening. She would arrive Sunday morning. CBC cameraman Colin Alison and soundman Alister Bell were on an airplane above the Atlantic flying back to Canada, having just finished a shoot in England. No sooner did they arrive on the tarmac in Toronto than they were told to book a flight to Zurich.

And that Saturday a scene was playing itself out in a conference room at the Bonaventure Hotel in Montreal that would make news around the globe.

For the dozens of media that had quickly assembled at the hastily called press conference, the three lawyers at the front of the room needed no introduction. They were a legal dream team: Gérald Tremblay, probably the best civil lawyer in the entire province; Roger Tassé, a former federal deputy minister of justice; and Harvey Yarosky, a criminal litigator without equal in the province of Quebec. Mulroney also hired Luc Lavoie as his public spokesperson. Lavoie was known by all the reporters in the room. A former journalist himself, he once worked for Brian Mulroney in the Prime Minister's Office. Now he would work again for Mulroney, speaking publicly on his behalf from his perch at National Public Relations.

Lavoie promptly introduced Gérald Tremblay, who walked to the podium and made a historic announcement. "Mr. Mulroney has given me a mandate to bring suit immediately against the authors of this libel. Monday morning we will file in the Superior Court an action in damages. We will be claiming $50 million damages from the authors of the libel, namely the government of Canada and the RCMP."

Tremblay appeared to blame Phil Mathias and the *Financial Post* for Mulroney's decision to sue the federal government. "We had no other choice when the whole matter was made public this morning by an article in the *Financial Post*."

Tremblay sat down as criminal lawyer Harvey Yarosky took his place in front of the cameras. He spoke slowly and deliberately. "Mulroney categorically and unequivocally states that he had absolutely nothing to do with Air Canada's decision to buy Airbus, nor did he receive a cent from anyone. He was simply not part of any conspiracy whatsoever in any way, shape or form. You may like or dislike his politics, but you cannot do this to a Canadian citizen."

Nor did he receive a cent from anyone.

Mulroney was claiming he was a victim of a reckless and irresponsible RCMP investigation. The following Monday, Mulroney formally sued the government, filing a Statement of Claim in a Montreal courthouse. His denials were unequivocal.

"Plaintiff has never received any of the alleged payments, in any form, from any person, whether named or not in the Request for Assistance, for any consideration whatsoever."

By Sunday afternoon, Trish Wood, Alister Bell and Colin Alison had arrived in Zurich. We packed the van for the three-hour drive to Lugano. Just as I was about to check out of my room, the phone rang.

"Hello. Mr. Cashore?" said a man's voice.

"Yes?"

"I heard you are interested in Brian Mulroney's Swiss bank accounts."

"Yes."

"My name is Emil. I am a Swiss banker and I think I have something you might find interesting."

My first reaction was to laugh. The accent seemed so ridiculous that I immediately figured the voice belonged to Alister Bell. The soundman was a great practical joker, as well as one of the best people to have on your team when you travelled. He was in a perpetually good mood; always solved problems that would inevitably arise on a shoot; and could sweet-talk anyone who was in our way into helping us. He cared deeply about the work he did and the documentaries we made, but he also insisted we have fun doing it.

"Thanks, but no thanks," I laughed and hung up.

The phone rang again.

"Why did you hang up?"

Now I started to wonder. Come to think of it, the voice did not sound like Alister at all.

"Sorry," I replied.

Emil had a proposal for me. He promised me that he had the bank accounts proving that Brian Mulroney got money on the Airbus deal. He worked for the Swiss Bank Corporation but he said he had a family and children. He would need some kind of compensation in return before he gave me the documents. He had a proposal. He would give us the bank records if we gave him $10,000.

I knew that we would never pay for information. The CBC had a strict policy against the practice. Still, I wanted to keep the dialogue going with Emil, to see whether I could convince him to hand over the information anyway. "Let me think about it," I said, still wondering whether this "Emil" was a practical joker or a real Swiss banker. I asked Emil for his number, but he would not give it to me. Instead, I gave Emil our cell-phone number (the entire team shared one phone) and asked him to call me tomorrow.

I told the rest of the crew about the call. Bell swore up and down he would never joke about something like that. Was it possible the voice really did belong to a Swiss banker with access to a Mulroney bank account? I called executive producer David Studer at home. He reminded me that we would never pay for information. But he advised me to keep talking to Emil.

"Don't say no," he said. "But don't say yes either. See if you can arrange to meet the guy."

We waited for Emil to call back.

On the trip to Lugano, Alister drove, Trish sat in the front passenger seat, and I sat in the seat behind her. Colin Alison was, as usual, fast asleep.

He was lucky, too; he could fall asleep in a car at the wink of an eye. That left the three of us to talk, which we did, non-stop, bouncing ideas back and forth, Trish filling me in on all the stories back in Canada, discussing the lawsuit, the coverage in the media, wondering why Mulroney refused to be quoted in any way about the story, why he had hired a PR person to do his talking for him. Most of all we speculated about who Emil might be. Three hours later we were pulling in to our hotel in Lugano, all of us looking forward to interviewing Pelossi on-camera that evening.

Pelossi told us he had changed his mind.

"I'm sorry," he told me. "I can't do it."

How I hated the job at times like this. If you counted the flights, the hotels and the overtime, the cost of sending a camera crew and host across the Atlantic from Toronto to Zurich, and then on to Lugano was adding up into thousands of dollars. The only reason that Wood and the crew had joined me had just gone up in smoke.

Pelossi explained that he was concerned about that law in Switzerland that forbids trustees—like him—from speaking out. It would look better for him if he talked publicly only after Swiss authorities had asked him for a formal interview. He was still waiting for Swiss police to officially request an interview. Pelossi assured us that we would still be the ones to get the exclusive interview with him, but he simply needed to wait. I expressed my concern about having to fly back to Switzerland a second time. In fact, I was not even sure I would be allowed to do it. I came up with a proposal that we do the interview now then agree not to air it until Pelossi gave his permission. Normally we would have just waited until he agreed, but there was no point in spending thousands to come back across the Atlantic again. Pelossi and his son, Mike, who was in law school and acting as his father's agent, agreed with my proposal, in principle, but wanted two days to think about it. As a compromise, we agreed to do the interview on Tuesday.

The *International Herald Tribune* was, for me, a refuge in a sea of German-language newspapers. I read it every morning over breakfast. On Monday morning I realized how far the story had spread. "Canada suspects

Mulroney got Airbus kickback," read the front-page headline, which also explained that Mulroney was suing the federal government for millions of dollars over the Letter of Request.

As I was making calls from my hotel room, the phone rang. It was Emil again.

"Hi, Harvey, it's Emil."

I told Emil that I had talked to my bosses and thought it was best that we meet in person. He suggested we meet Tuesday during the day. That wouldn't work; I would be out of town. I was beginning to think, again, that Emil was Alister Bell. I realized Emil only seemed to call when I was alone.

The next morning we drove to Lugano as planned and, armed with an agreement that we all signed, Pelossi did the on-camera interview. He repeated exactly what he had said before, this time using Mulroney's name. Pelossi was careful, precise. He stated, again, that he had no evidence that any money was paid into either of the Moores accounts, including the one code-named "Devon," over which he had written the initials B.M. But he insisted Schreiber told him that the two accounts were to be for the Canadian friends, and that the Devon account was intended for Brian Mulroney.

The next day we travelled to Bern, where we interviewed Pierre Schmid, director of the Swiss federal police office, and Pascal Gossin, who was with International Legal Assistance. The RCMP had hoped to see the banking records within a few months of its request and, had it been up to the Swiss police alone, that probably would have happened. But it was not going to be as simple as that. Karlheinz Schreiber had launched a court action in Switzerland against the release of his records. He would also begin to launch court action in Canada against the RCMP for the way they went about requesting the information. I wondered how Schreiber even knew that the RCMP had requested his banking information. It turned out that the Swiss Bank Corporation had given a copy of the Letter of Request to the account holders, Karlheinz Schreiber and Frank Moores. Not only did this mean that the account holders knew exactly what the RCMP wanted, they would also learn key details about the investigation. More important, getting a copy of the letter before any information was handed over gave the account holders time to launch court actions to try to stop the request altogether. It also gave them time to move their accounts to more secure locations. Schreiber fought back against the Germans too, who had already sent a similar letter requesting the same banking information. They were investigating Schreiber for bribery and tax evasion. All of this meant he was fighting the release of his records on two flanks—from the Canadians and the Germans. In Germany, however, there were no lawsuits, no leaks of letters to the media.

Then we drove back to our hotel, arriving late in the evening. We were all exhausted and had to get up early the next day to catch a flight back to Toronto. I went straight to my room, turned out the lights and went to sleep.

A ringing phone woke me up. Emil was on the line.

Now I was certain it was Alister on the line. The cellphone had not rung all day when we were together. Now I was by myself. How coincidental was that? Besides, the accent was not at all convincing. I decided to play along.

"We have to meet tonight," said Emil.

"Sure," I said. "Let's do it."

Emil gave me instructions about where to meet, something about a restaurant on the other side of the canal. He told me he would be wearing a green Swiss alpine hat with a feather tucked in the side. He gave me directions and an address. But I wasn't writing down a thing. I had no intention of showing up so Alister could have a good laugh at my expense. I hung up the phone and went back to sleep with a smile on my face. I could picture Alister outside in the dark, waiting for me to show up to tell me what a sucker I was.

The next morning Alister asked me if Emil had called back. So did Trish Wood.

"No," I lied, looking at them, wondering why they were taking the joke so far.

We flew back to Toronto, still wondering when we would broadcast the interview with Giorgio Pelossi. Still, in the course of a week, the entire story had changed complexion. The Phil Mathias story put Mulroney's name in the public domain forever. And the Mulroney lawsuit appeared to be an attempt to seize the agenda, to put the RCMP and the government on the defensive. The spin campaign was now resolutely in place. Luc Lavoie and his public relations firm led the charge. If Mulroney was going to win his campaign to clear his name, he would not just have to win in court; he would have to win in the court of public opinion. If Mulroney and Schreiber were going to present themselves as victims, they needed to create enemies. The list of people would include police officers, justice officials and certain journalists.

I was about to learn that one of those "enemies" would be me.

CHAPTER TWELVE
THE SPIN DOCTOR

To be sure, things started out looking incredibly awful for Lavoie and his PR campaign.

On the Monday after Mulroney's name was first mentioned, the Canadian Press published a story pointing out that the code name Devon was also—as we knew—the name of the street where Brian and Mila Mulroney had first lived after they were married in 1973. That night the CBC's *The National* filmed the Devon road sign, asking whether or not it was a coincidence. How far the story had come since the spring when, at *the fifth estate*, we had refused to report Mulroney's name, let alone the fact that he had lived on a street with the same code name as one of Frank Moores's bank accounts. National affairs reporter Jason Moscovitz repeated what Mulroney's lawyers told him on the weekend, that Mulroney "never received payment from anyone."

Never received payment from anyone.

That night another story on CBC News had the potential to derail the Lavoie spin campaign and the Mulroney lawsuit—and expose the flaws in what was about to become a massive spin campaign. CBC national reporter Neil Macdonald wondered who exactly had leaked the letter that—as Mulroney's legal team had said on the weekend—gave them "no other choice" but to sue the government. At the time, Mulroney's lawyers seemed genuinely angry that the letter had been leaked. Naturally, Macdonald assumed that the RCMP or the Department of Justice had leaked the letter. But Macdonald became suspicious after he interviewed Philip Mathias on-camera the Saturday that the *Financial Post* broke the story. When Macdonald suggested that the leak to the *Financial Post* reporter had come from a government source, Mathias appeared to correct him.

"Well, you're assuming it came from the Canadian justice system. I haven't said that and I am not going to reveal the source."

But then a CBC cameraman—angling for a better shot—happened to turn his camera to the letter Mathias was holding in his hands. Mathias reacted as if his hand were on fire. He quickly pocketed the letter and abruptly ended the interview. What the public did not know at the time was this: as account holders, the Swiss Bank Corporation had supplied copies of the RCMP's original Letter of Request to Schreiber and Moores. Naturally, the letters—in English—would have been translated into German. The letter Mathias had brandished in his hand before the camera, however, was in English. So it would seem that Mathias either had a copy of the original Letter of Requet submitted to the Germans by the Canadian Department of Justice *or* a copy of the SBC letter—the letter translated *into* German for account holders Schreiber and Moores—translated *back* into English.

Macdonald felt he was onto something. The following Monday morning Mulroney's lawyers filed the papers for the $50 million lawsuit. Included in the papers, of course, was the Letter of Request that Mulroney was claiming had libelled him. Mulroney spokesperson Luc Lavoie explained that the version they filed was "a translation that was done at the request of Mr. Mulroney's lawyers by a law firm in Switzerland." Interestingly, that version—the one Mulroney and his lawyers had translated at their request—was exactly the same as Mathias's version.

What seemed immediately clear was that the government had not leaked the Letter of Request after all. What was less clear was how reporter Phil Mathias of the *National Post* had come into its possession. That only raised more questions. Why would the people with the most to lose by the revelations leak the letter to Mathias? And how could Mulroney sue the government over a libel that either he perpetrated or that had been perpetrated by Schreiber and/or Moores?

Macdonald asked Lavoie for an explanation.

Lavoie was, of course, characteristically forthcoming. "I don't have to explain that and I am not going to attempt to explain that because all of this will be explained in court. But I want to be very, very clear and solid on one point. We have, we, the people around Mulroney and Mulroney himself, absolutely nothing to do with this document ending up in the hands of the media."

Mathias talked to the CBC about the issue.

"First of all, I have denied ever getting it [the Letter of Request] from Mr. Mulroney and I hope that's clear. Secondly, I am not going to talk about the source. Now, it could have come in a hundred ways, couldn't it? Maybe they leaked it to somebody else, maybe they leaked it to the Justice Department, who knows?"

Macdonald filed a story for *The National* on Monday night. A crucial element in the Mulroney libel action, he said, was "not that the Crown and police made unsubstantiated allegations to the Swiss. They have the right to do that. It was the fact that those allegations wound up in the hands of reporters."

Macdonald ended his story by summarizing a series of off-camera conversations he had had with Luc Lavoie. "Mulroney's spokesman first hinted it might have been leaked by Justice officials, then he called back to say that Justice officials had never been given a copy of the document, then he pointed out that it was prepared by Swiss lawyers originally, then he said it was all just a mystery."

Macdonald had exposed what looked like a fatal flaw in the Mulroney lawsuit. It's generally pretty hard to win a lawsuit for libel in which *you* leak the libel. If Mulroney had been involved in the leaking of the letter, then it meant that he had done so in order to have sufficient grounds to sue the government. Mulroney's lawyer, Gérald Tremblay, had already made it clear that the publication in the *Financial Post* prompted the lawsuit. It seemed almost impossible to fathom.

On Tuesday, a Phil Mathias story in the *National Post* suggested that Mulroney "faced enormous obstacles" in his lawsuit. On Saturday, November 25, Mathias wrote another story that suggested the Mounties may hit "red tape" in their pursuit of banking information in Switzerland.

"Before any details from the account can be released, Canada's request for information must survive a long legal process in Switzerland and pass the scrutiny of a Swiss prosecutor." The story pointed out that the Swiss were preoccupied with two competing values: "One is concern among foreigners that Swiss banking secrecy has been relaxed; the huge national banking industry relies on secrecy for much of its business, so reassurance is needed. The other is that the government is reluctant to snub Canada by lightly dismissing an investigation of a former prime minister."

The story quoted Michael Ritter, chief legal officer of Canadian Offshore Financial Services SA, based in Edmonton. Ritter had also been the highly respected former chief parliamentary counsel to Alberta. He was familiar with the legal-assistance process, the story read, as he used to be a Swiss banker himself. He was still a member of the Swiss Bankers Association. "The Swiss want to raise the legal-assistance process above the level of a fishing expedition," Ritter was quoted. His own clients were "disturbed by the idea there may be a fishing expedition going on in Switzerland."

Ritter explained that the Letter of Request was given to the account holders because Switzerland had a more "highly developed" concept of civil rights than Canada.[1]

I was intrigued by the *Post*'s repetitive use of the phrase "fishing expedition." It was the same phrase the *Toronto Sun* had used in its headline over Mathias's story a week before, a quote attributed to Schreiber's Edmonton lawyer. Now Ritter was using the same phrase. The term "fishing expedition" was obviously a loaded phrase designed to cast a negative light on the RCMP investigation. One could as easily have said the RCMP was simply asking questions about Swiss bank accounts, that they were following up on important allegations. Why dismiss it all as a "fishing expedition"?

At this time, investigative reporter Robert Fife entered the fray. Fife and I had worked in the Ottawa Press Gallery together. He had co-authored a book in 1991 entitled *A Capital Scandal: Politics, Patronage and Payoffs—Why Parliament Must Be Reformed*. Fife's book came out the same time as *Mulroney:*

---

[1] In 2008, Ritter was sentenced to ten years in jail for his part in an elaborate Ponzi scheme. It was also discovered that Ritter did not graduate from a legal program in London, as he had claimed.

The Politics of Ambition, the biography on which I had worked with John Sawatsky. John and I had been criticized by Mulroney's friend Pat MacAdam, but all that negative attention led to positive sales. Fife referred to all the publicity when he signed my copy of his book: "To Harvey, We're jealous that Pat MacAdam didn't go after us like he did you and John. Cheers, Bob F." His book had been heavily critical of Parliament, as well as the reporters who wrote favourable stories with the expectation they would be rewarded with leaked stories before the rest of the press gallery. "Writers who show a whiff of sympathy for the government viewpoint often receive special briefings or easier access to sources," he wrote. Fife reported that a CBC Ottawa bureau chief had once been unfairly accused of bias after other journalists, friendly to the Mulroney government, mysteriously leaked damaging information against him. Was the bureau chief really biased or, wrote Fife, "was the fine hand of Mulroney agents involved?" Fife concluded that "the columnists who had 'stumbled' on [the negative information] had all written several favorable columns about Mulroney at a time when he was under general attack and at 14 per cent [approval ratings] in the polls."

Fife wrote one story quoting Tory senator Marjory LeBreton that the Letter of Request had been "politically motivated" and that then prime minister Jean Chrétien had to have known about it. LeBreton claimed Justice Minister Allan Rock must have been responsible for the letter, and demanded that he step down.

Rock, according to Fife, claimed that the first time he heard about the Letter of Request was on November 4, 1995, when Mulroney's own lawyer, Roger Tassé, called him. In other words, Mulroney knew about the Letter of Request before Rock knew about it. Fife also reported that Allan Rock and Herb Gray, the solicitor general, denied that they or any government official leaked the Letter of Request to the *Financial Post*. "I have no reason to believe any leak came from the RCMP," Gray told Fife. Rock added: "We dealt with the Swiss government in the past and there have not been such leaks."

For the third day in a row, Fife filed a story, this time revealing that the "Americans" had warned the Tories in 1988 that "huge Airbus commissions were being paid to Canadians." Explained Fife: "A retired senior bureaucrat—who is not politically connected to Mulroney—said U.S. officials contacted him in November 1988 to complain that U.S. giant Boeing had lost out to Airbus. The source said the Americans were 'offended' by what they knew of the biggest civil aircraft deal in Canada's history. The U.S. State department knew of 'rich commissions being paid offshore' to Canadians, said the source who asked not to be identified. He quoted a top U.S. official as saying: 'This is the kind of [expletive] that goes on in the Middle East and Central America. This should not be going on in Canada.'"

Fife's reporting was so good I began to worry that he would beat me to the story. Still, that Friday the *Toronto Sun* complained about a "smear campaign" engineered by the CBC and directed against *Post* reporter Phil Mathias.

Their November 24 editorial read, in part: "Unlike careless journalists, Mathias did not simply rush into print with allegations, but first went to get Mulroney's side of the story (he denied any wrongdoing). He also carefully examined the documents he had obtained and reported the government's explosive allegations seemed to be based largely on media reports. It was fine work in the best tradition of tough, fair journalism. And yet ever since the story broke the CBC has been smearing Mathias through deceit and bush-league, ambush journalism. They are suggesting Mathias acted as a conduit for Mulroney so the ex-PM could then announce he was suing the feds."

The next day, November 25, Bob Fife named Giorgio Pelossi in public for the first time. "Tory insiders say Pollossi [*sic*] is a disgruntled employee who made unsubstantiated allegations against Brian Mulroney and former Newfoundland premier Frank Moores to get back at Schreiber," wrote Fife. He also quoted an anonymous Tory: "Basically this guy is out to get at Schreiber and the way to smear him is to throw a lot of big names out."

An opinion piece by William Thorsell, editor-in-chief of the *Globe and Mail*, appeared in the paper on November 25 and seemed to defend Brian Mulroney. "What is fuelling the conspiracy culture surrounding Brian Mulroney?" he asked rhetorically. "This week's revelations about Ottawa's unsubstantiated charges that Mr. Mulroney was on the take from three European corporations grows out of an extremely fertile field of dark, popular beliefs. Not even the absence of evidence to support RCMP claims in the Justice Department's letter to Switzerland has swayed most media or public opinion. Indeed, the primary response in the media has been yet more innuendo, suggesting that Mr. Mulroney is wriggling skillfully away again, to be unmasked another day." Mulroney was the first prime minister to personally pay for his food at 24 Sussex, Thorsell reminded readers, and suggested that all the personal attacks against Mulroney spoke more of the "conspiracy theorists" themselves. "Much of the story about Brian Mulroney is how and where the story got its spin. And who in the media will tackle that?" (I am guessing that he had not yet had time to read the *Financial Post* or the *Toronto Sun*, two newspapers doing exactly that.)

On the same day, a Saturday, in an article by Ross Howard, the *Globe and Mail* quoted former GCI president Greg Alford publicly for the first time. "There was no Airbus lobbying by GCI, none whatsoever," Alford told Howard. "I knew [Moores] well, and it [CGI] was a small enough firm. I would never say I knew absolutely everything, but Airbus was not a client . . . Until I read it in the papers I never heard of International Aircraft Leasing [IAL]."

That Saturday I was back at work in my office, typing up my notes, when the phone rang. Tower was on the line. He said rumours were flying.

"About what?" I asked.

He said I should take a close look at how money was raised in the Conservative Party.

"People are very nervous," he said.

On Monday, November 27, Trish Wood, the bosses and I held a meeting. Pelossi had now been named in public and so our agreement not to broadcast his interview had become moot. Pelossi had promised us that he would not speak to anyone before he allowed us to use his on-camera interview, even suggesting he would only have his wife answer the phone. But Tuesday morning, *Le Soleil* columnist Michel Vastel wrote a column that read very much like an interview with Pelossi. David Kaufman, the producer in charge of "Sealed in Silence," was already busy working on the next Airbus documentary in the edit suite with Gary Akenhead. They were told the story would go to air that night.

Brian Mulroney had refused to be interviewed, but Luc Lavoie agreed to speak on the former prime minister's behalf. Trish Wood and I flew to Ottawa for the interview, where we met Lavoie at his PR firm, National Public Relations. Lavoie argued that the RCMP should not call any Canadian citizen a criminal, even if it was only in a confidential communiqué.

Wood asked him about the Swiss accounts. "Does Mr. Mulroney have any connection at all to either of the Swiss bank accounts in question, namely 34107 and 34117 code-named Devon?"

"I categorically deny that he has anything to do with those accounts."

Short of time, we went to CBC studios in Ottawa and fed the tape via satellite to Toronto. At about the same time, my colleague Anita Mielewczyk, a brilliant and tenacious associate producer, was paying a visit to Frank Moores in Florida. Our sound recordist, Alister Bell, was with her and captured it all on videotape. Moores denied—again—that he had anything to do with Airbus.

On the plane back to Toronto I got caught up on that day's newspaper coverage, including Phil Mathias's latest story in the *Financial Post*: "Mulroney axed source of alleged bribes." Mulroney had actually killed the Bear Head proposal, according to Mathias, one of the deals that Schreiber had been promoting in Ottawa. In their letter to the Swiss, the Mounties had charged that Mulroney had received kickbacks on this deal *as well as* the Airbus deal. This "appears to seriously undercut the force's allegations of criminal activity by Mulroney while he was in office from 1983 to 1994," Mathias wrote. He seemed also to question Pelossi and our coverage: "Pelossi also appears to be the principal source for coverage of the Airbus affair on the CBC-TV program the Fifth Estate [*sic*]. People who know him well say Pelossi appeared in disguise on the program to allege Airbus payments to 'a Canadian politician.' But Pelossi is reported to have said elsewhere that he doesn't know where the money went after he handed the cheques to Schreiber."

I was shocked. Our program had spelled out clearly that Pelossi did not know where the money ended up. Mathias had made this point in his story two weeks earlier when he observed that our March broadcast stated that there was no evidence that any money was deposited into either of the Swiss accounts.

"Did the RCMP obtain most of its information from journalists," he asked, "particularly at the Canadian Broadcasting Corp.?" He quoted from the Letter of Request: "The RCMP has seen copies of the documents used in the preparation of the reports by the 5th estate [sic] and Der Spiegel . . ." He added, "Producers of the fifth estate could not be reached for comment."

It was unsettling to be charged by another reporter with having turned over documents to the RCMP—especially since it was untrue. In fact, when Mathias and I worked on the Regan story the year before, he told me he had given his entire file to the RCMP. Now he was criticizing the fifth estate for doing the same thing?

That night we broadcast our second story on the Airbus affair: "The Insider." I felt pleased that we had finally been able to show Canadians the source of the allegations. Viewers learned that Pelossi had proof that Airbus paid secret commissions to IAL, a shell company in Liechtenstein, and that he, in turn, passed the Airbus commission to Schreiber's personal account in Zurich, 18679 IAL. "But that's where the trail stops for Giorgio Pelossi," Wood told our viewers. "He doesn't know if Schreiber actually paid part of Airbus commissions to Frank Moores or anybody else."

Wood asked him if it was possible that all of this was done without Mulroney's knowledge.

"It's possible," Pelossi admitted.

"Is there any evidence as far as you know that money was paid into that account?" Wood asked.

"No," Pelossi responded. "I suppose, but I don't have any evidence."

"Mr. Schreiber suggests publicly that you are not an honourable man, that you are not telling the truth about this . . . he says you are just doing this because you are mad at him."

"No."

I wasn't sure how much clearer we could be about Pelossi, his evidence and his motivations. We also reported that Pelossi had been jailed briefly in 1986 on embezzlement charges unrelated to Schreiber, but that he had been released and the charges dropped. The next morning I got an angry phone call from Phil Mathias.

"That was a real number you did on Mulroney last night," he said. Mathias suggested we had insinuated that Mulroney got money from

Schreiber. I referred him to what we *actually* had said: there was no evidence he had received a penny.

"Harvey, as I see it there is a fork in the road," he said. He suggested he would continue examining flaws in the RCMP investigation while I appeared to be focusing on the Mulroney angle. "One of us is going to end up with egg on his face."

"There is no fork in the road," I said. "We should all be on the same road, the information road, wherever it takes us."

Mathias agreed.

I told him that I wanted to find out where more than $20 million in *schmiergelder* had ended up, plain and simple. If Mulroney was blameless I wanted to be the first one to prove it. But *somebody* had received the cash payments and it seemed to me pretty basic that as a journalist it was my job to find out. What made no sense to me, I told Phil, was why so many reporters were so convinced what *could not have* happened but who had no interest in finding out what *did happen*. The entire matter could be cleared up easily if the RCMP had access to Schreiber's bank accounts.

To get to *the fifth estate* photocopier you used to have to walk down a long corridor on the east side of the building to a small room tucked away just off of the atrium, a spectacular open indoor area that is the jewel in the crown of the broadcast centre. The CBC had been scattered about in various buildings around Toronto, but in 1993 we all moved into a single building, thanks to Brian Mulroney's Conservative government that had approved the construction. At the copier, I noticed someone had left a document on the glass. It was an internal memo from producer Larry Zolf to CBC management. I wasn't sure what to make of it. Zolf had had a long and distinguished career at CBC, but lately he had been flitting from one project to another. He was well known for fostering good relations with Liberal and Tory politicians, be they Pierre Trudeau or Brian Mulroney. Long before the Airbus story broke, Zolf had used his good relations with Mulroney to convince him to talk to CBC host Hana Gartner, on-camera.

As I read the memo in the photocopy room, I began to realize that Zolf was doing his own investigation, reporting to CBC manager Norm Bolen.

According to the memo, Zolf had talked with Sam Wakim: "What follows are the actual words Wakim used. Let me also note that here for the first time . . . Mulroney denies knowing Schreiber."

Wakim was a close friend of Mulroney's. They had met back in their student days at St. Francis Xavier University in Nova Scotia. Zolf quoted Wakim directly: "I think the charge that Mulroney leaked the story is nuts. It's like saying Canada sends its requests to the Swiss banks and the Swiss banks only give out information to clients, and Mulroney is a client with a secret account, so they send him the Canadian request and he, Mulroney, leaked it. That's all nuts!"

Zolf's interview continued for pages. Wakim blamed many of the rumours on Boeing, as others had done. "They did the old Ottawa act of blaming others, the other guys, i.e. Brian and Moores. Boeing told all of Ottawa Moores and Brian were thieves and liars. A Boeing guy walked around Ottawa saying Airbus used Moores to pay off Mulroney.

"Brian is mad as hell and keeping quiet. Keeping quiet for Brian is murder—it's a torture chamber for him. He can't talk to a soul. He can't say anything. . . . <u>Mulroney never met this Schreiber guy. Mulroney doesn't know Schreiber. Moores may have brought Schreiber around to a party, but that's all.</u> [Underlining Zolf's.]

"I'm a little hesitant to say what Moores does with his money," Wakim continued. "Still, Moores hasn't tried to bribe Mulroney with that money, that's for sure. Moores has been badly treated, but much of it is his own fault. Moores invites this stuff on himself. The other thing I wonder about is, is it an enemy of Moores getting even and doing all this to us."

Wakim ended his interview with Zolf on a philosophical note:

"All this is a great tragedy for Canada. These allegations are a disaster and hurt the country. It all hurts this place; people are leaving the country in droves. Separatism is splitting the country; now with the Mulroney affair, the whole world believes all Canadian politicians are crooks."

I returned the original to Larry Zolf.

"I think this is yours," I said simply, then walked away.

By the end of November, you could feel the tide turning in the Airbus coverage. The media were focused on Mulroney's lawsuit and allegations of conspiracies between the RCMP, the Liberals and certain people in the media. I tried not to get too distracted by it all. A colleague of mine once called stories that simply quoted this person and that person "noise." The better stories were the ones that contained hard information. Despite the daily coverage, there really was not much new information. Just lots of noise.

And so I did what I always did; I continued to pour myself into the research. My to-do list had grown to 258 items, mostly calls I needed to make to people in politics and the aviation industry. I heard there was someone named James MacEachern who worked for the PMO and later GCI. He sounded like a perfect person to talk to, though I had no idea where he was at the time. I made a note to myself: "Find James MacEachern—or did I before, and find out he was dead or something?" I also made a note to ask Max Ward, former head of Wardair, about a Christmas party attended by both Karlheinz Schreiber and former deputy prime minister Don Mazankowski. I really wanted to call Gary Ouellet again. The list of things to do seemed endless.

At the time, I was oblivious to a tidal wave of anger heading towards us at *the fifth estate*. It began as a ripple on Friday, December 1, when Don Mazankowski entered the debate, arguing there was an overt campaign to discredit Mulroney. "Brian's reputation has been horribly hurt. He's very distraught," Mazankowski told the *Toronto Star*. "It's an intensive smear campaign . . . the most intensive ever against a former Canadian prime minister . . . It's all part of an ongoing campaign to degrade the character of Mulroney."

Toronto Star reporter Dale Brazao tracked down Frank Moores in Florida, who said, "This story is going to end up as the biggest disgrace in the history of the media . . . This is all the doing of two or three so-called investigative reporters, who I consider scumbags, really." The whole incident "has been especially hard on the wife and my kids and my grandchildren."

Saturday, the *Sun*'s Bob Fife published an exclusive interview with Schreiber under the headline: "Mulroney bribe claim a hoax." Wrote Fife: "Accusations of bribery against Brian Mulroney are as much of a hoax as the Hitler diaries, German dealmaker Karlheinz Schreiber says." He quoted Schreiber directly. "As much as I am involved, as much as I know, as much as I have seen, Mr. Mulroney is totally innocent," Schreiber told Fife. "He [Mulroney] is involved in this as much as the Pope—nowhere at all."

Schreiber claimed—again—that he was not involved with the company IAL. "Where is the proof that IAL belongs to Mr. Schreiber?" he asked rhetorically. "Where is the proof that there is a signed agreement between Airbus and IAL? . . . Where is the proof that the bank accounts where the money was transferred belongs to Mr. Schreiber or Mulroney or Mr. Moores? Where is the proof? It's totally nonsense . . . I can tell you one thing, sir. You will laugh yourself to death pretty soon. I'm not joking." According to Fife, Schreiber planned to sue the CBC: "[Schreiber] was reluctant to discuss details of the allegations until the lawsuits are filed but stressed he is telling the truth that all the allegations are false. 'When I say something, it is the way it is or I say I don't want to speak about it. It makes no sense to lie.'"

A week later, Fife filed a story in which he accused a Justice Department official of "snapping" at him for refusing to provide more details about their investigation. The article, like others, repeated the mistaken suggestion that Pelossi had changed his mind about the Airbus commissions. "Pelossi now admits he has no direct evidence linking German dealmaker Karlheinz Schreiber to the kickback scandal," wrote Fife. According to the story, Pelossi could not prove Schreiber owned IAL, could not provide a signed Airbus contract, could not remember the name of the Airbus official he'd dealt with and could not remember the name of the Swiss law firm that retained on file the only signed copy of the Airbus contract. (In fact, Pelossi had already told me the name of the law firm and the Airbus official he had dealt with.)

That Sunday, December 3, 1995, my wife and I celebrated our son's second birthday. After we finished tidying up the party, I turned on *Sunday Report* to watch Wendy Mesley, who had assembled a panel to discuss the latest developments on the Airbus story: CBC reporter Neil Macdonald, *Globe and Mail* national reporter Paul Koring and *Globe* columnist Rick Salutin. Earlier, Neil Macdonald had reported that the RCMP had a right to spell out allegations to other police agencies while pursuing investigations.

He seemed to have changed his mind. "So when you see this happening, you know," Macdonald said, "it kind of makes you wince that someone is subjected to something like this and that what is nothing more than a police investigation takes on the clothing of something much larger."

Koring suggested that the RCMP had an obligation to more carefully craft its Letter of Request. "The difference is not that [Mulroney] is just another Canadian citizen. It is that the likelihood of this kind of thing getting leaked, because it relates to a former prime minister, is far larger. And I think there probably is an obligation on the sender of that letter to take that into consideration when it's being phrased."

"Well, look," said Rick Salutin, "when I listen to this I think, Who would you rather be? A kid trying to get away with a break-and-enter or stealing a bicycle, or a former political leader of a country? I mean, look what you've got going for you if you decide to pull something off or to steal something if you're a former leader. First of all, when you were in office, you made the laws. You could exert some influence of control over the police or the RCMP. Then in order to help you hide things, you have access to money and all these middlemen and wheeler-dealers that we find out can open accounts for you and shift money between Switzerland and Liechtenstein. And finally, if somebody comes up with something on you and charges you with something, you can call up all your buddies in the media and turn it into a story about how you're being persecuted by the media. Instead of what the real story is about."

Paul Koring interjected. "Well, wait a second. So far, there's not a scintilla of evidence of any wrongdoing. In fact, what we have is a mountain of denials."

Salutin suggested Koring had missed his point. "All I'm talking about is whether you're treated differently and whether there's this sort of . . . whether we should feel such sympathy and pity for the prime minister as opposed to those lucky ordinary criminals who don't have any of those perks going for them when they get investigated."

"Absolutely. Absolutely," agreed Macdonald. "Brian Mulroney can hire high-priced lawyers, he can launch legal counterstrikes. And you know, after what he's done and after the court case that he's launched, the Mounties had better be right. You know, if it turns out that the Swiss don't hand over that information or if it turns out that they're wrong, the Mounties and the Justice Department are going to have some explaining to do."

Salutin pointed out that the media—his fellow panellists included—appeared already to have come to the defence of Mulroney and Moores. "One of the things that's really interesting about this story is that Moores and Mulroney are claiming the media are persecuting them, but if you look at the media coverage, it's almost entirely about how these guys are being persecuted."

Koring suggested that the Liberals also had a lot of explaining to do. "Something else that we're going to need to find out is whether or not the new government, the Liberal government, is involved at all in the restarting of this allegation."

Luc Lavoie must have been pleased.

CHAPTER THIRTEEN
COUNTERATTACK

That Monday I trudged into work feeling a little shell-shocked. The dominant media event was the Mulroney lawsuit and not the Airbus story. As I walked down the street to the subway, it was all I could do to put the Mulroney lawsuit out of my mind, to try to keep focused on all the unanswered Airbus questions. Still, I had a reason to be optimistic. The previous week I got a phone call from someone who said he had something important to tell me about Airbus, Frank Moores and Air Canada.

I met Peter Macphail[1] at the cafeteria on the ground floor of the CBC building. He told me his job was to scour North America looking for airplanes at a bargain—typically, planes that had been seized by the US Drug Enforcement Agency. He'd buy them on the cheap, fix them up a little and resell them for a tidy profit. He also tried to broker deals of second-hand aircraft between one airline and another.

Macphail had two things to tell me, both to do with the sale of Airbus in Canada.

First, he took me back to Wardair's purchase of Airbus jets in the mid-1980s. He reminded me that Wardair had mysteriously cancelled its Boeing order in favour of twelve Airbus A310s back in 1987. I didn't need to be

1   Not his real name.

149

told that Frank Moores had been deeply involved in convincing Wardair to changes its mind. Macphail filled me in on what happened next at Wardair. Ever since the deal, things had gone downhill for the airline. The deal was supposed to help Max Ward compete with the national airlines, Canadian Airlines and Air Canada. After the federal government awarded Wardair landing rights in Europe, it looked as if the company might succeed. But there was too much competition in the marketplace. Wardair had borrowed heavily to finance Airbuses and it was having trouble making payments. By 1990 it was all over for Max Ward and the airline he began in 1952. Wardair folded into the western-based Canadian Airlines, and Max Ward went into retirement.

That was the end of Wardair, but not of the Airbus airplanes. Canadian Airlines had inherited the problem of what to do with the twelve Airbus A310s that no one in Canada seemed to want. Canadian Airlines put the A310s on the market, hoping to sell them as quickly as possible. They needed to get rid of the debt.

And that's where Peter Macphail came into the picture.

He and some partners initiated an elaborate scheme to broker the sale of five of the planes to Aeroflot, the Russian airline, in return for truckloads of vodka. Alas, the plan never materialized. But Macphail never forgot about the planes. He said his interest was piqued when he learned that the Canadian Armed Forces had purchased five of the twelve. He had sources in the Department of National Defence, he claimed, who admitted they hadn't wanted the planes. They were not military compliant and DND would have to pay millions to convert them. "They said what the hell are we going to do with a commercial airliner? We want an airplane that has a cargo door, we want an airplane that can do inflight refuelling." Macphail's sources told him the Mulroney government demanded that DND purchase the aircraft. The Canadian military paid $54 million per plane, Macphail said, even though Max Ward bought them new for only $42 million.

"So who got the difference and why?" Macphail said. "I mean, this is why I came down to talk to you. There is more to just what you are doing. It is much bigger. Somebody somewhere is getting awful friggin' rich." One of the DND A310s, he said, was converted into a VIP plane on which Brian Mulroney and other heads of state would travel.

"I believe there is something that went on before with either the purchase of the Wardair A310s, and definitely the transfer of these ten aircraft to Canadian [Airlines], with the five of the ten going to Canadian Armed Forces and one being made into a private flying apartment. Now, Harvey, in law, you and I know we have to prove things. But there are some things so blatant it just jumps right out at you and smacks and smells."

An Auditor General's report that would be released the following year appeared to back Macphail's claim. In 1996, the Auditor General of Canada raised concerns about DND's acquisition of the planes. It stated that a "directive" on the part of the Mulroney government had compelled the military to purchase the aircraft. "Prior to receiving this direction, the Department had no plans to replace the fleet before 1999," the report said. The AG report stated that DND paid a total of $265 million to "three aviation industry firms" for the five aircraft. "[The Canadian military] paid an additional $12 million for modifications," the Auditor General wrote. "This included the installation of operational equipment, reconfigurations to the interior section and [the] painting of each plane, and fitting one A310 with an Executive Interior for VIP transport. The government required that the fleet be capable of transporting dignitaries with a 'head-of-state' status." I would learn later that the Canadian military, following the purchase of five A310s, turned around and leased one of them to Thai Airways International. Karlheinz Schreiber also received secret commissions on the sale of Airbus aircraft to Thai Airways, leaving me to wonder if there was a connection.

Perhaps the Mulroney government could argue that it was merely trying to help a western-based company stay afloat. Macphail, however, saw it differently. Airbus had made an aggressive push to sell airplanes in Canada and now the Canadian government had intervened to help both a Canadian airline and Airbus Industrie itself. For a free-market party, it seemed like an odd rescue effort. I wondered why Canadian Airlines had even bothered to take over Wardair at all, if it meant they would be saddled with the A310s. I was later told that what Canadian really wanted was to take over Wardair's landing rights in Europe.

In any case, at the end of the day almost everyone involved in the deal came out a winner: Max Ward sold his airline at a profit instead of landing in bankruptcy; Canadian Airlines served landing rights in Paris; and the Mulroney government had its VIP plane for "heads of state." The only loser was the military and the Canadian taxpayer, who ended up footing the bill for those five Airbus aircraft and the costly renovation to them.

Macphail also had a story to tell me about Frank Moores and Air Canada.

Macphail knew that Moores had steadfastly denied any involvement with Air Canada or Airbus. He had seen our recent program, "The Insider," featuring the "jump" at Moores's condo in Florida. He wanted us to know there was far more to the story than we had realized.

Macphail said that he first heard the name Frank Moores while visiting Air Canada offices in Montreal in the late 1980s. He was there to speak to people involved in fleet acquisitions, including Ben Besner, a manager; his boss, Rob Peterson; and Peterson's boss, Chief Financial Officer Dennis Groom. Macphail wanted to discuss what was going on with the Airbus "transaction." He claimed that they replied, "Oh, Mr. Moores is looking after that."

His statement matched up with what I had already been told by three previous sources: the Air Canada executive who told me in the spring that Moores had complained to Air Canada about getting stiffed by Airbus; the Airbus salesman who told me that his colleague Anthony Lawler had complained about hearing of the "bagman" Frank Moores while on a trip to Air Canada's offices in Montreal; and the former Eastern Provincial Airways president, Keith Miller, who'd said that Air Canada chairman Claude Taylor was upset when he learned that Frank Moores and Air Canada President Pierre Jeanniot met privately about Airbus.

All this raised serious questions about what exactly Air Canada executives may have known about the Airbus commissions. The documents provided by Pelossi suggested that money would be deposited into the shell company in Liechtenstein *only after* Air Canada provided payments to Airbus. A logical question might be: If Air Canada executives knew about Frank Moores, did they also know about the secret commission arrangement he had with Karlheinz Schreiber and Airbus Industrie? And if so, did it mean they knew Air Canada may have paid half a million US more than they should have for each of the thirty-four Airbus airplanes that they had ordered? Air Canada had always officially denied knowing that Moores played any role at all in the deal.

In any case, I finally had a contact at Air Canada I could call. Dennis Groom had refused to speak with us, but perhaps manager Ben Besner might have something to say. Besner, however, had left Air Canada by then. I tracked down his home number.

Besner was happy enough to talk. He filled me in on the players at Air Canada, telling me that he had worked in the contracts office there. "I spent ten years being Air Canada's used-plane salesman," he said. Rob Peterson, he told me, was director of financing and reported to Chief Financial Officer Dennis Groom. By the time of my conversation with Besner, Peterson had become the chief financial officer at Air Canada. Besner insisted he knew nothing of Frank Moores or any role he might have played.

"We did everything on the orders of the executive management and Chief Financial Officer Dennis Groom." Besner had "never heard of Schreiber," either.

Besner, however, did have a lot to say about the Canadian government's decision to "bail out" Canadian Airlines by purchasing the A310s. He said it was "an insult to us at Air Canada . . . I was trying to market used L10-11s to the government." Besner repeated what Macphail had told me. "The Canadian government paid far too much for the [Airbus A310] planes." In those days, he said, the worldwide market for aircraft was collapsing. The Canadian military should have paid less for the Wardair planes, not more. Besner told me he thought we were doing good work and encouraged me to keep probing the story. But he couldn't help me with Frank Moores or Schreiber. Those names had never been mentioned, he said.

On December 7, 1995, the *Financial Post* published a scoop. Schreiber was about to sue *the fifth estate*: "German businessman Karlheinz Schreiber served notice yesterday on Canadian Broadcasting Corporation that he had been defamed in a Fifth Estate [*sic*] program dealing with the Airbus controversy." "The Fifth Estate," read the story, "indicated Schreiber was the person who allegedly passed secret commissions from French aircraft manufacturer Airbus Industrie S.A. to former prime minister Brian Mulroney." The truth is we had never alleged that Mulroney had received commissions from Schreiber. But there was more: "Schreiber and Mulroney have vigorously denied the Fifth Estate charges." What charges? I wondered. We hadn't made any charges.

In Canada, the first step in a libel or defamation proceeding requires a plaintiff to put the media outlet on "notice." I have received several "notices" of libel in my time as a journalist, but rarely did they escalate to lawsuits. Lawsuits are an expensive proposition for both sides. An ordinary citizen who feels libelled by a large media outlet is going to have a tough slog. If you lose, you could end up losing a lot more money than you could ever imagine. On the other hand, someone wealthy and powerful, like Karlheinz Schreiber, might figure he has nothing to lose. Headlines screaming that you are suing a media outlet can be fantastic from a media relations standpoint.

For the journalist, the first thing you wonder is whether or not you *will* get fired. While it is true that anyone can sue anybody for almost anything and for any reason, even an announced intent to sue can have the most confident journalist wondering if he or she has made a mistake. You worry about it almost daily. You wonder whether you could have phrased something differently, whether you could have been more fair, or more accurate, or something. You meet with lawyers to go over every word, every sentence, every possible interpretation of what you said. You are asked to provide all your documentation and notes. Often, in the middle of the night, you wake up and think, something is wrong, but you won't be able to put your finger on it.

There is a very practical benefit to suing a journalist. Almost every media outlet in Canada has a policy of not rebroadcasting or republishing any reports bearing on the suit, for as long as the litigation is pending. Moreover, the reporters generally are encouraged not to comment on any aspect of the story. There's a perfectly good reason for this. If a lawsuit ever gets to trial, the media outlet wants to prove that it behaved responsibly in the aftermath of the reports or broadcasts. If there was a libel, the news organization wants to do all it can to mitigate against any potential damage. This is a good idea if there is a potential problem, but a terrible idea if the lawsuit is designed merely to prevent journalists from doing their jobs. There seemed to be a lot of these kinds of lawsuits in the 1990s, as corporations began to fight back against investigative reports, both in Canada and the United States. This activity came to be known in academia as SLAPP lawsuits, Strategic Lawsuits Against Public Participation—lawsuits against both individuals who were protesting corporations and the media who were covering those protests. And, in my opinion, that's exactly what was happening with the Schreiber lawsuit. Trish Wood and I were called into a meeting with CBC lawyer Daniel Henry and *the fifth estate* bosses, and told not to talk to any of our colleagues in the media, for the time being. We were told to do our talking through our journalism. The only problem was that none of us knew what "the time being" meant. We hoped that Schreiber was just posturing; that he would not actually go ahead and file a lawsuit.

Meanwhile, it seemed as though everyone was beginning to run away from the Airbus scandal, even the minister of justice. The same day the *Post* published its story about Schreiber's intent to sue *the fifth estate*, the *Toronto Sun* reported that Justice Minister Allan Rock was suggesting the RCMP "shoulder the blame" if Mulroney was cleared in the Airbus scandal. If Rock was being quoted correctly, he seemed to be arguing that the RCMP would not be faulted for its investigation if it turned out Mulroney did get money from the Airbus sale, but would be in trouble if Mulroney did not get the money. The logic left me stumped. How would the Mounties know Mulroney got money or not if they didn't investigate? It was a Catch-22.

If some politicians were blaming the Mounties, some of my colleagues in the media started to blame me. My name first surfaced in print on December 8—in the first of a series of opinion pieces written by veteran *Ottawa Sun* columnist Doug Fisher. I knew Fisher fairly well. He was a former NDP member of Parliament, but, at some point after leaving politics, took a sharp to turn to the right, becoming a staunch supporter of many Conservative policies. His son Luke and I had worked for John Sawatsky back in the 1980s. The Fishers were a family of journalists. Luke's brother Tobias worked for CBC TV, his brother Matthew worked for the *Globe and Mail*. Their other brother, John, had worked for Don Mazankowski, Mulroney's deputy prime minister.

Fisher's column seemed to compliment me, sort of:

Some of my colleagues read the Airbus affair as confirmation the massive
public rejection of Mulroney extends to an urge he be punished. Without
denying the mass antipathy I prefer to see the Airbus case as a good example of what a dedicated production team with CBC-TV's great resources
can do, linking documentary and news expositions . . .

Then he mentioned me.

Few outside the CBC know the zealot in the Airbus pursuit. If it peters out
he may never be a household word. If the jackpot evidence is found he
becomes the latest Canadian Woodward/Bernstein. He is Harvey
Cashore, an engaging young man in his 30s who came east a decade ago
from B.C. (where his father is a cabinet minister) and got work as an aide
to John Sawatsky in his long preparation of the 1991 best-seller, Mulroney:
The Politics of Ambition. Then Cashore moved to CBC-TV and eventually
reached 5th Estate [sic], still with a fix on Mulroney. He, more than Mulroney's best known nemesis, Stevie Cameron (of On the Take) has made
Airbus the staple story for this winter. I'd wager 5-1 the Mulroney jackpot
won't be found.

I took all of this as a kind of backhanded compliment. But a public
wager about whether the jackpot would be found seemed a little too
sporty to me. The allegations reported by the *Financial Post* were serious,
and I was not sure whether it was fair to everyone involved, including Mulroney, to appear to be treating it so lightly.

A turning point for me came Sunday, December 10. Bob Fife's headline
in the *Toronto Sun* spoke for itself. "Devon a Swiss miss; key account said
to belong to Frank Moores' wife."

Fife's "Tory party and legal sources" had told him that the Swiss bank
account 34117 Devon, which had allegedly been set up for Mulroney, actually belonged to Frank Moores's wife, Beth. Further, Fife reported that the
Devon account never held more than 500 Swiss francs. Wrote Fife: "A
source confirmed that Moores opened two bank accounts at the Swiss

Bank Corp. in Zurich but neither was for Mulroney and neither had any-thing to do with secret commissions. 'The Devon account was for Beth Moores. There was never more than 500 Swiss francs in it,' the source said."[2]

A second "legal source" told Fife that the Devon account belonged to "Mrs. Moores." Fife then quoted Schreiber's Edmonton lawyer, Robert Hladun: "There's going to be a lot of trouble because a lot of people caused a lot of pain for a lot of people."

This was the first I had heard that the Devon account may have con-tained almost no funds at all. I wondered why Frank Moores had so vig-orously denied to us just that spring that he had had any Swiss account at all. Why had he not just said he had set up Swiss accounts but not for the reasons Pelossi had alleged? I looked, but could find no mention in Fife's story that Frank Moores had been lying for months about the existence of the Swiss accounts.

The suggestion that the Devon account belonged to Beth Moores seemed suspicious. Pelossi had written the initials B.M. just above "Devon" on the back of a Swiss banker's business card. True, B.M. could stand for Beth Moores. But logically, it made no sense to me. Pelossi had made the notations himself. He had always said that he wrote the initials B.M. on the business card in order to remind himself that the Devon account was des-ignated for Mulroney. If we were to accept the B.M.-means-Beth-Moores story, then we would have to believe that Pelossi had forgotten whom he meant when he had written B.M. in the first place, and that when he took a look at the business card a few years later, improvised that the B.M. stood for Brian Mulroney. It was a stretch. It made sense to suggest Pelossi made up the entire story because he was so angry with Schreiber, but suggest-ing that Pelossi had been confused about his own notation struck me as odd.

In any case, we were very concerned with reports showing how little activity there had been in the Devon account. We had always been clear that we had no evidence that any money had been deposited into the ac-count, of course. The broadcast was being spun, however, that we had

2 Both of Moores' accounts were set up in Canadian funds. The reference in the quote to Swiss francs is inaccurate.

linked the account to money and to Brian Mulroney. If Fife was right and there had never been much more than pocket change in the account, it could look like a strong wind through a house of cards. If the Devon account had been set up for big cash transactions, where was the money? There wasn't any, the detractors crowed. Rumours started circulating that *the fifth estate* had been duped.

Trish Wood, David Kaufman, Susan Teskey and I met in David Studer's office to discuss what to do. None of us knew what to say. "We never said money was paid into it," I feebly offered. We all knew we had taken a huge hit to our credibility. There wasn't much to be done except keep at it and make sure we get it right. I left Studer's office feeling pretty blue. We had worked hard on that story. We had not been reckless. Still—and this is the worst thing that can happen to a reporter—I had a moment of doubt. *Shit, what if I was wrong?* Back in my office, I thought about Fife's article. Okay, I argued, let's concede that there never was much money in the Devon account. What the article never addressed was, Why not? Why had it been set up in the first place?

Two days later, I sat down to watch *The National*. Another gale-force wind was sweeping through our Airbus story. CBC *National* reporter Neil Macdonald was reporting that "Mulroney and Moores have not been close for years."

"Brian Mulroney and Frank Moores used to be friends, all right," Macdonald reported, "but it was a friendship that crumbled quickly under the pressures of power. Moores began to snipe at Mulroney in 1987, in a long interview with the St. John's *Sunday Express*. People who were close to Mulroney at the time say he was angry about that article, that he considered it disloyal. And Mulroney was never one to easily forgive disloyalty. Margory LeBreton, now a senator, remembers that a few months after the article appeared, Mulroney asked her to check out rumours he'd heard that Moores was still taking shots at him.

"Oh, I guess we're talking eight or nine years, now, that there has been very little contact between the two gentlemen," LeBreton said.

"Moores himself," Macdonald concluded, "has said publicly that he and Mulroney have not spoken in five years. And timing is important, here. The Mounties, in their now-famous letter to the Swiss, say Airbus started paying its secret commissions in late 1988. Mulroney supporters point out that that was well after Moores took his first public shots at Brian Mulroney, and, they say, well after the two men stopped speaking to one another altogether."

I had heard the story of their falling-out as well, but had also heard that Mulroney had later invited Moores to both the prime minister's summer residence at Harrington Lake and 24 Sussex for a private party. Something didn't seem right. Even if Moores and Mulroney had had a falling-out, there was a lot of evidence that they were still on good terms. Besides, if Schreiber was the source of the *schmiergelder*, why would Moores be needed at all? In other words, what practical effect would a falling-out with Moores have had, since Mulroney and Schreiber were friendly? Perhaps this could explain why the Devon account may not have received any funds. Why give money to Moores when Schreiber could have just as easily given it directly to Mulroney? None of this meant any of this actually happened; I was just trying to figure out the logic of various scenarios. Still, we were all pretty sure that the attacks were going to be catastrophic for us at *the fifth estate*, just as soon as the definitive proof emerged that the Devon account held no money. I felt like a deer in the headlights.

Meanwhile, the mood at work was tense. Some colleagues at the CBC were shooting me looks in the halls. Some even spoke their mind. "You're making us all look bad," one told me. I didn't have the confidence to argue. I walked on. I got a horrible cold. In my state of depression, I decided to call Keith Miller, the former head of Eastern Provincial Airways who had helped me with my research in the spring. Miller had also appeared on-camera, albeit in shadow, to explain that Frank Moores was indeed involved in selling Airbus in Canada.[3] Miller wanted to remain in shadow out of concern that he might face retribution from his former friends in politics and in the airline business. Turns out he might have been right. Somehow, Frank Moores, among others, had figured out that Keith Miller was the man in shadow. He had received a series of bizarre phone calls from former Tories, he said, including one-time member of Parliament and lobbyist John Lundrigan. Lundrigan was a fellow Newfoundlander

---

3 In 2009, Keith Miller agreed to be identified.

who, like Frank Moores, had set up shop as a lobbyist in Ottawa after Brian Mulroney came to power.

Miller told me that Lundrigan had called him several times with an unusual request. He wanted Miller to call up Phil Mathias at the *Financial Post* and state that Frank Moores had nothing whatsoever to do with Airbus. Lundrigan told Miller that Mathias was a "good guy" and that they were fishing buddies. Miller told me he listened politely. Lundrigan wanted to help Moores squelch the rumours and knew that someone like Miller, well respected in airline circles, could help do that. All he had to do was make the call to Phil Mathias. Later, when Lundrigan realized the call had not been made, he phoned Miller back.

"I haven't called anybody," Miller said. He told Lundrigan he had no intention of calling the *Financial Post*. According to Miller, that's when Lundrigan exploded.

"I am sure that on that machine of yours—I am sure there are lots of calls that have been made to you from *the fifth estate*." Miller said he felt he had been set up. Somehow, Lundrigan had found out Miller had been the person "in shadow" in our show.

"Go fuck yourself," Miller told Lundrigan. He hung up, and they never spoke again.

"Jesus, man, every day there is something," Miller reflected. "All I did was tell you the goddamn truth. All I didn't want to do was go on TV, but I made that decision myself. I mean, shit, do I get castrated for telling you the truth?"

And then, perhaps sensing *my* despair, Miller gave me some avuncular advice.

"Don't forget they were lying in the goddamn sunshine for seven or eight years and then suddenly you came out of the weeds and start firing bullets at them."

"I will be happy when this is all over," I responded.

"Well, don't let them get you down," he said. "It won't be over for years."

CHAPTER FOURTEEN

SOMEBODY MUST BE JOKING

As 1995 drew to a close, the attacks on *the fifth estate* and me just never seemed to stop coming.

Friday, December 15, I received another phone call from Phil Mathias. He was writing another story about *the fifth estate* and its coverage of the Airbus story. Out of respect, Mathias said he wanted me to know that he was doing an investigation into the allegation that *the fifth estate* had turned over documents to the RCMP. He instructed me not to respond in any way. He simply wanted me to know that he would be asking my boss, David Studer, for a comment. Mathias called Studer later that day and, as we would learn from reading Saturday's paper, the denials didn't make much difference. He reported the allegation anyway.

Mathias had another scoop, however. One we had all been anticipating. Splashed on the front page of the *Financial Post* on Saturday, December 16, came confirmation that the Devon account—the one allegedly set up for Brian Mulroney—had never held a deposit of more than $500.

Frank Moores had provided the *Post* with a bank document showing that the account was opened February 4, 1986 (exactly as Pelossi had said). The story also reported that reviews of the Devon account balance sheets showed that no substantial funds were ever paid into it. (No mention was made, however, of whether there were any funds in the second account Moores had set up that day, 34107.)

He quoted Moores: "Brian Mulroney had absolutely nothing whatever to do with the Devon account or any other account of mine." Moores was not "in any way involved in . . . Air Canada's decision to purchase the Airbus aircraft," he added, "as a lobbyist or a conduit for illegal payments."

Moores had given power of attorney to his wife for both of the accounts. They were not for her, though. Beth Moores, he said, had nothing to do with the Devon account. "Moores said news stories that the account was opened for her benefit are not correct. He opened the account, he said, to hold the proceeds of European business deals that were planned, but did not materialize."

Moores also claimed that the code name Devon had nothing to do with the fact that Mulroney lived on Devon Street in Montreal in the 1970s. His ancestors, he said, had come from Devon, England. He had a living relative named Devon, too. He had two reasons to give the account the code name Devon, but it was certainly not because Mulroney had lived on Devon Street.

Mathias had no proof that we had given documents to the RCMP, but he reported the allegation, suggesting that our denials contradicted three newspaper reports.

"The RCMP's allegations rest primarily on similar claims made by a CBC television program, the Fifth Estate [sic]. Executive producer David Studer denies speculation in three newspapers that the CBC showed the RCMP its documents. That would be a violation of CBC policy and journalistic ethics," he wrote.

That same Saturday, William Thorsell, editor-in-chief at the Globe and Mail, hopped on the Mulroney bandwagon in an editorial defending the former prime minister. It was a "pity" that the Canadian Charter of Rights and Freedoms did not apply to RCMP investigations in foreign countries, he wrote. The RCMP was apparently not required to get judicial authority from Canada for the probe they initiated in Switzerland. They should have had, he argued. And at the Toronto Sun, Bob Fife interviewed Beth Moores, who claimed that the initials B.M. stood for her. "It was his [Frank's] account which I had signing authority on," she told Fife. "The B.M. was Beth Moores. It was never Brian Mulroney."

The next day Fife wrote yet another story critical of *the fifth estate*. Luc Lavoie told Fife that Mulroney had unjustly been called a crook because of an "institutional screwup" caused by the Justice Department, the RCMP and CBC TV's *the fifth estate*. "Sooner or later these guys will have to sit in the witness box and explain what happened," Lavoie said.

Fife also quoted Mulroney's friend, Senator Marjory LeBreton, who stated that *the fifth estate* was "out of control." (LeBreton was also quoted in the *Ottawa Citizen* saying she would support an inquiry into the Airbus scandal and how the RCMP and Department of Justice conducted itself.) In a story two days later, Fife quoted Tory leader Jean Charest: "The government will have to be accountable. It won't be good enough to claim it was some bureaucratic decision somewhere." Fife again took aim at *the fifth estate*. "The case against Mulroney was shaken on the weekend when ex-Newfoundland premier Frank Moores said he never opened a Swiss bank account for him as alleged by the RCMP and CBC's *the fifth estate*."

Things only got worse in the new year of 1996.

In a lawsuit, each defendant has to be served personally. At the CBC this means you either agree to meet a bailiff downstairs in the atrium, or, if you would rather not, the bailiff will come to your home, or track you down, and serve you with the papers. When I got a call from one of the CBC's security guards that someone was waiting downstairs to hand deliver a package, I knew what was going on. I elected to go downstairs and be served.

The Statement of Claim was written by Schreiber's Edmonton lawyer, Robert Hladun, QC. I skimmed the Statement of Claim quickly. Essentially, it stated that *the fifth estate* had falsely accused Schreiber of paying bribes and kickbacks and that, moreover, we had damaged his international reputation. As a result he had lost future business. Schreiber was suing *the fifth estate* for a total of $35 million.

Well, that was a relief, I joked to Trish Wood, since I could barely afford the mortgage on my house. The next day, Bob Fife delivered the cheerful news to readers of the *Toronto Sun*:

"German dealmaker Karlheinz Schreiber is suing the CBC for $35 million for implicating him in an alleged $20 million Airbus kickback scandal."

Yet again it was erroneously suggested that we had alleged that Schreiber gave money to Mulroney. "The suit arose after the CBC's fifth estate aired an item last March which quoted Swiss businessman George [*sic*] Pelossi as saying Airbus paid secret commissions to Schreiber, former prime minister Brian Mulroney and ex-Newfoundland premier and lobbyist Frank Moores."

The Schreiber lawsuit against *the fifth estate* was followed up by one from Frank Moores; his, however, claimed damages of only $15 million.

For my colleagues in the media, it was like blood in the water. The news unleashed a feeding frenzy of new stories. CTV reporter George Wolff, who was developing a good relationship with Schreiber, questioned Giorgio Pelossi's credibility because he'd been linked to Mafia interests (whereupon another dispute erupted between various news organizations about who was toughest on Pelossi[1]). *Globe and Mail* columnist Lysiane Gagnon wrote a story headlined, "The crude political witchhunt against Brian Mulroney." Gagnon also reported that the B.M. on the business card was for Beth Moores, that Mulroney and his government had nothing to do with the purchase of Airbus jets because the board of Air Canada made the decision, and that Justice Minister Allan Rock was at fault for the letter to the Swiss (even though there was no evidence put forward that he even knew anything about it). Doug Fisher, the *Ottawa Sun* columnist who had called me "engaging," wrote a series of critical columns, including one titled "Fairness falls victim to vampire journalism" in which he described the "blood lust" of "some" journalists towards Mulroney. "Like certain RCMP investigators, they are convinced that the previous government was riven with criminal conspiracies just waiting to be exposed." He suggested that the CBC needed to do some "soul-searching" since the Ottawa Press Gallery had now reached a "consensus" that the RCMP had "overstepped the mark." He went on to compare the standards

---

[1] And, as I said earlier, given that Pelossi had already admitted his role in a tax evasion, kickback and bribery scheme surrounding the Airbus commissions, wouldn't it make sense that he would also be involved in other similar, if dubious, activities? Why did these new allegations about other malfeasance suddenly make him not credible? Couldn't one argue it made him more credible, given it seemed to confirm this was the kind of thing he did for a living? In any event it was all off topic and not directly relevant to whether or not Airbus paid secret commissions, which they had.

of *the fifth estate* to the US tabloid television shows *Hard Copy* and *A Current Affair.*[2]

If there was a bright light in the media coverage, it came not from Canada, but overseas.

The German media had been following the Schreiber story as well. By the beginning of the year there had been several pieces in German publications about how the authorities had raided Schreiber's compound in Kaufering and seized documents. It wasn't just Schreiber who interested authorities. The home of Holger Pfahls, a former senior defence official connected to Schreiber, had also been searched, as had the homes of two Thyssen Industrie executives, Juergen Massmann and Winfried Haastert. Schreiber's lawyer in Germany, Stephan von Moers, told the media any work performed by Schreiber with regard to Airbus in Canada was done at the behest of Franz Josef Strauss.

In late December a story in the national German newspaper *Frankfurter Allgemeine* quoted von Moers saying his client was, in fact, involved in the Airbus deal in Canada. "That so-called 'necessary expenses' should flow to the customer was a recognized practice and accepted by the Department of Finance. The lawyer also confirmed that in one case Schreiber was involved in the transaction of such a payment."

It seemed as if there were two completely different scandals: in Canada, the focus was mostly on how the RCMP and *the fifth estate* had unfairly gone after Frank Moores, Karlheinz Schreiber and Brian Mulroney; in Germany, reporters were asking tough questions about Schreiber, his political influence and what he did with all his money.

The pending lawsuits precluded my reporting on the story, but I decided to call Pelossi. I wanted to find out if there had been any developments.

There *had* been. Pelossi told me that German authorities had recently visited him about documents they'd seized from Schreiber's compound. Specifically they wanted to confirm Schreiber's handwriting on a document. Pelossi told me that the investigators would not let him see the entire

---

2 When I called his office to explain my perspective, Fisher refused to come to the phone.

document—they covered the top and the bottom—but he confirmed to the authorities that what they had shown him was indeed Schreiber's writing.

Pelossi also wanted to clear up something with me: he said that he met Frank Moores's wife once, did not remember her name, but insisted that the B.M. on the business card stood for Brian Mulroney.

As far as I could tell, Pelossi seemed unperturbed by the numerous media reports attacking him. Instead, he observed that it must be Schreiber who would be feeling the pressure. In Germany, Schreiber would want to argue that he provided the "necessary expenses" to foreigners and therefore should not be taxed on the income (at the time it was, as I have said, legal in Germany to pay bribes and other "necessary expenses" to foreigners). In Canada, he would want to argue the opposite, that he did not pay kickbacks or bribes or *schmiergelder* to anyone, since that revelation could prove embarrassing, or worse, to the people who received it. Pelossi summed up Schreiber's predicament: "Schreiber is having to choose between betraying friends" or landing in hot water with the German tax authorities. One or the other.

I was lost, flailing around. I called anybody I could who might know something. In late January 1996, in the lull before the Mulroney lawsuit got under way, I made a call to Brian Walker, a former senior vice-president of sales and marketing for the now-defunct Wardair. Walker told me that he and Max Ward had had an enormous falling-out due, in part, to Ward's decision to purchase the Airbus aircraft.

"I was in Max's office when Airbus called. And Max said, 'We've made a deal [with Boeing], we can't go back on our deal. The deal is done, I am sorry.' And they proceeded to keep talking. And Max was making big-eye looks and he said, 'They really want this business.' And he put the phone down and he said, 'We are going to be buying Airbuses is what they tell us.' And they came over and they just took the price down to what they had to do get him [Ward] to go back to Boeing and ask for his money back."

Walker had not liked the idea at all.

"I was not in love with the airplane. It was totally wrong for what we were trying to do . . . the airplane didn't stack up to the 767 in terms of the number of seats you could get on the main deck. It's a great plane if you wanted to fly the cargo. But we were interested in [carrying] passengers."

Walker could see, however, that Airbus would not take no for an answer. "Airbus was going to have that order," he told me. "So it was as simple as that." Simple, because Airbus needed the sale for strategic reasons. "They [Airbus] had no major customers in North America," Walker said. "And they needed a showcase for the airplane. And they wanted to get a sizable fleet up and running somewhere in North America. And it has worked. Since that time Canadian [Airlines] is a major operator, Air Canada is a major, major operator of Airbus. You have got airlines down in the States now that are flying big fleets of Airbus. So I mean, that [the Wardair purchase] was a real foot in the door for Airbus. So it didn't really matter what Ward got them for, it served their purpose. And it allowed them to be able to quote manufacturers the operating statistics of the airplane operating within the North American environment.

"Airbus, you have to realize," he went on, "prior to getting into North America, had done a large majority of its business in the Near and the Middle East. You don't do business in that part of the world, I can assure you, unless you are paying something under the table. It becomes a natural way of doing business. And I believe probably Airbus had gotten that down to a fine art."

Walker was quick to point out that Max Ward was an honest businessman. His turnaround would have been based purely on the price of the plane.

I thanked Walker for his time. I told him that my goal was to discover where the Airbus millions ended up. "I can't help you with where Airbus's money went, I just can't tell you," he said. "I can tell you what I believe. I believe they [Airbus] would be very comfortable paying somebody money if they thought it would get them an order. I believe they wanted an order bad enough to crack Boeing and McDonnell Douglas's hold on this market, that they would have paid Santa Claus if they thought it would have helped."

Nothing seemed to be able to derail the narrative at play in Canada.

Karlheinz Schreiber and Frank Moores were suing CBC's *the fifth estate*. Brian Mulroney was suing the federal government. The amount claimed in damages added up to a combined $100 million.

Of the three lawsuits, Brian Mulroney's would soon take centre stage.

For starters, Schreiber's and Moores's lawsuits were crawling along at a snail's pace. I sensed that neither man had any intention of following through. By February, however, I had grown so restless at the slow progress that I wrote a letter to Daniel Henry, CBC's legal counsel:

> I don't know what stage the Schreiber lawsuit is at right now, but I won-
> dered whether or not we might try to advance the lawsuit as quickly as we
> can. I say this because it is my belief that Schreiber has sued the CBC partly
> because he thought it would be good public relations. People now won-
> der whether what the CBC said was accurate or not. Perhaps we should re-
> spond to Schreiber's lawsuit by saying, "Yes, he has the right to sue, but we
> also have the right to respond in a timely way to his accusations against
> us."
>
> The sooner people understand the information behind our story, the
> sooner I believe people will realize we were careful with our facts and our
> research. As well, our research demonstrates that Karlheinz Schreiber has
> misled the CBC and *Der Spiegel* magazine on several occasions. I believe it
> is in the public interest for people to know exactly what those instances are.
> The sooner the lawsuit proceeds, the sooner we can demonstrate exactly
> how Schreiber misled us.

What I had not understood at the time was that the CBC's aproach was basically to wait the process out. Why bother asking a plaintiff to hurry up a lawsuit when, if he was losing interest, we might inadvertently provoke him into a court case we might lose? It was a kind of let's-hope-the-whole-thing-blows-over approach. My issue was simple: the Airbus story was in the news almost every day and yet, as long as Moores and Schreiber were suing us, I wasn't allowed to talk on the record to other reporters. Worse, our Airbus stories were embargoed, meaning no one could ever watch them again, until the litigation was over. And lawsuits could take years to go to trial. That's because there are so many steps in between. First, we would have to prepare a statement of defence, then we would have to put together all our documents, then we would have to have "discoveries" of the various parties, then there would be case management, then there would be mediation to figure out if we could settle out of court, and then, and only then, would there be a trial. I realized that my two-year-old son would be in grade school by the time it was over. It seemed to me that Schreiber and Moores had already achieved exactly what they wanted. It hardly mattered whether they won or lost the lawsuits. We were silenced, but Schreiber, Moores and Mulroney were free to say whatever they wanted. On March 19, 1996, CTV's George Wolff broadcast a "CTV News exclusive." Schreiber's lawyer, Robert Hladun, was going to petition the federal court to stop the Airbus investigation: "Schreiber argues his rights as a Canadian have been violated by the Justice Department's request for financial information without first obtaining a proper search warrant from courts either in Switzerland or Canada." Schreiber was proving he would aggressively fight the release of his banking records everywhere, from Canada to Switzerland to Germany.

On March 21, I had a call from the *Globe and Mail*'s Paul Koring. He told me he had heard a rumour from Luc Lavoie that I had supplied the RCMP with outtakes of our interview with Giorgio Pelossi. As a matter of principal, TV journalists fight hard to prevent the police from getting their hands on their footage. Had I done such a thing it would have left me open to contempt, even ridicule, from my colleagues. The rumour alone was harmful. I wondered how many had heard the same story and not called me to check it out, who simply wondered if it was possibly true.

"The rumour is false," I responded.[3]

Mulroney seemed to want his lawsuit over in a hurry.

In early 1996, his lawyers had fought for, and won, an unusual appointment of a single judge to oversee the entire process, meaning that Mulroney's lawsuit was on a fast track for resolution. Lavoie spelled out the

---

3 Koring was simply doing his job by checking the story with me. He did not report the rumour.

strategy in public. "Our lawyers will do everything they can to keep it moving as fast as they can."

One problem loomed on the horizon: standing between Mulroney and his desire for a speedy victory against the federal government was the likelihood he might have to testify in court. Quebec civil procedure allows the defendants to examine the plaintiff in public, in a courtroom, as the first step in a lawsuit. That meant that the federal government could demand that Mulroney immediately answer questions, under oath, about his relationship with Karlheinz Schreiber even before the trial began.

The judge set April 17 and 18 as the dates for Mulroney's examination on discovery. I wouldn't go to Montreal, since I was off the story for now.

I circled the date on my calendar anyway.

CHAPTER FIFTEEN
STRAIGHT OUT OF KAFKA

There was a light snowfall Wednesday morning as the green GMC Jimmy pulled up to the sidewalk at the Montreal courthouse on Wednesday, April 17, 1996. The driver stopped long enough to drop off the eighteenth prime minister of Canada, and the other passenger, civil litigation lawyer Gérald Tremblay.

A gaggle of reporters followed Mulroney and his lawyer up the steps and into the building, surrounded by a team of security guards. Mulroney and Tremblay walked slowly as TV cameramen scrambled in front of them. Mulroney smiled and waved at bystanders; he looked confident and relaxed as he and his counsel walked to a nearby bank of elevators. Cameras were prevented from entering the courtroom, but one alert CBC cameraman filmed Mulroney briefly through a pane of glass. Everyone agreed it was one for the history books; no one could remember a former prime minister of Canada testifying under oath in a court case.

For the first time Mulroney was in the same room as RCMP sergeant Fraser Fiegenwald. The other named defendant, Kimberly Prost, had helped draft the Letter of Request to Switzerland. Fiegenwald and Prost each had their own lawyers in the room. Add that to five additional lawyers from the federal government and two lawyers for Mulroney.

A throng of Mulroney loyalists showed up, including long-time St. Francis Xavier University friends Sam Wakim and Fred Doucet, former cabinet minister Gilles Loiselle and Paul Terrien, a Mulroney speechwriter. Those who didn't arrive early had to sit in the overflow room, where a closed-circuit TV filmed the proceedings.

The media contingent included George Wolff and Rosemary Thompson from CTV News; Neil Macdonald, CBC; Bill Marsden, the Montreal *Gazette*; Tu Thanh Ha, the *Globe and Mail*; and Sandro Contenta, the *Toronto Star*. In all, twenty reporters crammed into the room, including an international contingent from the *New York Times*, Reuters and Agence France Presse.

Luc Lavoie was there as well. Despite the dreamlike coverage Mulroney was receiving in some outlets, several reporters in other major media had taken a more skeptical approach. They included the *Globe and Mail's* Stan Oziewicz and Tu Tanh Ha, the *Toronto Star's* Bill Schiller, and *Maclean's* magazine reporters Paul Kaihla and Stevie Cameron.

It must have been obvious to political veterans like Mulroney and Lavoie that if the former prime minister was going to win the lawsuit it would have to be won not only in the courtroom but also in both the political backrooms and in the public arena. Liberal justice minister Allan Rock was calling the shots. Allan Rock was widely considered prime ministerial material, and it was generally assumed he was contemplating a leadership run one day. He would therefore have a personal as well as a political reason to want to deftly stickhandle his way through the mess. On the one hand, he did not want to be seen as engineering a witch hunt against Mulroney; on the other, he did not want to be seen as giving preferential treatment to a former politician. One wrong move in either direction and his prime ministerial ambitions would be up in smoke. Perhaps that's why Lavoie's strategy might have been to publicly embarrass the Liberals into settling. The suspicion was reinforced the next morning in the *Toronto Sun*:

"PM's link to Airbus man."

"As former PM Brian Mulroney prepares to defend himself in the Airbus scandal," wrote reporter Bob Fife, "the *Toronto Sun* has learned that Prime Minister Jean Chrétien has a personal relationship with the key figure in the case.

"Chretien sent a warm birthday greeting to German dealmaker Karl-heinz Schreiber in March 1994—a year before the RCMP probe of Mulroney and the Airbus jets sale to Air Canada," wrote Fife.

The sizzle was out of the story by the second sentence, however. Anyone who has worked in and around Ottawa knows that politicians are always getting requests to send special birthday greetings, especially on a sixtieth birthday. "Aline and I are delighted to offer you our warmest greetings on the occasion of your sixtieth birthday," Fife quoted Chrétien writing. "It is our hope that this special day will evoke many cherished memories and fill you with great happiness . . . Kindest regards."

There must have been thousands of similar letters in circulation; Fife, however, described it as a "personal relationship." Even if there was a relationship, what did any of this have to do with the allegations against Mulroney? "The Liberals have privately revelled at Mulroney's link to an alleged $20-million bribery scam, which the RCMP say was engineered by Schreiber and Tory lobbyist Frank Moores."

"At a time when Brian Mulroney, 57, should be enjoying life as a respected private citizen," wrote the Montreal *Gazette*'s Bill Marsden, "the former prime minister has gone on the offensive to put to rest allegations that he's a crook . . . If he can convince the court and the public that he's being victimized, the government, the RCMP and in particular Justice Minister Allan Rock could end up looking like dangerous fools."

"What is the nature of the documents used by the CBC and *Der Spiegel*," asked the *Globe and Mail* in an editorial, "and how did the RCMP come into possession of them? The RCMP give no indication that they contacted Air Canada to determine whether anyone involved in Airbus experienced any political pressure in choosing the planes. Why? If there was no such pressure, what is the status of the alleged crime? Is it conceivable that the Commissioner of the RCMP did not authorize the action, given its explosive nature? Is it conceivable that Solicitor-General Herb Gray—who is responsible for the RCMP—did not authorize it on the same grounds? Is it conceivable that the Prime Minister's Office was not apprised of the action by Mr. Gray? How far up the chain of command in the Justice Department did authorization go for sending the RCMP material on to Switzerland? . . . Did any of them check with the PMO? . . . Why does the Criminal

Code protection against unreasonable search and seizure not apply to Canadians when the police or government seek evidence abroad? Why did RCMP and government officials accept the vague standard of proof laid out in Ottawa's letter in this case?"

It was odd that there had still not been a single question about where the money had gone. Nor a single suggestion that perhaps Canadians had a right to know more about why three European companies paid more than $25 million in greasemoney while doing business with the federal government.

It was because I was stuck back in Toronto that I had time to make a phone call to a freelance journalist in Germany named John Goetz.[1] Goetz would later tell me that he had been hired by *The National* to check me out and to see if there were any holes in *the fifth estate* story. That might sound absurd—a CBC program checking out another CBC program—but back in the mid-1990s there was a certain animosity between the two shows.[2] In any event, if that was how I came to meet Goetz, then it was all for the good.

Goetz, I would soon learn, was a force of nature. He had grown up in New York City, finished high school in Minneapolis, then, after graduating from Cornell University, travelled throughout Asia and Europe as a freelance journalist. In the fall of 1989, he decided to spend a couple of months

[1] My original partners had for the most part left the story by then. Mathias Blumencron had begun a rapid career path, eventually becoming editor-in-chief of *Spiegel*, and Jock Ferguson had moved on as well, working for a forensic accounting firm.

[2] Since that time the CBC has undergone a massive reorganization in its News Department. Back in the 1990s managers believed in a philosophy that was sometimes called "Show Culture." In this organizational model programs like *the fifth estate* were given significant autonomy to compete with other programs both within CBC and outside the corporation. The thinking was that internal program competition led to better results for the whole corporation. Still, this kind of independent culture meant there was little formal communication between various CBC News shows. This sometimes led to inefficiencies. For example, two or three CBC camera crews might show up at the same event, since these things were not centrally coordinated. Moreover, the competitive environment inevitably led to conflict within the CBC itself, as shows competed with each other to get the best stories for themselves. Today all CBC's news resources, from television, radio to .ca are all centrally organized. "Show Culture" is, for the most part, a thing of the past at CBC News.

reporting from East Berlin, having no idea that the wall was about to fall. That decision changed his life. He fell in love, learned to speak German, and has lived and worked in Berlin ever since. In 1994, he co-produced a story for *60 Minutes*, "The Ugly Face of Freedom," about anti-Semitism in western Ukraine. Goetz was opinionated, smart, charming and slightly mischievous. He had the unique ability to convince people to speak to him. With a laugh and a joke, he'd disarm his subjects and convince them that there was no harm in meeting for dinner, or a drink, to discuss a story, whatever it was. Goetz had figured out the Schreiber story was one that had a future for a dogged freelance journalist like him.

And on this day he had a new piece of information to share. We were discussing the arrest warrant that the German authorities had issued for Schreiber and wanted to know exactly what it said. Goetz said his sources told him that Schreiber was wanted for both tax fraud and tax evasion—including the secret commissions he received on the Airbus / Air Canada deal. It was an important piece of information. For the first time we knew that his arrest warrant was tied to the Canadian part of the story. But none of this would make the news that night. Mulroney's lawsuit was what mattered.

That Monday night the CBC's Neil Macdonald opened the national news.

"Portraying oneself as a little guy up against a big system cannot come naturally to anyone who's lived Brian Mulroney's life. But then, Brian Mulroney has had nearly six months to cherish his hatred of the Mounties and of Ottawa's legal machinery," observed Macdonald. "Mulroney talked about finding out that his own government had written Swiss authorities, calling him a criminal. He said he desperately tried to confront his accusers in the RCMP, but they ignored him. Mulroney said that as the Mountie accusations began to leak to reporters, it all began to resemble a scene from Franz Kafka's novel *The Trial*, in which a man is prosecuted for offences that are never really explained. 'You never know,' said Mulroney, 'when you'll be accused in the middle of the night by people unknown to you, someone who is judge, jury and executioner, who has declared you guilty without speaking to you. . . . It reeks of fascism,' he said, using a word he would repeat many times. 'If it could happen here, it could happen to any one of us.' Mulroney pointed at Crown lawyer Claude Armand Sheppard, his questioner. 'What in the name of God is going on? Who are these secret sources . . . who accuse me of being a criminal?'"

Macdonald said that Mulroney zeroed in on the RCMP and certain journalists.

"Brian Mulroney—seated directly across from seven Crown lawyers—despite his training as a lawyer, appeared to be incapable of holding his temper. He lashed out, went on the attack constantly, and interestingly enough, the RCMP sergeant Fraser Fiegenwald, who has been his nemesis throughout this, was sitting amongst those Crown lawyers. When Mulroney would make his allegations of police fascism, you could see Sergeant Fiegenwald's face redden.

"'Just you wait until I get your client, the RCMP, on the stand, under oath, and ask him about his secret sources,' Mulroney said."

Luc Lavoie was interviewed on-camera outside the courtroom, and he described how Mulroney felt after giving his testimony that day. "Well, he's very serene, and he's very happy that he could finally express in court the way he felt about what was done to him."

Macdonald told his viewers there were rumours that an out-of-court settlement was imminent: the government wanted out. Then Macdonald reported a new fact in the story. "Mulroney said he first met Schreiber informally in the early '80s and received him several times after becoming prime minister. Mulroney also said he'd also met with Schreiber since resigning as prime minister, usually over coffee in Montreal."

Coffee in Montreal? The remark caught my attention. It seemed to hang out there in Macdonald's report without any explanation.

The best advice my former boss John Sawatsky gave me was that a good investigative journalist always asks one basic question: "How did it come to happen?" All other questions flow from there. How *did* the coffee come to happen? How was it arranged? Who thought of it? What was discussed? What happened after the coffee? How many coffee meetings were there? When? Where? Why? And how does a former prime minister meet for coffee with a dispenser of *schmiergelder* anyway?

It seemed to me that reporters covering the trial had buried the most important piece of information—and instead dwelled on the theatrics in the courtroom. Why was it so important to focus on Mulroney lashing out at his critics? Wasn't that response predictable? Wasn't it more important what we learned about the relationship between Schreiber and Mulroney? And wasn't an unexplained coffee between the two men after Mulroney stepped down as prime minister rather intriguing?

Not a single media outlet raised any questions about the "coffee" that Mulroney had had with Schreiber after he was prime minister. At least, none that I could find. Some articles didn't even mention it. Every single story led with Mulroney's accusations of fascism against the RCMP. In his story "Mulroney scores points to clear his name," the *Gazette*'s Bill Marsden claimed that "Mulroney didn't balk at answering any question. At times, his garrulous nature shone through. His lawyers objected only eight times and even then Mulroney seemed eager to jump in." Many reporters focused on the misfortune that had fallen upon Mulroney and his family. "I've had my ups and downs in life. I've been successful and unsuccessful. I'm not a novice to controversy," read Mulroney's quote in the *Toronto Star*. "But this was the worst thing that has ever happened to me in my life . . . I have four young children, my mother is 85 years of age, my father-in-law is very ill—to have to explain to them what happened and what is going to happen is a painful thing. . . . I had to take my 10-year-old aside: 'Nicolas, in a little while it will be in the papers. They will say that the government of Canada will say that your father committed crimes and you will be harassed because of it.'"

When the green GMC pulled up to the courthouse for day two of Mulroney's testimony, both Nicolas and his father got out of the vehicle. Mulroney gave his son a hug goodbye in front of the cameras. Nicolas then hopped in the front seat and was driven away, presumably on his way to school. The second day went as well as the first. As government lawyers pressed for more details about his relationship with Schreiber, Mulroney again went on the offensive as he accused the Liberal government, a small coterie of journalists, and the RCMP of being out to get him.

During the lunch break, the media converged like a hungry wolf pack on RCMP officer Fraser Fiegenwald.

CTV reporter George Wolff approached him with cameras running in the halls of the courthouse.

"You were accused of fascist activities, of not giving the man a fair chance; you have no comment on that?"

Fiegenwald brushed by without answering.

Before he slipped into an elevator, Wolff asked another question. "No regrets, Mr. Fiegenwald?"

When the testimony was over later that day, Wolff and his cameras flocked to the former prime minister waiting outside the courthouse. "This was supposed to be the defence's opportunity to make some gains on you," Wolff stated in what turned out less a question than pro-Mulroney spin. "It seems perhaps you turned the tables. Is that your impression?"

"Well, I will leave those impressions to others," Mulroney said. "I testified honestly about what took place . . . There are gonna be some very, very interesting questions for some very unusual people."

"Like who?"

"Well, stay tuned." Mulroney looked around for an old friend. "Where's Sam?" he asked. Sam Wakim was eventually located, then Mulroney got in the car and they drove away.

Not everyone was enamoured of Mulroney's performance.

"With typical hyperbole," read an editorial in the *Toronto Star*, "former prime minister Brian Mulroney has accused the federal government and the RCMP of 'fascism' for pursuing corruption allegations against him. Slipshod, maybe. But fascist? Not to mention 'horrendous,' 'grotesque,' 'execrable,' 'poisonous,' and 'straight out of Kafka'?"

The editorial pointed out that the RCMP had a duty to investigate the allegations. "Nor would it have been proper for Justice Minister Allan Rock or Solicitor-General Herb Gray to have stopped the investigation, as some of Mulroney's former colleagues and his media apologists have suggested. . . . Contrast this with the views of John Crosbie, a minister of justice in the Mulroney government. He says Rock ought to have derailed the RCMP investigation of Mulroney because there was 'clearly' no evidence to support the allegations . . . We accept Mulroney's word that he was not involved in Airbus kickbacks, if there were any. But we cannot accept the suggestion the Mounties never should have pursued their investigation."

Over at CTV News, Mike Duffy was insisting that the "real" journalistic question in the Airbus affair is why the CBC looks to have given information to the RCMP. I fired off a note to my bosses, Susan Teskey and David Studer: "If Mike Duffy is concerned about false rumours spread by unscrupulous journalists he is doing exactly to us what he so despises in others."

On the afternoon of Mulroney's final day of testimony, I received a fax from the Privy Council Office (PCO) in Ottawa.

I stared at it in disbelief.

The PCO is at the top of the bureaucratic chain of command in Ottawa. All of its employees are civil servants, but it reports to and serves the Prime Minister's Office, which comprises political appointees only. The PCO falls under the purview of the Access to Information Act. In fact, I had made a request *more than a year before* asking for "any and all information" relating to Karlheinz Schreiber, including notes of discussions, meetings or any correspondence with Brian Mulroney or his staff.

Initially I had been told that the delays were the result of the PCO having trouble finding any records. Then someone was on holiday. Then there had been a meeting to discuss my request. Then they had collected records but a third party had objected to their release. Who? I had asked. What "third party"? No one would tell me. For months I had followed up with phone calls, but the delays continued. Finally, in February of 1996 I was told that the records were on their way. In April—two months later—the package had still not arrived.

Lo and behold, on the final day of Mulroney's testimony in Montreal—at exactly 2:42 p.m.—the package of documents arrived by facsimile. Much too late, of course, for any of the documents to be made public in time for Mulroney to respond to under oath.

My frustration boiled over when I read the materials. The PCO had obviously not given me the entire file.

The first document, labelled "Secret" and dated March 26, 1991, was written by Canada's top civil servant, Paul Tellier, to Norman Spector, a former chief of staff to Brian Mulroney, preparing him for a "possible call" from Karlheinz Schreiber. The correspondence was heavily blacked out, but this portion remained: "Currently there are restrictions in the Criminal Code and the Export and Import Permits Act preventing Canadian companies from exporting automatic weapons." Then, on June 18, 1992, Tellier wrote a memorandum directly to Mulroney stating, "I understand that in early May you met with Mr. Karlheinz Schreiber of Thyssen BHI to discuss his proposal to build (a word blacked out) peace-keeping vehicles (more words blacked out.) . . . Exports of this type of vehicle would raise issues of foreign policy and armament sales," wrote Tellier. This was the first time I had ever received any documentary evidence that Brian Mulroney had actually met Karlheinz Schreiber.

Still, that was all I received: two letters. I knew from my research there had to be more.

I was told that Schreiber had met Mulroney and his staff several times. I knew he had been buzzing around Ottawa for years on the Thyssen tank proposal. Schreiber had kept quiet about his involvement in the MBB helicopter deal and the Airbus deal, but he was always quite open about the Bear Head project.

So where were the rest of the records?

The cover letter to me from the PCO was, admittedly, apologetic. "Your continued patience and forbearance throughout the processing of this request are much appreciated. Any inconvenience the extended period of time it has taken to process your request is truly regretted." I immediately filed an appeal to John Grace, the Information and Privacy Commissioner, arguing that the PCO had withheld key documents:

My research indicates there were many meetings and discussions between Karlheinz Schreiber and the Prime Minister or his staff from the years 1984 to 1993," I wrote in my complaint. "One wonders whether the PMO appointments book was ever consulted to fulfill my request. In short I would suggest that my request, which first began more than a year ago, is still not close to being fulfilled.

I was angry. I had made a request for information using laws enacted by the Parliament of Canada in order to ensure public transparency in government. In my opinion, someone in the PCO had deliberately made a mockery of those laws. Isn't this what we'd expect from a banana republic, not from a modern western democracy?

For the next four years, my relationship to the Airbus story was what you could best describe as on-again, off-again.

Sometimes I would be motivated by all the unanswered questions, happen upon an interesting lead and pursue it doggedly for a day or two. Then I would meet a dead end and move on to something else with better odds of turning into an actual documentary. The Airbus story had been stressful and I felt as though I was able to escape it by focusing on other stories. I had been promoted from associate producer to producer in 1995 and was enjoying learning how to craft documentaries. My first documentary was about a botched police investigation into a Hamilton homicide incorrectly identified as a suicide. I continued to produce several documentaries a year: a toxic-waste disposal company that was sending failed treatments into the city sewer system, an investigation of a questionable fire at a plastics-recycling facility, a wrongful murder conviction in Nova Scotia and, one of my favourites, a profile of the Royal Military College hockey team, the Redmen,[3] in its quest to defeat their American rivals, the West Point Knights. I was also beginning to win awards for my work. John Sawatsky's schooling was starting to pay off.

Through it all, however, the Airbus story was always there in the background. Usually I forgot one story as quickly as I finished it, swiftly moving on to the next. But not with Airbus. Maybe because I knew we had failed at finding out where the money went. Maybe because I believed the media had been so badly manipulated. Maybe because I felt personally defeated. Or maybe because we were being sued for $50 million. If I had a breakthrough on the story I wouldn't just have another documentary; I might wipe out the lawsuits too. Whatever the reasons, and there were many, it was a story I could not let go. Or maybe it never let me go. Sometimes I was brought back into the story in ways not of my choosing.

Which is exactly what happened in the spring of 1996.

---

3 RMC has since changed the name of its sports teams to the Paladins.

For starters, Karlheinz Schreiber now appeared to be in a mood to proceed with the next step in his lawsuit. Perhaps empowered by Mulroney's public relations success in Montreal, we received an urgent legal "notice" from Robert Hladun, QC, in Alberta. It required us to produce our "Affidavit of Documents" within ten days. This is a fancy term that means we had to provide Schreiber with copies of all our notes, including records of conversations, names of sources, any documents or any other piece of information we had compiled while working on our story.

The idea of providing even a single page of my notes to Karlheinz Schreiber and his long-time lawyer, Robert Hladun, offended me to my core.

The law, however, was on their side.

Journalists are always taught to refuse to hand notes over to the police, but what many forget is that in a civil suit we almost always willingly hand over our materials. Sometimes journalists romantically suggest they would sooner go to jail than hand over their materials to a third party. But in a defamation case that option doesn't exist. All you would do is end up losing the lawsuit. Even the most notorious fraud artist, for example, has the legal right to obtain all your journalistic work product simply by launching a lawsuit against you, however groundless it may be. To me this was, and remains, the most offensive part of defamation law in Canada.

Still, the CBC had hired one of the best law firms in Alberta, Reynolds Mirth Richards and Farmer, and one of its best lawyers. Allan Lefever was not the kind of lawyer to rant and rave in a courtroom. He studied material carefully, was heavily detail oriented, spoke thoughtfully and had a razor-sharp mind. When he read through Pelossi's documents, he figured out a pattern in the bank accounts in Liechtenstein that I had not seen before. Lefever knew that I was concerned about protecting my sources, since people had risked their careers by speaking with me. So he came up with an idea that would at least work in the short term. He told me to go through all my notes and black out any information that might reveal a source. We would agree to release material to Schreiber, minus the blacked-out material. Still, the lawsuit would begin to eat away at weeks of my time. I would have to fly to Edmonton several times that year, frequently meeting Lefever's associate, Don Lucky, in their boardroom to catalogue and organize documents for their files.

And it wasn't just the lawsuits that pulled me back to the Airbus story.

A whole new group of media pundits began to march on the story, as if to trample *the fifth estate* straight into the ground. The first up was Susan Gittins. Gittins was a freelance reporter commissioned by *Saturday Night* magazine's editor-in-chief, Ken Whyte, to take a look at the Airbus media coverage. *Saturday Night* was owned at the time by Conrad Black's media empire.

On the phone, Gittins admitted that Phil Mathias was an old colleague of hers and insisted he had been unfairly criticized by others in the media over *his* coverage. She claimed it had been hard for pro-Mulroney stories to even get in print in the period after the Letter of Request was leaked. I asked her if she had read the *Financial Post*, or *Toronto Sun* or *Montreal Gazette* or listened to CTV News or read the *Globe and Mail*'s editorials. She countered with an observation that the *Ottawa Citizen*'s Greg Weston had trouble getting one of his pro-Mulroney columns into print (though it did actually get published).

"What day did you travel to go to Switzerland to interview Giorgio Pelossi?" she asked.

Gittins was referring to the interview we did with Pelossi back in the fall, when he came out of the shadows for the first time. She was wrong about my travelling to Switzerland to interview Pelossi. At the time I was in Switzerland, he had not yet agreed to an interview; but I sensed the drift behind her question. I had told Phil Mathias I was travelling to Switzerland the same day I left. I realized that at the time he must have thought *the fifth estate* was about to publicly identify Pelossi—or possibly even Mulroney. That might have explained why the *Financial Post* identified Mulroney on the Saturday—at least two days before we would be able to get anything to air.

A few days later, Southam reporter James Bronskill added more insight into the events of the previous fall, quoting a surprisingly candid Luc Lavoie, in a speech to the Ottawa chapter of the Canadian Public Relations Society: "The strategy was simple. . . . Either the story published by the *Financial Post* would be picked up by the media worldwide and Brian Mulroney would be described as a criminal, or the denial and the lawsuit would be picked up by the media worldwide and the story would be, 'The former prime minister of Canada is suing the government of his country for defaming him.'"

Looking back, I think this was about the time when the story began to fundamentally change who I was. Previously I had had an enthusiastic belief that the truth would prevail if journalists worked hard enough. That belief propelled me into journalism in the first place, back when I was twelve years old, living in Coquitlam, British Columbia, and established my public school's newspaper, the *Cape Horn Flyer*. It took me into high school, where I became editor of Centennial Senior Secondary's the *Catalyst*. And it convinced me to begin a career in journalism, far from home, at Carleton University in Ottawa. Now that belief was being shaken. Because my job as a journalist defined, in part, who I was, it meant in some ways I was becoming a different person. I became increasingly less optimistic, less enthusiastic, more defeated. And in itself that change in my outlook would have its own, if inevitable, consequences.

CHAPTER SIXTEEN
A VICIOUS CIRCLE

The showdown between the federal government and Brian Mulroney occupied the national stage throughout the spring, summer and fall of 1996. It was as if reporters were covering a sporting match, with each side trying to score points in the battle for public favour. One media survey revealed that the former prime minister was getting more ink than the sitting prime minister, Jean Chrétien. Everyone seemed to agree that Mulroney had the momentum. In the aftermath of his testimony in Montreal, the good news kept on coming for the former prime minister and, for that matter, Karlheinz Schreiber.

First, Mulroney won two important court rulings.

The first ruling that went Mulroney's way occurred when the RCMP and the federal government asked the judge to force Mulroney to disclose his long-distance telephone records, which would reveal who he'd called around the time of the Request for Assistance. The judge said no, Mulroney's telephone records were off limits. The second court ruling in Mulroney's favour occurred when the Mounties went to court to argue they should be allowed a delay in presenting their statement of defence. Imagine, they argued, if every time the police began to investigate someone, that person simply sued the police, and requested information about their case *while* the RCMP was investigating. How could they properly investigate? A failure to obtain an extension, they argued, "would result in public disclosure of the contents of an ongoing criminal investigation and would jeopardize the investigation." Again, the judge denied their request, telling them to file their defence immediately.

Schreiber, on the other hand, was having much more success in the Canadian courts than the Mounties. His lawyer, Robert Hladun, QC, had sought a federal court injunction in Vancouver to prevent the Mounties from having access to Schreiber's bank accounts in Zurich. Hladun argued that the Canadian Charter of Rights and Freedoms protected his client against unreasonable search and seizure and therefore the RCMP should have obtained a Canadian search warrant before it got permission to look into his overseas accounts. "The issue is: Do you have [Charter] protection from Canadian police when you are abroad?" Hladun asked the court. The judge agreed. Justice Howard Wetston ruled that the Mounties had no right to ask Swiss authorities to search and seize Schreiber's accounts without first obtaining prior Canadian judicial approval. "This ruling makes the government's [L]etter of [R]equest unconstitutional and therefore null," Hladun said, who added he would demand that the Department of Justice "cease and desist" efforts to obtain Schreiber's accounts. Mulroney's public relations spokesperson, Luc Lavoie, seemed overjoyed: "The letter was not only defamatory, it was also illegal," he told Phil Mathias at the *National Post*. In his article about the court victory, Mathias also quoted Schreiber who, by then, was living somewhere in Switzerland. (He did not attend his own hearing.) "My confidence in the Canadian court system has been confirmed," Schreiber told Mathias.

It looked to me as if almost every important court ruling was going in either Mulroney's favour or Schreiber's favour.

That spring I had an idea.

Based on my initial conversation with writer Susan Gittins, I believed that the *Saturday Night* article would take another kick at *the fifth estate*. I began to feel increasingly sidelined on the debate about the role the media played in the story, thanks to the Schreiber and Moores lawsuits that dictated I remain silent. Phil Mathias and Bob Fife kept writing stories; Mathias even won a National Newspaper Award for his Airbus coverage. And I was supposed to keep quiet? If I was depressed by this turn of events,

I took some comfort when I learned that the Canadian Association of Journalists (CAJ) gave me, Trish Wood and David Kaufman the award for the best investigative documentary of 1995 for our first Airbus story. And that's what inspired me to try to break our silence. I proposed that I write an opinion piece for the CAJ's *Media Magazine* about the Airbus story—and how the media had been so badly manipulated. David McKie, the editor, urged me on. I wrote up a first draft, then took it to my CBC colleagues for approval. To my surprise, everyone signed off, including CBC's media lawyer, Dan Henry, our Edmonton lawyer, Alan Lefever, and the lawyer handling our lawsuit with Frank Moores, John Koch from Stockwood Spies. (Lefever joked that he didn't see what more harm I could do.) I told McKie to go ahead and publish the article.

As my wife and I packed our bags for our annual summer holiday to British Columbia, I had reason to feel at least a little optimistic. But when I checked my voice mail in Campbell River, en route to Cortes Island, I learned that David McKie wanted to speak with me urgently. When I called him back, McKie said he'd had a phone call from Norm Bolen, head of CBC's Current Affairs Department. Bolen advised McKie that he didn't know what Harvey was "up to," but the article was not going to be published. It was simply too risky.

The story never ran.

Parliament resumed in the autumn of 1996 and the Mulroney libel lawsuit was back on the agenda. There were more news reports of a possible settlement, only to be stomped out by Justice Minister Allan Rock, who complained that private negotiations shouldn't be leaked to the media. Rock criticized Mulroney's team for falsely accusing him of being involved in the Request for Assistance when, in reality, he had only learned about it after Mulroney's lawyer told him. And government lawyer Claude-Armand Sheppard continued to argue that the Mulroney team was behind the leak that allowed Mulroney to sue the government. Government lawyers said they would subpoena journalist Phil Mathias to ask him who gave him the letter. Mulroney's team countered that by sending subpoenas to journalists like Stevie Cameron who, they claimed, had given documents to the

RCMP (Lavoie had arranged to have a CTV camera crew film the bailiff knocking on Cameron's door with the subpoena). Quoted in the Montreal *Gazette*, Cameron denied giving information to the Mounties, calling the subpoena "a big publicity stunt." The federal government's lawyer said it would subpoena the editor-in-chief of the *Globe and Mail*, Bill Thorsell, who had a close relationship with Mulroney; perhaps he might know about the leak to Phil Mathias. Then Mulroney's legal team announced it had subpoenaed another journalist who it accused of being too close to the RCMP—me. Later, I received a cheque in the mail for just over a hundred dollars, to cover the cost of a return bus trip to Montreal.[1]

That fall I was reminded just how far I had to go, even within the CBC, to restore my reputation. One morning a new colleague called me into her office after learning that she and I would be working together on the toxic-waste story I mentioned earlier. She wanted to give me a stern lecture.

"We are not going to do the kind of journalism you did on the Airbus story," she stated.

"What?"

"We are not going to do that kind of journalism," she explained again. She was opposed to character assassination and innuendo-filled journalism.

And I was in favour? I'd had enough. The CBC refused to let me write an article explaining my perspective, we'd taken numerous hits against us from reporters like Phil Mathias and Bob Fife and soon, I was pretty certain, *Saturday Night* magazine would be taking a dig too. Obviously our approach didn't seem to be working. The attacks were now coming even from within *the fifth estate*. I decided to confront the issue head-on, to find out what she meant by her admonition.

"What exactly did we say that you think we got wrong?" I asked her.

My colleague paused, and then admitted she hadn't actually seen any of our stories yet. She had based her reaction on what she had heard from others, and even then she couldn't be specific. I suggested she watch the stories.

---

1 I still have the cheque on my bulletin board at work. It is signed by Jean-Yves Lortie, an infamous political organizer from Quebec who helped topple Joe Clark in the early 1980s. (Lortie was dubbed "The Poodle" after his curly hairstyle.)

There was a bright side as I prepared to defend myself against the $35 million Schreiber lawsuit.

I found myself reading old notes again, studying the documents, finding things that I had forgotten about or missed the first time. I kept adding items to my chronology of events and looking over my list of contacts. Who hadn't I talked with yet? Sometimes I hoped Emil would call me back, the man who had claimed he had copies of Mulroney's Swiss accounts. I had read so many documents, they were burned into my memory. Certain events, I would never forget. Perhaps this was the beginning of what others would call my "obsession." If so, I had Schreiber's lawsuit to thank. One night, as I was poring over the interview notes—notes I would soon be forced to hand over to Schreiber's legal team—I was scanning for names of sources I would need to black out. It was tedious work. And boring. But suddenly I turned up a note—long forgotten—to call someone named Christian Graefe in Edmonton. Supposedly he had known Schreiber back in his Alberta days.

I decided to call him right away.

After the preliminary introductions, I asked Graefe about his relationship with Schreiber. He told me that he had indeed known Schreiber well in those days, but Schreiber eventually wore out his welcome. Graefe, who was close to several Tory politicians, had learned that Premier Peter Lougheed simply felt uncomfortable around him. Graefe told me that Lougheed soured on Schreiber after meeting him on a trip to Europe. "Schreiber tends to be very familiar, I gather, and Lougheed tends to be very reserved. Schreiber put his arm around Lougheed as they were supposed to walk into dinner and made a comment something like, 'Well, Peter, if you and I work together, we can really make music.' At which point apparently Lougheed said to his entourage, 'Gentlemen, I think we are in the wrong place.' And they left."

Graefe told me to call Irwin Zeiter, the owner of a bagel shop in Edmonton. It was as if he had been waiting for my phone call.

Zeiter said he first met Schreiber in Alberta in the 1970s when both were hoping to take advantage of the province's burgeoning economy.

Right away Zeiter knew two things about the Bavarian: he wanted to sell Airbus airplanes in Canada; and he was close to Franz Josef Strauss. Immediately after their first meeting, a chance encounter in Edmonton, Schreiber gave Zeiter a beautiful model of an Airbus.

"You see, when he came to Edmonton, he said that he had a contract to sell the Airbus. And he would get a very good commission."

Then Zeiter and Schreiber began working together on Schreiber's road-marking business, and soon Zeiter was getting invitations to visit Schreiber's compound in Germany.

"So he introduced me to all kinds of politicians. He used to give very nice parties, you know," Zeiter said. "[Schreiber] is a very down-to-earth person. He can tell jokes like nobody else I know. And he is very warm and very friendly. He is not the best-looking guy, but he is very friendly guy and everybody likes him. Because he tells you nice things and makes you feel good." Soon, however, Zeiter learned Schreiber had a unique modus operandi in business. "He always tried to get immediately in with the politicians. . . . He tried to buy up always everybody right from the beginning."

Now Zeiter was a bitter man. A former millionaire, he had lost his entire fortune after the real estate bust in the early 1980s. That's when he says Schreiber stopped calling him. "And I tried to get Karlheinz who could help me. He didn't. I am no friend of Schreiber. He left me high and dry and so I am no friend of his."

Zeiter said he would agree to appear on-camera any time. But for now he had to get off the phone. He had some bagels to make.

I was right about the *Saturday Night* magazine article.

"A Vicious Circle" took shots at almost every journalist who seemed to want to know where the Airbus money went: Stevie Cameron, Jock Ferguson, me and *the fifth state*. Here's a sample of what we were up against: "Mulroney's libel action goes to trial in January, and in the months since his court appearance, it's been looking more and more as if he was right—right to be incensed at the federal government, and right to blast the media.

"A close examination of the media's role in the Airbus affair, and their handling of the story, shows the journalists on the Airbus beat not as a noble bunch in high-minded pursuit of a corrupt prime minister, but, for the most part, as a pack running in circles after a scandal of its own making."

There wasn't much left to do but wait for the Mulroney lawsuit to begin in the new year, on January 6, 1997. I had received my subpoena to testify and was waiting to hear when I would have to show up. That's when I got a letter from National Public Relations, the firm representing Brian Mulroney. I opened it quickly, wondering what could possibly be happening now.

It was a Christmas card, with Luc Lavoie's handwriting:

"Harvey, all the best, Luc."

My initial inclination was to tear it up. Instead, I got a thumbtack and placed it on my bulletin board, right above my laptop.

It turned out to be the best inspiration I'd ever had.

CHAPTER SEVENTEEN
COLLATERAL DAMAGE

In the end, there was no trial.

The Sunday night before the court case was set to begin on January 6, 1997, word leaked out that Brian Mulroney had settled with the federal government. The official announcement would come the next day, but a "confidential" source close to the negotiations had called reporters and given them certain details about what was in the agreement. Luc Lavoie had been hard at work. He knew that *how* the settlement was sold to the media mattered as much as the settlement itself. And he knew that if he revved up his spin machine the day before the official announcement, he would get the all-important first word. Lavoie's message was simple: Mulroney had won; the federal government had backed down. Mulroney would get an apology and the government would pay his legal costs. No one had yet seen the agreement, or the wording, but it didn't matter. It was breaking news. The media lapped it up. That night Neil Macdonald's story on CBC's *Sunday Report* echoed a message that was reverberating across the country:

"Word tonight that Brian Mulroney's lawsuit against the federal government has been settled. Now, this is just an unconfirmed report at this stage; the official word from both Brian Mulroney's spokesman and from Ottawa is 'no comment' . . . We understand the deal was struck today and we understand that Brian Mulroney is happier tonight than he has been in a long, long time.

"It's been fourteen months, just over a year since the story that ruined Brian Mulroney's retirement," continued Macdonald. "He hasn't been seen much in public since, but sources close to Mulroney say he has gone from apoplectic, to obsessed, to merely fixated with clearing his name. As one friend put it, you pick a fight with this guy and he'll take your eyes out."

The next day, Justice Minister Allan Rock made the official announcement in Ottawa. He seemed almost oblivious to a brewing backlash as he bounced out of the government car parked on the south side of Wellington Street. It was a cold January day and he did not have a coat on, so he rushed from the vehicle and into the National Press Building, just across the street from Parliament Hill. He headed straight into the theatre where he sat down at a microphone, flanked by Solicitor General Herb Gray and RCMP commissioner Norman Inkster. Rock started out on the defensive, angry about the leaks from the Mulroney camp.

"Starting last night with leaks and spin about this agreement, there has been a lot of comment and speculation about what is in it," Rock began testily. "Let me start by telling Canadians what is not in the agreement. There is no $50 million damages payment to Mr. Mulroney, as he has been demanding for more than a year in his lawsuit. In fact, Mr. Mulroney has now dropped any claim to compensation for damages. This agreement does not stop the RCMP's ongoing criminal investigation into Airbus, or give anyone, including Mr. Mulroney, effective immunity from such an investigation. In fact, under the agreement, it is clear that the RCMP will continue its investigation in its entirety and it is now free to carry it through to whatever conclusion is appropriate." Rock pointed out rather self-servingly that both Mulroney and the government had agreed that he—Rock—had not been involved in the composition of the letter. Presumably, someone else would end up taking the blame.

Yes, there would be an official apology.

"Some of the language in the Request for Assistance indicates, wrongly, that the RCMP had reached conclusions that Mr. Mulroney had engaged in criminal activity. Based on the evidence received to date, the RCMP acknowledges that any conclusions of wrongdoing by the former prime minister were, and are, unjustified. The government of Canada and the RCMP regret any damage suffered by Mr. Mulroney and his family and fully apologize to them."

As far as settlements went, the government did not actually give up very much. They apologized only for the wording of a letter (that they had not leaked), agreed only to pay for Mulroney's legal fees, and specifically, said Rock, the federal government would not be paying for any of Mulroney's "media management advice" (meaning Luc Lavoie would not be getting any government money).

"There's no apology for the investigation," insisted Rock. "Police don't apologize for investigating. Police don't apologize for pursuing allegations. That's what police are for."

Rock sensed that there would be daunting questions about the government's paying out any money at all to Mulroney. What he may not have sensed is that the decision to apologize and pay Mulroney even a token settlement eventually cost him his political career.

"Some will ask why Mr. Mulroney's legal costs are being paid," Rock continued. "Let me explain. First, my own experience as a trial lawyer tells me that there is no such thing as a sure case. There are always risks in going to trial. I have already referred to elements of risk in this case, including some of the language in the letter, and the enormous cost of a lengthy trial. When public money is involved, we have an obligation to minimize risks. Obviously, we would have preferred not even to pay legal costs. But two events late last week convinced us that it was in the public interest to settle this case even if it meant paying legal costs to the plaintiff."

Two "events" had convinced the government to settle? Reporters listened closely as Rock asked his cabinet colleague, Solicitor General Herb Gray, to explain.

Gray pointed out that the government side had lost yet another key ruling, this one in Federal Court, which may have forced the RCMP to disclose confidential information in the Mulroney lawsuit. "This ruling, and other proceedings, have brought home to the RCMP the very great risk that testimony might be required that would have the effect of jeopardizing the entire investigation," said Gray.

Fair enough. The RCMP did not want to ruin their Airbus investigation. It was a good enough reason to settle and, in my opinion, the two cabinet ministers should have stopped there. But they didn't. Instead, they appeared to put much of the blame for the settlement on an unnamed RCMP officer, who had given confidential information to a "third party." Whatever happened was apparently so scandalous that it forced the government to settle with Mulroney and to pay his legal costs.

But what exactly had this RCMP officer done? Details were sketchy.

"While the Privacy Act prevents disclosure of the names of either individual involved," Gray said, "I can tell you that the commissioner has already initiated a Code of Conduct investigation and he will be available to you following this press conference to discuss the details of this process."

Rock and Gray were quick to point out that the "alleged" communication to the "third party" was not linked to the publication of the Letter of Request in the *Financial Post*, but that was as much as they would say. Still, it didn't take a rocket scientist to figure out that the Liberals were pointing a finger at Fraser Fiegenwald, the RCMP officer who began the Airbus investigation. To me, it seemed too convenient. The Liberals were looking for a way to escape from the Mulroney lawsuit almost from the beginning and now, on the eve of trial, they found a scapegoat: the hard-working RCMP officer who wanted to know where the money had ended up.

But if Allan Rock thought he could escape scrutiny by casting blame elsewhere, he was in for a shock. Reporters interpreted the settlement as the government admitting it had made a big mistake. They asked Rock if he was going to resign. "No, I am not resigning and I am not considering it," he protested.

On one level, the call for his resignation had been unfair. Rock had neither leaked the letter nor had he—as he was quick to remind—had a hand it its composition. In fact, he had not even heard about the letter until Mulroney's lawyer told him about it. So what had he done wrong? Rock had scapegoated the RCMP for the Liberals' decision to settle. Not his finest hour.

And the day just got worse for Rock and the Liberals.

Calls for Rock's resignation continued across the street on Parliament Hill from several MPs, the loudest from former Mulroney cabinet minister Jean Charest, now leader of the Progressive Conservative Party. And because the Mulroney team had sold the settlement as an overwhelming victory, many MPs and political pundits couldn't figure out why Rock's apology came across as half-hearted. Now Rock didn't just look inept, he looked callous too. "It was quite breathtaking," CBC commentator Rex Murphy summarized, "when you consider it cost two million dollars to reach that apology, how very little Mr. Rock was willing to apologize for. He wasn't apologizing for the Airbus investigation; he wasn't apologizing that the former prime minister was a target of that investigation; he wasn't apologizing that the RCMP were continuing the Airbus investigations, nor was he saying that in the continuation of that investigation, Brian Mulroney wouldn't be a target. As an act of contrition, the two-million-dollar apology was, let us say, several *meas* short of a full *culpa*." Murphy called the affair "a gargantuan botch-up of the most high-profile investigation since Hal Banks,[1]" and criticized the fact no senior officials took responsibility. *Globe and Mail* editor-in-chief William Thorsell continued that line of reasoning, appearing to suggest that the Mounties should have just walked away from it all. "But the investigation goes on," noted Thorsell, "and so, remarkably, does this Minister of Justice."

The media next zeroed in on the identity of the mysterious "third party" who had talked to Fiegenwald and the RCMP: *Maclean's* reporter Stevie Cameron. It was suggested that Fiegenwald had admitted on the eve of trial that he had, in fact, told Cameron that Mulroney's name was in the Letter of Request. What was the point of this? Mulroney had sued not because he was named but because of the way he was described in the letter. It was an important distinction. There was not a shred of evidence that Fiegenwald leaked the letter—either to Stevie Cameron or to Phil Mathias at the *Financial Post*. Indeed, he had refused to share the document with *anyone*. Instead of being commended for performing his job as a consummate professional, Fiegenwald was reassigned to "administrative" duties as he awaited his disciplinary hearing.[2]

---

1 In 1987, William Kaplan wrote a book about Hal Banks, *Everything that Floats*. The infamous 1950s-era union leader successfully fought extradition to Canada on charges of assault.

2 Years later, a new revelation (to be discussed later in the book) would better explain why Fiegenwald had been in contact with Cameron.

Allan Rock was soon shuffled to the Health portfolio.[3]

In Montreal, however, the mood was celebratory.

Luc Lavoie was seen flashing a V-for-Victory sign outside the courthouse where the lawsuit would have taken place. Gérald Tremblay, Mulroney's civil lawyer, was beaming with pride. "Mr. Mulroney's name has been vindicated and that's the only real thing he wanted," he told reporters. As for the fact that the RCMP was going to continue investigating, fine with him. "If they want to throw money down the drain, let them do it. There's nothing I can do," Tremblay told reporters.

And finally, for the first time since the scandal broke, Brian Mulroney was ready to talk to reporters. Mulroney stood outside his house in Westmount in the freezing winter weather to give interviews. Fourteen months ago the questions would have been all about his relationship with Schreiber, but on this day those questions would have seemed inappropriate, even rude. Now that reporters had opportunities to ask him questions, not a single person asked any about the Airbus affair.

One by one, reporters showed up with their camera crews. CTV got there first, and filmed the former prime minister as his son Mark stood nearby, smiling, in a blue winter jacket.

"We are very pleased with the outcome," the elder Mulroney said. "We achieved our objective, what we wanted. I wanted any stain whatsoever removed from my father's name."

"Are you surprised the RCMP hasn't said that they have dropped the investigation and they are continuing to say that you are part of that investigation?" asked the reporter.

Mulroney took the high ground. "From the very beginning we have said, Look, the RCMP can investigate and indeed they should investigate anybody from any walk of life they feel warrants an investigation. In my case they can investigate me until the cows come home. They won't find a single thing, because we have never been involved in anything untoward. So it won't just happen."

3 A Southam News poll later showed that nearly 70 per cent of Canadians thought the Liberals had done a poor job handling the lawsuit, yet also agreed that Mulroney deserved the apology and the settlement money. In other words, Canadians believed, based on the media coverage, that the Liberals had wronged Mulroney.

Later that night, Mulroney stood outside his home again, for another TV crew, this one from CBC News. And this time Mulroney's eleven-year-old son, Nicolas, was at his side.

"It was a terrible ordeal," Mulroney said. "We wanted to make sure that the good name that my father gave me was unsullied, and remained unsullied, and we have achieved that and we have got a settlement [for legal costs] that we are very happy with, and so what we want to do is turn the page and get back to our lives. . . . I was fighting for my family's reputation and honour and my own, for all the people who had supported me, and for the millions of Canadians who voted for me. This [investigation] was extremely unfair and we just wanted to make certain that that was clarified, once and for all, forever, for today and for history. It never happened. I had no involvement whatsoever, directly or indirectly in this [Airbus scandal], and that is what the government has finally acknowledged. And so now that it is done, the matter is passed, we hope the page has turned and we want to get on with our lives.

"Life goes on. And now that we have picked ourselves up from this and it's over, we turn the page to—and hopefully to—a happy future, to get on with the rest of our lives."

And with that, Mulroney and his son Nicolas turned around and walked into their house on Forden Avenue.

Allan Rock had apparently been so preoccupied with the Mulroney settlement and apology that he hadn't considered the possibility that both Karlheinz Schreiber and Frank Moores would want apologies too. And why not? If the government was apologizing for some of the wording in the Letter of Request, shouldn't they apologize to the two other "victims" named in the letter? Certainly that was how Frank Moores saw it. "I'm very upset and I'm also very angry," he told CTV's George Wolff. "I'm very angry that this sort of travesty could happen in a country which I've always been proud to be a citizen and still am." Moores's lawyer went further, telling CTV that his client also deserved a financial settlement from the government. "Surely they'll do the right thing," stated lawyer Edgar Sexton, who was at that time still suing *the fifth estate* and me for $15 million.

"Mr. Moores just wants fairness and justice."

Sexton also gave an interview to the *Globe and Mail* denying that Moores had received any Airbus money. "[Moores] certainly did not impede the RCMP investigation in Switzerland, and they got the information on his accounts and they've had it for several months. Obviously the accounts show nothing and substantiate the position of Mr. Moores, which has always been that he had nothing to do with obtaining the Airbus contract and that he got no money for it. As a result of all that, he also feels that he's entitled to an apology." Later he told the *Toronto Sun*, "I find it amazing that we have to ask."

Karlheinz Schreiber was somewhere in Europe, but he responded through his Edmonton lawyer, who told the *Toronto Sun* that his client had suffered "enormous damages." Schreiber too should get the same deal as Mulroney, both an apology and money for Schreiber's legal expenses. In fact, said Robert Hladun, Schreiber was contemplating his own action against the government. "He was quite anxious that there be a trial so that all the evidence would come out and everyone could see for themselves, in a courtroom, the truth—that this was all hogwash and a travesty of justice." Later, George Wolff managed to reach Schreiber by phone, so Canadians at least got to hear his voice. "The damages I've suffered in the whole thing are on the international level, reputation, a substantial amount of money," Schreiber told him. "I really think that the whole matter can be clarified in the interest of Canadians only in the proper trial in the courts."

And it wasn't long before questions surfaced about Schreiber's $35 million lawsuit against *the fifth estate* and me. Hladun claimed that the Mulroney settlement would help his client win his lawsuit against *the fifth estate*: "Mulroney deal helps Schreiber suit—lawyer; Airbus Affair," read the headline in the *Edmonton Journal*.

"We'll definitely be going forward," Robert Hladun told Charles Rusnell, *Edmonton Journal* reporter. "This [settlement] shows the allegations were complete nonsense." Rusnell reported, "The letter to Swiss authorities alleged that Schreiber, Mulroney and Ottawa lobbyist Frank Moores conspired to defraud the Canadian government." But then Rusnell made a critical error: "The Fifth Estate [*sic*] made the same allegation." No, we hadn't.

The next day Schreiber and Moores got their apologies.

On January 9, Allan Rock, and Philip Murray, the commissioner of the RCMP, wrote personal letters to Karlheinz Schreiber and Frank Moores. The letters contained brief outlines of the events leading up to the letter to Switzerland, and then a full apology: "Some of the language contained in the Request for Assistance indicates, wrongly, that the RCMP reached conclusions that you had engaged in criminal activity. Based on what is set out above, and as a matter of logical consistency, the Government of Canada and the RCMP fully apologize to you for that language, and regret any effect that it may have had on you or your family."

It turned out that Schreiber hadn't wanted the apology. He responded to the letter from Rock and Murray eleven days later, demanding that the RCMP shut down the investigation once and for all. The *Toronto Sun*'s Bob Fife had the story first. "'[That] reminds me of the nightmare years of my childhood when the Nazi regime set loose the Gestapo on the German public,' Schreiber said in his letter to Rock. 'I would not wish the enormous pain, suffering and embarrassment that you have caused for my friends and family on anyone. . . . You have acted deliberately and recklessly in sending out the Letter of Request without foundation, and today, sixteen months later, you feel the need to apologize.'"

The Schreiber lawsuit was what was largely responsible for my being brought back, in the spring of 1997, to the Airbus story. I had completed the tedious task of organizing and assembling all our documents and notes. Now all we had to do was turn them over to Hladun and Schreiber.

But that's when we came up with a plan that had the effect of stopping the lawsuit in its tracks.

We were willing to hand over our documents, but only at such time as Schreiber handed over his documents as well. Schreiber eventually coughed up some documents, hoping, we presumed, to be able to see our documents. But Schreiber's materials were woefully incomplete. We had assembled several bankers boxes of information and yet Schreiber had produced only a few documents of little value. And that's when our lawyer, Allan Lefever, spotted an opportunity. He reminded us that

Schreiber had signed a sworn affidavit stating that he had provided *all* documents in his possession. Lefever told us that under Alberta law, we had the right to examine Schreiber on his affidavit. This meant that the lawsuit would grind to a halt until Schreiber showed up in a discovery room in Edmonton to answer our questions. For the first time in a long time I felt as though we suddenly had the advantage. I couldn't imagine Schreiber ever talking about, let alone coughing up, his banking documents, which he would certainly have to provide in order for his defamation suit to proceed.

Sure enough, Hladun didn't seem so interested in pursuing the lawsuit anymore. Schreiber kept delaying his required trip to Canada. Finally, Hladun told us that Schreiber was too ill to travel overseas.

The lawsuit, for all intents and purposes, was over.

The headline above Phil Mathias's story in the *Financial Post* on March 13, 1997, said it all: "Court rules against Ottawa in Airbus investigation."

In yet another setback to the RCMP investigation, Federal Court of Appeal, in a 2–1 decision, confirmed a lower-court ruling that the Mounties violated Schreiber's Charter rights by trying to gain access to his Swiss accounts. Justice Allen Linden ruled that the Mounties should have first obtained a Canadian search warrant. In practical terms this meant that the Mounties were not going to receive Schreiber's bank account information any time soon. More than a year and a half had passed since the Mounties first requested the information and now they would have to wait even longer. The only option left was for Ottawa to appeal Justice Linden's decision to the Supreme Court of Canada. "The decision makes it harder to continue the federal investigation in Switzerland of the role alleged to have been played by former prime minister Brian Mulroney in the Airbus affair," observed Mathias. Bob Fife, writing in the *Toronto Sun*, seemed to agree. "Justice Minister Allan Rock has lost another Airbus case that puts in jeopardy an RCMP probe of the alleged kickback scheme." I couldn't argue with that logic. The investigation was, for now, seriously crippled. Ottawa eventually announced it would appeal. But who knew how long that would take, and whether the result would be exactly the same.

On March 20, 1997, *fifth estate* host Linden MacIntyre and I attended a dinner at Osgoode Hall in downtown Toronto for the opening of the Nathanson Centre for the Study of Organized Crime and Corruption, a new initiative launched by York University. We later produced a documentary about Mark Nathanson, the university's benefactor, and his murky offshore financial dealings in relation to a gold mine in Mali, Africa. The room was populated with judges, lawyers, academics, and journalists, including a reporter I knew from the *Globe and Mail*. After the dinner, he came up to me.

"Luc Lavoie hates your guts."

"What?"

The reporter explained that Lavoie had complained to him about my relationship with the RCMP, and had questioned my abilities as a journalist. I had already heard that Lavoie was talking behind my back and attempting to discredit my work to other journalists. Still, it startled me to hear how deep the animosity seemed to go.

As for the Mountie who started the investigation, Fraser Fiegenwald, he was charged with contravening the RCMP's Code of Conduct in late April 1997. The RCMP even issued a press release stating that an internal investigation "points to information that supports the allegation." The allegation being, of course, that he had given information to a journalist. Fiegenwald's lawyer, Don Bayne, vigorously denied that claim. "I've believed from the start that he's being made the scapegoat for events far bigger than his involvement in this," Bayne told Southam reporter Stephen Bindman. Bayne said that the "exhaustive" probe actually cleared Fiegenwald, as did a further review. But Fiegenwald was prevented from giving anyone a copy of the internal report. That too, would have been a violation of his oath. In the meantime, Fiegenwald would have to wait for his day in court, where he would have to plead his case in front of three fellow officers.

If found guilty, Fiegenwald could be dismissed from the force.

CHAPTER EIGHTEEN
A REAL CASH ORGY

On May 25, 1997, the RCMP wrote a cheque to Brian Mulroney for $450,000, the first instalment to cover his legal costs in his lawsuit against the federal government. That payment was followed on June 27 by another cheque in the amount of $450,000. And then on July 11, 1997, the RCMP sent a further payment of $300,000. At that point, a mediator, the Honourable Alan B. Gold, was brought in to decide how much more the RCMP should pay, and in particular whether or not Luc Lavoie's public relations expenses would be included. Allan Rock had specifically said they would not be part of the government's settlement, but Judge Gold begged to differ. On October 6, 1997, he ordered the RCMP to pay a further $806,000, $587,000 of which related to Luc Lavoie and his PR firm, National Public Relations. In the end, the Mounties paid Mulroney a grand total of $2,006,508.

Around the same time, the RCMP brass informed Sergeant Fraser Fiegenwald that it would not provide him with a lawyer to defend against the Police Act charges. The Mountie rank and file were so outraged on Fiegenwald's behalf that they planned a benefit barbecue to help offset the more than $30,000 that their colleague had already paid out in legal fees. "We want to show Fraser that we support him and his family," Corporal Serge Claveau told Southam News. "We also want to tell the commissioner of the RCMP that enough is enough. You have to give this guy a fair chance to defend himself against the accusations. We want him to have a fair trial." But later that year Fiegenwald gave up the fight. He decided to leave the force on his own. By leaving when he did, he escaped any chance of being found guilty by the tribunal, since the RCMP Act only applied to active members. Given the way events had already played out, Fiegenwald could be forgiven for thinking any judgment at this point would be contaminated by the politics that surrounded it. But he had also given up any chance he had of ever working on the Airbus file again. From that point on, his name would be synonymous with a bungled Airbus investigation.

It had been nearly three years since I was first brought in to help research the Airbus story and, while it began as an exciting project, it had morphed into a mostly stressful experience, particularly after the lawsuits against me and the CBC for tens of millions. Still, it felt as if I turned a corner in 1997. I felt more and more relieved. Mulroney's lawsuit was over. The Schreiber lawsuit was in limbo. The national media had for the most part stopped covering the story, at least on a daily basis. I stopped worrying about opening the newspaper to see yet another article critical of *the fifth estate* and me.

On May 4, 1997, our son Jeremiah was born. Massey, then three and a half years old, wore a T-shirt that said, "I'm a new brother."

There were, of course, other things happening in federal politics besides the Airbus controversy. On June 2, 1997, Prime Minister Jean Chrétien easily won his second mandate, with 38 per cent of the vote. No other party came close. Thanks to divisions in the Tory party, which began when Mulroney was in power, the right-wing vote was split in two. Both Preston Manning's Reform Party and Jean Charest's Conservative Party received roughly 19 per cent of federal support. The Reform Party began as a populist western conservative movement alienated by Mulroney's politics and personality. When internal bickering threatened to dismantle the Reform Party, a young Stephen Harper helped get the party back on track. "We are not here to fight Preston Manning," he told a party gathering in 1991. "We are here to fight Brian Mulroney and Jean Chrétien and Audrey McLaughlin."

I was wrong, however, if I thought I'd finally escaped public criticism on the Airbus affair.

In September of 1997 I received a letter from someone named William Kaplan, a Toronto lawyer and author who was writing a book about what had happened to Brian Mulroney during the Airbus investigation. He was a labour mediator in Toronto still teaching law at the University of Ottawa. He had also written several books, and edited other collections. Kaplan had a master's in history and a doctorate in legal history. As historian Jack Granatstein would later observe, he "publishes first-class work at a pace that puts law school professors and academic historians to shame."

I told my bosses about the letter, who then decided that CBC lawyer Daniel Henry would field all inquiries from Kaplan. I was specifically told not to call Kaplan. Then, on October 3, Kaplan left a voice mail on my telephone answering machine. I was again told not to return the call. CBC lawyers and senior managers huddled to try to figure out what to do.

As my anxiety began to increase to its previous level, I again found myself strangely attracted to the pursuit of the Airbus story. On the one hand, I braced myself for the attacks that were likely to come from Kaplan, and on the other, I felt inspired to prove him wrong. Perhaps I could even discover something so important that it might get mentioned in Kaplan's book. With my reputation on the line again, I was motivated to get back into the fray, to try to figure out where all that money ended up.

And that's when I started to focus on Germany.

Unlike the Canadians, as I have said, the Germans were making huge progress in their investigation into Schreiber. Prosecutors were developing new angles and journalists were writing even more investigative stories about Schreiber's greasemoney. Moreover, journalists in Germany were not attacking each other, as they were in Canada. If there was a competition amongst them, it was to get the story, not to discredit their colleagues. I also learned that journalists from different news organizations in Germany often shared documents with each other, seeming to understand that the most important thing was getting the story out.

One day, John Goetz, the American journalist working in Berlin, phoned me.

"Harv, there's been a huge breakthrough on the Schreiber story over here."

An article had appeared in the *Sueddeutsche Zeitung* (*South German Daily*) that was sending shock waves through the country. Veteran investigative journalist Hans Leyendecker had obtained confidential documents from the police investigation into Schreiber revealing explosive information of the middleman's secret business dealings. Goetz read the story to me over the phone, translating as he went. I typed notes as he spoke. Included in the documents were copies of some pages of Schreiber's personal Daytimers. There were references to more bank accounts, apparently with code names set up for politicians and others. And there was news of another Schreiber secret-commission deal, this one involving the sale of German-made tanks to Saudi Arabia.

I had to tell Goetz to slow down. I wanted to understand everything, to grasp every detail. I would go back and pore over those notes all day.

Leyendecker had reported that the Saudi tank deal included 188 million DM in secret commissions, spread around the world and handed out in cash to various recipients. The former German undersecretary of defence, Holger Pfahls, allegedly received 3.8 million DM (roughly $2.7 million CAD); the former treasurer of the CDU (the Christian Democrats), Walther Leisler Kiep, allegedly received one million ($740,000 CAD); Max Strauss, the son of the Airbus chairman, allegedly received $610,000 ($453,000 CAD); and Eric Riedl, a senior parliamentarian also involved with Airbus Industrie, was thought to have received $500,000 DM ($360,000 CAD). As well, the two Thyssen managers, Winfried Haastert and Juergen Massmann, were under investigation for possibly receiving kickbacks from Schreiber. "It is currently the most explosive investigative proceeding of the Republic, even though all of the accused dispute ever having received pay-offs," wrote Leyendecker, who described a "real cash orgy" in which Saudi Arabian sheiks also got money through shell companies in Liechtenstein and other offshore tax havens. Even former American president George H.W. Bush and Chancellor Helmut Kohl were named as being on the fringes of the story. Still, Leyendecker cautioned that the investigation, which began two years ago, was moving along slowly and that all the allegations were as yet unproven. There was still no proof, for example, that Eric Riedl received any money, despite the revocation of his parliamentary immunity during the investigation.

But it was clear that the spotlight shone on Karlheinz Schreiber.

"In the center of the game is Karlheinz Schreiber," wrote Leyendecker, "a former carpet salesman" who was close to the former Bavarian chancellor, Franz Josef Strauss. "If [German] companies had to carry out difficult business transactions, they gladly used his network of connections around the world," explained Leyendecker.

Then Leyendecker got to the part about the code names. I was fascinated to learn that Schreiber had given code names to various people he had given money to, in order to keep track of the secret payments he had made.

A diary notation on April 14, 1991—Max wg. LK—was thought to refer to Max Strauss and Walther Leisler Kiep. There were references to "Maxwell," "Stewardess," "Winter," and "Waldherr." To the investigators, "Maxwell" referred to Max Strauss, "Winter" referred to Thyssen executive Winfried Haastert, "Stewardess" to Stuart Iddles, the Airbus chief salesman, and "Waldherr" to Walther Leisler Kiep, the former treasurer of the Christian Democratic Union (CDU). Investigators believed that the notation "HO2" meant Holger Pfahls would get $2 million. They figured "LKI" meant Kiep would get $1 million DM. None of the evidence was conclusive, but they were important leads.

John Goetz and I chuckled. The codes seemed juvenile and easy to crack. But if we were giddy, it was probably because this was all a major breakthrough on a story that had for almost two years produced no tangible results. For the first time since Giorgio Pelossi had handed over the IAL documents, we were getting significant new information. And it didn't matter to us for a minute that someone else was breaking the story.

Goetz got to work.

A few days later he called me back again; he had obtained some of the police documents himself. He went looking through them for references to Canada and Airbus and came up with dozens more revelations.

The account Schreiber had allegedly set up for Max Strauss— "Maxwell"—had actually been set up in Canadian dollars. We wondered why. Then he read me portions from Schreiber's Daytimers. We didn't have the complete set, only a few pages, but there were intriguing details. One note said, "Brian in Germany." Did he mean Brian Mulroney? Another notation seemed to indicate Mulroney met Schreiber at the end of May in 1991, then perhaps again on December 4, 1991, in Ottawa. Another note said, "Tel Frank AB cancel." Telephone Frank Moores about an Airbus cancellation? Is that what he meant? And, if so, what on earth did *that* mean?

There was also a reference to a Marc Lalonde, along with the address 5440 Legare St; to "Stuart" and "Stewardess;" and one to "Fred" with a phone number that we knew to belong to Fred Doucet.

In the next few days I wrote letters to Leyendecker, and two of his colleagues at *Sueddeutsche Zeitung*, Conny Neumann and Michael Stiller. All three were actively pursuing the Schreiber story, and all three were keen to help. Michael Stiller called me one day with even more inside information. He said Schreiber had personally told him that all the "necessary payments" that he made on the Airbus sale went back to Canada. I was so grateful for this information that I sent Stiller and Neumann some of the documents we had received from Pelossi, as well as notes I made of my interview with Robert Hladun.

The document sharing was paying off. Goetz called me a few days later to tell me he had obtained a police witness statement from Hans Reiter, Karlheinz Schreiber's banker in Landsberg, Germany. I never understood exactly how Goetz received the document, whether he got it himself or, as part of a "trade" with another journalist, but it didn't matter. He had something to tell me.

"Schreiber's banker mentioned Mulroney."

Goetz explained. In his deposition Reiter told the German police that Schreiber had negotiated "numerous" business deals "of the most varied sort."

Reiter explained that in the early 1980s Schreiber had substantial debts with the bank in Landsberg. He described the situation as "difficult." However, the banker insisted, "Mr. Karlheinz Schreiber never lied to me in this regard." And to make the point that Schreiber was a man of his word, Reiter told a story about how he first heard of Brian Mulroney. "In 1982, I took on the task of arranging credit for Schreiber with a considerable amount of skepticism. My original skeptical attitude changed in the course of the year," he said, because "Mr. Karlheinz Schreiber's declarations always came through. . . . I would like to cite an occurrence in this context that still remains in my memory today. Mr. Karlheinz Schreiber referred to a Mr. Mulroney, who was unknown to me at the time, and told me, my friend Mulroney will be Prime Minister of Canada next year. This prediction actually came to pass."

I wrote a detailed note to the bosses, explaining the incredible new advances on the story—the Daytimer entries, the code names, the Reiter examination that mentioned Mulroney and even references to Airbus airplanes.

We decided, however, not to report the story.

Mulroney had just sued the federal government for $50 million and no one wanted a similar lawsuit on their hands, especially a media organization already being sued by Schreiber and Moores (even if the lawsuits were dormant). If we reported the contents of the Reiter affidavit in that climate we could see nothing but trouble coming our way. We would inevitably be raising questions about whether Mulroney had testified honestly at his examination for discovery, or worse, some might infer that Reiter was essentially saying that Schreiber got the Airbus deal because of his friendship with Mulroney. We knew that many of our colleagues in the media had already accused *the fifth estate* of trying to "get" Mulroney. This could all simply add fuel to their fire. And so, as much as we all would have liked to broadcast the information, we decided to wait. Maybe something even better would come up as well. But for now, I would have to get back to my others stories, ones that would actually get broadcast and not get us sued.

Then in November 1997 the *Toronto Sun*'s Bob Fife published a feature interview with Mulroney in which the former prime minister threatened to sue the federal government all over again.

There were, in fact, a series of articles by Fife about Mulroney.

The first was published Sunday, November 16, 1997: "Airbus called a setup" and "Grits needed scapegoat: Mulroney." Fife explained he had obtained an "exclusive" interview with Mulroney, who "attacked" Chrétien and other cabinet ministers, as well as the RCMP commissioner, Philip Murray. Mulroney claimed that Chrétien knew about the investigation before it was published in the *Financial Post*. Fife reminded his readers how hard Mulroney had worked to clear his name. "Like a grizzly bear poked with a stick, Mulroney roared and fought with a vengeance allegations that turned out to be fictitious."

I found the whole thing more and more mind-boggling. Mulroney had already won both the legal and the public debate; most Canadians were glad he got the money. The story had all but died. Why was he so angry now?

The article quoted Mulroney at length, furious over his conviction that the Liberals were out to get him. "Mulroney says he just wants to be left alone to pursue his business interests and raise his family," wrote Fife, which might seem a bit disingenuous in that Mulroney had just provided a lengthy interview to the *Toronto Sun* he knew would be splashed prominently across the front page of the newspaper. But perhaps Mulroney's last quote best explained his reasons for going public: "When they tried to besmirch my father's name and damage my children, that was the day they went too far. And anybody that tries it again—anybody—is going to encounter the same kind of treatment."

Was it a warning? *Anybody that tries it again.* It sure sounded like a threat to me.

But more surprises were to come. The next day, November 17, Fife quoted Mulroney demanding a Royal Commission into a "possible cover up" of the Airbus "fiasco." He demanded a public inquiry, and complained no one had taken responsibility. "The only way this can be dealt with is a royal commission of inquiry into this entire matter . . . You can give it a limited mandate to examine the conduct of the ministers and the key personnel and my own . . . so that the Canadian people will know all of the facts," Mulroney insisted.

Then came the revelation that Mulroney might sue the government again.

Wrote Fife, "Mulroney warned he may file another lawsuit against the government if it doesn't withdraw a September 29, 1995, letter it sent to Swiss authorities that accused him of accepting $5 million in kickbacks on the sale of Airbus jets to Air Canada."

Fife quoted Mulroney: "My lawyers have written to the commissioner of the RCMP and the appropriate ministers. We want that letter withdrawn . . . Now if we don't get that withdrawn, we will take appropriate action in the near future."

Back in January 1997, Mulroney had said publicly that the Mounties could investigate "until the cows come home." The settlement agreement specifically allowed the Mounties to continue their investigation. So why the sudden change of course in November 1997? I asked myself again.

The Liberal government declined to withdraw the letter, pointing out that Mulroney had already agreed to let the investigation continue. In any event, the RCMP weren't about to receive Schreiber's banking documents any time soon. They were still waiting to see how the Supreme Court of Canada would rule on whether or not their request for Schreiber's accounts had violated his constitutional rights as a Canadian citizen.

That Christmas I got another card in the mail from Luc Lavoie. "Harvey, all the best in 1998, your pal, Luc." I thumbtacked it on my bulletin board, right next to the card he gave me in Christmas of 1996.

January 1998 was the one-year anniversary of the Mulroney settlement and, for some reason, the commissioner of the RCMP issued a press release saying that if the suspects in the Airbus investigation were not charged, they would be publicly cleared. It was an unusual release, since police rarely publicly clear anyone who has not actually been charged with anything. Besides, it seemed to me that the only way Mulroney, or anyone else, could be cleared would be for the Mounties to find out where all the money went. If Mulroney did not get any of Schreiber's money, then it would make sense to clear him. But that's not what the press release said. The press release said that the suspects would be publicly cleared if they were not charged. I wasn't even sure how you could do that.

At the same time, two columnists decided to weigh in again as well, both with vastly different approaches to the Mulroney story. *Globe and Mail* editor-in-chief William Thorsell complained about the Letter of Request yet again: "The letter that should have never been sent lives on," he wrote, insisting, as he had before, that the Mounties should never have sent the letter to the Swiss requesting the accounts. Southam's Andrew Coyne, however, provided a perspective that I had never heard in the mainstream media.

"One year later, it is still hard to see what all the fuss was about," he wrote. "Contrary to innumerable press accounts, it has never been established, nor has the government ever conceded, that it had no evidence to support the allegations against Mulroney—only that it did not have enough evidence. This is hardly earth shattering. If there were enough evidence to convict, presumably the police would have no need to make inquiries. The presumption of innocence, we should remind ourselves, is an obligation upon the courts—not the police. To be sure, the letter is a flimsy business, offering little more than half-remembered versions of television documentaries in support of its claims. Had Mulroney been convicted on this evidence, had he even been charged, the affair would be worth all the outrage it has excited. But as things stand, we are left with nothing but a bit of private correspondence between two countries' legal authorities, such as one imagines are exchanged every day in the course of their duties. Had it never been leaked, there would have been no libel."

Coyne then took issue with the Canadian court rulings that had ruled Schreiber's rights had been violated when the RCMP tried to access his Swiss accounts without a warrant. "One might simply say that if you want the protection of Canadian law, it is usually safest to remain on Canadian soil, where it applies. No one, after all, is forced to open a Swiss bank account."

We decided we would meet William Kaplan, who was writing what we expected would be a sympathetic book about Mulroney. So one day in February, David Studer, Susan Teskey, David Kaufman and I met him in one of the CBC boardrooms.

The meeting was a disaster from beginning to end. I pulled out my tape recorder, as I always did. Kaplan strenuously objected. "I tape all my interviews," I said.

"But you're not doing the interview."

Kaplan confronted me with a question that I wasn't at all prepared for. "Did you get a phone call from someone named Emil in Zurich?"

Emil in Zurich? I had always wondered about the mysterious Zurich banker named Emil who said he had copies of Mulroney's secret accounts to give me.

"How do you know?"

Kaplan told me that Schreiber had told him the entire story. Schreiber was the one who had called me at the hotel in Zurich, putting on a fake accent, pretending to be a Swiss banker who would release Mulroney's bank account information as long as I paid him a bribe. Schreiber told Kaplan that we had made arrangements to meet at a location in Zurich that he knew to be just outside a brothel. Schreiber—Emil—had told me he would be wearing one of those cliché green Swiss hats with the feather on the side. That's because Schreiber had arranged for a CTV reporter and his camera crew to film the meeting from a hidden location. The plan was that I would show up, the cameras would catch me making the hand-off, and I would promptly be on the national news paying a bribe to Schreiber. Then, of course, I would have been fired. At that moment I was so thankful that I had thought Emil was a practical joke. As a result, I never even attempted to show up at the meeting. Even if I'd had no money in my hands, it would have looked bad, me staring at CTV cameras in the dark, trying to explain what I was doing.

I told Kaplan the entire story was true except for the part about me showing up for the payoff. Wouldn't there be videotapes anyway if I had? Kaplan had to agree. He moved on.[1]

Kaplan believed we had been unfair to Mulroney. He alleged we had overstated the evidence against Mulroney. We insisted we had been very careful and reminded him to go back and look at the transcripts. I gave my speech about wanting to know where the money ended up.

I admit I sounded sanctimonious. I believed Kaplan had an axe to grind, an agenda. If I hadn't been so defensive I might have found a way of better explaining my perspective. Kaplan and I concluded the interview each more distrustful of the other than when we began. At least that was over, I thought. I hoped that I never had the experience of meeting him again. A couple of days later someone had leaked the details of our meeting to the satirical magazine *Frank*, which portrayed Kaplan as a Mulroney sycophant. No doubt this made Kaplan even more suspicious of *the fifth estate* and me. Upon reflection, it is hard to objectively say which of us may have behaved more badly. It was that close.

1 Later that day I called Alister Bell to apologize. For more than three years I wrongly believed that he had played a practical joke, despite his protestations to the contrary.

CHAPTER NINETEEN
MR. CLEAN

I t was beginning to look like the never-ending story.

In early 1998 I observed that three and a half years had gone by since Pelossi first contacted the media about the Airbus story. Yet neither the authorities in Germany nor Canada had obtained the bank documents from Switzerland. There were the inevitable complaints about how long the RCMP was taking, but that criticism was hardly justified. If they didn't even have the bank documents, how could the police get to the core answers? As Sergeant Fraser Fiegenwald explained before he left the RCMP, obtaining the bank documents should have been the beginning of the investigation, not the end. In the meantime, I learned the RCMP had assigned new officers to the investigation, since I would get the odd call from my contacts to tell me that the Mounties had visited them. That's how I learned that two inspectors named Graham Muir and John Dickson were working together on the file. Another inspector, Peter German, later joined them, as well as Ray Brettschneider, who also had the advantage of speaking German. I would continue to hear through the grapevine that they had interviewed Air Canada executives, cabinet ministers, political aides and Airbus salesmen.

I never gave up believing that we at *the fifth estate* were on the verge of doing another program on Airbus. By 1998 it seemed as if CBC executives were becoming less concerned about the $50 million in lawsuits that were still, technically, hanging over our heads. Schreiber was still refusing to show up for his examination for discovery on his affidavit of documents in his lawsuit against us. Frank Moores had done nothing to advance his lawsuit after filing the initial papers back in 1995. David Studer told me that if I presented an important new development we would definitely consider doing another story. Still, we all knew that the bar was raised. We would have to show that we really did have important new information.

On March 20, 1998, the Supreme Court of Canada finally heard the case of *Schreiber vs. the Attorney General of Canada*. Attorney Robert Hladun argued that the RCMP should not have been allowed to obtain his client's overseas bank accounts without a proper judicial warrant. Federal government lawyers argued that the Canadian Charter was irrelevant to whatever decision the Swiss made to release or not release the accounts. The judges reserved their decision.

Also at the end of March 1998, I was given permission to work exclusively on Airbus research for a while, along with associate producer Sheila Pin. We hoped that we could produce a story for the fall, about the "spin" campaign, how the Letter of Request was leaked, and the new developments in Europe.

In Germany there seemed to be a new revelation every week. Goetz had learned about a journalist who had suffered repercussions after writing an investigative report about Schreiber in the 1970s, linking him to an oil deal in which bribes were allegedly paid to Franz Josef Strauss. But the journalist couldn't prove certain details, was ridiculed as a result, and had to leave the profession.

"He is now a massage therapist," Goetz said.

"That sounds more relaxing anyway," I replied.

Goetz had also discovered that the German authorities had sent a Letter of Request to Canada. The Germans were asking the RCMP to conduct searches in Canada on their behalf. Goetz had also been on the phone to Jörg Hillinger, the chief prosecutor on the Schreiber file. Hillinger also reminded Goetz that Germany had a statute of limitations in place for crimes like bribery and tax evasion. They did not have a lot of time left for their investigation into Schreiber. Even now, they could not prosecute him for any crimes alleged to have been committed before 1988. As the months passed in their investigation, they would have to abandon any leads that were more than ten years old.

Goetz said that Hillinger was already upset that the media had broadcast details of his investigation. "Hillinger is very angry with journalists," Goetz told me. He explained that any unauthorized leak of information to the media could prompt a judge to shut down the entire investigation. "Schreiber may have an argument the whole investigation is disqualified. That would be like taking three years off Hillinger's life and throwing it in the garbage can."

But the leaks kept coming from someone inside Hillinger's office.

In May 1998, journalists at *Sueddeutsche Zeitung* were given a copy of a letter Schreiber had written to a tax official in 1996, only a few months after the Airbus scandal first broke. The letter was not so much a legal argument about why he was innocent as it was a patriotic plea. It was addressed to the head of the revenue agency in Augsburg, Anton Gumpendobler, and began with complaints about the leaks coming from his department. "Why is information constantly passed on to the press? For supplementary income?" Schreiber suggested. (A letter Schreiber wrote to the authorities complaining about leaks to the press was itself being leaked to the press.) "I would also like to remind you that in the mid-80s [Airbus] was on the brink of bankruptcy," Schreiber wrote in his ten-page letter. He hinted that any further prosecution of him and others could damage German companies. "Would you and your colleagues want to participate in a shop floor meeting at Thyssen, Airbus Industrie or MBB?" He ended his letter: "The English say: 'Right or wrong—my country'! I love this country and in particular, the Free State of Bavaria."

Schreiber was arguing that he had done everything politicians had asked him to do—help sell German products abroad. He believed that the very governments that had used him as a middleman were now coming after him. What Schreiber did not seem to appreciate was that Germany had begun to clamp down on the old and cozy relationships between politicians and businessmen. Germany would soon criminalize bribes to foreigners, following the lead set by the United States a long time ago. Schreiber was, in a way, a victim of Germany's new approach to politics and business.

On May 28, 1998, the Supreme Court of Canada ruled that the RCMP had not violated Schreiber's Canadian Charter rights. This decision meant that the Mounties' Letter of Request to Switzerland was not illegal after all. The decision was unanimous. The 6–0 ruling blew out of the water the two lower-court rulings in Schreiber's favour. The Supreme Court ruled that Schreiber should not have expected Canadian Charter rights protection for business dealings in another country. If he chose to do business in Switzerland then he should be governed by the laws of Switzerland. The new justice minister, Anne McLellan, was satisfied, telling reporters, "We're just very pleased today that the Supreme Court has upheld the Letter of Request procedure that we used."

And Schreiber seemed to be losing in Switzerland too.

In the summer of 1998, a Swiss court ruled in favour of Germany, explaining that there was ample evidence that Schreiber had engaged in offences that would allow the Swiss to co-operate. An appeal court in one Swiss province ruled that Schreiber's coded accounts "can with little imagination and through more than coincidence be tied to the fellow accused [Winfried] Haastert, [Juergen] Massmann, [Holger] Pfahls, [Walther Leisler] Kiep and [Max] Strauss." For the first time in years it looked as if finally the bank documents might be released. For the moment, however, Schreiber had launched a last-minute appeal in Switzerland and so, for the time being, the Swiss were releasing nothing. Still, the tide was turning. The bank documents would be released, of that we were almost certain.

We were even getting breakthroughs in Canada. I had waited three years for them, but in 1998, I finally received the requested Access to Information documents from the Privy Council Office—all relating to Brian Mulroney, Karlheinz Schreiber and Bear Head Industries. There were more than a hundred pages.

The documents left no doubt that Karlheinz Schreiber had great access to Brian Mulroney, his cabinet and a host of civil servants. They all amounted to a monumental leap forward in our understanding of the influence that Schreiber exerted while in Ottawa.

The first document was dated February 14, 1986.

A heavily redacted memorandum to Mulroney from the clerk of the Privy Council, Paul Tellier, was the first evidence that the Bear Head project was on the horizon. Tellier was preparing Mulroney for possible questions in the House of Commons after the *Globe and Mail's* Jeffrey Simpson had reported that Mulroney's cabinet was split over the proposed Thyssen plant in Cape Breton, Nova Scotia. "The Thyssen proposal pits Cape Breton's need for jobs against some of Canada's general policies barring arms exports," wrote Simpson, noting that West German laws prohibit the export of military equipment to "regions of tension," including Israel, and Arab states bordering on Israel.

The next document was a letter of protest to Mulroney from Sidney Spivak, national chairman of the Canada-Israel Committee, who told the prime minister he was "profoundly" disturbed by the Thyssen proposal.

There was another memorandum from 1988 to the prime minister from Tellier, this one saying that the Thyssen proposal was still active and that Senator Lowell Murray, responsible for the Atlantic Canada Opportunities Agency (ACAO), had met with officials from Thyssen to discuss the issue. There was a letter to Mulroney from the two Thyssen executives, Juergen Massmann and Winfried Haastert. They wrote Mulroney on February 1, 1988, saying that "the location near Port Hawkesbury, Nova Scotia will allow us to supply the Canadian market, enter into competition in the American market, and enable the export overseas of a diversity of products, subject of course to the receipt of appropriate Canadian export permits."

There was also a "confidential" memorandum written by a civil servant, Ernest Hebert, on June 15, 1988, to Derek Burney, Mulroney's chief of staff, relating to German chancellor Helmut Kohl's upcoming visit to Canada. "Attached for the Prime Minister's attention are 1) a brief on the Thyssen issue." [There was a "part 2" but it had been blacked out.] Still, this briefing confirmed the Thyssen issue was discussed at the highest political levels in both countries. "It is necessary to arrive at a decision on this matter soon so that Thyssen may plan its US strategy," wrote Hebert.

Then came a document titled "Understanding in Principle." It was dated September 27, 1988, and appeared to be an agreement between Schreiber and the Mulroney government to build a light armoured vehicle factory in Cape Breton. Yet one clause seemed to negate the agreement itself. "The understandings set out in this Understanding in Principle do not create any enforceable, legal or equitable rights, nor obligations . . ."

The document was signed by three Mulroney cabinet ministers, the Honourable Gerald Merrithew, minister responsible for the Atlantic Canada Opportunities Agency, Robert de Cotret, minister for regional industrial expansion, and Perrin Beatty,[1] minister of national defence, and Karlheinz Schreiber, for Bear Head Industries.

I knew from what Giorgio Pelossi had told us in 1994 that a letter of comfort had triggered payments of $2 million to the Liechtenstein shell company IAL, to be used as "success fees." Now we had the actual document. But it seemed so inconsequential that I wondered why it had triggered anything, let alone a sizable "success fee."

The rest of the file was filled with documentation and correspondence showing that Schreiber had an endless series of meetings over the years with politicians and bureaucrats. Fred Doucet came on as a lobbyist for Schreiber, Elmer MacKay was helping write letters and putting in a good word, as were others, but in the end the proposed light armoured tank facility never got the go-ahead. The question, it seemed, was, why had all those meetings taken place over so many years with the project never once moving forward? (In fact, the correspondence continued into the new Liberal regime, where Marc Lalonde continued the lobby effort.)

In May 1998, I decided to try Stuart Iddles again.

Perhaps now the former Airbus vice-president would be willing to talk. I learned he had bought a villa in Puerto Vallarta, Mexico. I made some calls, only to end up talking to Brock Squire, his former real estate agent, with whom Iddles had had a falling-out. Brock Squire told me that Iddles had bought a property called Casa Las Estacas, one of the "trophy properties" in the resort town. He had paid $1,750,000 for it, "all in cash." Squire told me the funds were transferred from a Swiss account with Lloyds Bank. "I understand from him that his arrangement with Airbus was rather

---

1 At the time I read Perrin Beatty's signature on the document, he was still president of the CBC.

laissez-faire," Squire told me. "Their salaries were quite modest relative to the responsibilities they had. . . . Management looked the other way if they [Airbus salesmen] were doing whatever kind of deal on the side with whatever country they happened to be dealing with. I think that's where they actually made their serious money from what I could gather." Iddles once confided in Squire that he had a problem moving cash around Europe. "He told me at one point he was stopped in an airport in Switzerland, in Geneva, I believe, and he had several million dollars on him in a briefcase." For the first time in a while I felt as if I wasn't just poking around the edges of the story. It seemed possible that the money that Iddles used to pay for his home in Puerto Vallarta might have come from the Air Canada deal. Certainly the timing seemed right, as the Air Canada money started to flow in just before Iddles bought the property. If so, I was getting to the heart of my question: Where did the money go? Maybe part of the answer sat on that cliff in Puerto Vallarta.

That summer I travelled to Montreal to meet Keith Miller . . . again.

The former airline economist, who had been so helpful to me in the early days of my research in 1994, had a few more stories.

First, Miller told me that the old Tory lobbyist, John Lundrigan, had once confided to him that Moores was going to earn $30,000 per Airbus plane delivered to Air Canada. Multiplied by thirty-four planes, it meant Moores would have received $1.2 million.

Second, Miller had heard that Moores had made a voluntary disclosure to Revenue Canada in 1995 fessing up to the taxman on all his undeclared income in those Swiss accounts. By using the Voluntary Disclosure Program, Canadian taxpayers can admit they filed false tax returns without incurring any penalty, and, more important, avoid possible criminal charges. Miller had heard Moores declared $1.4 million. Given that Moores was still, technically, suing the CBC and me over allegations he received Airbus money, I had to marvel at his chutzpah. If the story was true, it meant Moores was publicly denying he got Airbus money, yet privately confessing to the Canada Revenue Agency that he had. And third, Miller told me that he had recently played golf with Moores in Florida. He got a call out of the blue from Moores, who suggested they play at the Loxahatchee in Jupiter. Miller realized that Moores had something on his mind. Moores wanted to know what Miller remembered about those meetings back in 1986, when Moores was trying to convince Miller to join the Airbus team.

"Did I mention money at the meeting in Toronto?" Miller said Moores asked. "Yes," Miller responded, without really understanding why Moores needed to know. As the golf game continued, it was clear Moores had a few things he wanted to get off his chest.

"Schreiber stiffed me on the Airbus deal," Moores told Miller.

Miller asked Moores why he didn't sue Schreiber. Moores said that he couldn't—there were no signed contracts. Then, just after the game had finished, Moores looked Miller straight in the eye and said, "Brian Mulroney did not get any of the Airbus money. At least not from me."

Moores never again asked Miller to play golf.

John Goetz also called me that summer to tell us that Hans Reiter—Schreiber's hometown banker—had agreed to talk. We had already obtained Reiter's examination to police, in which he mentioned Brian Mulroney's name, so *the fifth estate* bosses immediately agreed to pay for Goetz's airline ticket from Berlin to Munich. Since we knew Reiter was going out on a limb by talking with Goetz, we made sure not to mention the banker's name while approving the travel.

As soon as Goetz arrived at Reiter's office, he could tell something was wrong. Reiter was there, but so were several lawyers from the Landsberg bank. They told Goetz to hand over his copy of Reiter's affidavit and demanded to know where it came from. Then they threatened to file a formal complaint against Goetz for having possession of a confidential document. Goetz had to get out of there. He bolted for the door.

The Airbus file had begun to take over my life again. Only the year before, I had been relieved it was fading away, but now, with the revelations out of Germany and the Supreme Court ruling that looked to pave the way for the release of Schreiber's bank documents, I began to fixate once more on finding out where the money went. I badly wanted *the fifth estate* to do another story. I made a couple of pitches to my bosses. I thought we could report all the new information that we had learned from our own Airbus investigation: the Reiter affidavit in which Mulroney's name had surfaced; the story about Stuart Iddles and his alleged Airbus cash; the Frank Moores tax problem; the quote by Schreiber's lawyer, Stefan von Moers, that his client had paid greasemoney on Airbus to Canadians; the fact that Schreiber was now a fugitive from German justice; the new Daytimer entries which showed the middleman had used code names to indicate payments to anonymous recipients.

The answer came back: Not now, but keep at it.

It was a sensible decision, but I was frustrated. The story had advanced so much from our last documentary in 1995. Why didn't we report what we knew? Studer probably understood better than I that the climate was not right. Not yet. We would have been accused, again, of carrying out a vendetta, of not knowing when to stop, of being "out of control."

Some continued to accuse me of being obsessed with the Airbus file, but at the time I didn't see it. I thought we had enough new information that needed reporting and now I just needed to find out even more to convince the bosses. I came to believe that I was almost there, that one day I would get that piece of information that would allow them to change their minds. Sometimes this preoccupation manifested itself in benign ways, sometimes not. One day I looked up at the clock and realized it was after six. I figured I'd better get home. I took the subway, as usual, and then opened the door to the house.

"Sorry I'm a little late," I said cheerfully.

Alisa was in tears. She was wearing her white choir shirt and black pants. She had makeup on. What for? Then I remembered. She had practised all year with the East York Choir to sing at a benefit concert. The event was taking place that night. She couldn't leave until I came home because of the boys. Shit.

"Couldn't you remember this at least?"

She left the house then sped away in the car, hoping she could get to the concert in time for the intermission.

If the climate in the summer of 1998 was not quite right for another *fifth estate* Airbus story, it was just perfect for the publication of William Kaplan's book *Presumed Guilty: Brian Mulroney, the Airbus affair, and the Government of Canada*.

Saturday Night magazine published an excerpt of Kaplan's book on its front page—the same magazine that, under editor-in-chief Ken Whyte, had published Susan Gittin's anti–*fifth estate* story just the year before. On the front of the magazine was a caricature of Brian Mulroney sporting a white muscle shirt, a pierced left ear, large biceps and a big wide grin. Then, in big yellow letters it read: "MR. CLEAN."

There was a subhead: "What do you do when you're called the most reviled Prime Minister ever and then you're accused of being a crook? You fight back."

Kaplan quoted people like former transport minister John Crosbie, who criticized Trish Wood as host of *the fifth estate*'s Airbus stories. "Nothing I said could shake her faith in the proposition that the former prime minister was a master criminal who had lined his pockets while in office," Crosbie alleged. (Kaplan seemed not to notice that he was allowing Crosbie himself to make an unsubstantiated allegation against someone's personal integrity—exactly the kind of thing he complained that others had done to Mulroney.) Kaplan also quoted former deputy transport minister Ramsey Withers (who had left government to join GCI immediately after the Air Canada board had voted to approve the Airbus purchase). "I told Wood that what she was alleging had not happened. I told her that she was heading into trouble." Crosbie and Withers were good people to talk to. One was a former transport minister when Air Canada was looking at purchasing Airbus aircraft. The other was a former deputy transport minister. It seemed to me Kaplan had asked the wrong questions.

Kaplan himself made an error when discussing our original *fifth estate* program, critiquing us for allegedly implying that Mulroney took money. "Pictures of a former Canadian politician who once lived on Devon Street in Westmount figured prominently in the broadcast. It did not take much detective work to conclude that the identity of the person Pelossi and *the fifth estate* were referring to was Brian Mulroney." Kaplan was dead wrong about that. Our broadcast never mentioned anything about Mulroney living on Devon Street. (We had actually made a decision not to report that his old street bore the same name as the code name on the account in Zurich.) Kaplan repeated the suggestion that Stevie Cameron was an RCMP informant, which she had vehemently denied; he suggested that I and my colleague Jock Ferguson might also have given documents to the police.

In the conclusion to his book, Kaplan theorized that Schreiber had leaked the Letter of Request to Phil Mathias in order to direct attention on to Brian Mulroney and away from himself. I didn't believe the theory, but I did wonder if Mulroney might have presented the theory to Kaplan as a way of distancing *himself* from Schreiber.

Right after the *Saturday Night* magazine article appeared, both Phil Mathias and Bob Fife had their own Airbus stories in their respective newspapers.

On October 25, 1998, Bob Fife had an exclusive interview with Frank Moores under the headline "A case of spite or justice? Former Newfoundland Premier Frank Moores is feeling like a scapegoat." Wrote Fife: "Frank Moores always lived life to its fullest and played for keeps. But as it turns out, his most unforgivable sin was knowing Brian Mulroney . . . Moores, too, has been bitten by the fangs of a dubious RCMP investigation that many now suspect was fuelled by Liberal partisanship and anti-Mulroney rancor." Moores, said Fife, readily admits his "wild days" as a party animal ended in 1979 when he met his wife, Beth. "There isn't a lot of laughter in his life these days," Fife added. "Moores's care-free spirit has been crushed by the heavy hand of a police force that appears determined to reek [*sic*] revenge for Mulroney's victory in the Liberal government's Airbus fiasco."

The RCMP investigation in itself was devastating to the former Newfoundland premier, Fife reported. "In an exclusive interview from his home near the Rideau Lakes, Moores argues the continuing criminal probe against him is vindictive, petty, financially crippling and without foundation. He maintains the Mounties are on a fishing expedition—if not a witchhunt—to find incriminating evidence against him to justify the botched Airbus affair."

Then Fife criticized *the fifth estate*.

"The probe began in 1995 on the basis of a now discredited CBC report by *the fifth estate*," he said.

A now discredited CBC *report by the* fifth estate.

Our *fifth estate* report had not been discredited. Our work was solid, meticulous and fair. And even if he disagreed, why did he not point out specifically what he thought we had said that was wrong, rather than rely on generalizations?

According to Fife the B.M. account referred to Beth Moores. Odd that Frank Moores had long ago insisted the account had not been opened for his wife. "The RCMP's case largely fell apart when it turned out the 'B.M.' account belonged to Beth Moores," he stated. "Moores certainly didn't behave like a man involved in a bribery scam," he continued, "he did not resist Mountie demands to obtain his Swiss accounts, and contacted Revenue Canada to settle any outstanding taxes." Fife stated that Moores's other personal Swiss account supposedly "contained under $1 million."

"The amounts are not such that you'd be using them to bribe somebody," Moores told Fife.

Holy shit, I thought. The suggestion that individuals could not be bribed for sums less than $1 million came as a surprise.

Moores complained to Fife that his offshore accounts were still frozen, calling it a "vindictive delaying tactic." He also stuck to his story that he did not receive any money related to Airbus or Air Canada, but admitted for the first time that Schreiber paid him commissions for lobbying for a German firm "connected" to Airbus, though it was unclear exactly what that really meant. The point was not pursued.

On October 27, 1998, two days after Fife's defence of Moores, Phil Mathias wrote an article in the first edition of Conrad Black's new *National Post* about author Stevie Cameron and her new book, *Blue Trust: The Author, The Lawyer, His Wife and Her Money.* (The *Financial Post* had been blended into the *National Post*, which meant Phil Mathias was now writing for Conrad Black's paper. Black had named Ken Whyte the new editor-in-chief of the *National Post*, transferred from *Saturday Night* magazine.) *Blue Trust* detailed the life of a Montreal tax lawyer named Bruce Verchere, whose clients allegedly included Brian Mulroney. Cameron wrote about an affair that Verchere had had with the daughter of novelist Arthur Hailey, as well as Verchere's subsequent suicide at his Montreal home.

Mathias told his readers that Mulroney was considering legal action over the book. "Brian Mulroney, the former prime minister, is considering a lawsuit for libel against author Stevie Cameron over the way she has weaved his name into her new book *Blue Trust*," wrote Mathias. He quoted his source, Luc Lavoie. "We're reviewing the book very carefully because Mr. Mulroney will not tolerate any more smears." Mathias explained that the book described how Verchere was "familiar with offshore banks and clever about setting up complicated corporate mazes to shield ownership [of money] . . . from prying eyes." Verchere was also on the board of the Swiss Bank Corporation. Mathias noted that was where "the now disproven Mulroney account was allegedly opened."

The following month, on November 21, Phil Mathias had another story about Stevie Cameron in the *National Post*, this one a feature-length profile with the headline "Stevie Cameron just can't let go of Brian Mulroney." It seemed to me that Phil Mathias couldn't let go of Stevie Cameron. The article was full of references to her "obsession" with the former prime minister. Mathias quoted *La Presse* columnist Lysiane Gagnon who said Cameron "has tried for years to link Mr. Mulroney to criminal wrongdoing with a ruthlessness that has more to do with outright obsession than investigative journalism." The historian Michael Bliss was also quoted. "There's no doubt at all that the prime minister was personally honest," Bliss told Mathias.

As for the Airbus affair, Mathias stated there was "no evidence" Frank Moores received Airbus commissions and insisted that when it came to Airbus "there's no tainted money to trace."

I took a different approach. There *was* an Airbus money trail that needed tracing. I was certain of it. And soon there would be a development that made me think we were getting close.

PART III
RUPTURE

CHAPTER TWENTY
CLOSING IN

In January 1999, five years after first asking the Swiss, the Germans finally got Schreiber's bank documents. The Airbus story would never be the same again.

Schreiber's ability to battle the Canadians and the Germans in the courts for as long as he did *was* remarkable. He had hired a team of high-priced lawyers in three countries who fought battles on several different fronts; a Charter of Rights argument here, an abuse-of-process charge there, behind-the-scenes political overtures, and appeals to higher courts whenever possible. Schreiber knew as well as everyone that if Switzerland refused to turn over the bank documents to Germany and Canada, he was virtually safe from prosecution, and so was everyone else. It was that simple. But early in the new year of 1999 he lost his final appeal in Switzerland. German authorities, at least, would soon be getting their hands on his bank documents. (If there was a ray of hope left for Schreiber, it was that the RCMP still had not received their copies. The Swiss courts had not yet ruled on their application.)

In Germany, the media were back on the story.

"Switzerland releases Schreiber's bank records," read the headline in *Sueddeutsche Zeitung*. Hans Leyendecker had the story again, with a subhead that read: "The Department of Justice sees 'Substantial Suspicion' against business agent, who apparently also bribed politicians." The Swiss judgment indicated that Schreiber's own lawyers did him no favours. "The complicated statements by Schreiber's lawyers" served to "further conceal the facts and to increase existing suspicious factors."

Conny Neumann followed the Leyendecker story with another break-through report: that the German investigation had reached into Canada. "The state attorney's office has widened its investigation all the way to Canada in the so-called Airbus Affair," she wrote. German authorities, wrote Neumann, were asking their Canadian counterparts to conduct a search of Schreiber's residences in Ottawa and Calgary, as well as some banks and other offices. The request for the Canadians' help had got stuck somewhere in Bonn, but now it looked as if it was proceeding. Neumann also reminded her readers about Schreiber's legal status in his home country. "Schreiber has evaded arrest in Germany by fleeing to Switzerland, and has always maintained he had nothing to do with IAL."

John Goetz and I were more than intrigued about the new angle in the Canadian investigation. We wanted to get our hands on all the documents—the materials the Canadians would hopefully provide to the Germans, the 1991 and 1994 Daytimers seized by the police, any more investigative interviews like the one we had obtained from Schreiber's German banker and, of course, the Swiss banking documents. But how?

There had to be a way. If the Swiss were now releasing the documents to the Germans then surely there would be many copies floating around Europe, from the Swiss police, to the German Justice Department, to the Augsburg prosecutors near Munich. From that moment on we made it our goal to get the documents.

Jörg Hillinger and his team of prosecutors must have been happy. Having worked tirelessly for years interviewing one witness after another, finally they had in their grasp the crucial information to discover where Schreiber's *schmiergelder* might have ended up.

In Canada, however, the wheels were turning more slowly. The RCMP still had not received copies of the bank accounts from Switzerland, and, international law being what it was, that had prevented the Germans from forwarding *their* copies directly to the RCMP. The Mounties would have to wait for the Swiss to rule on their case first. Despite all the damaging

stories breaking in Germany, it was as if an invisible wall across the Atlantic was blocking the documents from being published in Canada—at
least as far as newspapers like the *National Post* were concerned.

On February 22, 1999, just three days after *Sueddeutsche Zeitung* reported
that the German investigation had reached into Canada, the *National Post*
published another story critical of the RCMP. "Sources say the Mounties
have not progressed beyond their 1997 admission that there's no evidence
of wrongdoing by Brian Mulroney, the former prime minister. The investigation's cost is now estimated at several million dollars," wrote reporter
Phil Mathias. He neglected to explain that it was actually Schreiber who
had held up the investigation through a series of court challenges aimed
at keeping his bank documents out of their hands. Mathias quoted former transport minister John Crosbie who criticized the Mounties for their
"incompetence."

"I would say this investigation will be continuing through much of the
next millennium . . . ," Crosbie told Mathias. "They've [the RCMP] even
been around to interview some of my [former] staff. That's so that they
can say the thing is continuing. But they asked my staff nothing new—
just the same old stuff."

Mathias also called Schreiber in Switzerland, reminding him that the
RCMP investigation had actually begun ten years ago (Mathias was counting from the time the RCMP first looked into the allegations in 1988 and
1989 but came up empty). "Mr. Schreiber said: 'Isn't that funny? Ten years!
Jesus Christ!'" The allegation is a "crazy hoax." According to Mathias, former Mulroney cabinet minister Elmer MacKay complained that the RCMP
was tapping his phone for "ass-covering, face-saving" purposes.

On March 3, a freshman member of Parliament rose from his seat in the
House of Commons to demand that the government shut down the RCMP
investigation. Peter MacKay was not only the Conservative Party's justice
critic, he also happened to be Elmer MacKay's son. He also had his own personal connection to the story: owing to his father's good connections with
Karlheinz Schreiber, MacKay had worked for Thyssen Industrie in Germany.

"Mr. Speaker," blustered Peter MacKay, "the RCMP investigation into
the Airbus affair has cost Canadian taxpayers nearly $4 million and counting.
Despite the fact that investigators have absolutely no evidence to justify

chasing these false allegations, they have stepped up their efforts. This amounts to a vindictive and politically motivated pursuit of a former Prime Minister. In light of this ongoing embarrassment for this Liberal government, when will the solicitor general stop wasting taxpayers' money and call off his Liberal posse?"

Solicitor General Lawrence MacAulay rose to remind MacKay that it would be inappropriate for any government to tell the RCMP what to do. "As solicitor general I do not direct the activities of the RCMP."

"Mr. Speaker, he should tell that to a former solicitor general," MacKay responded, pointedly referring to Allan Rock as well as implying—incorrectly—that Rock had directed the RCMP investigation. "For years now Canadians have witnessed this farcical saga that resulted in a forced half-hearted apology to Mr. Mulroney, followed by RCMP investigators then continuing and expanding the investigation," MacKay said. "When will the government cut its losses, put an end to this ill-founded investigation?"

MacKay huffed and puffed but the Liberals refused to interfere. Five days later, he again rose in the House. "Brian Mulroney is innocent of all wrongdoing and yet the Liberal government will not cease and desist the RCMP investigation. The Liberal government has a vendetta against the former prime minister which stems from the Liberals' days in opposition. There are growing concerns that the current prime minister's legacy might pale by comparison. The Liberals' plot for revenge is continuing to cost the taxpayers significant dollars, $4 million and counting." In fact, had the Liberal government ordered the RCMP to shut down its investigation then *that* would have been the scandal. Peter MacKay would rise in the House of Commons again. In the meantime, he had some powerful allies in the media. Leading the charge was Conrad Black's *National Post*.

On April 1, just five weeks after MacKay's tirade in the House of Commons, reporter Philip Mathias weighed in again with an article critical of the RCMP: "Ottawa refuses to withdraw allegations against Mulroney." It was a reference to the RCMP's decision not to withdraw its Letter of Request to the Swiss requesting Schreiber's bank accounts. "The refusal [to withdraw the letter] comes despite the fact that the Canadian government announced publicly it had no evidence of any wrongdoing, and apologized to Mr. Mulroney, on Jan. 6, 1997."

Confusingly, Mathias then claimed to have obtained a letter from Carla Del Ponte, Switzerland's chief prosecutor, indicating that the Canadian government's apology related only to "the wording of the request for judicial assistance." Mathias seemed to be suggesting that the Canadian government had not properly informed the chief prosecutor in Switzerland of the terms of its settlement with Mulroney. Yet the statement was accurate. Of course the government apologized only for the wording. That was, in fact, the foundation of Mulroney's lawsuit—not that the letter had been sent but that the wording had libelled him. The RCMP was allowed to continue its investigation. So why would anyone care that the letter be withdrawn now? In his settlement with the government, Mulroney had never demanded such a thing. In fact, post-settlement he had even encouraged the RCMP to continue their investigation.

In his story of April 1, 1999, Mathias reported the familiar explanation that the infamous Devon account had been opened for Beth Moores, Frank's wife, and *not* Brian Mulroney. "When the Airbus controversy broke, Mr. Moores revealed that the Devon account was actually opened for his wife Beth Moores (B.M.)." This, despite the fact that it was the same Mathias who had dismissed that assertion back in 1995, when he wrote: "Moores said news stories that the account was opened for her benefit are not correct." Mathias quoted Schreiber saying that the reason the government refused to withdraw the letter was because of a "a simultaneous face-saving and ass-covering action to protect the politicians," a charge that sounded eerily similar to Elmer MacKay's quote five weeks earlier.

The next day the *National Post* ran an editorial, "Contempt of Court," stating that Brian Mulroney was not the only person who had suffered from the botched RCMP investigation: "Karlheinz Schreiber, the financier, was also tarred as a crook in the infamous letter. He has now launched two lawsuits, both winding their way through the Canadian courts. One asks that the letter of request be withdrawn and that the Swiss be informed of its falsehoods. The other seeks $35-million in damages for libel."

The *National Post*'s coverage was becoming more illogical by the minute. The lawsuits they referenced against the CBC were hardly winding their way through the courts, as Schreiber had refused to show up for his examination and it had actually sat dormant for nearly two years. Curiously, the paper neglected to mention anything about the outstanding arrest warrant in Germany for Schreiber on charges relating, in part, to his Airbus dealings in Canada.

The editorial surmised that the Justice Department would not withdraw the RCMP's Letter of Request to Switzerland because it "hopes that the investigation will come up with some evidence of some wrongdoing by someone (preferably a Canadian) that would enable the investigators to recover some face." Whether it was true or not that some Mounties were "hoping" to find wrongdoing, wasn't it their job to pursue allegations of wrongdoing? "At stake," concluded the *National Post* editorial, "here is nothing less than the rule of law; and its equal application to all—including present and former government officials."

The next day, April 3, 1999, the *National Post* published a third in a series questioning the continuing RCMP investigation. "Frank Moores," wrote Bob Fife (now working on the same paper as Mathias), "the former premier of Newfoundland, has accused the RCMP of dragging out its investigation of him in the so-called Airbus affair in order to take revenge for having to apologize to Brian Mulroney over its handling of the matter." The story repeated almost verbatim allegations Moores had made to Fife in his previous story: "The cost of this has been absolutely unbelievable. I don't mean just in dollars. The big thing is the boards you could sit on, advisory boards I would have liked to be involved in, but now no one will touch you with a barge pole." Again Fife reported that Moores insisted the B.M. account belonged to his wife, though Moores had specifically said earlier he did not open it for her.

At the same time as *National Post* reporters were coming to the defence of Moores, Mulroney and Schreiber, former *Toronto Star* reporter and Mulroney adviser Bill Fox published his book, *Spin Wars*. He included a chapter on the media's Airbus coverage, which was enormously critical of *the fifth estate*'s contribution—singling me out by name. Fox commended Bob Fife for his coverage. "While other journalists were racing around Europe, looking for breaks in the Airbus case, Fife was breaking pivotal stories 'just using the phone.' He says it was clear to him that Staff Sergeant Fraser Fiegenwald was working closely with . . . the fifth estate." Fox wrote that Fife believed there was a "hatred" of Mulroney that existed in the Parliamentary

Press Gallery and that it had influenced how media like the CBC had treated Mulroney. "We were persecuting this guy based on the fact that we didn't like him. That is really dangerous in a democracy," Fife told Fox.

According to Fox, Mulroney blamed me, in part, for all that had happened to him. Fox wrote that Mulroney had "identified three journalists as 'key' to the Airbus travails—nemesis Stevie Cameron, the fifth estate co-host Trish Wood, and the fifth estate producer Harvey Cashore." Mulroney was quoted saying he believed CBC employees (unnamed) had acted as "RCMP informants." Luc Lavoie was also quoted saying CBC and *the fifth estate*'s Airbus coverage was "scandalous": "Airbus, which had the potential to bury Mulroney, in the end afforded the former Tory leader his first real opportunity to start the process of refurbishing his reputation . . . Mulroney, Lavoie, and his legal team achieved a significant victory in this particular media-relations war. We will never see its like again."

On April 6, 1999, Phil Mathias called.

We hadn't spoken in months, but he wanted to make sure I had seen the recent stories in the *National Post*. I had, I assured him. Mathias also said he had heard that I might have information that he should include in a future story. (I remembered that I had complained about Mathias's reporting to a mutual acquaintance.)

"All you have to do is read *Sueddeutsche Zeitung*," I snapped.

I didn't stop there. I asked him why his stories were so one-sided. I questioned why he had been so eager to write that Giorgio Pelossi was in jail for six months (without being charged), but not so eager to write about the outstanding arrest warrant for Schreiber. Wasn't that a double standard in his reporting? Why not tell his readers that Schreiber was a fugitive from German justice?

Since the warrant dealt with tax evasion and not bribery, Mathias said, "it's not relevant to Mulroney." I told him that sounded like a rather convenient argument, designed to justify to himself why he had withheld important information from his readers. How did he know what exactly was relevant to Mulroney and what was not? Why not simply report events that seemed to be in the public interest, as journalists are supposed to do?

"The Airbus story is only a story to the public if we can show bribes were paid to Mulroney," Mathias insisted.

"Well, we're always going to disagree on that point," I told him, adding that it was in the public interest to know where the money ended up, whether or not bribes were actually paid. "Why don't you ask Schreiber where the money went?" I asked.

"I have, but he won't tell me."

"Then why don't you report that he won't tell you where the money went?"

"Schreiber says it's none of our business."

Sometimes I would stare at pages from Schreiber's Daytimers for hours on end. I had collected the pages from our German friends, and was convinced there were clues in the handwriting that I had not yet understood. If I read them and reread them, I mused, perhaps I would learn more, spot a lead that had so far eluded me. There were mentions of meetings with Mulroney; there were many references to Frank Moores and to Fred Doucet, Mulroney's former chief of staff. Elmer MacKay was mentioned throughout. Lots of German contacts. Claude Taylor, the former Air Canada chairman, was mentioned once, as was Jean Pierson, the former head of Airbus. (I later wrote Pierson a letter about his mention in the Daytimers, but he refused, as always, to talk.)

There was one particular page that I always returned to. On January 19, 1991, on the right-hand margin of his Daytimer, Schreiber had done some simple math. First, he added up three numbers—393, 393 and 200. At first, it looked as if Schreiber was adding up three separate commission payments that he had received on the delivery of three particular A320s to Air Canada. (Air Canada paid for each of the thirty-four Airbus planes separately, as they arrived in Canada over a period of a few years.) I knew I could check these amounts because Giorgio Pelossi had given us copies of invoices that had come from Airbus Industrie that he channelled through the Liechtenstein shell company IAL then into Schreiber's personal account in Zurich, 18679. Sure enough, Airbus had indeed sent two separate payments of $393,000 USD, plus another for $200,000 in the period immediately leading up to Schreiber's Daytimer entries. It was a perfect match and proved to me, without any doubt, that Schreiber had received Airbus commissions.

Those three commissions came to a total of $986,000, which he wrote down simply as 986. He then divided the 986 by two, writing down 493 CAN. In a column directly underneath, he wrote 246 KS, 123 Maxwell and 123 Stewardess. Underneath that column and just to the left he wrote 246 Frankfurt. Had Schreiber designated half the Airbus commissions to Canadians and half to Europeans? The first time I saw this math I ran into Susan Teskey's office.

"The math in Schreiber's Daytimer . . . It's exactly what Pelossi said!"

By now Pelossi had been thoroughly discredited in the Canadian media. But this evidence was in part a confirmation of what he had told us. Pelossi had always said that Schreiber told him he was going to give half the Airbus commissions to European friends and half to Canadian friends. This math showed Schreiber doing exactly that—dividing the commissions into halves and then quarters.

German authorities had already identified "Maxwell" as likely being Max Strauss, the son of the Airbus chairman, "Stewardess" as Stuart Iddles, the former VP of Airbus, and "Frankfurt" as Frank Moores. KS was undoubtedly Karlheinz Schreiber.

Schreiber had assigned the European share to three people—himself, Maxwell and Stewardess. That came to a total of $492,000, half the overall amount. He had assigned 493 to CAN.

But where had that money gone? He'd assigned 246 for Frankfurt, but that still left $247,000 unaccounted for. The Daytimer didn't provide any additional clues.

I decided to call Stuart Iddles again, in Puerto Vallarta. "Sorry to bother you again, it's Harvey Cashore calling from CBC Television in Toronto. I have some Daytimers of Karlheinz Schreiber from 1991 and you show up in them quite a bit. And there are some payments—"

"Look, I am sorry, I am not going to discuss that business. I have very clear instructions from Airbus. I am not willing to discuss it in any way. I am sorry. So please don't waste my time."

"The thing is—"

Then he hung up.

It was an optimistic period in the investigation.

We had all gone through some pretty emotional ups and downs, in particular my bosses, David Studer and Susan Teskey. There were days when we felt isolated and bruised by the constant attacks. But now we were guided more by the positive developments in Germany than by the diatribes at home. But then, at the time of greatest optimism in the story, tragedy struck the Augsburg prosecutor's office.

On April 26, 1999, Jorg Hillinger was driving his car when he veered off into the direction of oncoming traffic, and was hit by a large transport truck. He died instantly. John Goetz called me with the shocking news. Hillinger had spent the last four years of his life running the Schreiber file and making sure it stayed on track. We wondered what his death meant for the future of the investigation. Did anybody else have the determination to see it through? Ten days after his death, we had the answer. John Goetz was on the phone.

"Harv, Massmann and Haastert have been arrested. They're in jail." Goetz was referring to the two Thyssen managers who we knew well, as they were closely involved with Schreiber in the Bear Head project in Canada. "There might be even more arrests," Goetz added.

It turned out that four days before his car accident, Hillinger had issued arrest warrants for the two men. They were eventually arrested about a week after his death, on May 3 and 4. Goetz explained that both Conny Neumann and Hans Leyendecker were going to have a big story in the paper the next day. There were rumours that Leisler Kiep, the treasurer of the Christian Democrats, and Holger Pfahls, the senior defence official, might soon be arrested. Goetz also told me that the arrest warrant for Schreiber would soon be "upgraded" to tax fraud and bribery of a public official. Everyone knew that Schreiber was living in Switzerland, but until now the charges weren't strong enough for the Swiss to consider extraditing Schreiber to Germany. A police source in Switzerland told Conny Neumann that new charges might be enough.

"It looks good that he could be extradited to Germany," the source told her.

The news was coming fast. For years nothing had happened. Now two people were in custody. We were a little frantic back then, wondering if there was anything new on the Canadian front, and wanting to be the first to report it. Goetz explained that Leyendecker had the best documents. Maybe he would agree to an arrangement with a Canadian journalist—a journalist such as myself—since we were not directly in competition. We needed to trade something with him, but what? Goetz had already called Leyendecker, who wondered, correctly, what was the value of swapping anymore. "Did I get anything from you of any value?" he asked Goetz. He had a point. Still, I collected all the documents I could think of that might remotely seem relevant, and shipped them off to Goetz, who then shipped them off to Leyendecker.

"This could be the beginning of a major event," Goetz told me. "You have to get over here."

The next day, May 7, Leyendecker and Conny Neumann shared a joint byline in *Sueddeutsche Zeitung*. They explained that the two Thyssen managers, Haastert and Massmann, were accused of failing to pay taxes on greasemoney they had received from Schreiber "in connection with the sale of war machinery." There was also a reference to Canada, stating that investigators were looking into Schreiber's involvement in the sale of Airbus planes to Canada.

Then Goetz and I got some great news of our own. Goetz had been trying for weeks to get a copy of the Swiss high court decision that paved the way for the release of the bank documents. He got bumped from one Swiss canton to another, making dozens of phone calls to locate the written judgment, finally discovering it was in a courthouse in a Swiss canton called Graubünden. That was the easy part. Then Goetz had to find someone who had the authority to release the court's decision to a reporter. Goetz kept on getting the runaround until one day he spoke to a friendly-sounding clerk who told Goetz he could have the judgment as long as he paid the 20 Swiss franc processing fee. That was a problem. Not the money, but how to get it transferred. No one knew how to get it done, short of Goetz travelling to Switzerland in person. Finally, Goetz figured out he could wire the money through the post office, which he did, then crossed his fingers, hoping to see the document arrive in the mail. It did.

The package arrived only one day after the arrests were announced in the German media. It was a happy coincidence. Goetz read it through quickly, and then called me in Toronto.

"You have to get this translated right now," Goetz told me.

We hired not one but two German students from the University of Toronto to make the translation go faster. When they finished, it was clear there was indeed something new. There, on the front page of the document, was a brand-new angle on the story.

Another Canadian had a bank account in Switzerland!

It wasn't immediately clear who the Canadian was; the document itself only referred to people by their initials. I had never heard of a court not using real names in a situation like this. I guessed the courts weren't as open as they were in Canada.

Still, the more I read, the more I realized to whom it might be referring. It was easy to tell, for example, that "K.S." was Karlheinz Schreiber. "B.S." was obviously Bärbel Schreiber, his wife. But then there was a third person, someone described as "O." living in the USA.

Later in the document he was identified as the "Canadian lawyer O." That's when I knew. "O" must have been Gary Ouellet. He was both a Canadian lawyer and he was living in the United States.

Tower had once told me that Gary Ouellet could unlock the Airbus mystery if he ever talked. I remembered Ouellet's conversation with me in 1994, when he failed to convince even himself that he had not worked on the Airbus file. There was also the story that Keith Miller had told me— that Gary Ouellet and Frank Moores showed up in a meeting with Pierre Jeanniot at Air Canada. And, of course, Ouellet was close to several cabinet ministers in Ottawa, as well as to Brian Mulroney. I also knew by now that Ouellet had declared bankruptcy in 1994. At the time, Ouellet would have been required by law to list all his worldwide assets, but there was absolutely no mention of the Swiss account in the court records in Quebec. If Ouellet had any money in that account when he declared bankruptcy, he had quite possibly defrauded the Canada Revenue Agency.

The document itself contained a crystal-clear summary of the allegations against Karlheinz Schreiber, stating that authorities in Augsburg were engaged in a "criminal" investigation against "K.S." and five others. The summary referred to the Bear Head project in Canada and the Saudi tank deal, alleging tax fraud, trade tax fraud and corporate fraud. It explained how Schreiber, his wife and Gary Ouellet had all fought the Germans' request to obtain their banking documents.

The court also stated that the Germans alleged Schreiber had forged an invoice for one of his companies on May 7, 1991. A lower court had concluded Schreiber had been engaged in "willful deceit of Revenue Authorities" that included "the fabrication of falsified contracts and forged invoices, [and] the use of various accomplices." The court also stated that the "central role" played by Schreiber was not being denied, nor did Schreiber deny sums of money flowed into the accounts. Schreiber's lawyers had argued, however, that the payments were "passed on to foreigners." If true, this meant Schreiber wouldn't have to pay taxes on them.

Sueddeutsche Zeitung continued its reporting. On May 14, 1999, another story about Schreiber—"Suddenly everything falls perfectly into place"—outlined how cash withdrawals from Schreiber's bank documents lined up perfectly with meetings between, for example, the middleman and Juergen Massmann, "as if by coincidence." The paper also described how Holger Pfahls had apparently been carrying around 470,000 DM only two days after he had met with Schreiber. German authorities claimed that Schreiber had "built a house of lies to mislead the German financial authorities."

It was an interesting day in Canada too, if for completely different reasons.

Peter MacKay rose in the House of Commons demanding—again— that the RCMP stop their Airbus investigation. "Letting this case fester and bumble on is not an option. The solicitor general should tell Canadians when he will put an end to this futile investigation." MacKay didn't seem to want to take no for an answer. Two weeks later he was at it again. "The atrocious Airbus investigation makes the Canadian justice system the laughing stock of the international community." Liberal parliamentary secretary Jacques Saada reminded MacKay that he was, in effect, suggesting that politicians run the police. "The only cases that I am aware of where the legislative branch tells the judicial branch what to do are in banana republics. I do not think Canada qualifies as a banana republic."

Undeterred, MacKay rose again.

"Mr. Speaker, this debacle continues and the Department of Justice continues its attempts to cover its tracks in what could go down in history as the biggest political witch hunt of all time. It is an international embarrassment," he said, his voice reaching a crescendo. "When will the government cease and desist in its malicious and vindictive obsession to besmirch a former prime minister?"

At *the fifth estate* we were increasingly intrigued by the developments in Germany and how they contrasted with developments here in Canada. By the end of May, 1995, *the fifth estate* bosses decided I should get on a plane to Berlin.

I caught an overnight flight, and arrived in enough time to check into my hotel, then walk to the trendy Prenzlauer Berg district. I found my way to the Prater beer garden on Kastanienallee, where I met John Goetz in person for the first time. A gap between his front teeth gave him a friendly smile, but his eyes were serious. We shook hands, ordered a beer and then sat down for a long conversation. We had a busy schedule ahead of us—a trip to Munich to meet Michael Stiller and Conny Neumann at *Sueddeutsche Zeitung*, then to Cologne, to see Hans Leyendecker, who lived in nearby Leichlingen.

But first we travelled to Augsburg, in Bavaria, where we met with Reinhard Nemetz, the chief prosecutor who had taken over from Jorg Hillinger. He worked in one of those old European-style buildings with high ceilings, not yet refurbished. His office furniture was falling apart, for which he apologized profusely. Nemetz was as helpful, to a point, giving us an overview of German law as it relates to bribery and fraud, along with a few general observations about the investigation. It was clear there wasn't a chance he was going to give us any documents. We didn't even ask.

It was obvious, too, that Nemetz was concerned mostly with getting Schreiber back to Germany. On that topic, he was remarkably open. He told us he was thinking of changing Schreiber's outstanding arrest warrant to include extraditable offences from Switzerland. But he said there was a danger that if he did so, Schreiber might flee to Canada. Still, if that were to happen, Nemetz pondered the idea of arresting Schreiber en route, in the airplane. Nemetz wouldn't talk about the German legal aid request to Canada, nor did he reveal anything about what might be in the bank documents. He was, it seemed, a man who played by the rules. That didn't stop us from trying.

"Did Canadians receive Airbus commissions?" we asked.

He responded cryptically, saying there "could be" matters of interest to Canadians. Then he grinned. "It is clear certain amounts did not stay with [Schreiber]," he said. Nemetz also said that the RCMP had not asked the Germans for any help with their investigation. That had us somewhat confused, since Nemetz seemed eager to help them. "As soon as the Canadian authorities ask us I would be happy to give them what I have."

We asked about "O." We showed him a copy of our document, then he checked the version he had on his desk, which contained the entire name. "Would it be a mistake to report that 'O' is Gary Ouellet?" we asked, still needing confirmation for our theory.

"I can't say anything," Nemetz insisted, then, apparently seeing the looks on our faces, added something else. "You don't have to be that intelligent to figure out who it is."

Goetz and I made a few calls trying to locate Gary Ouellet, then found out he was working with a Dutch magician, Hans Klok. At that moment Klok was touring Europe, which meant Ouellet had to be in Europe too. We put a call in to his production company and left a message. Ouellet couldn't be more than a short plane ride away. But we never did get a callback.

Still, the research trip to Germany just kept getting better.

In Munich, Conny Neumann and Michael Stiller let me photocopy more of the Daytimer pages they had collected. Then Goetz and I went to visit Leyendecker, taking the train up the Rhine Valley to Cologne, passing through vineyards on picture-perfect mountainsides. Leyendecker was the Bob Woodward of Germany, a well-respected investigative journalist who had a track record of breaking big stories. When we got to his house he made us wait in his living room for twenty minutes. We had a bad feeling until we realized he was photocopying dozens of documents for us.

We did not know it then, but buried inside that stack of paper lay a clue that would take us to the heart of the Canadian story.

Leyendecker talked to us about what he knew about the Canadian angle. He also said something about how Schreiber was supposed to get an additional $4 million in 1994 from Airbus but that there were complications and the money never came. He told us about a letter that Schreiber wrote to Frank Moores referring to a supposed $1 million "loan" he had given the former GCI lobbyist. The German authorities said the $1 million was not a loan at all, but, rather, income that Schreiber paid to Moores. Schreiber had written the letter, the Germans claimed, in order to help Moores fool Revenue Canada. Income is, of course, taxable; a loan is not.

Leyendecker said that Schreiber had once told him that German businessmen did not get any of the Airbus money. It all went to other countries. Schreiber specifically told Leyendecker that he would always protect the Canadians. "I will never tell those names," Schreiber had informed Leyendecker.

When we were about to leave, Leyendecker wanted us to know that for a long time he had doubts about the Schreiber investigation.

"I was wrong. I thought there was nothing to this story. I did not think the investigators were very smart. I was wrong."

CHAPTER TWENTY-ONE
BRITAN

When it came to speaking publicly about the Airbus affair, Brian Mulroney was judicious. Ever since his name was attached to the controversy in 1995 he had always had Luc Lavoie, his PR person, available to speak on his behalf. When he did choose to speak for himself it was usually for a reason, like when he held court with his son Nicolas outside his house in Westmount after the lawsuit settlement in 1997 or, later that year, when he gave an exclusive interview to Bob Fife demanding a Royal Commission into the government's handling of the Airbus affair. Since then he had hardly been heard from, particularly on television, where his comments would have had the biggest impact. So it was a bit unusual when the CBC's *The National* advertised it would be broadcasting an exclusive interview with Brian Mulroney on the evening of June 2, 1999. The interviewer was Brian Stewart, the senior CBC correspondent who had reported on the Airbus lawsuit in the mid-1990s.

"One hears stories that you're still furious there's an investigation under way," Stewart said. "You're thinking of maybe even launching another suit?"

Mulroney didn't deny the possibility. "Well, the only way to launch a suit is to go ahead and do it. I don't talk about it. I never talked about the last one until we had it done." Mulroney then raised an argument that

Peter MacKay had recently raised in the House of Commons: Why did the Mounties shut down their investigation into Bre-X, the infamous gold "salting" stock scandal, and yet continue the Airbus investigation?

"I must tell you I find it somewhat ironic," the former prime minister said, "that the RCMP has been investigating this for some five years where to the best of anybody's knowledge and information, no one has suffered, no visible crime has been committed that anyone was aware of, even remotely, and they're unrelenting in their pursuit of whomever or whatever. And yet two weeks ago in the face of the greatest fraud in the history of Canada, the Bre-X scandal, where $6 billion was stolen from investors, where life savings of ordinary Canadians were wiped out, where people committed suicide in the face of such enormous personal loss that they sustained by the fraud artists in the Bre-X matter. Then the RCMP announces: after two years they're shutting the books, they're calling off the dogs and that's the end of it. Whereas in other investigations, including the Airbus matter, they've got lots of time—and by the way they said they wanted to save public money, they didn't want to spend any more public money, and yet they got nine or ten people going around the world, still trying to look into the Airbus matter. And I got no problem with that, except I find it interesting, Brian. They've got nine or ten people going around the world year after year, talking to everyone and his brother about this. And they can do it until the cows come home as far as I'm concerned, they won't find a single solitary thing. There's nothing, as far as I'm concerned, was ever done wrong . . . [T]hey go around the world, but they don't come down the street to see me."

"You still haven't heard?" asked Stewart.

"Never. They've never come to see me. They've been to see everybody else . . . I'm surprised they haven't knocked on your door. They've been to see everybody else around the world, yet they haven't come down the street to see me."

"What do you think is going on here?" asked Stewart. (Mulroney had once suspected the Liberal government of encouraging the Airbus investigation.) "Do you believe that now or do you think it's the RCMP just basically afraid to admit they're going nowhere? They don't know how to get off the back of the tiger?"

"My suspicions and my views, I expressed in the court action. The government settled, was forced to apologize, to pay $2.1 million in fees. And to make an important statement in writing: they stated in writing that, and I am paraphrasing, we do not have nor have we ever had any information to justify any allegation of wrongdoing by Mr. Mulroney. That's a pretty significant statement. So it raises the question, why is this ongoing? Now, as I say, they can do it until the cows come home."

The day after Mulroney gave that interview I attended a conference for investigative journalists in Kansas City organized by the Investigative Reporters and Editors (IRE). The IRE was the organization that put *Der Spiegel* in touch with Canadian journalist Jock Ferguson way back in 1994.

I flew to Kansas City with my CBC colleagues Gerry Wagschal and Matt McClure. When we arrived at our hotel we met a journalist from the Montreal *Gazette*, William Marsden, who had written those sympathetic stories about Mulroney during the lawsuit days. Marsden had been a reporter at the *Gazette* for years, having already done more investigative stories than the three of us young CBCers combined. He seemed to know who I was. "You sure got that Airbus story all wrong, didn't you?" I told him that there was a lot going on in Germany that might change his mind on that front. The four of us hung out most of the conference, attending seminars during the day, eating barbecue ribs and listening to blues at night.

A journalism conference allows reporters to swap war stories and get advice about their own projects. One evening, Wagschal, McClure, Marsden and I had a long discussion about the state of journalism in Canada. Then we turned to the topic of Airbus. I told them that the media had been victims of a serious spin campaign, the likes of which Canadians had probably never seen. I argued, as I always did, that Canadians had a right to know where the money ended up, wherever it ended up, and that, until the RCMP got copies of the accounts, how could anyone be sure of anything? I told them about the Swiss court judgment in which it was revealed there was another account, identified as Mr. O. I said I believed it belonged to Gary Ouellet. Marsden seemed interested. He asked me to play golf with him on Friday, which I did, and we talked more about what was happening in Germany. He suggested that he and I write an article together for the Montreal *Gazette*. I thought it would be a great idea and looked forward to discussing it when we got back to our offices.

On Monday, Marsden called. "I'm sorry. My bosses say they don't want you to co-write the article. They think you're just too biased to write a story for the *Gazette*."

It was an insulting remark, but the kind I'd heard too many times now to count. Fine with me, I thought, we were going to do the story on our own anyway.

"But I'm going to do the story myself," Marsden added.

I felt the blood rushing from my head. Marsden was going to break my Gary Ouellet story ahead of me? He knew that I couldn't produce a story until the fall when *the fifth estate* was back on the air. He could do a story for the paper anytime.

"That's my story, Bill," I complained vociferously.

"Well, you shouldn't have told me about it then."

"We were at a journalism conference. Those were confidential discussions."

"No they weren't." Still, we all knew Marsden had a point. There was no explicit agreement that he not use the information.

I got off the phone. The Gary Ouellet story was a huge breakthrough for us. It was the reason that Studer paid for my trip to Germany. Now I had just blown the whole thing. I actually thought what I had done might be a firing offence. I called Gerry Wagschal and Matt McClure, and they couldn't believe it.

In a panic, I called John Goetz and told him what had happened.

"Well, the good news is there is no way Marsden's going to get the court document."

I calmed down; Goetz was right. We probably couldn't get it again ourselves, it was that complicated. We had already given the document to Stiller and Neumann and *Sueddeutsche Zeitung*, but we knew they wouldn't report on it until we gave the green light. But, just to be safe, Goetz phoned them to warn that Bill Marsden might be calling them looking for it.

And that's exactly what happened.

One day Goetz called to tell me Stiller got a call from Marsden, who asked about getting their copy of the Swiss court judgment. Goetz told me Stiller was ready. "Actually, there is a journalist in Toronto named Harvey Cashore. The document belongs to him. You should call him. Would you like his phone number?"

I could have hugged him.

Still, I knew I had to fess up to my indiscretion. I told David Studer what had happened. To my eternal relief, he told me not to worry. For a while I even convinced myself that Marsden's story wouldn't appear, hoping that he'd be embarrassed by the idea.

It wasn't to be.

Marsden's story about the Swiss judgment appeared in the *Gazette* a month after the conference, and there, several paragraphs into his story, was *my* story. "The court's judgment revealed the curious fact that one of the plaintiffs challenging the Germans' right to examine the accounts is a Canadian with the initial 'O.' Details of the story of 'O' are sketchy. All we are told is that he is a Canadian lawyer with a Zurich bank account that the Germans wish to examine as part of their investigation into tax evasion and secret commissions." Marsden didn't come out and say "O" was Ouellet, but he may as well have, reporting in the next paragraph that "Quebec City lawyer Gary Ouellet ran an Ottawa lobbying company called Government Consultants International."

It was impossible to describe how I felt seeing *the fifth estate*'s hard-earned scoop in the Montreal *Gazette* under the name of Bill Marsden. I have never had an experience like that in my entire career, either before or after. I had talked to journalists in Germany all about my Airbus research, and they had talked to me about theirs. We had shared documents back and forth. We all understood that we would not scoop the person who had obtained the information in the first place. We had all benefited immensely from that kind of working relationship. If there was a lesson to learn that summer it was simply that some journalists play by a different set of rules. And when you find out, you remember who they are.

A couple of days after the Kansas City conference, I picked up the phone and called Gary Ouellet's wife, Renee. Gary hadn't lived in Quebec City for two years, she said. She insisted she didn't know anything about any bank account in Switzerland. She confirmed that Ouellet was travelling in Europe with Klok but said he should be back in Los Angeles at the end of the month. She then suggested I call his business line and leave a message, which I did.

The next day I called Ouellet's assistant, in Holland, on her cellphone. Gary Ouellet, she said, was in the same room, but too busy to talk.

"Yes, but you know, can he call you back because as you hear maybe, he is in the middle of rehearsals right now. Is there a way he can call you back?"

I asked if I could call back.

"He is going to be practically rehearsing all night. So I don't know."

I was optimistic that we would soon get a chance to talk to Ouellet. Perhaps he would not want to talk to us, but what was to stop us from tracking him down? He had a schedule for his magic tour, and it would not be hard to find out where he might be in the months ahead. Still, we waited to see if he would call back himself.

In the meantime, I called Schreiber's Swiss lawyer, Heinz Raschein. Perhaps he might know where Ouellet was, or at least confirm if the "O" referred to in the court documents was actually Ouellet. I told him that I had received the court judgment where he had acted as the lawyer for Ouellet and the Schreibers. I wondered if he had a phone number for Gary Ouellet.

"The only way I have to get in contact with Mr. Ouellet is Mr. Schreiber," Raschein told me.

In the middle of June I began hearing rumours that Schreiber might have made a recent trip to Canada. I had also heard that he was working in the food industry—of all things—with Greg Alford, the former vice-president of Bear Head. I called Alford in Toronto. "I heard somewhere about a pasta business or a potato-chip business that you folks were involved in, something like that. Or am I completely off the wall?"

"I didn't realize I was the story," Alford responded.

"I thought Schreiber was involved in it as well."

"Listen, I will call you back when I have time, right now I am with people."

That summer the satirical magazine *Frank* also reported that Schreiber had been spotted in Canada. It was possible. We knew that he would have been concerned that the charges in Germany might be upgraded to an extraditable offence from Switzerland. But I wasn't sure why Canada would be any safer. We had an extradition treaty with Germany. I tested the theory by placing a call to John Harding, an Ottawa businessman who had appeared in Schreiber's Daytimers. Maybe he would know if Schreiber had been in Canada recently.

"I am not going to comment on that. I am not in a position to be talking about him," Harding said.

"Just tell me it is not true, that *Frank* magazine is wrong."

"No, I won't do that."

On June 11, 1999, MP Peter MacKay once again was up in the House of Commons demanding that the RCMP shut down its investigation into both Brian Mulroney and his friend Karlheinz Schreiber.

"When will the government withdraw this spurious letter of baseless allegations against Mr. Mulroney sent to Swiss authorities and call an end to the ill-founded Airbus investigation?" An exasperated Jacques Saada, the parliamentary secretary, appeared incredulous. "I will repeat for the fifty-first or fifty-second time the same answer: the federal government has no intention of meddling in the decisions of the RCMP, of conducting an inquiry or of stopping an inquiry. It is not our role. Ours is a legislative role. The RCMP's is an investigative role. We have no business meddling, especially since this investigation was recognized in the agreement reached with Mr. Mulroney at the time. I really do not understand why my colleague opposite cannot comprehend that."

Karlheinz Schreiber had a serious civil suit against the federal government for $50 million, said MacKay. It was time to settle, he said. "My question is for the architect of Airbus, the deputy prime minister. Does the Liberal government intend to settle this matter the way it did with Mr. Mulroney, or does it intend to be dragged kicking and screaming through the courts before facing a final costly, humiliating verdict?"

The stack of documents I brought back from Germany sat unread on my desk for a few weeks. Part of the delay was the need to get them translated; also I had been assigned to work on another story about the Canadian brothers who had turned into fraud artists south of the border.[1] By the middle of June I decided to skim through the documents. I couldn't understand the words, but I could identify the names, account numbers and code names.

I noticed the usual code names. "Frankfurt" for Frank Moores, "Stewardess" for Stuart Iddles, "Jurglund" for Juergen Massmann, "Winter" for Winfried Haastert, "Maxwell" for Max Strauss, "Waldherr" for Walther Leisler Kiep. Once in a while I would type a German word into Babel Fish and get enough of a translation to understand the gist.

That's when I saw it. On a page of an Augsburg prosecutor's report dated February 6, 1996, I noticed the word "Britan."

Was it a code? I flipped to the end of the document and saw the signature of Jorg Hillinger, the former head of the Augsburg prosecutor's office.

"Was bedeutet Britan 200.200?" It appeared Hillinger had written down a list of questions for André Strobl, Schreiber's account manager at the Swiss Bank Corporation, where many of the secret accounts had been set up. I typed out the phrase and plugged it into Babel Fish. It came back as, "Which means Britan 200.200?" The translation wasn't perfect, but I got the point. What does Britan 200.200 mean?

What *did* it mean?

I pored over more documents. Britan popped up again, in an *Aktenvermerk*—(memorandum), along with the names Jurglund, Holgert and Frankfurt. Next to Britan 200.200 was written *Telefonverzeichnis* (telephone book). I deduced that the investigators had seen Britan 200.200 written down in Schreiber's personal telephone book, which they must have seized when they raided his compound in 1995.

In the investigators' notes, every code name had its corresponding real name attached. But not Britan. I placed a call to Goetz. He immediately called Hillinger's replacement, Reinhard Nemetz, the prosecutor who we

[1] The Dickinson brothers had defrauded dozens of U.S. investors. We did the story in 1999 after one of the brothers had agreed to a prison-house interview.

had seen back in May in Augsburg. Did they know what Britan stood for? Goetz called me back with the disappointing news. Not only would Nemetz not tell us anything, we had no right to have those documents in the first place.

"You have those documents illegally!" Nemetz had yelled at Goetz.

What we had was a code name we had to crack. Schreiber's normal pattern was to add or subtract consonant. If so, Britan *could* be Brian. Even so, what did that mean? Why would Schreiber use a code word for Brian? Logic steered us to one tantalizing possibility: German authorities had already proven that Schreiber had attached code names to sub-accounts with money intended for individuals. It seemed a fair question: Did Schreiber set up a sub-account named Britan? If so, was it for Brian Mulroney?

In his court case against the government, Mulroney had denied receiving any alleged payments for any consideration whatsoever. His lawyer reiterated repeatedly his client had not received a cent *from anyone*. He had had a "cup of coffee" with Schreiber after leaving office, he had testified, but that was it. The idea that Schreiber had set up an account for Mulroney was preposterous.

I had to put the question on hold. I still had that other documentary to finish. Then came the summer holidays.

Alisa and I were looking forward to spending time with our two children. Jeremiah had just turned two; Massey was five and a half. Alisa and I both had jobs that demanded long hours of prep work, and so the summer break would be a chance to unwind. On many occasions, after the boys had gone to bed, we would both work well past midnight. I had a tendency to be a workaholic at the best of times; perhaps there was a good reason. Those one-year contracts at CBC meant we never knew what our future held; I was half expecting to get a call one day that the gig was up. So it was partly fear of losing my job that made me work around the clock. That year, however, I finally became a full-time staff employee. Still, I was aware of the journalistic axiom that you are only as good as your last story. I am competitive by nature, and working in that kind of environment only made me more so. That summer I resolved to put as much distance between my work and my family holiday as possible. I even left a voice-mail message at the office telling callers that I would not be checking for messages and therefore, "please do not leave one."

I could feel the stress leaving my body as we drove up Vancouver Island's main highway to Campbell River en route to Cortes Island. That summer, Jeremiah's grandfather and I taught him how to hold a fishing rod. Massey and I hiked to the top of the mountain next to the bay on our property, burying a message under a pile of rocks for any future visitors. The boys and their cousins discovered that "Pirate" Cortes had left a trail of clues, which we followed to a treasure box full of chocolates. And my mother helped Jeremiah and my brother's children bake a carrot cake for the Cortes fair, where the kids got their faces painted, then drank organic smoothies mixed up in a blender powered by a bicycle. Through it all I was oblivious to the storm brewing in Europe: the Germans had quietly issued an urgent Interpol warrant. They were closing in on Karlheinz Schreiber.

The Airbus scandal was returning to Canada.

CHAPTER TWENTY-TWO
ARRESTED

Something was going on.

I realized when I returned from the West Coast that there were an unusually high number of Airbus clippings to catch up on. For starters, European journalists were reporting that Holger Pfahls, the former assistant secretary of defence, who had also been the chief of Germany's counterespionage service, had evaded an arrest warrant on charges of corruption and tax evasion from cash allegedly received from Schreiber. Pfahls had been located in Taiwan, and told the Augsburg authorities he would return to face the music. He purchased a return ticket but apparently got cold feet. He never boarded his connecting flight. Karlheinz Schreiber also had escaped arrest; authorities seemed to have lost his trail too.

In August, Schreiber's lawyer, Robert Hladun, launched legal action in Federal Court aimed at preventing the RCMP from obtaining Schreiber's bank records. The clock was ticking. Switzerland's high court had recently ruled that the RCMP, like the German authorities, was entitled to have the bank documents. Hladun had intervened, however, to stop the process. He asked the court to consider his "final" appeal. Opposing the motions were the RCMP and the Justice Department. The *Globe and Mail*, oddly, interpreted the action as the government itself *reviving* the investigation. "Ottawa renews Airbus probe," read the headline. "'It's been nearly five years that the investigation began,'" Mulroney spokesman Luc Lavoie was quoted. "'How long does this have to go on, this kind of carnival . . . this is veering into surrealism, into insanity.'" Lavoie said that Mulroney was "enraged" that he was still under investigation and was asking his lawyers to consider "all his legal options."

Phil Mathias and I were on the phone again—again we debated the latest coverage. We had an odd relationship, Phil and I. One day a civilized conversation, then a debate, sometimes angry words, followed by periods of no communication at all, then rapprochement. I told him that it looked to me as if Mulroney didn't want Schreiber's accounts made public, for reasons I couldn't understand. I pointed out that Mulroney could have spent the last four years demanding that Schreiber open his bank accounts in order to show he received no money, not demanding that the RCMP shut down their investigation.

"If Mulroney has nothing to hide, why hasn't he publicly called for Schreiber to open his accounts?" I had asked. His answer came on August 20, in a story in the *National Post*.

"Brian Mulroney, the former prime minister, has stepped up efforts to persuade Karlheinz Schreiber—the man at the centre of the Airbus affair—to release his confidential Swiss bank accounts to the Canadian government so the matter can finally be put to rest."

This was the first time I could recall that Mathias, or anyone else, had written about Mulroney wanting Schreiber to open his accounts; I wasn't sure where the "stepped up" came from. Luc Lavoie also made a statement I found odd. "Nothing would make Mr. Mulroney happier than to have these documents opened up so that his innocence would be clear forever." I wondered why they hadn't said *that* back in 1995 when they sued the federal government. According to Mathias, Mulroney, while vacationing in South Africa, had telephoned his former chief of staff, Fred Doucet, and asked him to "organize another approach" to Schreiber. Doucet then called someone else, Mathias wrote—an unidentified "former cabinet minister" in Mulroney's government, "a man who knew Mr. Schreiber"—to ask him to ask Schreiber to release the documents. I presumed that cabinet minister was Elmer MacKay. If it was him, I wondered why he couldn't be named. Mathias wrote that "over the last three years, Mr. Mulroney has interceded with Mr. Schreiber several times, both directly in telephone calls, and through intermediaries."

Until now, Mulroney's public strategy had been to demand that the RCMP's Letter of Assistance to the Swiss asking for copies of Schreiber's accounts be withdrawn. He had even threatened to sue if that didn't happen. By August 1999, however, the Germans had Schreiber's bank accounts, and it appeared the RCMP would soon have them as well. Now Mulroney was calling for them *to be released*? Author William Kaplan, in his 1998 book, *Presumed Guilty*, reported that attorney Robert Hladun, in October 1995, had taken a close look at the Swiss accounts and had seen nothing linking them to Mulroney. Perhaps Mulroney now felt it was safe to make the suggestion.

In the same article, Phil Mathias reported that Schreiber himself had no intention of releasing his records to the RCMP. After all, why had he spent about $2 million in legal fees to block their release to both the Germans and the Canadians? "It's a matter of principle," Hladun said. Observed Mathias, "Others doubt that anybody would spend so much money just to establish a point of principle."

Aside from his latest appeal to the Federal Court in Canada, Schreiber had also launched a new appeal to the Supreme Court in Switzerland. A decision was expected to come in September. "If either [court] rules in Mr. Schreiber's favour," wrote Mathias, "the Airbus affair will likely come to an end."

Maybe. But I doubted it.

It was hard to keep on top of all the articles and opinion pieces that were popping up in the mainstream media in August, almost all of which were driven by the Mulroney spin machine.

The *Globe and Mail*'s editorial "When will the Chretien government and RCMP stop persecuting Brian Mulroney?" stated, "The careless, baseless exercise of political and police powers against Canada's former prime minister continues under a surrealistic aura of 'due process' and 'normal procedure.' Shame." Phil Mathias published another article pointing out that the Canadian government had paid $64,000 to a Swiss law professor, Nicholas Schmidt, who had argued the RCMP letter was "legally sound." (The Canadians had to hire the Swiss professor to counter Schreiber's court challenge there.) Former conservative prime minister Joe Clark, now enjoying a rebirth as leader of the Conservative Party, also wanted the RCMP investigation shut down. "I think people have had enough of this, what appears to be an organized pursuit of one man based on partisan matters," Clark told the *Ottawa Citizen*, coming to the defence of the man who toppled him for the leadership of the party in 1983. And Peter MacKay, by then the Conservative house leader, once again blamed Jean Chrétien for the RCMP investigation. "I think the Prime Minister is battling shadows and it is a narcissist chasing his nemesis. He is very, very concerned that Mr. Mulroney has rehabilitated his reputation almost entirely and is going to continue to do so," he told the *Toronto Star*. One Mulroney confidant had suggested that Prime Minister Jean Chrétien was so spiteful he not only inspired an RCMP investigation, it also explained why he was making it impossible for Conrad Black, the Canadian media baron, to receive a peerage in Britain. "Things don't get much more extraordinary in politics than this," wrote a reporter for the *Halifax Daily News*. "The prime minister of the day is immersed in deep legal imbroglios with the former prime minister and with the owner of almost half the newspapers in the country."

On August 24, I called Giorgio Pelossi. Maybe he had heard something. Indeed he had. "The word is," he told me, "that Schreiber has left Switzerland and is in Canada permanently."

The last time we had actually produced an Airbus story on *the fifth estate* was in the fall of 1995. Four years had gone by and I had nothing to show for all my work on the file. A big fat zero. I had had many successes on many other stories (including a story that revealed the wrongful murder conviction of Nova Scotia teacher Clayton Johnson, who had been falsely accused of killing his wife; and a story that shed light on Pepsi Canada's secret lobby campaign to spike its kids' drink, Mountain Dew, with caffeine by convincing Health Canada to drop a ban on the additive in non-cola soft drinks), but my interest in Airbus had produced absolutely nothing. In the years since the last *fifth estate* item had appeared on Airbus, my son Massey had gone from an infant to a toddler to a budding little hockey player. Jeremiah wasn't even born when the whole thing began. Perhaps a saner person would have walked away from it all. I recalled the economic theory known as the law of diminishing returns, which means that some-times you get to a point in your work when you have exhausted most of the opportunities and, if you continue, you are doing nothing but butting your head against the wall; you are getting fewer and fewer results for an increasing amount of work. By any business model, I was well into the law of diminishing returns. So why did I keep at it?

I needed a break. And I got one. On the morning of August 31, 1999, I was on the phone with John Goetz to discuss possible next steps and to divide up a list of people to call. Hoping a European journalist might have more success, we had decided Conny Neumann should call Gary Ouellet. She would also call Schreiber's lawyer, Robert Hladun.

I told Goetz that Phil Mathias had yet another story in the paper, more about how Schreiber believed the Canadian government had no right to see the accounts and that Brian Mulroney was now asking that he cough them up. The article was a longish feature, tucked away on page nine, and detailed the history of the feud between Pelossi and Schreiber. Readers were reminded how Pelossi had claimed Schreiber told him he was going to bribe Brian Mulroney. The story concluded that there was no evidence for that allegation and suggested the RCMP was on a "fishing expedition." He also reported that Schreiber recently had lost his latest attempt to block release of his banking accounts at the Federal Court in Vancouver. He would appeal that decision, he claimed.

There was a crucial piece of information missing from the story. Math-ias had known Karlheinz Schreiber was living in Canada. He did not tell his readers, but Mathias had met with Schreiber in Toronto to research the story we were all reading. (What's more, the two men met again on Au-gust 31, the same day that Mathias's article appeared in the National Post.) The two men had had coffee together at the Prince Hotel in Toronto. We know this because that's what Schreiber was doing when the RCMP swooped down and arrested the middleman.

The RCMP press release came out over the wires soon after: "Acting on behalf of German authorities, the Royal Canadian Mounted Police today arrested Karlheinz SCHREIBER at a Toronto hotel. Two RCMP officers made the arrest around 6:00 p.m. this evening." The release stated the Germans wanted him to face charges of evading more than 25 million DM in taxes. The press release went on, "Following the arrest, SCHREIBER was taken to the RCMP's Toronto North Detachment in Newmarket, Ontario where he was fingerprinted and photographed. He is currently being held in a Toronto detention centre." The release also stated Schreiber would be arraigned in court at 361 University Avenue the next day at 10 a.m. I called my colleague Howard Goldenthal.

"Schreiber's been arrested."

Goldenthal had not worked on the Airbus story, but he was a friend. He had heard all about the story from me over the years and was indirectly responsible for John Goetz and I working together. We decided to head out to the Metro West Detention Centre, the closest jail to the Newmarket detachment.

Before I left, I made a flurry of calls.

One was to *the fifth estate* host Linden MacIntyre. (Trish Wood had left the CBC the previous year, and MacIntyre would be the new on-camera presence on any future story.) Then I called David Studer, followed by a call to Susan Teskey. I called John Goetz too, even though it was 2 a.m. in Germany. Then I ran to my car, picked up Howard at his condo in downtown Toronto, and we headed out to the detention centre on Disco Drive near Pearson International Airport.

It was about 9 p.m. when we arrived; the night was warm and muggy. We could see lights through the main entrance, security guards, but not much else. We parked in the public lot and waited, for what, we didn't know. Somewhere behind the nondescript brick walls of the single-storey facility, Schreiber was spending his first night behind bars. Tired of waiting, we walked up to the main entrance and asked the security guards if we could visit. They said we would have to come back during visiting hours. And no, they would not confirm if Schreiber was inside. We went back to the car. Three hours later, having seen nothing, we left. Frankly, never had it been so exciting to be sitting in a parking lot for hours looking at a brick wall.

I left my house at 6 a.m. the next morning and drove back to the detention centre. I met up with a freelance cameraman the CBC had hired for the occasion. I knew Schreiber would be transported to the downtown courthouse that morning and hoped we could film him getting into the police van. I realized our competition, CTV, had the same idea when their cameraman walked up next to us. Through a window near the loading garage we could see prisoners being escorted to vans. It looked promising. We waited for two hours hoping to see Schreiber until, exhausted, the CBC's freelance cameraman went back to his van for a nap. That was exactly the moment Schreiber, in handcuffs and escorted by burly guards, was ushered into a police van. I yelled at the cameraman, but he was sound asleep. I felt like a fool. Luckily for CTV, their cameraman captured the scene.

I ran to my car and hightailed it to the courthouse on University Avenue. Phil Mathias was standing on the steps to the side entrance of the building. He noticed that I arrived at almost exactly the same time as the police van. "Funny how you knew exactly when to show up," he said. "How are your RCMP friends doing?" he cracked, implying that the Mounties had tipped me when to arrive.

In his front-page story that morning, Mathias wrote that the *National Post* had been interviewing Schreiber when the RCMP arrested him at a Toronto hotel. Mathias wrote that Schreiber "normally" lives in Switzerland, but that he was in Toronto "marketing an instant-spaghetti cooking machine to restaurant chains. Yesterday, he traveled to Barrie, Ont., where he plans to set up a factory to make the machine. Mr. Schreiber's first stop on the way home was the Prince Hotel in Toronto."

I made my way up the escalators and into the courtroom on the second floor, which was by then packed full of spectators and journalists. German reporters were still mostly en route. I noticed Stan Oziewicz from the *Globe and Mail* and John Nicol from *Maclean's* magazine, both of whom would write solid in-depth articles on the Airbus affair and Schreiber's arrest.

Robert Hladun looked weary, having just got off the red-eye from Edmonton. He also looked out of place; as he was not a member of the Ontario bar, he could not wear robes like the other lawyers in the room. Then Schreiber entered the courtroom from the prisoners' entrance, still handcuffed. Unshaven and looking confused, he appeared to be even more exhausted than his lawyer. When Justice Frank Roberts asked him if he had anything he wanted to say, he responded simply, "I don't know what to say." The court was told that German authorities had filed a detailed arrest warrant, which we would later learn included allegations of bribery, income tax evasion, and aiding and abetting criminal breach of trust. Charges related to the Saudi tank deal, as well as the three deals in which Schreiber earned his "success fees" in Canada: the MBB helicopter deal the Airbus deal, and the Thyssen Bear Head project.

The most pressing issue for the court was whether or not Schreiber would get bail in Canada while his team fought extradition to Germany. Hladun asked that the matter be dealt with two days later on Friday; the judge agreed. Schreiber would be spending at least another two days in jail. He needed an Ontario-based lawyer.

The next day, Mathias had another well-placed scoop in the morning paper. "Swiss find no link to Mulroney in accounts: Bank records of man at centre of Airbus probe contain no mention of former PM," blared the headline on page one of the *National Post*. "A letter sent last week by Swiss authorities to Brian Mulroney states that there is nothing to link the former prime minister with Swiss bank accounts held by German businessman Karlheinz Schreiber, the man at the centre of the Airbus affair." Mathias quoted directly from the letter: "'Please note that none of the bank records so far produced or yet to be produced involve accounts of Mr. Mulroney's.'" Mathias wrote that he had "obtained" a copy of the letter from Mulroney's lawyers to the secretary-general of the Swiss Justice Department. "'Our client wishes to know,'" he quoted the letter, "'how the Swiss authorities involved are participating in what appears from our client's perspective to be a political attack rather than bona fide legal cooperation.'" The argument sounded nothing like Mulroney's earlier assertions that had hoped the bank records would soon be released to prove his innocence.

Courtroom 2-3 packed up quickly that Friday morning. I had come early, sat at the back and watched the room fill up. We had all heard by now that Schreiber had hired one of the best defence lawyers in the country, Eddie Greenspan. The well-known litigator had recently successfully defended former Nova Scotia premier Gerald Regan against charges of sexual assault. Robert Hladun was in the courtroom as well, looking a lot more rested. I saw him walk up to Phil Mathias, shake his hand and say something I couldn't make out. Then Schreiber was escorted into the courtroom, again in handcuffs, surrounded by five security guards. Later they took off the handcuffs, allowing Schreiber to fold his hands across his chest.

I figured I'd ask Mathias a question while we waited for the judge to arrive. "Now do you believe Schreiber got commissions on the Air Canada deal?" Mathias shrugged. It was Schreiber's position that he'd worked on the Wardair deal, he said, and had received commissions from the Air Canada deal, but did not actually do any work on it.

Court was called into session. Justice Roberts, who had a murder trial to oversee, was promptly replaced by Justice David Humphrey. Stevie Cameron, sitting nearby, whispered to me that Justice Humphrey's son practised law with Brian Greenspan, Eddie Greenspan's brother. Small world.

The lead Crown prosecutor, Tom Beveridge, began by arguing that Schreiber should not get bail. He was most definitely a flight risk and had, in fact, been fleeing an arrest warrant in Germany when he came to Canada.

Eddie Greenspan countered that his client had property in Canada, had never been charged or convicted of anything his entire life, and besides, the German charges were nothing more than disagreements with the German tax department. He also raised concerns about whether these "allegations" were more properly suspicions, which hardly motivated actually arresting someone.

I noticed Schreiber turn briefly and appear to smile at Phil Mathias. Schreiber then put on his glasses, consulted a piece of paper he had taken out of his glasses container, then took off the glasses.

Beveridge countered that in Germany, "suspicions" carried the same legal gravity as a "charge." He insisted Schreiber was on the run from German justice; he reminded the court Schreiber had not returned to Germany even for his mother's funeral. That assertion seemed to bother Schreiber. He put his glasses back on, took out the piece of paper and looked at it again, intensely.

Greenspan countered that Schreiber had been a Canadian citizen since 1982; he owned property in Canada that he'd purchased in 1989; on May 6, 1999, he began residing in Toronto's upscale Yorkville district.

Then Inspector Peter Henschel, an RCMP officer from A Division, Commercial Crime, in Ottawa, testified that he was nearby when his two colleagues arrested Schreiber at the Prince Hotel. German investigators had been able to locate Schreiber, he explained, by tracing a call from his mother-in-law's residence in Germany to a cellphone in Canada. German prosecutors had asked the RCMP to intervene and they had moved swiftly. As Henschel provided more details about Schreiber's arrest, Eddie Greenspan left his spot in the courtroom and walked over to Phil Mathias sitting in the public gallery. He briefly whispered into his ear.

Henschel described the contents of Schreiber's Louis Vuitton bag, which they seized after the arrest. He testified it contained more than $10,000 in Canadian currency, almost $6,000 in US funds ($8,952 CAD), 10,000 in Deutschmarks ($8,014 CAD), 7,370 Swiss francs ($7,250 CAD), 435,000 Italian lire ($353 CAD), 6,250 French francs ($1498 CAD) and a few British pounds. Henschel testified that he told Schreiber he should not really be walking around with cash like a bank. The bag also contained emergency blankets, a cigarette lighter, cognac glasses, five key rings, a gold Rolex watch, three cases of medication, two access control cards, a German hunting licence and a chequebook. Henschel explained that Schreiber had filled out a document for his rental suite in Yorkville as being for a Mr. and Mrs. Herman, with the additional notation "Do not post or reveal to public." His emergency telephone contact was Greg Alford, to whom I had talked only a few months before in my efforts to locate Schreiber. I realized now Schreiber had probably been right beside him when I called.

Henschel said Schreiber was rather talkative following his arrest: he could not believe that Canada would extradite him on a tax matter. "What are the allegations?" Schreiber repeated the question several times. If he had known this would happen, Schreiber told Henschel he would never have come to Canada. "I was so very naïve. I cannot believe this has happened. I have failed." Henschel read from one of Hans Leyendecker's stories in *Sueddeutsche Zeitung* where a friend of Schreiber's had quoted him saying, "They will never get me."

I thought I recognized Schreiber's wife, Bärbel, in the audience. I asked her if she was Bärbel. "No," she said quietly. I gave her my business card and walked away.

If Schreiber really was on the run, Greenspan summarized, why had he hired two lawyers to fight the charges against him in Germany? He also noted that Massmann and Haastert had since been released from custody, so they had bail also, didn't they? He pointed out that Schreiber had made dinner reservations at the Four Seasons Hotel on August 16, 1999, under the name "Schreiber." Greenspan also told the court that Schreiber was actively suing the CBC and had also filed a lawsuit against the federal government on May 4, 1999.

Prosecutor Tom Beveridge countered that Schreiber was always "one step ahead of the law," that he lived under temporary accommodation in Toronto under an assumed name, and used a cellphone not registered to him. While in Canada he had even avoided returning to his Ottawa town home. Beveridge described Schreiber's Louis Vuitton bag as an "escape kit," noting the variety of currencies it contained. In the strongest possible terms, he implored Justice David Humphrey, "You cannot possibly consider releasing him."

The judge reserved his decision for the following Tuesday. Schreiber would have to be in jail for a few more days at least. From almost anyone's perspective Humphrey had a monumental decision to make. If Schreiber was denied bail, he may as well have waived his right to fight extradition to Germany, since being in jail in Toronto would have had the same effect as being in jail in his homeland. But if Schreiber was granted bail, his lawyer would surely fight the extradition tooth and nail; draw the process out as long as possible, perhaps even years. Schreiber was sixty-five years old.

The story had entered a new phase: suddenly other reporters were flocking to cover the real story again. This was good news, certainly, since it was where I believed the focus should have been all along. But it meant I was now entering a much more competitive environment. No longer did we have the playing field to ourselves. A *Maclean's* reporter told me he had been given permission to go to Germany. A CBC radio reporter I knew might be travelling to Europe too. Who else would be going? I began to worry that some other journalist would get a big break on the story when we, at *the fifth estate*, had done all the hard work.

I knew I had to crank up my efforts.

I went to the clerk's office at the courthouse and photocopied everything in the Schreiber extradition file. Then I faxed it all off to my colleagues in Germany, Conny Neumann and Hans Leyendecker. Friday marked the beginning of the last long weekend of the summer, Labour Day holiday. I cancelled all my personal plans. Alisa and the boys had to spend the last weekend of the summer without me. I spent the weekend holed up in my office going through the documents, reading as much as I could, typing up interviews and putting new facts into my rapidly expanding chronology of information. (A colleague of mine, Robin Benger, would later tell me that what stands out for him about that time is coming to pick up something from his office late in the evening and seeing me there, alone, working away in my dimly lit office.)

I called Leyendecker to brief him on what had happened. He told me the investigation had crossed into France, where authorities were assisting the Germans with their Airbus investigation. I hoped we could interview Leyendecker as part of a new story on Airbus; he told me he would be happy to help us out. I called Gary Ouellet's old law partner, Ghislaine Levasseur, who was intrigued to learn that Ouellet had a bank account in Switzerland. He reminded me that Ouellet had filed for bankruptcy. He knew Ouellet was in L.A. but didn't know where exactly. I made a note to myself to retrieve the tapes of Allan Rock's now-famous press conference where he apologized to Mulroney.

I was so concerned about being scooped by other media that I sent David Studer, Susan Teskey and Linden MacIntyre an email. What if someone else found out that Gary Ouellet had a bank account in Switzerland, or obtained the Daytimer entry showing that Schreiber was dividing up the Airbus commissions? At the time, Airbus was still denying that it had paid Schreiber any money at all; the Gary Ouellet angle would have added an eyebrow-raising new perspective to a story many thought was a hoax. But that wasn't the only thing on my mind. I knew we had that lead that no one else had, the code name Britan. I thought it so sensitive I didn't dare write it down in a note. On the holiday Monday I talked to both Studer and Teskey, who came up with a simple recommendation.

"Get on a plane to Germany."

I knew they were right. The story was beginning to break everywhere. Senior reporters were back on the story in Canada and in Germany. We had a head start on our competition in Canada, but for how long?

On a personal level the story was taking its toll.

I had just cancelled all of our plans for the Labour Day weekend, and now I had to tell my wife that I would be flying to Germany, again on a moment's notice, for how long I couldn't say, again. She seemed resigned to it, but reminded me what I already knew.

"You will miss Massey's first day of school. You won't be able to go back and change that."

"I don't have a choice."

Looking back, I realize I did have a choice. I believed my job was on the line, my reputation and the story. I wouldn't ever be able to say I went to my son's first day of grade one. Was I being inhumanly selfish? The choice I made? I got on that airplane to Germany.

I was also going to miss the last day of Schreiber's bail hearing. My colleague Anita Mielewczyk attended in my place.[1] She had also worked on the story in 1995, jumping Frank Moores at his home in Florida.

I was in Germany by evening, and Anita gave me the headlines. Schreiber got bail. The judge was about to make his decision that morning, when two former cabinet ministers came forward to support Schreiber's bail application: former Mulroney cabinet minister Elmer MacKay, and former Liberal cabinet minister Marc Lalonde.

It was, as Canadian Press reported, a "surprising turn of events." Judge David Humphrey had said he had concerns about releasing Schreiber, but that they were removed after MacKay and Lalonde each put up $100,000 in bond money. Humphrey noted that both cabinet ministers had at one time been involved in portfolios that administered the law. "It goes without saying that both these honourable men have more to lose than $100,000," said Humphrey as he announced his decision to grant bail. "They are obviously

1 CBC lawyer Dan Henry and other media lawyers successfully fought Eddie Greenspan's argument in court that there be a publication ban on the bail hearing.

satisfied that [Schreiber] will abide by the rules because their personal integrity is on the line."

Outside the courtroom, Elmer MacKay had explained why he came forward. "He's a man of his word, I have known him for some time and I find him to be a good friend. That's as far as it goes. And I don't desert my friends."

Schreiber's jailhouse paperwork was completed the next day and he walked out of the courthouse wearing a smart green-plaid jacket and tie, with his wife at his side; Eddie Greenspan was close by too. For the first time Canadians got a glimpse of just how charming Schreiber could be. He had been swarmed by dozens of reporters and cameramen, yet within minutes had organized them into an orderly semicircle.

"Mr. Schreiber, how does it feel to be free again?" asked one.

"It's wonderful. As a matter of fact it is like a second wedding to see my wife again; she is the centre of my life. My great love." He suddenly noticed the reporters scrambling over each other to get close to him. "May I have a recommendation, if you move a little bit backwards, and you are not hitting this, you all can hear much better. Let's all be polite. You have me here; I stay here for you."

Schreiber had a message to deliver to his Canadian friends: "Now, it is I think a great pleasure, honour, to have friends. I have always had friends in my life. And I will never let a friend down. So they came here to get me out. I will never do anything to harm them."

I will never do anything to harm them.

Schreiber, apparently, had made some new friends in jail.

"It was a horrible experience for me to be in jail. I am sixty-five years old and never a charge, was never a day in jail, never punished for anything. For nine years I was a judge in the Supreme Court in Munich for commercial affairs. Now I saw the other side. But I have to express my greatest admiration to the officers in the detention centre. Yes, I have seen better hotels in my life but many hotels around the world could send their employees there for training purposes. The way they operate they are strict with their rules, yes, but they are human. But they have very very difficult, what can I say, kind of guests from around the world. So I learned something I would have never seen in my life, [which] means nothing, is only negative in life. Most things have a positive aspect as well."

After a question from the media about the "suspicions" against him, Schreiber explained how the German authorities were pretty unreasonable when it came to taxes.

"Today it is very common in Germany when you have problems with taxes, total mess in the country. They can just go and grab you wherever [they] want . . . I came here [to Canada] to clear up certain things," he said. "I think quite frankly that the Canadian government and the RCMP are badly misused by certain people from Europe."

"Sir," asked one journalist, "do you think that because you have begun legal proceedings against the federal government that they arrested you, that there is some kind of personal—"

Eddie Greenspan interrupted. "I don't think there should be any comment by Mr. Schreiber about any feelings he should have about these matters. It will all be discussed in court in due course at the appropriate time."

"Mr. Schreiber," said another, "you were quoted as saying not too long ago that perhaps it was a mistake that you came to Canada. You never thought that this would happen to you. How do you feel today?"

Again, Greenspan interrupted. "I don't think that Mr. Schreiber should be commenting on whatever quotes have been attributed to him. Everything that occurred in court has occurred. He is now a free man and we are going to meet the matters before the court."

Schreiber looked at Greenspan; he wanted to answer. "But if you allow me to say so, I don't regret that I came to Canada. Not at all."

"I don't regret that you came either," said Greenspan with a smile.

"Even though you have been arrested now," another reporter asked, "you are going to have to go through an extradition hearing here, you don't regret coming here?"

"No. I have fallen in love with this country. Why would have I become a Canadian? I was completely safe in Switzerland and I came here. So why not?"

"You thought you were safe here too?"

"Yes, but the time has come with all these things around me, the 'mysterious dealmaker,' have to be cleared up. I would now come back to Mr. Greenspan. I think you can imagine that after these days, I just want to stay alone with my wife and my friends for a while." Schreiber pulled out a piece of paper on which he had written some points about his case. "I have a little list here, which I prepared in jail, nine pages, all for you. But my request is you don't hound me today, you leave me alone, you get an invitation, whoever wants, make it to Mr. Greenspan, I will be available."

When one of the reporters asked about the pasta business he was hoping to develop, Schreiber's eyes lit up. "Maybe it is the biggest business, the largest business I have ever done. Very very interesting for the Canadian agricultural scenario, the restaurants, and for jobs, and for the export of business."

"What are you going to do tonight?" asked another.

"Do you see these little scars here?" Schreiber said, pointing at his nose. "This is where here I have normally a ring. My wife carries me around, she will tell me what to do. I thank you very much for your attention. You've been very kind. And I hope it stays this way. Let's team up and get something done nice." Schreiber walked across the street to a waiting taxi, the reporters flocking after him. He had one more thing to say. "I started out very poor in a small village, nine hundred people, poorest parents. I know what it means to work every day hard. This is what you do to feed your families. I admire you, have a good day."

At about exactly the same time that Schreiber was complimenting the work habits of Toronto journalists, John Goetz and I were in a meeting in a city in Europe. We were interviewing someone close to the German investigation, who we hoped might tell us something more about the code name Britan. And he did, sort of. We were told that Britan 200.200 did not refer to an actual bank account at the Swiss Bank Corporation, since it was not the numeric system they used. The person we spoke with reminded us that Schreiber had also written the number Britan 150.150 and Britan 100.100 in his phone book, but no one had a clue what they meant either.

Goetz and I turned our attention to the revelation that Gary Ouellet also had an account in Switzerland. Perhaps Airbus money, we theorized, was funnelled through Ouellet's account instead of Frank Moores's accounts. "I can confirm there is a Ouellet account," the source said. "The

Ouellet account received Airbus money." But our source wouldn't say how much or when. "Look at Schreiber's Daytimer and his phone listings closely," the source urged us. "Some accounts are hidden in the phone numbers." The source also knew that Elmer MacKay and Marc Lalonde had been witnesses for Schreiber at the bail hearing in Canada. The Germans already knew of Lalonde and MacKay as their names had appeared frequently in Schreiber's 1991 and 1994 Daytimers, the ones they had seized from his Kaufering residence back in 1995.

The source also said that the German investigators were upset to learn that Schreiber's Canadian lawyer had said there was a "human rights" problem in Germany. The RCMP had kept them informed of developments in Canada, calling the Augsburg investigators at 11 p.m. to tell them that Schreiber got bail. Their real concern now was Germany's statute of limitations. If Schreiber was successful delaying his extradition to Germany, the charges could expire.

The source also reminded us that the Canadians had still not responded to their letters. "[The Germans] are shocked and surprised that the Canadians have not answered their legal aid request, and that the Canadians themselves have not asked them anything. They have really interesting things to tell the RCMP. If the Canadians ask, they are going to tell them. Why don't they ask? Why haven't *they* made a legal aid request to Germany?"

For a few days John Goetz and I drove around Europe. We paid a visit to Hans Leyendecker again, who informed us that a "good source" told him that Schreiber left Switzerland after being frightened about the possibility of being extradited to Germany. "Schreiber some day felt frightened that the Swiss authorities would give him to the Germans, and he was thinking to go to Canada. He thought nobody could get him there because he has a Canadian passport." Leyendecker said Schreiber told him personally that the Germans "would never get him."

Goetz and I also knocked on doors in Zurich and Bern, hoping to speak to bankers and police officers. We spoke to Pascal Gossin from the federal Swiss police department, who told us that the *National Post* story claiming that the Swiss police had said Mulroney had "no link" to the Swiss accounts was not, technically, accurate. Rather, the Swiss police had said there was no account in Mulroney's name. The Swiss had not said, either way, whether there was a link or not. We also got an interview with Eric Riedl in Munich, the parliamentarian who knew Schreiber and Helmet Kohl, the former chancellor, and who had been involved in pushing Airbus in North America. He told us he never met with Mulroney and did not know anything about his involvement. Sometimes we'd get a small piece of information, sometimes an all-out refusal to talk. Overall, it was a frustrating experience. We were having almost no luck in our quest to obtain the bank documents. Everyone, it seemed, had a copy of the documents by now—all the German investigators, the Swiss police, the Swiss Justice Department and who knew who else—but no one would let us near them.

Reinhard Nemetz, the chief prosecutor in Augsburg, agreed to give us an on-camera interview, albeit in German, outlining the bribery case against Holger Pfahls. "We strongly suspect, based on various records and bank documents . . . that Mr. Schreiber had paid 3.8 million DM to a former state secretary in the federal ministry of defense."

We left Augsburg, and got on the autobahn for Zurich.

On a whim, we decided to make one of those long-shot phone calls on our cellphone. To our surprise, the person at the other end of the phone agreed to meet. But he was in a location that would require an airplane ticket, so we called the office in Toronto and spoke to Susan Teskey. I explained that this was a potentially significant development, but I still needed approval to spend the money.

"Will you pay for Goetz to fly there?" I asked.

"What do you think?" she laughed. "Good luck."

Goetz and I were delirious with the possibility that we might have another important source on the story. We drove to Zurich in our rental car, admiring all the Mercedes and Porsches that were flying past us, reaching speeds well over 200 kilometres an hour. That night, after Goetz and I checked into our rooms in Zurich, we found an outdoor café on a cobblestone street in the old part of the city. We caught a glimpse of the gold clock at St. Peter's Church shining in the night on the edge of the Limmat River.

We talked about everything that night.

We wondered what it would be like to be Karlheinz Schreiber, one minute powerful and rich with friends in high places, and the next minute fighting extradition to Germany to face real jail time. Goetz explained that the old Bavarian political style, upon which Schreiber owed his fortune, was rapidly coming to an end. Franz Josef Strauss had died in 1988 and his successor, Max Streibl, had died just last year. They had left behind them a kind of political culture that quietly condoned the mixing of business and politics. In 1993, the so-called "Amigo Affair" had engulfed Bavaria with revelations that politicians had rewarded their friends with government money. Streibl himself resigned as premier after allegations that he gave defence contracts to his "amigo" Burkhart Grob, who wined and dined the premier at his villa in Brazil. As it grew, the Amigo scandal became synonymous with the old Bavarian political elite.

"So, really, Schreiber is the last amigo," Goetz summed up.

Goetz and I talked a little about our lives, our careers, and how we ended up where we were. I talked about how hard it was to travel, to be away from my family, sometimes not able to tell them when I would return home.

Goetz paused. "My wife and I just split up."

I bought him a drink, the finest single-malt Scotch on the menu.

CHAPTER TWENTY-THREE
"THE CANADIAN"

I came back from Europe more or less empty handed.

We had done one on-camera interview with the chief prosecutor on the case in Germany and we'd had a bunch of background conversations with people who hadn't told us much, but that was it. We did, however, have that one tantalizing new development: the new source in Europe who had agreed to meet Goetz.

I had to return to start pre-production on the documentary. The bosses had given us the green light. After nearly four years of not reporting, we were now going ahead with a documentary that would focus on what we had learned about Karlheinz Schreiber. It was a gutsy decision. I don't know if CBC has ever produced a documentary about anything while still facing outstanding lawsuits on the same topic, let alone for $50 million and one of the most controversial in Canadian politics. The decision to proceed was made by many, but none deserves the credit more than executive producer David Studer.

What all this meant was that I had to start shifting gears from the research phase of the story and into the production phase. First, I needed to distill the evidence that we had accumulated from the last four years. As I reviewed key evidence, I realized just how much new information we had in our files. We could now prove that Schreiber had received the Air

Canada/Airbus commissions and that he had divided them up according to a formula largely consistent with what his accountant had claimed. We could show that Schreiber had written down, in his Daytimers, the names of key Air Canada officials, Airbus officials and Canadian politicians. We could show that Schreiber had used a system of code names for people to whom he had given cash payments. We could show that Hans Reiter, the banker in Germany, had provided a sworn statement that Schreiber told him his "good friend" Mulroney would come to power. We could show that another Canadian, Gary Ouellet, had also opened up a mysterious Swiss bank account, and like Schreiber, had fought the release of his bank documents to the RCMP. And we could show that two people had been arrested for allegedly receiving kickbacks from Schreiber, that a third— Holger Pfahls—had fled Germany.

Yet, on its own, this evidence wasn't enough. Since television documentaries depend as much on who will appear on-camera as on the new information, I made a list of people who had already agreed to speak on-camera: Brock Squire, the Puerto Vallarta real estate agent who'd told me that Stuart Iddles, the former vice-president of Airbus, bought an expensive villa entirely with cash from a Swiss bank account; Hans Leyendecker, the German journalist, had agreed to speak about Schreiber and the alleged bribe to Holger Pfahls, as well as explain to us that Schreiber had bragged that the Germans would never catch him; Professor Erich Samson, one of Schreiber's German lawyers; and Michel Drapeau, a retired Department of National Defence colonel would talk about how the deputy minister, Robert Fowler, did not like Schreiber, nor did he approve of the Bear Head project, but had had meetings nevertheless because of Schreiber's connections to the Prime Minister's Office. In addition, Reinhard Nemetz, the chief prosecutor, had already given us an interview.

It wasn't a bad list, even if Schreiber himself was still refusing to speak with us. (We had placed several calls to his lawyer's office asking for an interview and each time were told it was not going to happen.) I began to believe that we had a pretty good documentary in the making.

We also hired a German translator, Sue Burkhardt, who went through that stack of German documents and made more precise translations of those documents where we saw the code name Britan. Meanwhile, John

Goetz was making progress with our new source in Europe, who we began calling "The Canadian," which made us laugh every time we said it, because the sobriquet wasn't remotely accurate.

"The Canadian has agreed to give us everything in his file," Goetz told me almost as soon as I returned from Europe.

"Do you really think he will?"

"I don't know."

For now, Goetz had some interesting details.

German authorities had issued a new arrest warrant against Schreiber, adding more serious charges. They alleged that Schreiber had threatened to cause harm to Giorgio Pelossi, the accountant who'd kick-started the entire scandal. "Somebody someday is going to pay for this at some time," Schreiber was quoted as saying in one report, but it wasn't clear in what context he was being quoted and by whom. "There is the danger that the suspect if he is not under arrest, will take his already announced threat and put it into reality," wrote one of the German investigators.

Giorgio Pelossi also called me in September to say he remembered being in the GCI offices in 1988, the same year that the Airbus deal and Thyssen deal occurred, and that "Karlheinz introduced me to all the lawyers there." Pelossi also thought he met Fred Doucet at the same time. It was November 1988 and George H.W. Bush was elected president. He told me they all partied until two or three in the morning.

I decided to write up a research report, called it, "Where did the money go?" I gave it to Linden MacIntyre to use as a kind of primer for his entry into the story.

We actually were getting closer to finding out where the money went.

We knew now that Stuart Iddles had already received payments, and we knew that the Strauss family probably received millions as well. A recent report in *Sueddeutsche Zeitung* had suggested that investigators had now confirmed that Schreiber gave about $5 million to the Strauss family from Airbus deals in Canada and Thailand. The state prosecutor argued that the Strauss family lost millions on Schreiber's real estate deals in Canada and that the "weapons dealer" used the Airbus commissions to repay them. (There was also a story floating around Europe about how Max Strauss once bragged out loud at a dinner party that the Strauss family had found a way to get their money back on the Alberta real estate losses. That comment made the other Alberta investors furious; some even threatened to sue Strauss and Schreiber.) We also knew that the $5 million that Schreiber received from Airbus in 1988 either went to pay off his own personal debts or was for his own personal use, and was not split up according to the 50/50 formula he used later on.[1]

Linden MacIntyre's entry into the Airbus story benefited us all.

He was an experienced investigative journalist, as thoughtful as he was determined. He would take me for a beer and explain his Jesuitical philosophy, the foundation of which seemed to be that everyone, no matter who they are, has a reason for behaving the way they do. MacIntyre's point: dig as hard as you can, but always look for all perspectives. In this sense, MacIntyre's view of journalism married up nicely with that of my old boss, John Sawatsky. Sawatsky also came at journalism from the point of view that reporters should be non-judgmental; the facts are supreme. Sawatsky believed that journalists should be aggressive in the gathering and reporting of those facts, whatever impact they may have on the individuals affected, positive or negative. It is, of course, impossible for journalists to escape our own biases and inadvertent judgments as we make decisions about how to pursue a story. Still, if we are seeking to understand and enlighten, then hopefully our judgments will take a back seat.

As well as his journalistic philosophy, MacIntyre had another more practical perspective on the Airbus story. He was a Cape Bretoner, from the same neck of the woods as Fred Doucet, the Mulroney aide (later a lobbyist), and Doucet's brother Gerry, the GCI lobbyist. MacIntyre also went to St. Francis Xavier University in Antigonish only a few years after Brian Mulroney and his friends passed through the same halls. Early in his career, MacIntyre began to work as a reporter in Nova Scotia, and got to know Gerry Doucet, who was attempting a run at the leadership of the provincial Conservative Party. Doucet lost by a hair. His second-place finish left him

[1] In some ways the Thai Airways deal mirrored the Air Canada deal. In his Daytimers, Schreiber can be seen dividing up those commissions equally between himself, "Maxwell" and "Stewardess." Both Strauss and Schreiber were in touch with Pitak Intrawityanunt, a "special adviser" to the Thai cabinet.

with a trail of debts, no real job after politics and several hungry mouths to feed. Then his wife left him. He began a law practice in Nova Scotia, and then, when Brian Mulroney came to power, he joined the lobby firm GCI. Not a bad thing to do if your brother is Mulroney's closest confidant and one of his senior policy advisers. But Fred and Gerry Doucet declined to speak to anyone about the Airbus story.

Schreiber appeared to be enjoying his notoriety.

A few weeks after his release on bail, he was spotted at the Four Seasons, then at Vaticano, one of the best Italian restaurants in the city. Sometimes he would stop by the Coffee Mill for a bowl of goulash soup. Schreiber was friendly with all the waitstaff and managers. He knew all the employees; he asked about their backgrounds, their children, their work. Sometimes he'd tell a joke and make everyone laugh.

But Schreiber had a ruthless side.

He would never harm his friends, that much was true. But watch out if you stopped being his friend, as the current premier of Bavaria, Edmund Stoiber, was about to realize.

For Edmund Stoiber, a past association with Schreiber would come back to haunt him. When Schreiber got into trouble with the Augsburg prosecutors, he assumed that Stoiber would come to his rescue. Schreiber had written Stoiber several letters requesting that he review the Airbus files. The prosecutors in Augsburg did not know what they were doing, he said. Stoiber's response was to tell Schreiber to send whatever information or complaints he had to the prosecutors. Schreiber, who valued loyalty above all, felt betrayed by the chilly formality of his friend's answer. Schreiber told *Stern* magazine that he was a victim of Stoiber's "clean-up" campaign in Bavaria. "It's all political after all," he said. "He [Stoiber] wants to build a profile and show people how he deals with the amigos." But he suggested the premier was being hypocritical, alleging that Stoiber "of course" was part of the Airbus negotiations (hinting perhaps that Stoiber might have known about Schreiber's secret side contract to grease the sale). Schreiber would later allege that he provided 2 million Deutschmarks to the Christian Social Union (CSU) in the 1980s; as a result, Stoiber faced an official probe; he denied any wrongdoing.

"Corruption is as persistent as prostitution," Schreiber told *Stern*. "Even today no business runs on its own. You have to do something." Schreiber explained that even if he wanted to, he could not necessarily prove who he paid greasemoney to, as one does not normally get a receipt for such payments. That explanation was not going over well with the German tax authorities, who demanded he prove the payments happened in order to avoid tax evasion charges. "Had I done it differently I would have been dead a long time ago," Schreiber said, explaining that he could have been a liability to certain people if they thought he had proof. Still, Schreiber was crudely dismissive of the prosecutors in Germany.

"They have nothing. They only have a code, but no evidence. That will blow away under the butt like a fart."

I was beginning to feel swamped by all the work I had to do in preparation for the documentary. I asked the bosses for help, and they found me Kit Melamed. She was the original associate producer who had worked so diligently on the Airbus story back in 1988, along with Eric Malling, and had recently returned to work for *the fifth estate* after a stint at our competition, *W5*. Melamed came from a prominent journalistic and political family. Her father was the legendary *Toronto Star* reporter Val Sears; her brother, Robin Sears, had been a prominent New Democratic Party apparatchik, having served as Bob Rae's chief of staff when he ran the provincial NDP in Ontario. Robin Sears and Kit Melamed were proud of their maternal grandfather, a founding member of the Co-operative Commonwealth Federation (CCF), the forerunner of the New Democratic Party.

I was thrilled that Melamed was joining the Airbus team. She got to work. She remembered she had a confidential source of her own from way back, and promptly called him again, getting even more confirmation that Moores had lobbied for Airbus.

Someone on our team needed to call Pat MacAdam, one of the St. Francis Xavier University alumni who had become part of Mulroney's inner circle. Kit agreed to make the call. An hour later, she came to my office.

"Max Strauss met with Mulroney."

Now, *that* was interesting. Max Strauss's father had paved the way for Schreiber to earn millions in *schmiergelder* on the Airbus and MBB helicopter deals, but only if Mulroney's government approved those purchases. Could it be that neither Schreiber nor Max Strauss ever mentioned Airbus or MBB when they met with Mulroney? MacAdam wasn't actually in the meeting, so he couldn't say one way or the other. But it seemed likely that the topic would have come up. Or, put another way, why wouldn't Schreiber and the young Strauss have mentioned their interest in Airbus to Mulroney? Air Canada would make the decision whether or not to purchase Airbus jets on its own, but that decision would then have to be approved by a variety of federal government departments and cabinet. So what harm could it do if Schreiber put in a good word with Mulroney?

MacAdam was eager to defend both Schreiber and Mulroney, telling Kit that he sent a fax to Elmer MacKay after he put up bail money for Schreiber. "I wish that my financial resources had allowed me to do the same. Karlheinz is a decent guy," MacAdam said.

MacAdam's conversation with Melamed was a breakthrough interview. First, it allowed us to interview someone who would defend Schreiber and Mulroney. We wanted to show all perspectives in our documentary and were discouraged that so far we had been unable to find someone close to Mulroney who would appear on-camera. MacAdam changed all that. Second, the interview provided us with a glimpse into the Schreiber/Mulroney relationship that we had never before understood.

The next week Kit Melamed and Linden MacIntyre flew to Ottawa and interviewed MacAdam on-camera. MacAdam said that Schreiber "administered" the Strauss family's businesses in Canada and the United States, and that he would "often come up here [Ottawa] with Franz Josef Strauss's son, Max, and visit his trapline. Pay courtesy calls on people.

"[Schreiber] was a close friend of Mr. Mulroney's. They knew each other long before Mr. Mulroney became an MP and leader of the Opposition. I don't know where they met, maybe through the Strausses. And he'd pay a courtesy call on Mr. Mulroney," MacAdam said. "I was the gatekeeper then, and kept the appointments, and he'd come in with Max Strauss and say hello, and leave."

And how often did Schreiber meet Mulroney back then? "Oh, maybe five, six, seven times a year. [Schreiber] travelled extensively. The U.S., Europe, Canada. He had homes in Ottawa and Alberta, [and] Germany."

MacIntyre asked specifically about Max Strauss.

MacAdam recalled a phone call—from either Elmer MacKay or Bob Coates—asking if Mulroney had time to visit Schreiber and the younger Strauss. "I asked [Mulroney]," MacAdam said, "he said 'sure.' So they came into the office and I left them alone.... I don't think Strauss had any business with the government of Canada. But the father, Franz Josef Strauss, was a good friend of Mulroney's years gone by."

MacAdam also said he would bump into Schreiber from time to time after Mulroney became prime minister. The middleman never failed to talk about his special project, Bear Head, which Schreiber believed would build safer military vehicles than the ones the Canadian Forces currently used. MacAdam wanted the world to know that both Mulroney and Schreiber were outstanding people. "I don't think they [the RCMP] will get either one of them, you know," adding that he was not using the word "get" in a pejorative way. "They're both honest, decent men," he went on. "I would have no hesitation in going out in the desert if Brian Mulroney or Karlheinz had the water. I wouldn't be afraid. I trust them implicitly."

There was something about the Max Strauss story that intrigued me. By now I had read through Mulroney's 1996 examination on discovery a few times and had remembered there was an exchange about the Strauss family. I went back to the transcripts and found the section, reading with fascination a particular exchange between the government lawyer, Claude-Armand Sheppard, and Brian Mulroney, as he was asked about his relationship with Karlheinz Schreiber:

Sheppard: And was he [Schreiber] known to you as a friend of Franz Josef Strauss?

Mulroney: He was not known to me as that, but I subsequently read that he was known to Mr. Strauss. I did not know Mr. Strauss myself, nor did I know any of his family.

Sheppard: You talk about Schreiber's family?

Mulroney: Strauss's family. This is Strauss like in the waltz.

The exchange was intriguing on a couple of levels.

First, it contradicted MacAdam's very clear memory that Max Strauss came to visit Mulroney when he was leader of the Opposition. It even contradicted MacAdam's assertion that Mulroney knew Franz Josef Strauss. I tended to put less weight on what MacAdam said about the father because no specific anecdote was attached to the memory, but the memory of the son visiting was clear and precise. It was also noteworthy that the information came from someone who was defending Mulroney. My guess was that MacAdam had no idea that Mulroney had testified this way in his discovery in Montreal.

Second, it was interesting that Mulroney denied knowing Strauss or "any of his family" when he was not even asked that question. Why deny something you are not asked?

Sheppard must have found it interesting too, because later in the day he returned to the same topic.

"This morning I had asked you whether you were familiar with the relationship between Karlheinz Schreiber and Franz Josef Strauss, and I remember that you responded and made some reference to the composer as well. I'm not sure I understood your answer correctly this morning. You found out at a later date that there was a relationship between Mr. Schreiber and Franz Josef Strauss, is that what you indicated this morning?"

"Yes," Mulroney replied, "I was advised in some circumstances that Mr. Schreiber, in Alberta, when he was in Alberta, very successful business apparently in Alberta, was, had been either a representative of, or associated with, in some way, in some of the Strauss interests. I can't tell you beyond that."

"Is it not a fact that Franz Josef Strauss was the chairman of Airbus?" Sheppard asked.

"I knew of Franz Josef Strauss; I didn't know him personally, I never met him, but I knew of him as the premier of Bavaria and as a minister of finance in the Federal Republic. I had no idea what his other occupations may be," Mulroney replied.

"Britan" was a bank account after all.

A new document surfaced from Germany that showed that Schreiber had set up rubrik accounts, or sub-accounts, in Canadian funds, for at least three other people, including Britan:

46341.2 Rubrik "Fred"

18679.5 Rubrik "Marc"

46341.5 Rubrik "Britan"

All of the above accounts were sub-accounts of the main Schreiber account in Zurich, 18769 IAL. German investigators' notes had already identified Fred as likely being Fred Doucet, Mulroney's close friend. And they had identified Marc as Marc Lalonde, the former Liberal cabinet minister who had put up bail money for Schreiber. As Schreiber had not chosen codes for those accounts, only actual first names, it seemed obvious for whom they were intended. But who was Britan? If the German investigators suspected someone, they hadn't said.

Still, we now knew for certain that Britan was a sub-account created by Schreiber and that it also had a specific account number associated with it. Now, more than ever, we focused our attention on finding out who it was for, and what kind of money was in the Britan account.

On September 25, 1999, Phil Mathias published a profile of Schreiber in which he alluded—for the first time—to the missing Airbus money. "Mr. Schreiber's public face is a super salesman of aircraft, tanks and an instant spaghetti-cooker. He fascinates the media because he allegedly received $13.2-million in unexplained commissions from the sale of 34 Airbus aircraft to Air Canada in 1988. Where the money ended up is unknown." I wondered whether or not he had developed a new perspective on the story from the last time he insisted that there was "no tainted money" to trace. Gone were the attacks on *the fifth estate* and the convoluted critiques of the RCMP.

In another article that day, Mathias wrote about the new allegations filed in Schreiber's extradition case where it was alleged Frank Moores received Airbus commissions after all. "Jesus, this is like the Energizer Bunny. It never stops," Mathias quoted Frank Moores as saying. "You can use my first denial or my fiftieth," he said. "I have never received any commissions from the Airbus sale." As for suggestions that Schreiber had set up a sub-account—"Frankfurt"—in his name, Moores denied it. "That doesn't make sense," Moores told Mathias. "Why would anybody set up a secret account for me to receive commissions when I already had accounts in which I have received commissions?" Moores complained about the leaks coming from the German investigations. "Have you ever heard of a Revenue Department carrying on their campaign in the press," Moores told Mathias. "One of the things I find absolutely incredible is that a Revenue Department could go so public before any charges have been defined."

It was time to pay a visit to my old source Tower.

Tower gave me four new pieces of information: 1) A businessman named Michael Cochrane, a former vice-president of finance at Air Canada, had been approached to put up bail money for Schreiber. He declined. 2) Greg Alford, Schreiber's vice-president at Bear Head, was also involved in lobbying the government to purchase Airbus aircraft. "Greg was a lot more involved than people realize." 3) Nothing happened in the Prime Minister's Office without Fred Doucet knowing about it; and 4) Schreiber personally donated $13,000 to Jean Charest's 1993 leadership campaign.[2]

Then John Goetz called.

He told me "The Canadian" had agreed to meet again. This time Goetz was led to believe he might even get a chance to look at the bank documents. John wanted to know if we would pay for the plane ticket.

---

2 Years later, Schreiber would testify before a parliamentary inquiry that he donated $30,000 to Charest's leadership campaign. Looking back, my guess is that I mistakenly heard "thirteen thousand" when Tower probably said "thirty thousand."

I asked the bosses. We already had the makings of a substantial documentary. Was it really likely we would see the bank documents? Every major news outlet in Germany and Canada was trying to get them. Was it possible we would succeed when no one else had? It was a long shot. Teskey and Studer approved the expense.

On the day that Goetz met with "The Canadian," I couldn't think of much else. Based on the time difference I figured we might hear something around noon Toronto time. But the time kept marching on. I hung around my office phone, not wanting to miss the call. There were several false alarms. Then at about 4 p.m. the phone rang. I picked up.

"Harv, Harv, I have the bank documents."

Goetz explained that he had taken the bank documents back to his hotel room, but he had promised "The Canadian" he would not photocopy them.

"What about Britan—do you have the Britan account?"

"Yes, I'm looking at it right now."

Goetz told me the account showed a deposit of $500,000 Canadian on July 26, 1993. That was about a month after Mulroney stepped down as prime minister. The very next day there was a cash withdrawal of $100,000 from the account. Then another cash withdrawal of $100,000 on November 3, 1993, another cash withdrawal of $50,000 on July 21, 1994, and a final cash withdrawal of $50,000 on November 21, 1994.[3]

A total of $300,000 in cash was withdrawn from the Britan account in a period spanning sixteen months. As excited as we were about that development, we were in a race against the clock to get all the other information out of the bank documents. First, Goetz tried copying them by hand then faxing the sheets to us, but it was taking too long. Then I had an idea.

"Read them out loud."

I told Goetz we would tape his voice, and then re-create the documents after transcribing our conversation. Kit and I would also take notes, but with the tape as backup. Goetz began reading the documents, line by line.

3 November 21 also happened to be the same day that Schreiber shut down his Zurich accounts, transferring them to a mirror account in Liechtenstein, under his wife's name.

He read every date, every transfer, every cash withdrawal and every deposit. By 9 p.m. the recitation was over. It was 3 a.m. in Europe and Goetz was exhausted. I was hungry but could not eat. Despite the enormous media frenzy in Germany and Canada, the cbc's *the fifth estate* was the first news organization in the world to obtain Schreiber's secret Swiss bank accounts.

We didn't stop there.

Kit Melamed and I stayed up the rest of the evening putting the names of the various accounts on recipe cards, then tacking them to her office wall. On each card we jotted down transfers in and out of each account. Each transfer had a transaction number that matched up with the account from where it came, or where it went, so we jotted down those numbers as well. The wall filled up quickly. Another recipe card was for Frankfurt, one for Britan, one for the Canadian funds account, one for the U.S. funds account, one for the account in Liechtenstein that held the secret commission from Schreiber's Canadian deals. And on it went. We tacked up more cards for Marc and Fred and Winter and Jurglund and Maxwell and Stewardess. When that was all done, we matched up the transfers between accounts, putting a string between one thumbtack and another. It was exciting work, as we slowly began to see the money transferred from this rubrik to that rubrik. When the last piece of string was put in place we looked back at our wall, a spiderweb of sheer excitement.

We followed the string backwards from the Britan account, wanting to know where that money may have come from. The string from Britan went first to the Frankfurt sub-account. From there it went to the Canadian funds sub-account. From the Canadian funds sub-account it went to the U.S. funds sub-account. The string from the U.S. funds sub-account took us out of the Swiss Bank Corporation in Zurich and into the IAL account in Vaduz, Liechtenstein. And from Vaduz, Liechtenstein, the money trail took us to Paris, to the Banque Française du Commerce Extérieur, where Airbus had deposited the money it had skimmed off from the cheques it received from Air Canada.

"Britan got Airbus money!" we yelled. Suddenly we were more subdued.

"Shit." We knew the implications.

What happened next would lead to the unravelling of the friendship between Karlheinz Schreiber and Brian Mulroney, and eventually the revelation of a secret that for years the two men had agreed never to talk about.

CHAPTER TWENTY-FOUR
TOO DAMN STUPID

W e knew we had to ask Brian Mulroney for an interview.

It would have been irresponsible for us to broadcast details of the Britan account and not ask Mulroney about it. That much was obvious.

It was, however, a tricky proposition.

We knew that whether or not the former prime minister received any money from Schreiber, he would not exactly welcome an interview request of any kind from *the fifth estate*. If Mulroney did get the money, he would not be pleased about the information possibly coming out. And if he did not get the money, it would be understandable that he would find more questions on the Airbus story entirely unpleasant. We still did not know which of the two scenarios applied to Mulroney, but we knew we had to ask.

The question was how to do it. There was some history between Mulroney and me, and we had to think carefully about how to proceed. I had already heard from third parties that Luc Lavoie had spread rumours suggesting I had too cozy a relationship with the RCMP. I was even told that Lavoie hated me. And I had learned from reading *Spin Wars* earlier in the year that Mulroney had blamed me for what had happened to him.

In the beginning I thought all I had to do was convince Lavoie and Brian Mulroney that I did not hate the former prime minister. Eventually I came to understand they probably knew it all along. The problem was not that I hated Mulroney; the problem was that they *needed* me to hate Mulroney. Otherwise their spin would never work.

David Studer and I drafted and re-drafted a letter to Brian Mulroney, along with CBC legal counsel Dan Henry, one of the unsung heroes of *the fifth estate*'s Airbus coverage. Henry was tough and demanding, but always saw the value of our story, even wanting to push some elements forward when we ourselves were not so certain.

My letter to Mulroney, dated October 8, 1999, was uncomplicated:

Dear Mr. Mulroney,

 The Canadian Broadcasting Corporation's programme the fifth estate is gathering research for a story concerning Karlheinz Schreiber and some of his business activities in Canada and abroad. In the course of the research we have come across some new information which we would like to discuss with you in an interview. It is our sincere objective to understand the facts as best we can, and it is for this reason we are hoping to speak with you. This is not to suggest that we have come to conclusions about this information, rather the opposite. We believe that the more perspective we can get on our information the more complete our story will be.

   Sincerely,

   Harvey Cashore

It was about 4 p.m. when I printed out the letter and walked over to *the fifth estate*'s fax machine. I tripled-checked every word to make sure there were no spelling mistakes. Then I dialed the fax number at Ogilvy Renault, Mulroney's Montreal law firm. I paused before I hit the Send button. I was nervous. There would be a reaction from the former prime minister, but what? Finally I pressed the green Send button and saw the paper slip into the machine.

Then I headed off to Pearson International Airport.

Air Canada had given us permission to film the A320 Airbuses land on the tarmac and dock into their gates. I did not get back to my office until late in the evening. It was then that I learned that Luc Lavoie had called my house twice, and had left three voice-mail messages for me at work. I was already late getting home to begin the Thanksgiving long weekend, but called anyway.

"It's been a long time," Lavoie remarked.[1]

"Four years," I agreed. "But I got your Christmas cards."

The small talk was soon over.

"What's going on?" Lavoie said.

I explained that I wanted to speak with Mr. Mulroney about "some information" that had come up in the research.

"I guess you are going to have to settle with speaking with me," Lavoie told me. "Whatever information needs to be checked, ask me and I will find out." He made it clear: Mulroney wasn't talking to me. "Because he just doesn't do that. Don't take it personally, he doesn't do it."

"Oh no, I don't take any of this personally. This isn't personal. I am just trying to understand this."

Lavoie asked me again what this new information was. I responded carefully. "Well, I mean, look, this is obviously a little awkward for me, and this is delicate, and I am treating it that way. We have some information that we have obtained about Karlheinz Schreiber's bank accounts. And one possible interpretation of these facts that we have obtained, and I have to stress *possible interpretation*, might be, and I have to stress *might be*, that one of them was intended for Brian Mulroney."

"That one bank account or one entry in the bank account or what?"

"No, that one rubrik," I said.

"One rubrik in the account?" he asked, getting it exactly right.

"Let me stress that I am not suggesting this is so, I am just—"

"I understand. I understand. But that is through deduction that you come to this conclusion?" Lavoie asked.

"I have not come to any conclusion."

"No, no, but I mean, let's not call it a conclusion, but that you've come to this possible interpretation."

I was so concerned that I might say the wrong thing and get sued for

---

1 For a complete audio recording of the Luc Lavoie interviews go to www.cbc.ca/fifth/moneytruthandspin.

another $50 million that I worried about agreeing to anything Lavoie was saying.[2]

"I believe it's possible that one interpretation may be that one of these rubrik accounts was intended for Brian Mulroney."

"I see."

"I have to stress all over again I am not saying this is a conclusion."

On and on we went, Lavoie trying to get information from me, me trying to get an interview with Brian Mulroney. I told Lavoie that we were not going to air the following week, so Mulroney could put some thought into what he wanted to do. Still, Lavoie told me he needed something more to report back to Mulroney.

"I need more than this. Like, you have seen his accounts, Schreiber's accounts? I mean, don't forget, Harvey, I mean as far as we are concerned, we never had anything to do with any of this stuff. So I would like to know, what could lead anybody to interpret anything as meaning that it [the money] might have come to Mulroney?"

I tried again to tell Lavoie that I would explain it all to Mulroney.

"As I'm saying, Harvey, he won't speak directly to you. You are going to have to settle with me." He added: "I have always been a straight shooter with everybody . . . You give me information, I will check it out and get back to you. It's that simple . . . Pass me the information and I will check it out as much as I can. You are not going to get directly to him. This is not going to happen."

"So what you are saying, if I am hearing you correctly, is you want *me* to tell *you* all the specific new facts that we have obtained?" I asked.

"Yes, and I can actually, if that is worrying you, I can actually give you an undertaking in writing if you want that I won't share it with any other reporter anywhere in the world. So I mean I am not going to spread anything around. It is not my purpose here. My purpose is to get to the bottom of it. So if you wanted a commitment on my part of that sort, I will give it to you."

2 The lawsuits that Moores and Schreiber filed against us had been dormant for months, but there was nothing to stop them from resurrecting them at any time, and nothing to stop anyone else from launching a new lawsuit.

By agreeing not to talk about the new information, I quickly concluded that Lavoie was making an offer that I should consider. "Can I get back to you on that?" I said. "That is something I will have to mull over."

I got off the phone and consulted Dan Henry and David Studer. They decided I should try once again to get an audience with Mulroney. I called Lavoie back the next day, now the Saturday of the Thanksgiving long weekend.

Lavoie sounded a little more impatient than last time. Mulroney was upset, he said, and that getting a letter like this on a Friday before the Thanksgiving long weekend was no fun. "He is not going to give an interview nor have a conversation with you or any of your colleagues about this."

"Right," I said.

"But I mean you don't trust me from what I can hear," Lavoie said. His offer of confidentiality still stood. "I told you yesterday, I am not going to spread it beyond Mr. Mulroney. It is the canal to him. That's his wish and that is the way things will go. And you know, regardless of anything else, I guess I am a straight shooter. I am not going to fuck around with you. I am not going to go and spread anything to colleagues of yours or anything like that. I promise. You have my word for it." Lavoie tried to get some information from me. "What you said it was, if my understanding is correct, is you had seen Schreiber's accounts. Am I right?"

I paused, not sure how to answer.

Lavoie pressed. "We know they are in Germany, so you have seen the accounts?"

"I have seen some information about his [Schreiber's] banking records."

"Okay. So you are not saying you have seen the accounts."

"I don't want to say that I have or that I haven't."

"Okay. And in it there is a section, I don't know what words you used," Lavoie said, "what did you call it?"

"A rubrik."

I again pleaded with Lavoie to let me talk to Mulroney.

"It is just not going to happen. I actually told him that you asked to speak with him. He won't. So."

"Can I ask why, what the stumbling block is?"

"What the stumbling block is? He doesn't speak to journalists about this. Period. It is simply that. And to be honest with you, and he hasn't said that, but I guess I am interpreting his mind, when I say that he has been kind of bruised by at least one of the stories on *the fifth estate* about this. So I mean, one could understand why he is so careful."

Lavoie and I debated the stories in 1995 for a while. Then I simply suggested we talk again on Tuesday and, for the time being, enjoy the Thanksgiving weekend. Lavoie's response provided a revealing psychological insight into Brian Mulroney's predicament.

"Really, put yourself in his shoes. This has been destroying his life for four years. I guess I get the feeling from his voice that he just can't take it anymore."

Lavoie urged me to give him something more to go on. I told Lavoie that nobody else besides me was at work and that I couldn't consult my bosses to see how much I should reveal. I told him I would try to call him back in an hour or so.

"Okay. And please get my point. If only for human reasons, try and see if we can deal with it this weekend. Nothing is going to happen beyond you and me and him [Mulroney]. But I am trying to help his life a little bit here. He is going nuts."

I got off the phone, called David Studer and Dan Henry, who again told me to tell Lavoie we wanted an in-person interview with Mulroney.

I called Lavoie back.

"I guess my feeling is that I want to speak with Mr. Mulroney," I said. "I will talk to him right now. I will be at the phone. I will be right there to talk to him. I don't want to leave him hanging on anything. But I do want to talk to him."

"Okay. I have talked with him after we spoke. And I tried to convince him to do that. It was negative. If only, the only positive thing I can say, is he said, 'Try and get me some more [information] and I will see if I speak with him.' I told him everything I knew. He said, 'On that basis I am not speaking with him. If there is anything more serious than this—'"

"Any more serious?" Wasn't this serious enough?

Lavoie corrected himself. "Well, any more specific."

He pestered me to offer up just a bit more information. "But why don't you give me a little more? Don't give me everything. Give me a little more.

I will get it over to him and see what he does," Lavoie said. "I am not playing a game here. I am just telling you."

It seemed we were making progress. If I was going to give more information, I wanted clarification on their agreement not to speak to anyone else. "You are saying that Mr. Mulroney and yourself will not speak to journalists and other people about this so that it would not get out into the public discussion. Is that what you are saying?"

"Exactly. And that is very firm." He repeated, "We won't use it, share it with any other news organization, with anybody else . . . We just want to know what it is about."

Lavoie wanted to know when we were going to air with the story. I told him the airdate was likely November 20.

"So it's a week and a half from now?"

"Yes."

Lavoie and I hung up. The plan was to talk again the next day. But he called again later that night. He said he could now promise that if we told them what we knew, Mulroney would not seek an injunction to prevent broadcast nor would there be any attempt to seize documents.

I suggested we talk about it again tomorrow.

Lavoie was persistent. "Why not tonight?"

"I want to sleep," I said.

"Yeah, so do I. But my Thanksgiving weekend is dead anyways."

"Yeah, so is mine."

I felt like our frosty relationship had begun to thaw. I could better understand where Lavoie was coming from and remembered that he was, after all, doing his job as a paid PR person for Mulroney. What he said was true, in a way. I had ruined Mulroney's weekend, Lavoie's weekend and mine. I decided to tell him a little more.

"Well, can I ask you a couple of things?" he asked. "Does [Mulroney's] name appear in any document that you have seen, showing that he has received money from anybody. And if so, what kind of money are we talking about?"

The question got me thinking. If Mulroney had not taken money from Schreiber, why would he care to ask what *kind* of money we were talking about? But if he had taken money from Schreiber, was it possible Mulroney, through Lavoie, was wondering how *much* of the money we had found out about?

I paused. "I am not trying to be—I am trying to figure out—"

"His name or a code name?"

I paused again. "Okay, you are very smart to have asked me that last question."

"So there is a code name that looks like him?"

"There is a code name," I said, "that if you looked at it, you might say that."

"I see. You might, because it sounds like his name, it's spelled like his name?"

"It is very close to."

"Very close to his name," Lavoie repeated.

Our conversation took an unexpected turn. Lavoie had something important he needed to tell me. "Because, can I tell you on my part, something totally off the record?" Lavoie asked.

"I hesitate to say yes to off-the-record things, but if you mean not for attribution, I am happy to hear something not for attribution," I responded.

"No, off the record, really, because it is an opinion I want to express."

"If you think it is not newsworthy and it is not, it is just a side point, I would be happy to hear it, sure," I said, "if you are trying to help me understand something."

Lavoie began. "We believe, but we don't want this to be spread around in any way, shape or form, that Karlheinz Schreiber is the biggest fucking liar the world has ever seen. That is what we believe."[3]

It was a shocking statement, even if off the record. Until then I had assumed that Mulroney and Schreiber were still friends. They had known each other from the early 1980s, met several times while Mulroney was in office, and even had a cup of coffee after he left office. And it made me wonder, too, whether Mulroney thought Schreiber was talking to us. I had never implied that Schreiber had spoken to us, only that I had obtained his

3 I explain later in the book why I made the decision to use this quote.

bank documents, but it now looked as if Mulroney might have thought Schreiber had given them to us.

"We are very afraid," Lavoie continued, "that this man was quite capable of using anybody's name to get money from somebody else. We have no proof of that; we have no evidence that would lead us to believe that. But this is the way we feel about it. And that is certainly why Mr. Mulroney is so nervous."

Mulroney was nervous, Lavoie seemed to be saying, not because he had received Airbus money, but because he was worried Schreiber claimed he had.

We went back on the record.

I told Lavoie that this was exactly the kind of perspective we needed to hear from someone on-camera. He declined. "I can't say it on the record anywhere because it is libellous to say that we believe somebody is a liar. I don't have any evidence that he is. But we are led to believe by the events as they unfold that the guy is a bullshitter."

I asked Lavoie if there was anybody who could speak on-camera and say the kinds of things he was getting at.

"You see, I mean, one of the myths here, Harvey, one of the myths here, all along is that Mulroney and Schreiber were somehow close. They were not. They never were."

"What was their relationship?" I asked.

"It was very minimal. Their relationship was that the man was pushing for a project in Nova Scotia, especially on Cape Breton Island." Lavoie talked about the history of the Bear Head project and the involvement of key players like Elmer MacKay, Fred Doucet and even Liberal senator Allan MacEachen. Lavoie noted that Phil Mathias had claimed in a recent article that Schreiber was involved in Mulroney's 1983 leadership bid. Lavoie said that Mulroney had no personal memory of this, had gone back to his files to check and found nothing.

"So the myth once again is that they were close. They were not close. They were never close. Actually, they were not. It would be totally wrong to describe them as friends. Because they were not friends. They were acquaintances who had learned to know one another through this project that he was pushing using any means available."

I sensed that I was about as close to talking with Mulroney as I would ever get. Surely what Lavoie was saying to me had come from his briefings with him.

"How did they first meet from your perspective?"

"I don't know the exact answer to that, but he said they never [met] before he was elected prime minister. And on this I would refer you to the transcript of his examination on discovery in April of 1996. This transcript is public."

"Yeah, I've read it."

"And he was under oath. And he said there everything I guess that one can say about his relationship with Karlheinz Schreiber." Recalling the cup of coffee after he left office, Lavoie added, "And he said he met him once after he left his job as prime minister, here in Montreal at the Queen Elizabeth Hotel."

Finally, I had my chance to ask about that coffee.

"Why would he even meet him once? What was the occasion?"

"You mean at the Queen Elizabeth?"

"Yeah."

"Oh, the guy was in town, called Mulroney and said, 'I would like to meet you because you know I am still pushing the [Bear Head] project that you guys rejected. And I am pushing it with the Liberals and I would like to know what you think about it, because I think I am changing locations and I want to make the project happen now in Quebec.' So Mulroney thought it was a funny thing and he said he went and had a coffee with him. That is it."

Mulroney thought it was a funny thing to go have a coffee with Schreiber? That was the reason they met?

Lavoie told me the story about the one and only time he spoke to Karlheinz Schreiber.

"It was in the spring of 1996. I was sitting in my office; it was then in Ottawa. And the phone rang, out of the blue, around six o'clock. And there was this man with a very thick accent, because he has got this very thick accent, which to me was hard to understand. I am French-Canadian. I guess I don't get English as well as anybody else who is anglophone. And then I said, 'Who is speaking?' It was clearly a long-distance call.[4] And he says, 'Karlheinz Schreiber here.' He sounded to me like he was drunk but I can't prove that. And he was just laughing and saying, 'I read all about you, and people send me clippings and you are always quoted in there and I wanted to tell you that you are doing one heck of a job' and so on and so forth. And so I jumped on the occasion and I said, 'Where do you think this is heading, sir?' He said, 'This [the Airbus investigation] is all a hoax, this is all a joke. In due time people will find out that this was all a hoax and a joke,' and so on and so forth. And that is the extent of what I got from him. I spoke to the guy once in my life; that is all I know."

I reminded Lavoie that Schreiber had once claimed that he wasn't even involved in the Airbus deal. Lavoie told me he had asked Schreiber the same question. "I asked him specifically. I asked him specifically if he had anything to do with the Airbus thing. He says, 'No, no.' But I mean, talking to a drunk guy who is sort of laughing on the phone . . . And he was telling me he was having a glass of champagne while he was speaking to me. That's all I know of him. Now, I mean, on the other hand the guy has never done any harm to me. I have no problem with him personally."

Lavoie added that he had spoken with Norman Spector, Mulroney's former chief of staff, about Schreiber. "'Norman' I said, 'Did you meet him?' He says, 'Yeah, I did twice.' I said, 'How was he?' He says, 'Well, he thought bureaucrats were all a bunch of assholes.' And he says, 'He was very pushy for his project.' And then he ended . . . I remember the word . . . he says, 'He was your typical hustler.' That's all he told me."

I returned to Lavoie's earlier suggestion that Schreiber may have been a liar and that he may have claimed he had paid people, like Mulroney, when in fact he did not.

Lavoie took the argument a step further, even suggesting that Giorgio Pelossi, the man who for years had been vilified by the Mulroney team, may have been telling the truth after all. Lavoie reasoned that if Schreiber was lying now about giving money to Mulroney, then maybe he had lied to his accountant as well, telling Pelossi that some of the Airbus money was for Mulroney when really it wasn't.

---

4 I assumed this was a reference to a not-so-clear phone connection.

"Why is it that Pelossi was saying what he was saying?" Lavoie asked me. "I don't know this Pelossi guy. Even if I knew him it wouldn't change my mind, he probably didn't make up the entire thing he said. He probably, he might, I shouldn't say he probably didn't make up. He might have not made it up. He may have heard that. Right?"

Lavoie's theory made sense, in a way. If Schreiber had lied in his bank records about giving money to Mulroney, then he could have just as easily lied to Pelossi about giving money to Mulroney. It was, however, a dramatic shift away from their earlier spin that Pelossi made up allegations against Schreiber and Mulroney in order to embarrass his old boss, with whom he was engaged in a bitter struggle. In one fell swoop, Pelossi had gone from a discredited accountant with Mafia ties, to someone who maybe was telling the truth all along about what he was told. At least, this was the new theory about Pelossi, as proposed by Luc Lavoie.

Lavoie explained. "So if one is to assume that [Pelossi] may have heard that, and believe me, we haven't spoken to Pelossi . . . then what the hell is this about? And the only thing one can think of is, it could be somebody that was trying to convince somebody else that he needed money for a third party which might have been a head of state or a government, therefore getting more money for himself. It could be that. We don't know that. And I want to be very careful here. We do not know that. But if ever there is the name of Brian Mulroney anywhere [in Schreiber's accounts] it has to be that. Because there never was any money. And to think otherwise is really to not know Mulroney."

Lavoie hammered home the point.

"He is too smart to do something like that. It is just too dummy. It is too damn stupid. He wouldn't do that."

Lavoie and I were getting along so well now that neither of us seemed to want to get off the phone. We talked more about the Bear Head project. Lavoie reminded me that Mulroney had said he killed the project, and yet still met with Schreiber afterwards because Schreiber didn't take no for an answer. Schreiber was close to Liberals like Marc Lalonde and Allan MacEachen, he said. As for the Airbus allegations: they were just that, allegations. Lavoie never saw Frank Moores or Gary Ouellet in the PMO in all his years working for Mulroney. As for the possible falling-out between

Frank Moores and Mulroney, Lavoie said that the fact that Moores was at Harrington Lake for New Year's Eve eight months after the falling-out was alleged to have happened was not all that important. They could have been in the same room, Lavoie suggested, and yet not talked to each other.

I remembered to ask about Mulroney's relationship with Gary Ouellet, without telling Lavoie about our discovery that he too had a bank account in Zurich.

"I think they have known each other from days at Laval University," he said. "I first met him [Ouellet] when I was still a journalist and he was a chief of staff to Benoît Bouchard, when Bouchard was a junior minister. I don't know how long he was in there, no more than a year, probably less, in the early days of the government. Bouchard was a very junior minister. And I met this guy who was quite a pleasant guy actually, quite a funny guy. Then I knew that he was a lobbyist in Ottawa with the group, whatever it was called, GCI or something like that. And frankly that is about it. What the relationship was with Mulroney, certainly it was a friendly one, going back years. But that is about it."

As the conversation was winding down we turned to a discussion about my objectives. I tried to tell Lavoie why I thought the story was so important to Canadians: "The Canadian public deserves to know the answer to that question."

"The answer to what question?" Lavoie said.

"Where did the Airbus commission money go? Where did it go? And there is one person who has the answer. And that is Karlheinz Schreiber."

"Karlheinz Schreiber?" Lavoie responded.

"Yeah. He's got the answer."

"He's not giving it?" Lavoie asked.

He's not giving it? I did not fully appreciate until later that Lavoie must have thought we were already speaking to Schreiber. He must have immediately regretted ever having made the "fucking liar" comment. If Schreiber hadn't been speaking to us, calling the middleman a "fucking liar" might have backfired.

"I want to find out where the money went, wherever it went," I repeated.

"Yeah, but it didn't go to Mulroney."

"You say that, and I've heard you say it."

"He said it himself, under oath."

"Right."

"So it would be major perjury, right?"

Kit Melamed had been busy poring over the bank records. According to her calculations, the total cash withdrawals from Schreiber's Canadian accounts alone amounted to $1.1 million. There was $236,000 in various cash withdrawals out of the Marc account, and more than $400,000 out of the Frankfurt account. The DM account saw a total of 3 million in cash withdrawn, and of course there was the $300,000 out of the Britan account. And none of the above included any non-cash transfers to other bank accounts. Those transfers also climbed into the millions of dollars. But it seemed the Germans were right. Indeed it *was* a real cash orgy.

Four days had passed since Lavoie and I had talked and I had yet to hear back about the next steps. I called him at the number he'd given me to reach him in South America. The urgency seemed to have left his voice. "I am just touching base from our calls on the weekend and am wondering whether you have any thoughts from your end," I said.

"Not really. Not really. What about you?"

I told Lavoie that we did think it was important that we give Mulroney the information about the account.

"You are talking about the same information you had when you spoke on Saturday, right?" Lavoie wanted to know if I would be showing the documents to Mulroney, or bringing a photocopy.

"Not a photocopy of it, we will be bringing our notes, notes we have compiled in the course of putting together the evidence that we have come across. But I don't think we will be bringing a copy of a bank record."

"Why not? Why not?" Lavoie said. "Why not, why not, we are talking about really serious stuff here."

"I can put some thought into it. I am not saying no. I just thought we would bring the information. But you are saying you want to see the documents? The actual documents?"

"Yeah."

"I think we could probably do that," I said.

"Can I know," Lavoie asked, "if you have documents? You do have documents?"

"We have some documents."

"You should go very—you have some documents in there?"

"We have some documents, yes."

"Yeah, it is not just people talking or whatever."

"No. Not at all."

"And you are still going for next Wednesday?" he said.

"Yeah, the twentieth." I wasn't sure why he needed the date confirmed. Then I blundered. I told Lavoie I simply wanted Mulroney's perspective.

Lavoie exploded. "His persp— I mean, Harvey, let's be clear about one thing. His perspective is pretty fucking clear. He never received a penny connected with any of this stuff. So I mean there is not much of a perspective that he can put onto this, except to go, 'What the fuck is this?' That's essentially it." I got the point. "It is a fucking good perspective because he said it under oath. And the former prime minister of a country like Canada doesn't go under oath to say something like this, and lie about it. You don't lie about this stuff. And to think otherwise is pretty close to being insulting . . . I mean, the guy goes under oath in front of the whole world to see and he says, 'I have got fuck all to do with this' . . . That is the only perspective you'll ever get. I mean, there is no other way of looking at it. It is not like, 'Oh, let me analyze this.' There is no analysis. It is really fucking clear. There is no possible analysis. Who the hell has used his name? . . . Don't forget one thing: Under oath, in front of the whole world to see, a former prime minister of Canada said that he had nothing to do with this transaction. And he received nothing . . . I mean, how is it that the former prime minister of Canada says under oath, 'I have got nothing to do with this,' and all of the other people who were involved with this transaction say, 'He certainly did not intervene with anything.' How come it is that you cannot come yourself to the conclusion that if his name was anywhere, it was being used by somebody else. It should be a natural conclusion. That is my point. Why would you think otherwise? Why," he asked, "would you think he is a crook?"

CHAPTER TWENTY-FIVE
FUCKING LIAR

In the week leading up to our broadcast on Wednesday, October 20, it seemed as if the entire *fifth estate* staff was on the story. Sheila Pin, who had worked with me the year before, flew to Puerto Vallarta to interview Brock Squire about Stuart Iddles. Linden MacIntyre had flown to Germany to meet up with John Goetz, where they interviewed the German journalist Hans Leyendecker, then filmed MacIntyre explaining parts of the story as he spoke on-camera in front of various locations in Switzerland and Germany. Production manager Alex Powell was lining up freelance cameramen from Mexico to Alberta to Germany. Kit Melamed continued full-time on the story and associate producers Howard Goldenthal, Declan Hill and Anita Mielewczyk were helping out wherever needed. Editor Gary Akenhead was sitting in a dark edit suite with me, putting all the pictures and interviews together, working quickly and brilliantly, in order to get to air on time. Susan Teskey and David Studer were providing editorial advice as the pieces of the documentary puzzle began to fall into place.

On October 16, the Saturday before our Wednesday-evening broadcast, I had another call from Luc Lavoie, who was still in South America. Mulroney had changed his mind, he said. He didn't want to see our bank documents after all. Lavoie told me that if we went to air with the information we had we would have to "live with the consequences." Something had happened to change Mulroney's mind. We wouldn't know the whole story for several years, but we were about to get part of the answer very soon.

Kit was doing her best to get an interview with Karlheinz Schreiber. But Eddie Greenspan, Schreiber's lawyer, was giving us a rough ride. Greenspan was insisting that we interview him, not his client, but we declined the offer. For two reasons. First, we wanted an unrehearsed response from Schreiber about the contents of his bank documents. Second, we already had an interview with one of Schreiber's lawyers, Erich Samson, in Germany. We didn't need yet another lawyer speaking on his behalf.

We told Greenspan that Schreiber had already done interviews for German newspapers and was therefore quite capable of talking to us as well. Greenspan countered that "no other media" has been as adverse to Schreiber in the past as *the fifth estate*. On Monday, October 18, just two days before our broadcast, Greenspan fired off a letter to Kit Melamed and me. He reminded us that Schreiber was suing *the fifth estate* for $35 million and demanded again that he be interviewed, this time stating the interviewer had to be Harvey Cashore[1] and not Linden MacIntyre. We refused. Greenspan had no right to dictate who would be doing the interviewing; besides, we only wanted to speak with Schreiber. Greenspan and CBC lawyer Dan Henry fell into a spirited exchange of letters that day, but Henry stuck to his guns.

What Greenspan did not know was that we already had teams in place closely watching Schreiber's apartment. If Schreiber was not going to agree to an interview, then we would find him on the streets of Yorkville and speak to him anyway. Four years earlier we had jumped him outside his home in Kaufering, now we were hoping to jump him at his home in Toronto. Declan Hill and Howard Goldenthal were pulled off other stories to monitor the front entrance and back exit to Schreiber's upscale apartment. On Monday, October 18, Hill showed up at 6 a.m. and did not leave his post until just before midnight. To no avail. Tuesday morning Hill and Goldenthal were back at their posts, joined by cameraman Mike Wasilewski and soundman Larry Kent. In those days *the fifth estate* had only three cellphones to share among the staff. If Schreiber was spotted,

---

1   I still have no idea why Greenspan wanted me to be the one to interview Schreiber.

Hill or Goldenthal were to call me and Linden MacIntyre, who would then get in a cab and rush right over.

On Tuesday morning, I was with Gary Akenhead in the dark edit suite. Linden MacIntyre was in another part of the CBC building filming what we call "studio."

Howard Goldenthal was on his stakeout when out of nowhere comedian Jackie Mason appeared and asked for directions to "the expensive shops." Goldenthal pointed him in the direction of Holt Renfrew, just down the street. "Thanks!" Mason replied.

Then Declan Hill got himself into a bit of a pickle.

He had no idea that as he watched for Schreiber to emerge from his luxury apartment, he himself was being watched—by the security team at the jewelry store underneath Schreiber's building. He had been hanging around the location for so long that the owners thought he was casing the joint. There had been a rash of jewelry-store thefts and the owner panicked, calling two police officers, who rushed to the scene. How do you explain to a police officer that you are not about to rob a jewelry store but actually waiting to "jump" Karlheinz Schreiber? Somehow Hill managed to do it. As it turned out, he got himself out of that bind just in time. His cellphone rang.

It was Mike Wasilewski. "Schreiber's on the move."

Declan thanked the police officers, excused himself and ran up an alley hoping to spot Schreiber. Larry Kent and Mike Wasilewski, meanwhile, were already following him down the street. That's when they called Linden MacIntyre.

"We're on his tail now," Wasilewski said.

MacIntyre and I raced to the fourth floor to tell the bosses that the jump was happening.

"You can't do it yet," senior producer Susan Teskey replied.

MacIntyre and I had not understood that the CBC News management team had decided to give Schreiber until 5 p.m. that day to agree to an interview. They wanted to bend over backwards to be fair to Schreiber. We complained that we had bent over backwards since early September to be fair to Schreiber.

"What if he's going to the airport?" MacIntyre said.

We worried Schreiber might have figured out what we were doing and was headed to the airport for a flight to Ottawa, the only other place he was allowed to travel under his strict bail conditions. We knew there was a 3 p.m. flight. Eventually we agreed we could jump him before five but only if he was going to the airport.

Mike Wasilewski—by now acting more like a race-car driver than a CBC cameraman—picked up MacIntyre at the Broadcasting Centre then sped to the airport. They looked in vain for any sign of Schreiber's car in the huge parking lots at Pearson International Airport. They may as well have been looking for a needle in a haystack. Their cellphone rang. It was associate producer Howard Goldenthal.

"Schreiber just went inside Eddie Greenspan's building."

On a hunch, Goldenthal had decided to head down King Street to Eddie Greenspan's offices. He was also in Yorkville when Schreiber was spotted, and hopped in a cab. When he got there he saw Schreiber's vehicle in the back parking lot of Greenspan's building. Goldenthal sat across the street in an Indian restaurant that had a clear view of the front entrance. Linda Guerriero, a new associate producer at *the fifth estate*, joined him so it wouldn't look like he was doing what he was doing—staring intently at the entrance to Greenspan's office.

Schreiber was still inside when MacIntyre and the camera crew pulled up. They waited until exactly 4:45 p.m., when the door opened and Schreiber reappeared on the street. MacIntyre, Kent and Wasilewski quietly tailed Schreiber as he drove through rush-hour traffic, up University Avenue, eventually making his way to an address on Lowther Avenue in the Annex district of Toronto.

I got MacIntyre's call in the edit suite. They were now waiting outside a house on Lowther. Luckily, there was enough distance between the door of the house and Schreiber's car that the camera crew would have plenty of time to approach him. I asked MacIntyre for the address. I did a reverse search on the Internet and came up with the name Michael Cochrane— presumably the same Michael Cochrane who (with Elmer MacKay) had been asked to put up half the bail for Schreiber and who was, at one time, a VP of finance at Air Canada.

MacIntyre, Kent and Wasilewski had been waiting for nearly two hours outside the house when the cellphone rang. It was Susan Teskey.

"The jump is off. Don't do it." Teskey told MacIntyre there was to be an emergency meeting scheduled in David Studer's office for eight that evening. I was still up in the edit suite with Gary Akenhead. *Shit*, I thought. *Now what?* Akenhead kept on editing while I went downstairs for the meeting.

Linden and I sat on Studer's couch, joined by Dan Henry. Kit Melamed sat in the chair next to the couch, and Susan sat in the chair next to David's table. We formed a kind of circle. A roomful of pissed-off journalists. We had worked hard to get in a position where we could confront Schreiber with questions about the Britan account, and now the rug had been pulled out from under us. We demanded to know what was going on.

Studer had something to tell us. "Mulroney has threatened to sue the entire board of directors of the CBC."

"Jesus," I whistled.

Mulroney's lawyer, Gérald Tremblay, had written a letter to the chair of the CBC, Guylaine Saucier.

We knew the implications. Because the CBC is a Crown corporation, we have strict measures in place to try to ensure that journalistic independence is protected. Senior executive management has no editorial control over the content of our stories; and frequently when complaints are directed to the president of the CBC—as Airbus had complained in 1995—the response generally is to forward the complaint to the programmers. By sending a threatening letter to the chair of the CBC, Mulroney and his lawyer probably knew it was landing on the desk of a government appointee.

What does the letter say? we asked.

We were handed photocopies, then sat in silence as we read.

Tremblay acknowledged my letter to Mulroney of October 8, 1999. He reminded Saucier that the CBC had nearly been sued along with the RCMP back when Mulroney had been named in the Letter of Request to the Swiss authorities in 1995. "Because of the dubious role played by *the fifth estate* and its agents in the promotion and eventual promulgation of the suspicions against Mulroney, we strongly recommended your inclusion as defendants in the above mentioned libel action. This recommendation was vetoed by our client because of his disinclination to include members of the media in this matter at that time."

According to Tremblay, his client had no account in Switzerland, and he had not been involved in either the Airbus or MBB helicopter deals and that "the above mentioned information is indisputably true and has never been challenged. Any attempt by the CBC to state or suggest or imply anything to the contrary would be false and libellous. In that event, legal action against you, your directors, officers and agents would be immediate."

In other words, they were threatening to sue individuals, not just the corporation.

> There is a responsibility on you to ensure your producers and journalists act in a fair-minded and balanced manner. There is also a responsibility upon you and the leadership of the CBC to ensure that your agents and/or representatives are not participating in a vendetta against Mr. Mulroney and his family. Any evidence of such malice will result in a lawsuit seeking a condemnation for exemplary and punitive damages. . . . Please govern yourselves accordingly[2]

MacIntyre was incredulous. "But what's this got to do with jumping Schreiber?"

We all began to talk at once, voices getting louder.

The letter from Mulroney was just the tip of the iceberg, explained Studer. The heated exchange of letters between Eddie Greenspan and Dan Henry about interviewing Schreiber had escalated. Senior managers from CBC News had become involved. Apparently insufficiently aware that *the fifth estate* had been trying for weeks to arrange for an interview with Schreiber, they hit the panic button when they heard we were sitting outside a house in the Annex *about to jump Schreiber*. Concerned about offending Greenspan, they suggested we stop the jump, for now. In

---

2 That story has a happy ending. It turned out that McCarthy Tétrault was representing the CBC on several important files. Tremblay should have checked before he sent the letter to see if there was a potential conflict. CBC lawyers noted that *their* law firm had sent *them* a letter threatening to sue for libel. The CBC wrote Mulroney a letter directly telling him that it would not be responding to the letter from McCarthy Tétrault and that he should get a new lawyer.

the middle of the meeting we were joined by senior manager Sig Gerber, my boss's boss, always a proud defender of the CBC's investigative journalism.

By the end of the meeting everyone's nerves were frayed. To date, the Airbus story had dragged in its wake a depressingly rich number of lawsuits and no one—me included—wanted another. But it had been—*was*— a hugely important story. Tempers flared. Then cooled. Eventually we all realized what was at stake. By meeting's end everyone agreed it had been a mistake to cancel the jump. There were apologies all around the room. The managers were sorry; the journalists were sorry for overreacting. We would try again tomorrow.

That, however, was a problem. We were going to air next day. How did we know we would even get another chance for a jump? I left the meeting and returned to the edit suite. Then I called home to tell my wife I would not be coming home that night. Her silence said enough. Again, I told myself there was no choice. We had to work around the clock in order to finish the documentary. Alex Powell would stay overnight as well, working to organize the camera crew, the jumps and other logistics. At about 3 a.m. I got CBC security to let me into Studer's office, where I could sleep on the same couch where we had all had the heated discussion. I slept for three hours, then went back to the edit suite where Akenhead was still working. We counted down the time we had left. In order to make it to the Maritimes, the documentary had to be finished at 8 p.m. that night. We had only fourteen hours left before we aired our first Airbus story in four years.

A few hours after my catnap, I noticed everyone began arriving at the office for the beginning of the workday. Pulling an all-nighter is a strange experience. You see everyone else come to the office fresh and raring to go. But for you, nothing really has happened to separate one day from another. You still feel like it's the day before, though you have a knot in your stomach from the lack of sleep.

At around 9 a.m. Studer called me to the edit suite.

"Can you come to my office?" When I got there, he explained that after getting off the subway at Union Station he had picked up a copy of the *National Post*. "Take a look at page three," he said, tossing me the paper.

I read the headline: "Mulroney lawyers vow to sue CBC if program defamatory: Today's 'fifth estate' to focus on Airbus affair."

"The program," wrote reporter Phil Mathias, "is expected to report that the word Britan appears in banking documents belonging to Mr. Schreiber, the man at the centre of the Airbus affair. Britan is allegedly close to the word Brian. That similarity allegedly suggests a connection between the two men, *the fifth estate* is expected to imply."

Mathias took us to task for "allegedly" suggesting there was a connection between Brian and Britan: "Others have pointed out that Britan is also similar to the name of a country, Britain, and a region of France, Brittany. It is also close to the name of the Britta [*sic*] water filter and other commercial products. Robert Hladun, Mr. Schreiber's Edmonton-based lawyer, said jokingly that Britan may be a reference to Britney Spears, one of the music stars most admired by the 65-year-old Mr. Schreiber."

Bells went off in my head. In my conversation with Luc Lavoie over the Thanksgiving weekend, I *never told him* the actual name of the coded account. I only said it was *close to* Mulroney's name. So how could Mathias have known to call it the *Britan* account? Who told him?

Schreiber, Mathias wrote, was suing *the fifth estate* for $35 million. Attorney Robert Hladun suggested our newest program might increase the claim for damages, since we could be bringing into the picture evidence of "malice."

The article went on: "Both [Schreiber] and Mr. Mulroney have denied that any money has ever passed between them. However, the so-called Airbus affair has generated a series of allegations against Mr. Mulroney, each one followed by revelations that prove the allegation to be false." Schreiber's bank accounts were "leaked to the media" by "German authorities," the article stated. I looked up when I finished reading it.

"Turn to the editorial page," Studer told me.

The lead editorial in the *National Post* that day was titled "Gone Fishing."

CBC's flagship, *the fifth estate*, plans to air a program tonight that raises questions about former prime minister Brian Mulroney's conduct during the so-called "Airbus affair." Tonight's program is expected to break the tittilating news that the word "Britan" shows up in banking documents belonging to Karlheinz Schreiber, who was arrested recently in Toronto for alleged tax evasion in Germany. Sources will suggest that "Britan" is code for "Brian." Such sensationalism comes 10 years after the RCMP opened its first investigation into the claim—eventually disproved—that bribes were paid by Airbus Industrie SA to secure a $1.8-billion Air Canada contract. It comes six years after a second investigation into the matter was launched in 1993. And it arrives five years after a Justice Department official asked the Swiss government for evidence against Mr. Mulroney on the ridiculous grounds that he was "a criminal" engaged in corrupt activities during his tenure in office—until the Liberals were forced in 1997 to pay $2-million in compensation and to concede grudgingly that "any conclusions of wrong-doing by the former prime minister were—and are—unjustified." It is a testimony to Mr. Mulroney's tolerance that he has not, until now, sued any media outlets for persistently reporting on this affair. That may now change. His lawyers warn that any suggestion of malice in the fifth estate documentary will result in a lawsuit. This is reasonable enough; for the relentless investigation of Mr. Mulroney is itself a scandal, and a growing one. . . . If they continue much longer, somebody's bound to get caught. Will it be one of Mr. Mulroney's accusors?

"What do you think?" Studer asked.

"Well, they certainly broke the agreement," I said. I was, of course, referring to Lavoie's solemn commitment, repeated many times, that neither he nor Mulroney would talk about the information I had given him over the phone. Studer felt exactly the same way.

"What do we do about it?"

I had an idea. It was unorthodox, and something I had never done before in my career, but I felt we had to consider it. "David, I taped all those conversations with Lavoie." He knew what I was getting at.

Because Mulroney and Lavoie had broken their agreement, we considered the possibility that we were now entitled to use Luc Lavoie's off-the-record quotes. And because Lavoie had offered a perspective in his conversation with me that was not mentioned in the Phil Mathias article, we wondered whether the public should hear that perspective too.

I went back to my office and found the relevant section on the tape of my conversation with Lavoie:

We believe, but we don't want this to be spread around in any way, shape or form, that Karlheinz Schreiber is the biggest fucking liar the world has ever seen. That is what we believe.

We had to think carefully about the implications of broadcasting that clip. Normally I tape conversations only for accuracy. When I taped Lavoie, I had not the slightest interest in using it for broadcast. I just wanted to make sure my notes were accurate.

But the *National Post* article and the accompanying editorial changed everything.

David called a meeting with Linden, Dan and me. I had taped all my conversations with Lavoie, I explained. At one point in the tape, I said, Lavoie had called Schreiber a "fucking liar." We needed to know the legality of broadcasting an audiotape made without someone's knowledge. According to Dan, we would be allowed to do so.

Okay, that was hurdle number one. Hurdle number two was more complicated. We needed to confront the ethics of broadcasting the clip. What was the right thing to do?

For part of this discussion we brought in Bobby Culbert, the head of all of CBC News, and Sig Gerber, the head of Current Affairs. We showed them the *National Post* article, told them about the prior agreement between Lavoie and me and our belief that he—and by extension the Mulroney camp—had broken, and our discussion to broadcast the incriminating clip. It was our call, they said, but CBC News management would support our decision, whatever it was.

After the brass left, it was only Linden MacIntyre, David Studer, Dan Henry and me left in the room. Given the pending litigation and the *threats* of litigation, it would have been so easy for Henry to advise against it. He decided to approve. In fact, if the decision backfired, we could all be in big trouble. Still, the person with the most to lose, by far, was executive producer David Studer. All decision-making at the program began and ended with him. He was the one who'd given the green light to broadcast the story in the first place. He had a difficult call to make, and not much time to do it. In many ways, it was easy for the rest of us to say yes, since we knew that ultimately the responsibility ended with him.

"Let's do it," he said.

I raced back to the edit suite. Kit was assigned the job of transferring the clip from my audiotape to beta tape. She tracked down a still picture of Lavoie and built a ten-second insert towards the end of the documentary.

The phone rang. It was Declan Hill.

"I'm in a taxi following Schreiber. We're going down Avenue Road."

"He must be going to Eddie's office!"

I called Linden.

"Get to Eddie Greenspan's office as fast as possible."

Later I pieced together what happened. Hill and Howard Goldenthal had been in Yorkville since the early morning. Howard was covering the front entrance of Schreiber's building, and Hill the back. Mike Wasilewski and Larry Kent were close by near a parking lot. It was at that point that Hill spotted Schreiber's car driving away. Not wanting to lose sight of Schreiber, he flagged down a taxi.

"I've wanted to say this my whole life," Hill told the taxi driver. "Follow that car!" And it seemed the taxi driver had wanted to hear that his whole life, too. He sped away in hot pursuit of Schreiber.

In the meantime, Hill called Wasilewski to tell him to make his way to 144 King Street as soon as possible. That meant that four cars from different directions were speeding to Eddie Greenspan's office.

The timing was perfect: Schreiber pulled into a small parking lot adjacent to Greenspan's law offices. Wasilewski pulled up seconds later and parked illegally on the street directly in front of Schreiber's car. Hill's taxi arrived seconds later. And just as Mike Wasilewski and Larry Kent jumped from the van to roll film of Schreiber, Linden MacIntyre roared up in his taxi a split second later. When Schreiber got out of his car, he saw Hill, the camera crew and MacIntyre, all converging at almost exactly the same moment.

"Have you anything at all to say about the Britan account?" MacIntyre asked Schreiber as they walked briskly along the street towards Greenspan's office. "Anything at all to say about the Britan account, Mr. Schreiber? Can you tell us why you had code-named accounts naming Canadians, Mr. Schreiber?"

Schreiber pointed a finger at his head and waved it in a circle, as if to suggest MacIntyre was crazy.

"You don't want to speak to us?" MacIntyre asked as Schreiber ducked into a doorway and disappeared into the building.

The rest of the day was a blur. Gary Akenhead went home to sleep while the edit was transferred to what was called the "heavy suite," where the last-minute touches get made to the documentary.

In this case we had more than a few final changes. We still had to film two more pieces to camera, and we had to insert the Lavoie clip and the jump of Schreiber. Editorial assistant Virginia Smart spent the day updating the script, in time for us to issue a press release to our colleagues in the media about the latest revelations.

Linden MacIntyre and I grabbed a sandwich on the run, and then went with the camera team to film outside the courthouse. MacIntyre read his "stand-up" as he looked into the camera.

But who is Britan supposed to represent? If Schreiber followed his previous pattern for code names, adding or subtracting consonants, Canadians could be forgiven for thinking it might yield the name Brian. The only Brian who has been publicly associated with the Airbus affair is the former prime minister. Whoever Schreiber had in mind, we have no evidence that Mulroney ever knew that Schreiber set up a bank account with a code name similar to Brian. He [Mulroney] will not talk to us, but he has stated under oath that he never had a Swiss bank account, nor was one ever set up on his behalf. We also have no evidence that Mulroney received a single penny of any of those Airbus or Thyssen commissions.

We got back in the van and drove to Yorkville, where we positioned our cameras on Cumberland Street, just outside Schreiber's apartment. We filmed MacIntyre explaining how Schreiber had ended up living here.

"Karlheinz Schreiber and his wife Barbara[3] eventually settled into a posh Yorkville hotel in Toronto as Mr. and Mrs. Herman. In effect, he'd become a fugitive from German justice, suspected of having evaded taxes on several business deals, including the Air Canada / Airbus commissions. He's hired lawyers to fight the allegations and he now claims that, while he did

---

3 Schreiber's wife's formal name is Barbara; we would come to learn Schreiber always called her Bärbel.

receive the money, he gave much of it away to others, which means he wouldn't have to pay taxes on it."

I brought the tapes with the stand-ups back to the heavy edit suite to be inserted into the documentary.

Time was rapidly ticking away. A team of people had assembled in the large dark room on the seventh floor, filled with dozens of TV monitors and edit machines. Brigitte Thompson, the associate director, was there making sure that our times were all accurate, that we had the proper English subtitles over the German interviews, and that all the commercial breaks were in the right place. She sat in the middle of the room, her back towards us, looking very much like the pilot of an aircraft.

Finally, with barely ten minutes left before we had to feed the documentary to the Maritimes, we were ready. We could hardly believe it.

"That was a little too close," Thompson said to me by way of colossal understatement.

Suddenly Susan Teskey noticed something about the jump of Schreiber. On the raw tape, he was filmed going all the way into the building, with the door closing firmly behind him. But on the edited version, the door hadn't yet closed before we cut to another scene. It wasn't perfect but we could live with it. Teskey could not. She was a perfectionist.

"Make the door close," she told the editor.

"But we only have eight minutes left."

"You can do it."

The editor began a complicated process of laying down the tape again, timing backwards from the end. But as time started ticking down, the editor froze. Literally. I didn't realize what was happening. The editor was not moving. He had panicked.

"We're going to go to black."

"Get Lorne," Brigitte said.

Lorne Mullins was a veteran editor who had been through many high-stress situations. He arrived a few minutes later and figured out what to do. I remember his hands spinning back and forth as he worked several edit machines at once. He made the changes with seconds to spare.

Everyone breathed a sigh of relief. We had made it to the Maritimes.

Howard Goldenthal had a condo on Church Street in Toronto and we all piled into cabs to watch the show at 9 p.m.

Linden MacIntyre handed me a glass of Scotch. We talked about the decision to air the Lavoie clip. He told me what Conn Smythe, the legendary owner of the Toronto Maple Leafs, had once said: "If you can't beat them in the alley, you can't beat them on the ice." We fought this one in the gutters, MacIntyre told me. "Sometimes you have to do that."

I appreciated his words of wisdom. But as I watched the documentary—presumably along with hundreds of thousands of other Canadians—I felt a tinge of regret. Had we done the right thing? I prided myself on sticking to my word, even in the toughest situations. Now I had broadcast an off-the-record quote; a breach of promise justified solely because the other party had broken their promise first. Wasn't that like a child in a schoolyard fight insisting "he hit me first"? Yet I knew that if we had not broadcast the clip, the bully would have won. I managed to convince myself all over again that we had done the right thing.

Besides, there was no turning back now.

At about the twenty-five-minute mark of the documentary, Canadians saw a picture of Luc Lavoie, and heard the audio recording that would forever change the direction of the story.

"Karlheinz Schreiber is the biggest fucking liar the world has ever seen. That's what we believe."

I felt like I had taken off my Boy Scout uniform.

CHAPTER TWENTY-SIX
RETURN OF THE MOUNTIES

I thought this time was going to be different.

The *National Post* aside, I believed that our Britan-account story would force our parliamentary institutions, the justice system and the media to deal with the reality that the old Airbus story now required some new answers to some pretty important questions.

I believed the Britan-account revelations would lead to tough questions in the House of Commons, and demands that Mulroney answer specific questions about whether or not he had received that cash from Karlheinz Schreiber. Maybe someone would demand an inquiry. I tried to imagine the repercussions for a U.S. president linked to a similar scandal.

In fact, virtually nothing happened. There was no meaningful response from Parliament or the justice system. Even the media seemed unmoved.

True, nearly every paper in the country picked up the CP wire story the next day, which stated that *the fifth estate* had reported that a coded bank account called "Britan" had been the repository of Airbus commissions. But in almost all cases the stories played inside the paper with little of their own original reporting. The *Globe and Mail* simply republished the CP story on page six, the *Vancouver Sun* on page seven. The Montreal *Gazette*'s story, on page fourteen, was the best of all of them, going into much more detail

317

about what was in our broadcast. But that was about it. Few reporters were assigned to follow up or probe more deeply. The Parliamentary Press Gallery was virtually silent. No one seemed to want to touch the story.[1] The only paper to follow up in any substantial way was the *National Post*.

"The program broadcast on Wednesday on *the fifth estate* about Karlheinz Schreiber and the Airbus affair has raised allegations that the CBC acted unethically," wrote reporter Phil Mathias. "Luc Lavoie, a spokesman for Brian Mulroney, the former prime minister, says a remark he made about Mr. Schreiber being 'the biggest fucking liar the world has ever seen,' was taken out of context, and caused him intense embarrassment. 'I have never heard Mr. Mulroney describe Mr. Schreiber that way,' he told the *National Post*.

"Mr. Lavoie made that remark, he says, after being assured the conversation was off the record. It was an angry reply, he said, to the suggestion that Mr. Schreiber had bragged to other people about money going to Mr. Mulroney. The context was removed before the remark was broadcast, Mr. Lavoie complained." Mathias quoted Eddie Greenspan stating that we had not allowed Schreiber the right to reply: "Their conduct is outrageous," said Greenspan. "Had I come on and had I given answers . . . [on Mr. Schreiber's behalf] that show would have been a non-story."

Greenspan criticized us for how we dealt with the Britan-account revelation. "If you had an account that said McIntyre, there's a 'c' in it so you could say Schreiber paid something to the president of Canadian Tire. That's the game of Scrabble they get into. In my view the fifth estate is out of control," Greenspan said. "I may pursue this by means of a lawsuit." The story ended with the suggestion that Schreiber might also sue the German authorities for releasing his bank records to *the fifth estate*. The

---

1 One of the few columnists to go against the grain was Stephen Kimber, a professor of journalism at King's College in Halifax. He would write several columns for the *Halifax Daily News* including the following observation in January 2000: "Karlheinz says the Germans have got it all wrong. He says he came to Canada because he likes it here. And of course there's nothing to those scurrilous allegations. But no, he doesn't want to go back to Germany right now to set them straight. Sounds reasonable to me. After all, if Karlheinz's word is good enough for the editorial writers at both the *Globe and Mail* and the *National Post*, it sure as hell should be good enough for thee and me."

National Post had once criticized the CBC for speculating who leaked the Letter of Request. Now, without any evidence to back up its claim, the newspaper was doing its own speculating about who leaked us the bank documents.

As fate would have it, Phil Mathias and I would meet only a few days later at Schreiber's extradition hearing, which began on Monday, October 25.

When I walked into the courtroom that morning, Mathias was sitting in the front row next to Stan Oziewicz from the *Globe and Mail*. I sat down in the middle directly behind Karlheinz Schreiber, who was sitting two rows ahead. He wore a navy blue sports coat with gold buttons, dark grey slacks and a red tie with white polka dots. The ubiquitous Louis Vuitton bag was at his side. Even though we were both looking in the same direction, I realized we could see each other in the reflection of a pane of security glass separating the public gallery from the lawyers. I looked at him, he looked me; he promptly stood up and switched seats.

The legal arguments quickly escalated to such arcane complexity that I wondered what I had done wrong to deserve such torture. During a coffee break, I was standing in the hall when I noticed Mathias approaching Schreiber.

"How are you?" I heard him ask Schreiber.

"You should go to Augsburg to have a press conference with Pelossi," Schreiber joked.

Oziewicz wandered by, shook my hand; Mathias shook my hand, too It was very awkward.

"Thanks for the publicity," I kidded him, hoping some humour might break the ice. "I appreciate it."

Mathias didn't seem amused. "It wasn't me. Greenspan called me. He's obviously a fan of yours." A short time later—on the way back into the courtroom—Mathias stopped me. He seemed angry. "I hope Dan Henry thought your story was fair," he snapped. He stared daggers at me.

"Are you all right?" I asked.

He walked away.

By early November, John Goetz was back in Toronto to cover the Schreiber story for German television. He stopped by my office to discuss the latest developments.

The phone rang. I could tell from call display that it was Luc Lavoie.

"Answer it," Goetz suggested.

Lavoie was in a surly mood. He left no doubt that he felt betrayed by the broadcast of the "fucking liar" clip. He vehemently denied that either he or Mulroney had broken their end of the agreement. "I have a piece of information for you. Mulroney never spoke to Phil Mathias in his life. Not once. Not once. Never spoke to him. Ever."

"What about you?" I asked.

"I never spoke to any other *media*. I never did." Lavoie insisted that when Mathias called him about the story, he mentioned nothing about his conversations with me. Still, I wondered if he had had a different understanding of our confidentiality agreement. He only said he hadn't spoken to other *media*. Did he speak to anyone else? I reminded him that he said they wouldn't talk to *anyone*.

"No, no. I never said anybody else," Lavoie protested. "I said I would never speak to any other *media*."

Lavoie was dead wrong. The audiotape proved it. He had specifically said he and Mulroney would not talk with reporters or "anybody else." Otherwise, indeed, it would have been an empty agreement. As it happened, Lavoie admitted that he *had* told Mulroney's lawyers about our conversation about the coded account, without holding *them* to our agreement.

"This I said to them [Mulroney's lawyers]," Lavoie said.

"You did? And did they undertake not to repeat that to anybody?" I asked.

"I didn't make that kind of agreement with them."

As far as I was concerned, that was a de facto admission Lavoie had broken our agreement. By not telling Mulroney's lawyers that they were bound by some understanding, it was easy to see how the confidential information I shared with Lavoie ended up in the *National Post*.

"Why did you decide to shaft me the way you did?" Luc asked.

I told Lavoie I had to get off the phone to go pick up my children from daycare. I wondered why he and Mulroney were so upset anyway. After all, wouldn't the explanation that Schreiber was a liar *help* their argument that Mulroney did not get the Britan-account money?

On November 12, 1999, lawyers at the federal Department of Justice signed an order called an Authority to Proceed, which officially confirmed Canada's intent to allow Germany to seek Schreiber's extradition. For an extradition to proceed, the federal government would have to agree that the charges in Germany were similar to possible charges Schreiber might have faced were the offences committed on Canadian soil. German Justice Department officials listed the corresponding Canadian laws that would apply to Schreiber. They were: income tax evasion; making false or deceptive statements in an income tax return; defrauding the government of income tax revenues; uttering forged documents; defrauding the government of Saudi Arabia; defrauding Thyssen Industrie AG; corruptly accepting a secret commission; giving to an official a loan, reward, advantage or benefit as consideration for co-operation, assistance or exercise of influence in connection with a matter of business relating to the government.

In Germany, meanwhile, the Schreiber affair had broken like a sudden storm across the front pages of the country's newspapers. Only recently had former German chancellor Helmut Kohl celebrated the tenth anniversary of the fall of the Berlin Wall, for which he could justifiably claim an important role. But a parliamentary committee had initiated a probe into how Walther Kiep, the former Kohl party treasurer, ended up in a restaurant in St. Margarethen, Switzerland, with Schreiber, with a briefcase that later would be revealed to contain 1 million DM.

"We suspect money was paid into accounts of the Christian Democratic Union party and not declared," chief prosecutor Reinhard Nemetz told the media. Kiep himself stated publicly that he did not keep the money himself, and that the party leadership was kept informed. Eventually Kohl admitted he *had* received cash payments on behalf of the CDU from anonymous donors, but refused to name any of them. Angela Merkel,[2] the general secretary of the CDU, wrote in an open letter in the *Frankfurter Allgemeine Zeitung* that Kohl should resign from the Bundestag and leave politics. "We have to take the future into our own hands," she insisted. The crisis in Germany continued for months and led to the creation of three separate parliamentary inquiries.

In mid-November, the *National Post* published a story that claimed Schreiber was launching a "landmark" $1 million lawsuit against the Canadian government for wrongful arrest, which had caused him "personal" injury and "mental" distress. "This is the first time the government of Canada has been sued over 'wrongful' extradition proceedings, according to Mr. Schreiber's lawyer Edward Greenspan." The paper quoted Greenspan: "We're going ahead full steam."

In fact, Greenspan would be launching *another* lawsuit—against Linden MacIntyre and me. On December 1, the CBC received a letter from Greenspan stating that our November broadcast had defamed Karlheinz Schreiber: "The use of edited and out of context words 'the biggest fucking liar this world has ever seen' are not only defamatory and malicious, but bring odium, contempt and ridicule upon the character and reputation of Karlheinz Schreiber." Unless we paid Schreiber $2 million in damages, wrote Greenspan, he would "commence legal proceedings against us."

We were now facing two lawsuits from Schreiber: the first a $35 million suit for the 1995 story we broadcast about Airbus; the second for $2 million alleging defamation because of the "fucking liar" quote. The CBC's legal department hired John Rosen, a well-known Toronto lawyer with a reputation for his strong courtroom performance. Rosen, in turn, brought on board civil litigator Robyn Ryan Bell at Bennett Jones.

Towards the end of December 1999, I had to begin preparing to defend the latest Schreiber lawsuit. We called it the "fucking liar" lawsuit, to

2   Angela Merkel became chancellor of Germany on November 22, 2005.

differentiate it from the *other* Schreiber lawsuit. Once again I had to go back into my files and print out and photocopy everything that was remotely relevant to the litigation. It was depressing, in a way, because it was both time consuming and counterproductive, as it took time away from my real job, to get documentaries on-air.

Goetz called to tell me he had met with Herbert Leiduck, a billionaire developer from Cologne who recalled a particular conversation he'd had with Schreiber on his yacht in the Mediterranean in 1993. "Schreiber said that he had the Canadians in his pocket, all of the Canadians from the government," Leiduck told Goetz. Leiduck also said that Schreiber bragged about being responsible for the Airbus deal with Air Canada. "Airbus wanted him because of his contacts to Canadian politicians," Leiduck said. Leiduck clarified that while Mulroney was the only Canadian politician Schreiber actually named, the middleman was never specific about who was in his "pocket." Leiduck told Goetz that he figured Schreiber was simply bragging, and did not make too much of the claims until he read about the controversy a couple of years later.

It was around this time that author Stevie Cameron suggested we write a book together—a biography of Karlheinz Schreiber. Her publisher, Macfarlane, Walter and Ross, had already committed to an Airbus book, and Cameron was suggesting we team up. Stevie had been a huge supporter of my work in the last four years, telling people that I was the reigning Airbus expert, and offering me kind words when the going got tough in the face of the attacks from Lavoie et al. When Phil Mathias published his unflattering review in the *National Post* of Cameron's 1998 book, *Blue Trust*, I called her and told her not to pay any attention to it. The Schreiber book seemed like a good idea. I would bring the previous *fifth estate* research to the project; she would bring hers. We had our work cut out for us. The publisher wanted the book to come out in the fall of 2000, which meant we had to have the manuscript finished by the summer. We had a vast amount of organizing, collating and writing left to do. For Cameron, it would be her full-time commitment. She would begin work on the manuscript early in the new year. I planned to work evenings and weekends.

When *the fifth estate* season ended I agreed to devote even more of my time to the book and get more involved in the writing.

Just before Christmas of 1999, I found myself in the gift shop down the escalators from the atrium in the Broadcast Centre. I stood staring at all the Christmas cards when I remembered the ones Luc Lavoie sent me in 1996 and 1997, still pinned to my bulletin board. Suddenly I had an urge to find the most expensive card in the shop. It was lined with gold trim and sprinkles. I paid more than $6 for that card, and then took it up to my office.

"Dear Luc," I wrote. "All the best in 2000, your pal, Harvey."

Then I put it in the mail.

CHAPTER TWENTY-SEVEN
THE PIERRE HOTEL

The story was taking a toll.

Somewhere along the line it began to define who I was. I would get a break on the story and be in a good mood for a week. There would be a setback and I would be in a funk. Sometimes I looked forward to a time when the story might finally be over; I wouldn't have to ride such highs and lows. This contrasted, however, with my determination to get to the bottom of the story, and to find out where the commission money went. Perhaps I would never get the answer. What then?

I kept on telling myself that next year would be different. Next year I could slow down. Next year I could finally relax.

As it turned out, next year was going to be different, but not in ways that I had hoped.

Early in 2000, colleagues Linda Guerriero, Victor Malarek and I found ourselves on the outskirts of Edmonton, in the home of Steve and Joan Kurylo. They had been friends of Schreiber back in his Alberta days, but we were there that day to interview Steve Kurylo about his experience in the Elk Velvet Antler business. I can trace back the ideas for a few of my non-Airbus stories to calls I made while on the Airbus file, and this was one of them. I had contacted Kurylo to talk about Schreiber at first, but then found myself learning all about Elk Velvet Antler pills. Turns out there are dozens of farms all over Alberta, where elk are raised exclusively for the "medicinal" effect of their velvet antlers. That day Kurylo took us through his large acreage where elk roamed like cattle; then we hopped on an all-terrain vehicle and drove up to a laboratory where we put on white sanitary outfits. Kurylo showed us how they crushed the velvet antlers to form tiny pills, which were then shipped to customers around the world. Our story was an exposé on the bogus study by a University of Alberta professor who claimed the pills caused a spike in testosterone.

As we waited for the camera crew to set up for the interview with Kurylo, we talked over the kitchen table about what it was like to know Schreiber back in those early days in Alberta.

Joan Kurylo remembered she had some old photo albums and dug them out of the basement. There were pictures of the inside of Schreiber's compound in Kaufering, just outside Munich, where Schreiber hosted a costume party for the Kurylos and other Bavarian guests. Giorgio Pelossi had been there too, wearing what appeared to be a pirate outfit. Schreiber was costumed as a clown. Former Alberta politician Hugh Horner was wearing a funny hat while bowling. In one photo Schreiber was cooking on the barbecue while wearing traditional Bavarian lederhosen. There were pictures from Alberta too: Schreiber playing the accordion by the campfire, Pelossi smiling from the upper bed in a Winnebago, Schreiber and Pelossi on a private Alberta government jet. Joan pointed to a picture of an attractive woman with short auburn hair and said she was Renata Rauscher, Schreiber's longtime girlfriend, who had suddenly left him in the early 1980s. Joan told me that she always figured they would split up as the woman had a "sad soul." Schreiber had treated her as a "trophy wife," she told me.

As we reminisced, Steve Kurylo told me that Schreiber was one of the most meticulous men he knew. Wherever he went on a business trip, he always carried a three-ring binder with him. He was the same way on holidays. Even if he was staying at a hotel for only one night, Schreiber would always empty his suitcase and carefully arrange the contents in their proper place—shirts and underwear in the hotel dresser, pants hung up in the closest, toiletries bag carefully laid out in the bathroom. While on the Kurylos' visit to

Kaufering, Schreiber had showed them the guns that he and Renata carried with them "at all times" while in Germany. Schreiber had explained that he was worried about his personal safety. Renata needed to carry a gun as well, in case someone tried to kidnap the girlfriend of a dealmaker like Schreiber.

In Germany, meanwhile, the Airbus scandal continued to unfold. Wolfgang Schäuble, current leader of the Christian Democrats, admitted he too had accepted a cash payment from Schreiber in the amount of 100,000 DM (approximately $70,000 CAD), which he claimed he promptly turned over to the party's fundraisers. As he had at first strenuously denied even knowing Schreiber, there were calls for his resignation. Schreiber would later tell Stan Oziewicz at the *Globe and Mail* that the money he gave to Schäuble in 1994 related to the "success fees" that Thyssen Industrie gave him for the Bear Head project in Canada.[1] Schreiber also explained that he gave the money to Schauble because he felt sorry for him (an attempted assassination in 1990 had left the politician permanently paralyzed and confined to a wheelchair). Schäuble blamed the former party treasurer, Brigitte Baumeister, for not properly registering the cash in the party books. No one was buying Schäuble's explanation; eventually he stated he would not stand for re-election. Kohl faced even more criticism when, after saying he had never met Schreiber, a photo surfaced of Schreiber attending a luncheon for Brian Mulroney hosted by the German chancellor in Bonn on June 13, 1991. (The *Globe and Mail* reported that Luc Lavoie would not comment on the photo that put Schreiber, Mulroney and Kohl at the same head table.[2]) Another senior CDU official, Manfred Kanther, admitted that the party had set up secret accounts in Switzerland and Liechtenstein in which they had hidden millions of dollars.

There was even a suicide. Wolfgang Hullen, who had been in charge of the Christian Democratic Union's party finances, was being investigated by

---

1 Despite the *Globe and Mail*'s rigid anti-RCMP and anti–*fifth estate* editorial position, Oziewicz continued to write solid investigative-style stories.

2 Lavoie would later tell me that Schreiber was not an invited guest and that Mulroney had asked Lavoie to give up his seat so Schreiber could attend the luncheon at the last minute.

prosecutors for "breach of faith," when he killed himself in his Berlin apartment on January 20. The German flag flew at half-mast over the Reichstag the next day, a symbol, perhaps, not only of the mourning of a life, but the despair in which all politicians now found themselves, in what had become the country's largest postwar scandal.

Back in Canada, all those outraged Tories once demanding a public inquiry had fallen silent. Gone was the chorus of people once demanding a parliamentary investigation into how the RCMP had handled the Airbus affair—including Peter MacKay and Brian Mulroney. No parliamentarians from any party seemed to want to deal with what was, by any objective measure, a significant story of political corruption.

Still, Canada was, in some ways, the centre of attention. Schreiber was vigorously fighting extradition to Germany from a courtroom in Toronto.

In January 2000, he was back in court. The public gallery was packed with reporters from virtually every major newspaper and TV station *in Germany*. I would sometimes drop by the courtroom on University Avenue on the way to work and talk to German reporters, or just sit quietly at the back of the room, soaking up the atmosphere and watching Schreiber. He talked to everyone, it seemed, except to me. At a break during one of those hearings in Toronto I first spoke to Greenspan. Rather, he spoke to me, trying to engage me in a discussion about why I was so obsessed with the story and why CBC had paid for me to take twenty-six trips to Europe.

"Twenty-six trips!" he yelled.

(The comment was interesting, not because it was true, but because I knew its source: Phil Mathias. Earlier Mathias had complained to me about my travel to Europe, as if to suggest, I suppose, that I had misspent public money in pursuit of the story. "How many trips have you made to Europe?" Mathias had shouted at me caustically. "Twenty-six," I shot back, never thinking he would believe such a ridiculously high number, or that he would repeat it to Schreiber's lawyer.[3])

---

3 Mathias later wrote Greenspan a note telling him that he had not understood that my comment was a joke. Then Mathias wrote me a note stating that he was "always happy to clear up any misunderstandings." (If you added up the flights I had taken to Europe between 1994 and 2000 while researching and producing three separate Airbus stories, the actual total comes to five.)

"I just want to know where the money ended up," I told Greenspan as a group of reporters looked on.

"Well, I know where a lot of it is now," he said.

We all laughed. Greenspan is one of the most high-priced defence lawyers in the country, and we all knew he wasn't representing Schreiber for free.

In late January 2000, John Goetz called to say he noticed a small but interesting story tucked in the back pages of *Der Spiegel* magazine. The RCMP had recently conducted raids at various locations in Canada in their probe of the sale of German-made helicopters to the Coast Guard back in 1986. The article was brief but intriguing.

Generally, for the Mounties to secure permission to execute a search warrant they need to provide evidence a crime *might* have taken place, not absolute proof that it had. Still, we were curious what exactly the Mounties were alleging. We already knew that the helicopter deal had triggered the first instalment of the secret commissions that flowed into Schreiber's and Moores's Zurich bank accounts, but we did not know a lot more than that. We had spent far more time probing the Airbus and Thyssen deals than the MBB deal, probably because the commissions in the helicopter deal (only $1.2 million) paled in comparison to the Airbus deal (well over $20 million U.S.). Still, whether it was one million or twenty million, we knew the raids in Canada were a significant new development.

I knew where to start.

Der Spiegel had reported that one of the raids took place in Fort Erie, Ontario, where MBB Helicopter—now called Eurocopter—had an assembly plant. That was enough to remind me to call Helge Wittholz, the former president of MBB Helicopter Canada Ltd. I had known of Wittholz for some time. Back in 1994 one of my Ottawa contacts had told me to call him, but I had waited until December 1999 to make the call. Wittholz and I had a short but friendly chat, but then agreed to talk more in the new year.

Now seemed like a good time to call.

The RCMP had been to see him on a few occasions, Wittholz told me. He remembered a Sergeant Fraser Fiegenwald from a visit in 1995. After Fiegenwald was forced out, two new Mounties came to see him, he said. They asked even more questions about the contract the Coast Guard signed with MBB Canada. Wittholz told me that the contract with the Coast Guard specifically banned secret commissions under a clause called "No bribes, etc."

Wittholz had met Schreiber a few times in Canada. He said Schreiber was always talking about his close relationship to "The Old Man"—Franz Josef Strauss. "Schreiber was the confidant and dealmaker for Franz Josef Strauss, there is no doubt in my mind," Wittholz said. "I mean, the story was very simple." He explained that he did not know Schreiber was involved until after the deal was done. "We fought it tooth and nail," he said. "We were even told to stay out of it," Wittholz said, referring to orders from the German parent company, MBB Helicopter.

Wittholz had something else on his mind. After insisting he had no evidence and that it was only a rumour, he told me a story that, if true, was far bigger than the sale of a few helicopters to the Canadian Coast Guard. Wittholz claimed the Coast Guard deal might have been tied to the dumping of Joe Clark as leader of the Progressive Conservative Party back in 1983. He said he first heard about the possible connection after asking his bosses in Germany why they were paying secret commissions. "The explanation for all of this was that when Mulroney took over the leadership of the Conservative Party and ousted Clark, that at that time, the CSU, the party of Franz Josef Strauss, provided money to do that."

There had, of course, been rumours circulating for years that foreign money had helped dump Joe Clark as leader of the Progressive Conservative Party. But this was a whole new wrinkle. "And they expected, if [the Tories] would get to power," Wittholz continued, "that they would later be reimbursed by deals where commissions would be paid by German companies. You follow what I am saying?" Wittholz asked. I said I did. "So a party on the right is giving money to a party on the right in another country—and getting reimbursed when they get to power." Wittholz laughed. He said the story came from a reliable source: a man named Kurt

Pfleiderer, the head of the Helicopter Division of MBB. One day, when Wittholz was questioning Pfleiderer about the legality of the secret commissions, he said his boss finally exploded.

"This is normal business practice and if you don't like it, you should go and sell ballpoint pens!" Pfleiderer had told him. "Honestly. That really hurt," said Wittholz. "I was really disappointed in that man."

Wittholz said he had documents to help prove his point, but did not want to share them for now. "I don't want to get into that. I mean, I gave it to the people that I hoped will get to the truth," he said, referring to the RCMP.

Our conversation wrapped up. Wittholz told me that he would be "very happy" if the "real" dealmakers were exposed. "For me," he said, "Schreiber was a middleman. He was just tasked to do all these deals. Strauss was the one with 'all the power.'"

Afterwards, I felt both exhilarated and disappointed. If foreign money really had helped dump Joe Clark, then I was working on a story of historic proportions. It *felt* like it had the ring of truth. Why would the president of a helicopter company in Germany even make up such a bizarre story if it wasn't true? Still, I had to consider: Wittholz would not talk on the record, and refused to give me the incriminating documents. He had sounded very frustrated: "Honestly, I am sick and tired because *nothing is happening.*"

Wittholz had refused to turn over the documents, but I figured with a little spadework I would find them. At least, whichever documents he had already turned over to the RCMP. I reasoned that the RCMP probably had used the documents to support its application for a search warrant. Documents filed in support of a search warrant are in the public domain. If only I knew when or where the application was made.

The next day I called Mathias von Blumencron, the *Der Spiegel* reporter who had written about the raids against Eurocopter, and with whom I had worked so closely in 1994. He told me he had a copy of the one-page search warrant application the RCMP had submitted to Schreiber's accountant in

Alberta. That would provide details about where exactly the RCMP had obtained warrant approval. I needed Blumencron to cough it up, but I would need to trade something for it.[4]

I had recently obtained a 100-plus page Record of the Case against Schreiber (which had been deposited as evidence in Schreiber's extradition case in Toronto). It outlined new and specific details about the bribery, fraud and tax evasion charges against Schreiber. On its face it might not have seemed like a fair trade. There probably wasn't anything in it Blumencron didn't know already. It was also a public court document available to anyone who asked. But it was all I had.

We made the trade.

The application had been filed by an RCMP inspector named Allan Matthews. It requested that the RCMP be allowed to search Schreiber's accountant's office in Alberta. Investigators would be searching for any documents relating to the sale of helicopters to the Coast Guard, particularly paperwork involving Frank Moores, Schreiber and International Aircraft Leasing. The search warrant alleged that Messerschmitt-Bolkow-Blohm (MBB) did "commit the indictable offence of fraud" and "did by deceit, falsehood or other fraudulent means, defraud" the government by placing the economic interests of Canada at risk. The RCMP was alleging that because MBB had paid secret commissions to Schreiber and Moores and passed that cost along to the Coast Guard, the Canadian taxpayer paid too much for the helicopters.

The document confirmed that approval for the search warrant was obtained in Ottawa. The only problem, Blumencron told me, was that he

---

4   Blumencron did not tell me how he got a copy of that search warrant application, but in my opinion the only source could have been Schreiber. This particular copy was the one provided to Schreiber's accountant in Calgary. I doubted very much that the accountant, who was still on good terms with Schreiber, would have given it to *Spiegel* without Schreiber's permission. As for why Schreiber gave it to Blumencron, I suspect it was intended to send a message to German politicians to lay off, unless they too wanted to be brought into the case against Schreiber. After all, at the time of the payout of the secret commissions, MBB was owned in part by the Bavarian government and two other provinces in Germany. It looked as if German politicians had implicitly or explicitly approved the secret commission payments as a way of selling German products.

had already called the courthouse—they told him that the supporting documents had been ordered sealed.

I couldn't get the Wittholz documents after all.

I had not spoken to former Mulroney cabinet minister Frank Oberle in nearly five years, but when his name surfaced on some dinner receipts relating to Bear Head—receipts entered as evidence at the Berlin inquiry—I called him up again, and asked him about Schreiber. He gave me a blunt, honest overview of Schreiber's modus operandi around the world.

"[Schreiber] obviously worked with monies given to him by large industries to grease the skids and facilitate some of the sales. And obviously the German government, knowing that these monies were paid to him, want their share for taxes. And that is his main problem. He paid out large sums of money I assume for international sales. In his view he didn't do anything wrong. He did what the international business climate demanded." I asked what Oberle meant by "greasing" the skids. "Well, obviously paying bribes and doing things the way other countries deemed to be normal business practice. We don't, obviously."

In early March 2000, I wrote a memo to Studer and Teskey summarizing the new evidence we had collected on the Airbus story. I mentioned the RCMP search warrant against MBB and allegations they had defrauded the Canadian government; the photographs of Schreiber from Steve Kurylo; a published photograph from the *Globe and Mail* of a luncheon that included Brian Mulroney, former German chancellor Helmet Kohl and Schreiber; the Herbert Leiduck interview in which the German industrialist repeated what he had said in a sworn affidavit: Schreiber had bragged he had paid off Canadian politicians; how we had even more of Schreiber's Daytimer entries (in particular, pages showing Schreiber's handwritten notation of a $50,000 cash withdrawal from the Britan account, as well as notations of meetings with people like Fred Doucet, Elmer MacKay, Frank Moores and others); and finally how Mulroney may have given misleading testimony in Montreal at his sworn deposition in 1996 when he testified he had not met any members of the Strauss family, an assertion contradicted on-camera by his own friend Pat MacAdam. I suggested we could broadcast more of the Luc Lavoie tapes, which included the insightful comment that Mulroney "can't take it anymore" after learning that we had obtained a coded account that looked close to Mulroney's name.

I reminded them of Bruno Schirra, a German reporter to whom I had been introduced, who had the kind of access to Schreiber that certainly I—and even Goetz—could only dream about. Schreiber educated Schirra on two different kinds of corruption: level one and level two. Level one payments were of a general nature, not for any specific reason. Level two corruption was more direct and more specific. Monies would be paid to individuals so that a government would make the "right" decision.

At about the same time, I had an idea how we might unseal the MBB search warrant. Dan Henry agreed, but he would need to know where the documents were being stored for the plan to work. I made a cold call to the Ottawa courthouse, and told the clerk I wanted to obtain the documents used in support of the MBB search warrant, dated December 17, 1999. She looked up the case on her computer. There had already been an application made to unseal the search warrant, she said. *Shit*, I thought. Somebody had beaten me to it. I got her to give me the transit company waybill number—*and* the name of the Toronto lawyer who had made the application: Paul Schabas from Blakes. Kit Melamed told me that Schabas was the *Toronto Star*'s media lawyer. If Schabas was representing the *Star* on this, then it meant that another media outlet had had the idea before we did.

I called him right away. Schabas refused to reveal the name of his client, but told me it was not the *Toronto Star*. That was a relief. I deduced that his client must have been Eurocopter; a phone call to the helicopter company confirmed it.

I thought about what do to next. The Ottawa court clerk had told me that Schabas would be making an application before a judge to unseal the search warrant materials. I wanted to be there when he made the application in court. I walked to the courthouse on University Avenue, only a ten-minute walk from the CBC building. I had become friendly with one of the senior clerks there and asked him if there was anything on the schedule for an application to unseal the MBB search warrant materials. My contact went back to his desk, looked inside a couple of files, then returned to the counter.

"March 20," he told me.

I circled the date on my calendar, planning to drop by the courthouse that morning on my way to work.

On March 13, I wrote another note to Susan Teskey: Goetz had a source who might be getting copies of Schreiber's complete 1991 and 1994 Daytimers. Getting the entire collection seemed like a dream. I told Teskey what an enormous breakthrough this could be. "We know from past experience that Schreiber almost always makes a notation in his Daytimer when he takes cash out of his bank accounts."

A few days later Goetz was in Toronto filming another story for German television when he swung by my office with a "present"—photocopies of every page from the 1991 and 1994 Daytimers. Goetz's source had come through!

Among the names referenced in the pages were Helmet Kohl and Brian Mulroney. There were dozens of references to his Swiss banker, André Strobl, and friends like Elmer MacKay, Marc Lalonde, Frank Moores, Fred Doucet, Gary Ouellet and Bobby Hladun. The margins were crowded with what looked like mathematical computations, some of which made sense, some which didn't. I came upon the name Ben J. Besner in tiny handwriting. Besner was the Air Canada manager I had spoken to in 1995, after a source had tipped me that Besner might know something about Frank Moores's role at Air Canada. But when I called Besner at the time, he told me he knew nothing about Moores or Schreiber. I called Besner.

He had no better memory of Schreiber this time than when I'd talked with him in 1995. "I never met him. I haven't got a clue who he is. Not a clue."

"Have you ever talked to him?"

"I don't think so." I wondered how his name had come to appear in Schreiber's Daytimer. "If my name was in the Daytimer then someone else from my office would have been there as well."

He did not elaborate.

The most significant entries in the Daytimer were from the periods November and December 1994. Bank documents showed that cash had been withdrawn from the Britan account on November 21, 1994. In his Daytimer for that day, Schreiber had made a note of the withdrawal: "50 Britan CA." Other names had been scribbled in the margins.

"Greg Alford NY."

"Kathi—Pierre NY."

Greg Alford was Schreiber's long-time assistant on the Bear Head project. I had no idea who Kathi and Pierre were. I made a note to myself. "Kathi—Pierre NY? What's this about? Is Kathi a word in German? And who is Pierre?"

It was in the same two-month period in 1994 that Giorgio Pelossi went to *Der Spiegel* and *the fifth estate* with the Airbus documents. By then Mathias Blumencron, Jock Ferguson and I had already been working on the story. Schreiber's Daytimer entries seemed to suggest that he had become aware of our work and was growing more preoccupied with the unwanted attention. There were numerous notes to call contacts at Airbus and references to a phone call from a "Blumencrom" at *Der Spiegel*.

There were several references to Mulroney. On November 9, when he made a note to call former girlfriend Renata Rauscher, he also wrote, "Spiegel re Mulroney meeting." His notes for November 10 made it clear he was trying to get in touch with Mulroney. He wrote, "Doucet," for Fred Doucet, then "Brian," leaving blanks for Mulroney's "OF" number and his "HO" number. On November 14, 1994, in the entry for 10 a.m., Schreiber wrote: "Brian 2 + 4." On November 18, 1994, he wrote, "Doucet re New York." Was Schreiber planning a trip to New York with Fred Doucet? A November 21 entry notes that he had taken money out of the Britan account. Again, on November 23: "Doucet re New York." November 24: "Fax Airbus letter." On November 27, Schreiber made a note to call, or speak with,

Elmer MacKay, the former Mulroney cabinet minister who would later put up bail money for Schreiber and whose son had been a vocal critic of the RCMP and had lobbied for years to shut down the Airbus investigation.

I flipped to December.

On December 4, Schreiber jotted down a flight number from Munich to New York. I turned the page back to November 21, where he had written "NY" and "Britan 50." I realized that "Pierre" mentioned earlier was not a reference to a person but to the famous hotel in New York City, just off Central Park.

But what really stood out was an entry on December 8 at 10:30 a.m.

"Brian."

CHAPTER TWENTY-EIGHT
FOR THEIR EYES ONLY

Normally in the morning I exit the subway at St. Andrew station and walk five minutes to the CBC building on Wellington Street. But on March 20, 2000, I got off two stops earlier at Osgoode, the closest exit to the court-house on University Avenue where I knew that Eurocopter would be making arguments to try to unseal the RCMP search warrant materials. As best I understood, Eurocopter wanted to know if there were any weak elements in the case that they could exploit in their defence. Unsealing the documents would help them find out. I wanted to know what was in the documents to see if there were any new leads on the story. So we had the same goal, perhaps, yet vastly different objectives.

Before we arrived at the real business of the day, Justice Edward Then's court would have to deal with some procedural housekeeping: what the court calls, "to be spoken to's." By the time that had been dealt with an hour or so later, I was one of only four people left in the public gallery.

Several gowned lawyers were sitting in front of me. Two were to my left. I would later learn they were Paul Schabas and a colleague. Schabas had greying hair and wore glasses, looking much as he had sounded on the phone, polite and studious. On the right side of the room were the Crown attorneys on the case, Trevor Shaw and Michael Bernstein. They were in charge of shepherding the Eurocopter case through the court process, and to lay a charge if they so decided. Also present was Inspector Allan Matthews, RCMP Commercial Crime, the officer who had applied for the search warrant. Behind Matthews were three bankers boxes—presumably containing copies of the documents Helge Wittholz, the former MBB Canada president, had refused to give me.

We were reminded that proceedings were being held in camera, meaning that media could not attend. Justice Then, noticing spectators in the public gallery, wanted to know who we were. Three of my public gallery colleagues introduced themselves as an attorney and two law students, one of whom later told me he was about to article with Eddie Greenspan.

"Who is that?" Justice Then asked, pointing at me and looking at Crown attorneys Shaw and Bernstein. They looked at me and shrugged. Paul Schabas and his co-counsel looked at me and shrugged too. I didn't know if I was allowed to talk.

Finally the judge addressed me directly. "Who *are* you?"

"My name is Harvey Cashore, I work for CBC Television, I am a producer with the program *the fifth estate*."

"Why are you here?"

I mumbled something about this being an issue in the public interest. I was a problem, it turned out. My attendance meant that the judge would have to hold a hearing within a hearing—to determine whether or not the public should have access to this proceeding.

Crown attorney Trevor Shaw turned to me. "You do know that there is a publication ban on these proceedings?" he said.

"I do now," I replied.

Justice Then asked both the Crown and MBB lawyers to state their opinions on a proposed publication ban. First, the Crown argued that their investigation would be derailed if the information in support of their search warrant became public. Paul Schabas said he was representing Eurocopter, of course, but as a media lawyer had a strong belief in the public's right to know. Eurocopter was neither consenting to nor opposing the Crown motion, he said, but reminded the judge of the options. He suggested to Justice Then that he could allow the media to attend, but reserve the right to suspend proceedings as necessary and resume the hearing in camera. That sounded like a reasonable compromise to me. Schabas reminded the judge that the burden was on the Crown to prove why the proceedings should be under a publication ban, or worse, as the Crown was arguing, that the media should be excluded from even attending. In effect Schabas was saying the Crown's application was rare and that they had better have good reasons for it.

CBC lawyer Michael Hughes would later join the debate, and arguments about banning the media from the room continued well into the afternoon. During one of the breaks, RCMP inspector Allan Matthews introduced himself. He asked me when our next story was going to air. I told him I did not know yet.

It was after 4:15 p.m. when Justice Then gave a brief oral decision.

"The application to exclude the public is granted," he ruled. "That is all I proposed to say." He added, "It is open I believe to the CBC to monitor the proceedings as it sees fit, except by attendance."

Except by attendance? Then just how were we supposed to monitor the proceedings?

I was livid. The next day I called Crown attorney Trevor Shaw to ask what he meant when Justice Then said CBC could "monitor the proceedings." Shaw told me to ask my lawyer. I told him my lawyer also had no idea.

"I can't talk to you," he said.[1]

While skimming Schreiber's Daytimer, I came upon the date September 26, 1991, and the name Don Cameron. Cameron had been premier of Nova Scotia from 1991 to 1993. I wondered if he would remember what the entry meant.

Cameron was in no mood to talk. "I have got nothing to add to that," he said to me on the phone. "I am not in public life anymore and I am sick with a bad flu right now and so I am not in a very good mood, to boot."

"Is there a better time to call back then?"

---

1 The CBC would later be granted permission to attend the hearing, though still covered by a publication ban, which lawyer Dan Henry continued to fight to overturn.

"No, I am not going to talk to you, do you understand? You understand, do you?"

"Okay, and you understand that I have some information here in which your name comes up—and you don't want to talk about it?"

"Whose name comes up?"

"Your name."

"Look, you can do what you want to do. Just better make sure you are right about it. That is all I got to tell you."

"That is why I am calling you."

"I got nothing to say."

Der Spiegel's Mathias Blumencron was back in Toronto in mid-April for another meeting with Schreiber. We met up afterwards. Blumencron told me Schreiber was still furious with Lavoie over his "fucking liar" comments that we had broadcast back in November. "Schreiber said he wants to grill Luc Lavoie the Kaufering way, slow heat with flame strokes," Blumencron told me. "I think the relationship is not the best between Schreiber and Mulroney."

Schreiber told Blumencron that he had heard Lavoie and I had had our conversation in person, and not on the phone; he said that I got Lavoie drunk and tricked him into making those comments.

What else? I asked.

"I could create the most horrible Watergate here in Canada when I want to," Schreiber said. Of course, Blumencron said Schreiber refused to provide details. He handed me a thick package: the document file Canada had sent the Germans in support of its Request for Assistance. I opened the package at home that night. It included copies of cancelled cheques, invoices for "services rendered" and documents showing a money trail from the German arms manufacturer Thyssen Industrie to several lobbyists close to Mulroney.

The next morning I arranged the documents in chronological order. International Aircraft Leasing in Liechtenstein had received its first grease-money payment from Thyssen on December 31, 1987, after the Nova Scotia government provided Schreiber a written commitment on Bear Head.

They confirmed that IAL had received a second payment of $2 million on October 25, 1988, after the federal government signed that Understanding in Principle with Schreiber on September 27, 1988.

According to the documents, Schreiber himself had created false paperwork to obscure the money trail. On April 28, 1988, for example, he had his Calgary company, Bitucan, invoice one of his Liechtenstein companies, Merkur Handels. "To invoice you for services rendered regarding your industrial project in Indonesia. Please remit Can. $50,000." There was, in fact, no Indonesian project. Schreiber needed to create the invoice to provide a pretext for moving the Thyssen greasemoney into Canada. A credit/debit sheet also revealed that Schreiber paid his lawyer, Robert Hladun, $50,000 on May 18, 1988, followed by another payment on June 8, 1988, of $10,000. Presumably these were legal fees Schreiber owed to Hladun.

On October 20, 1988, Schreiber drew up another false invoice for the phony Indonesian project. "To invoice you for services rendered regarding your industrial project in Indonesia. Please remit $710,000."

On November 2, 1988, Fred Doucet billed Schreiber's Bitucan $90,000 "Re: Professional Services." That same day, his brother, Gerry Doucet, billed Bitucan $90,000 "For services rendered by Gerald Doucet." On November 8, Frank Moores billed Bitucan $90,000 "For services rendered." (Gary Ouellet would also bill Bitucan $90,000, but not until December 1988.) And on November 10, 1988, Government Consultants International billed Bitucan $250,000 "Re: Consulting Services Rendered."

Then on November 15, 1988, Bitucan employee Erika Lutz sent out the $90,000 cheques to Frank Moores, Fred Doucet, Gerry Doucet and Gary Ouellet. GCI itself received payment in the amount of $250,000. The payments came to a total of $610,000. German investigators were able to show that Schreiber kept an additional $100,000 for himself, bringing the total to $710,000—exactly the amount that had been transferred from Liechtenstein to Canada for the so-called "Indonesian Project."

Moores billed Bitucan once more on May 17, 1989, for $60,000. When the invoice arrived in Calgary, however, Lutz sent Schreiber a handwritten note requesting approval. "Karlheinz, asking your okay for payment." On May 30, Schreiber faxed her back a note, also in his handwriting: "Has been done. Destroy invoice." (It appeared someone forgot to do that.)

On October 10, 1989, Bitucan invoiced Merkur an additional $110,000 "Re: Industrial Project in Indonesia. To invoice you for professional service rendered." On January 29, 1991, Fred Doucet sent an invoice directly to Merkur for $30,000. On March 25, 1991, Merkur cut a cheque, No. 124, to Doucet for the $30,000 that he had requested.

Again, there was no project in Indonesia.

On April 12, 2000, I took the 11:30 a.m. train out of Toronto's Union Station destined for Montreal. I arrived at 5 p.m. and went straight to my room. My instructions were to wait for a phone call from a former Schreiber associate who refused to be identified. I met him two hours later in the lobby of the Queen Elizabeth Hotel. Bill Dunbar[2] looked like a diplomat and wore a smart suit and trench coat. Dunbar escorted me outside the main doors of the Queen Elizabeth where his driver was waiting for us in a luxury SUV.

It hit me that I was in the back seat of an SUV in Montreal with no cellphone, no idea where we were going and no idea, really, who Dunbar actually was or what he was planning. We made our way down St. Catharines Street, turned up St. Marc and pulled up in front of Kalenka, a Russian restaurant. I was relieved; we were simply on our way to dinner.

I pulled out my pen and pad and got to work.

Dunbar bragged that one of his closest friends was involved in running arms in Central America. He told me he met Schreiber in Central America and that they tried to do some business together. Schreiber had bragged about his connections to Franz Josef Strauss, Dunbar said. Schreiber invited him to Europe, where he visited Kaufering. They also visited Pelossi in Lugano. Dunbar told me a story about a woman named Rita Santalla. Rita, an attractive Cuban-born American who lived in Costa Rica, got to know both Schreiber and Pelossi. She had some kind of role with Schreiber's companies in Costa Rica, but it was not clear exactly what. Dunbar claimed that Santalla might have caused friction between Pelossi and Schreiber. After Pelossi had confided in her about the Airbus deal with Air Canada,

2 Not his real name.

Santalla told the Lugano accountant that Schreiber was taking advantage of him. She wondered why Pelossi got so little when Schreiber got so much; maybe he should do something about it.

Dunbar's story was second-hand, and therefore not completely reliable, but it seemed to suggest that Santalla might have influenced Pelossi's decision to take Airbus money from the accounts in Liechtenstein without telling Schreiber. That decision, of course, eventually led to their falling-out and Pelossi's subsequent decision to go public with the Airbus documents. And that, in turn, led to the very public Airbus scandal. Did it mean, then, that the entire Airbus controversy could be traced back to a mysterious woman from Central America?

I was trying to eat my borscht and take notes at the same time. I noticed Dunbar staring past me to someone in the restaurant. At the next table sat two women. Dunbar winked, which prompted them to join us. He told me to put away my notepad and pen. We would finish up tomorrow. The women were introduced, and Dunbar ordered a round of drinks. Natasha sat next to Dunbar; Mikaela sat next to me. They both spoke with Russian accents. "I'm so sorry," Natasha repeated to Dunbar as she draped her arms around him: I wasn't sure why she was sorry and she didn't elaborate. Mikaela was smoking Davidoff cigarettes and staring at me. She was, admittedly, stunningly attractive. She put her hand on mine.

"Don't look so serious," she said.

They talked about going to a nightclub, The French Kiss, but Dunbar suggested a Russian club on St. Catharines Street. We all piled into the SUV, Natasha and Mikaela on either side of me in the back seat. Mikaela's leg crept up onto mine. Five minutes later we arrived at the entrance to the nightclub—an unmarked door, then a hallway leading up some stairs to a dance floor. There were couches at the far end, tables for eating and pool tables but, strangely, except for two bartenders, the place was nearly empty.

Mikaela brought me to the dance floor. She whispered in my ear and told me that she was not normally like this.

"What are you normally like?"

"Normally I am completely naked."

I left Mikaela standing by herself on the dance floor, which set off a daisy chain of angry looks. Obviously I had insulted them.

"I think we should take you back to the hotel," Dunbar told me coldly. Within minutes we were back in the suv and I was being unceremoniously dumped off at the Queen Elizabeth. I looked at the clock. Nearly 1 a.m., which meant it was 7 a.m. in Germany. I called Goetz to tell him what had happened. We speculated about what might have really been going on.

"That was a honey trap!" he said.[3]

Sami Jadallah, a Riyadh businessman, was a name that appeared frequently in Schreiber's Daytimer. His name had surfaced at the Berlin inquiry earlier in the year as having given Schreiber a huge loan back in 1988. I found him living in a suburb outside Washington, D.C. When I asked him about the loan, Jadallah claimed there never was one. He never loaned Schreiber a penny, he said. Jadallah said he was not entirely surprised that I might think so, and told me a story to explain what had happened. One day in 1994, he said, he got an unexpected call from Schreiber asking to meet at the Mövenpick Hotel at the Zurich airport. Schreiber had an unorthodox business proposal.

"He told me he was having some problems with the tax authority, you know. And he mentioned some money to me."

Schreiber offered to pay Jadallah a substantial amount of money if he would help Karlheinz with a plan to deceive the German tax authorities. Schreiber's idea was complicated; it involved creating a false loan agreement with Jadallah and making it appear as if Schreiber had borrowed millions of dollars from the Riyadh businessman on October 1, 1988. This way Schreiber could say he owed money to Jadallah for the putative loans and claim that his greasemoney was actually a business expense, not income. Therefore he would not have to pay taxes on it.

"Schreiber said if I can sign some papers or something like that, or to say that if I am asked that he owes me money," Jadallah told me. "And I said, 'Are you serious?' Schreiber said 'Yes.' I said, 'I will not do it. This is a fraud. You know. This is serious business.'" According to Jadallah, Schreiber simply dropped the subject. He reached into his Louis Vuitton bag, Jadallah

---

3   I still have no idea why Dunbar may have wanted to trap me, but it does seem oddly plausible.

said, and pulled out a brochure for a pasta-making machine called Spaghet-tissimo. Schreiber told him he had obtained the patent from Thyssen In-dustrie. He said it would transform the pasta business. It was surreal: one minute Schreiber was discussing how to commit tax fraud, he laughed, the other how to revolutionize the spaghetti-manufacturing industry.

"That was the last time I heard [from] him," Jadallah told me. "In any case, I tell you, if he says that he owes me the money, he can give it to me."

Towards the end of May, I decided it was time to call Fred Doucet. There were so many new questions to ask about the dozens of times he was men-tioned in Schreiber's Daytimers, and in particular the references sur-rounding Schreiber's trip to the Pierre Hotel in New York City. I called his Ottawa office but never expected him to personally answer. It caught me by surprise and I stumbled through my introductions and intentions. He wanted no part of any discussion about Schreiber or anyone or anything else.

"I will pass on all of that," he said.

"Because we have new evidence—"

"I will pass on all of that." Then he hung up.

CHAPTER TWENTY-NINE
THE LONG HOT SUMMER

Karlheinz Schreiber's extradition case dragged like a push me/pull you: a couple of days of hearings would be followed by an adjournment for some legal reason or other, followed by another few days of hearings, followed by another adjournment for any host of other reasons. A scheduled witness suddenly was unavailable. A lawyer was busy on another case. Another arcane legal point had to be researched. By the time the hearing resumed at the end of May 2000, nine months had passed since Schreiber's arrest. Incredibly, the extradition hearing had hardly begun.

Some German journalists got back on planes to Toronto for the resumption of the extradition; others simply stayed at home, waiting for Schreiber to come back to Germany.

Christian Nitsche, a television journalist with *Report Munich* in Bavaria, made the trip. I had first met him the previous September and now, on the Sunday before the Monday court hearing, my wife and I had him over for a visit. He told me he wanted to talk in private. I put my youngest son, Jeremiah, into his green wagon and walked with Nitsche to the Danforth, Toronto's Greek district. I noticed that he took the battery out of his cellphone. Then, when he made sure that Jeremiah was sound asleep, he turned to me.

"You need to be careful, you have children."

I laughed away his comments. He told me he was not being paranoid. He said that "something" had happened to a colleague's car back in Germany. Now he worried he was being followed and that his phones were tapped.

"Look out behind you," he warned.

Toronto Star legal affairs reporter Tracey Tyler wrote a story on the Monday and quoted the Augsburg chief prosecutor, Reinhard Nemetz, as being optimistic that the Canadian courts would proceed expeditiously with the case. "The Canadians are aware of . . . our very strong feelings that extradition should happen very quickly," he said. "I cannot imagine, for that reason, that the extradition case could take years."

In court, Greenspan seemed to be throwing everything at the wall, accusing Giorgio Pelossi, *the fifth estate*, Stevie Cameron, the federal government and the RCMP of committing grievous wrongs against his client. He also argued that Canada's International Assistance Group (IAG) would have a difficult time being objective with his client because Schreiber happened to be suing them for wrongful arrest. The IAG "hates my client's guts," he said. Greenspan also referred to some "explosive material" he came across while pursuing Schreiber's lawsuit against the federal government. A legal technicality prevented Greenspan from discussing this information in another courtroom, but he was hoping to find a way to introduce it nevertheless.

The hearing dragged on, and it became apparent that in defending Schreiber, Eddie Greenspan meant to defend Mulroney as well. "In my opinion" Greenspan said, "the Canadian government shamelessly went after a former prime minister of this country and Mr. Schreiber." Odd, as I was under the impression that Mulroney and Schreiber were not exactly on the best of terms. Was this a message of reconciliation?

Schreiber's extradition hearing was adjourned after just two days as the judge considered whether to allow Greenspan to explore the conduct of Canadian officials as it related to Schreiber's arrest.

In Ottawa the next day, Peter MacKay rose in the House of Commons, this time in support of Karlheinz Schreiber. "Mr. Speaker, while we know the minister of justice [Anne McLellan] cannot comment on the specifics of the extradition case involving Karlheinz Schreiber or the million-dollar slander case that has been launched by him against her government, could she assure the House none of the irregularities that existed in the first instance, which forced the government to settle out of court in an embarrassing way, exist this time around? Does she honestly feel that the actions of her department are in full compliance with Canadian and international law?"

The new justice minister, Anne McLellan, responded: "Mr. Speaker, as the Honourable member knows, this matter is before the courts at this time. Therefore it is inappropriate for me to make any comment in relation to it."

That summer, I decided to call Marc Lalonde.

He was one of the few Liberals Schreiber had come to know in Canada. His name had appeared several times in Schreiber's Daytimers. In 1991, Schreiber had set up a sub-account called "Marc"—which might refer to Lalonde. The account showed cash withdrawals of tens of thousands of dollars. Despite the fact that Lalonde (and Elmer MacKay) put up bail for Schreiber, we still did not know much about his relationship to events. He seemed to have flown beneath the radar.

When I talked to Lalonde on the phone, I asked how exactly he had come to meet Schreiber.

"How I first came to meet him? That would have been when he was actively here with Bear Head and he was also involved in trying to sell Airbuses to Air Canada," Lalonde said. He insisted Schreiber hired him, but not on Airbus—only on the Bear Head project. Lalonde said the biggest obstacles on the project had to be the legality of exporting this kind of military equipment. "I was knowledgeable about the problems in that regard arising out of Canadian legislation . . . But Germany also had restrictions. These restrictions are not exclusive to Canada. They tend to be taken collectively and for NATO." In fact, the *Globe and Mail* had reported allegations back in the 1980s that Thyssen saw the proposed Canadian-based plant as a way of circumventing German law and exporting weapons to the Middle East. I asked Lalonde about that.

"Yeah, maybe, maybe; but again: So what? You have that all the time. Multinational companies establishing subsidiaries in other countries for all kinds of purposes . . . [If] it would be allowed under a subsidiary, that may be the case, it happens all the time." Lalonde told me that Frank Moores had been the one to introduce him to Schreiber. "I got a call from Frank Moores asking me if I would see him."

Frank Moores, the former Conservative premier, was calling Marc Lalonde, the former Liberal cabinet minister, to arrange a meeting with Schreiber in 1988 about Bear Head? Given that the project needed support from two Conservative governments, one provincial and one federal, why on earth did Frank Moores want to bring in Marc Lalonde, a Liberal?

"That is the question I asked myself," laughed Lalonde.

So Moores did call Lalonde, but I wondered if the call really was only about Bear Head. Schreiber and Moores were involved with the Air Canada/Airbus deal in 1988 and Lalonde was well positioned to help out on that file. Air Canada was still a Crown corporation and populated by appointments made during the former Liberal government—in which Lalonde had been a high-profile cabinet minister. I asked Lalonde if Airbus ever came up in discussion, even if in passing.

"So far as I discussed Airbus with Mr. Schreiber, this is what I would have told him . . . that our experience was, my experience, having been in the government before, that Air Canada would make its choice on the basis of the merits of the deal."

I had an idea. I was convinced that Lalonde knew far more than he was admitting. I guessed that if he were involved in the Air Canada deal then he would have had to have met Stuart Iddles, the vice-president of marketing for Airbus who had worked so closely with Schreiber. I asked Lalonde if he could compare the role that Schreiber played on the Airbus sale with the role that Stuart Iddles played. "I mean, some people say that [Schreiber] played a big role," I suggested, "some people say that no, Stuart Iddles played a bigger role. What would he say was the role that he played is what I am wondering?"

"I don't know, honestly," Lalonde replied. "I don't know how big a role he played. Obviously a middleman. What role exactly he played compared to Iddles, his name?"

"Yeah."

"I don't know."

Iddles, his name? Perhaps I was wrong. It looked as if Lalonde did not know Iddles after all. I asked Lalonde to describe his relationship with Air Canada president Pierre Jeanniot.

"Pierre Jeanniot I have known him for thirty years. I knew him before I got into politics. As a young official at Air Canada, very very competent and able individual. And very honest. I always have a lot of time for Pierre Jeanniot. I have always had a great deal of respect for him."

"And what did he make of Schreiber?" I asked.

"What did he make?"

"Yeah, what was his sense of Schreiber?"

"You better ask him," he said. "I didn't ask him. . . . I did not ask him what he thought of Schreiber. And even if I did again, even if he had told me something, I would say go and ask him. I never did discuss Schreiber with him."

If Pierre Jeanniot and Marc Lalonde were good friends, which they were, and if Schreiber was trying to sell planes to Air Canada, which he was, and if Lalonde and Schreiber were now working together on Bear Head, which they were, wouldn't it have made sense that Lalonde would at least mention Schreiber's efforts to Jeanniot—at the very least to put in a good word? I had noticed a particular entry in Schreiber's Daytimer in 1994 that seemed to link Lalonde to Airbus and Air Canada. I told Lalonde that it said "Greg/Marc/BHI/AC/ABI." Greg stood for Greg Alford, Marc for Marc Lalonde, BHI for Bear Head Industrie, AC for Air Canada, and ABI for Airbus Industrie.

Why would Schreiber connect Lalonde to Air Canada in 1994 if he had not helped Schreiber on the file?

"Might have been," Lalonde admitted. "Might have discussed whether there were further opportunities for further sales I suppose. I know there were discussions of further sales to Air Canada and to Canadian [Airlines]. We may have discussed that at that time."

It seemed odd to deny that he worked on the Air Canada file but then to suggest that Schreiber and he *could* have discussed it. I tried to clarify: "And would you have made calls to Air Canada on his behalf as well?"

"Uh, no," Lalonde said. "David Angus, my partner, is on the board, and we were conflicted about acting for anybody in connection with transactions at Air Canada."

I asked Lalonde to give me his take on why Airbus Industrie had agreed to give Schreiber $20 million if Air Canada bought the A320s. "What would Airbus expect Schreiber to do for that kind of money?"

"That's a funny question to ask me."

"Why?"

"Well, you better go—I am not acting for Airbus—I do not know their way of doing business. And I cannot comment about what could have gone on in Airbus's mind," Lalonde said.

"But did Mr. Schreiber ever talk about the contract that he had [with Airbus]?"

"No."

I asked about the Marc sub-account in Schreiber's bank records. "Did Schreiber ever give you a cash envelope, or cash?"

"You have to be kidding."

In July 2000, Justice David Watt ruled against Eddie Greenspan's request that Schreiber's extradition be allowed to examine the RCMP's Airbus file. Despite the setback, the *Toronto Star*'s legal affairs reporter Tracey Tyler suggested a strategy. She quoted Greenspan as saying that this was the beginning of many future legal challenges. "One of the beauties of the law is that it has many avenues to bring arguments," Greenspan told Tyler. "I never look at a clock when I'm involved in a criminal case; I just look at the due process of law." But it seemed Greenspan was very much looking at the clock, and the calendar. Exploring every possible legal angle had the effect of slowing the hearing down. Even if he lost the small battles, he was actually winning the larger one: keeping his client free on bail in Canada. Germany's statute of limitations laws also worked in their favour. The charges might simply expire if the extradition took too long.

I was nearly done with my portion of work on the Schreiber biography, which would be published as *The Last Amigo*. I wanted to interview Phil Mathias. He told me he had some concerns about how I might view his role in the story. He wanted me to provide "written questions." Otherwise he refused to co-operate. Turns out, he wouldn't be the only one. Not by a long shot.

Bobby Hladun, Schreiber's Alberta lawyer, reminded me that I was a named defendant in one lawsuit and a material witness in another. Pierre Jeanniot refused to be interviewed again, stating he had done enough interviews already. Elmer MacKay also declined. "Information and background, which I have, may be utilized in future when events unfold, or the situation becomes more definitive," MacKay wrote Stevie Cameron and me.

Frank Moores's lawyer, Edgar Sexton, refused to talk. By the summer of 2000 he was a federal judge. I recalled that back in January 1997—when attacks on *the fifth estate* over its Airbus coverage was at its most virulent—Sexton had publicly stated that Moores never received any Airbus money. He had told the *Globe and Mail*, "Obviously the accounts show nothing and substantiate the position of Mr. Moores, which has always been that he had nothing to do with obtaining the Airbus contract and that he got no money for it." I wrote him a letter explaining that I had some important details of the story I needed to clear up. "I have banking information which I believe demonstrates that the facts as stated in [your] quote are false." Sexton responded to my letter with one of his own, in which he stated that it would be inappropriate for him to say anything at all, as he was now a judge:

> I have considered your letter of June 21, 2000. During my practice as a lawyer, I occasionally made statements to the press on behalf of clients concerning confidential information related to me by the clients. When I did so, it was on my clients' instructions and based upon my review of the information they provided to me and any other information at my disposal. I did not at any time make a statement to the press that I had reason to believe was untrue. Clients' right to confidentiality prevent me from

discussing further their affairs publicly. Furthermore, as a judge, it would be inappropriate for me to make any comment on client matters in which I was engaged as counsel prior to my appointment to the bench.

In August, Peter MacKay responded to a written request from my co-author, Stevie Cameron, and me explaining that he too would not discuss the matter.

I did work for a short time [approximately five months] for a company for which I understand Mr. Schreiber was on the board of Directors. While in the employ of the company, I did not see, speak to, or correspond with Mr. Schreiber directly or indirectly. Any suggestion of illegal, inappropriate or illegitimate relations with this man is completely without warrant and would be vexatious.

Interesting, because we never even hinted at the possibility of illegal activity. All I wanted to know was why he rose in the House of Commons so many times to try to shut down the RCMP investigation.

It would be a long summer.

The biography of Schreiber had turned into more of a struggle than either Stevie or I had expected. The publisher decided to delay publication for four months, which meant I continued working on it throughout the summer. I told my wife we had to cancel our holidays that year.

"I have no choice. I have to get the book finished."

When my annual leave was over, I went back to *the fifth estate* and worked mostly on other stories. It felt refreshing to be off Airbus for a while. But only for a while.

In early September, Brian Mulroney was back on television, again speaking with Brian Stewart on CBC's *The National.* In his previous interview with Stewart in June 1999—prior to Schreiber's arrest—Mulroney had suggested he might sue the Mounties again. Fifteen months later, he seemed to have charted a new course—a new message. I wondered if it was a message directed less to Canadian viewers and more to Karlheinz Schreiber.

Stewart had asked Mulroney about his friend:

"Well, Mr. Schreiber was never a good friend of mine. He's a man I knew. And I regarded him as—and he was introduced to me, and he had a reputation of accomplishment. And things have to be placed in perspective. You have to look at this now seven years earlier, and his reputation was unflawed, he had achieved a great deal in the business community. And what is sad about this is the assumption people presume guilt on his part and on the part of others. Mr. Schreiber should be presumed to be innocent. And moreover, he has a wife and a family. And the personal dimension of this should not be lost on people. He is a Canadian citizen who has the right to be presumed to be innocent. And yet because of all of the rumours and gossip and innuendo there is a tendency to presume that people have done something untoward. And so, look, life takes its toll on all of us. And this has not been a pleasant experience for anybody, and I'm sure not for Mr. Schreiber and his family, and I believe that they, too, are entitled to the presumption of innocence as I was and as other people are."

"What's your feeling currently about the Airbus scandal and the ongoing investigation that seem to have no end," Stewart asked.

"I just don't know. I just don't know, it just goes on and on and—"

"Do you even think about it much anymore?"

"I just don't know where it is, Brian, and we'll just have to see, see where it leads."

Four days after Mulroney's CBC TV interview, on September 9, Schreiber launched a lawsuit against Mulroney's spokesman, Luc Lavoie, for the "fucking liar" comments broadcast on *the fifth estate* the previous year. Schreiber was demanding that Lavoie pay him $300,000 in compensatory damages. Was it a coincidence that it was an amount exactly equal to the cash withdrawals from the Britan account? Interestingly, the statement of claim that Greenspan had prepared had dropped the item arguing that Britan was not Brian.

In the most bizarre turn of events to date, however, Luc Lavoie and I found ourselves defendants in lawsuits launched by Karlheinz Schreiber.

CHAPTER THIRTY
TIME, PLACE, WEAPON

I had unfinished business.

It had been nine months since Helge Wittholz, the former president of MBB Helicopter Canada, had first told me about how foreign money and influence may have helped dump Joe Clark as leader of the Progressive Conservative Party—and that the secret commission contracts with International Aircraft Leasing may have been a kind of quid pro quo for those involved in helping to make it happen.

I had not convinced him to speak on-camera back then, and hadn't been able to get my hands on the documents he had provided to the RCMP. By November, my other *fifth estate* projects were winding down, and I began thinking about the Wittholz angle. I couldn't just leave *that* angle hanging; he'd made a shocking allegation that, if true, might change the way we viewed Canada's political history.

I told David Studer that I wanted to return to the Airbus story, explaining the fresh angle. Not only did he agree to resurrect the story, he actually assigned more people to work on it—concurring that this might be our last kick at the can. My *fifth estate* colleagues Howard Goldenthal and Jennifer Fowler officially joined the Airbus team for the next four months, working alongside Linden MacIntyre, John Goetz and me.

Fowler and Goldenthal pieced together what had already been reported about the dump-Clark movement. They also re-interviewed key players. They learned that the pivotal moment for Clark had come at a leadership review convention in Winnipeg in January 1983, when delegates voted 66.9 per cent in favour of Clark's continued leadership. For Clark, it was not enough; he had wanted at least 70 per cent support. Brian Mulroney attended the Winnipeg convention as one of many delegates from Quebec. After the vote, a pro-Clark MP from Quebec, Roch Lasalle, blamed Mulroney. "He was behind it," Lasalle said. "[Mulroney] is the master of consummate hypocrisy," he said, referring to rumours that Mulroney had worked behind the scenes to undermine Clark, all the while supporting him in public. Newspapers quoted former party president Michael Meighen as saying that if only sixty-five more people had voted in favour of Clark, "that's all it would have taken to bring him up to 70 per cent," he told the *Globe and Mail*.

The race *was* that close.

Which meant that any foreign influence *could* have made all the difference. Indeed, allegations that offshore money had influenced the vote had been around from the beginning. Dalton Camp, a respected party strategist, told the *Globe and Mail* in 1983 that sources had told him that "foreign interests" had helped topple Clark. Camp publicly complained to the newspaper that this was "certainly alien to the party system" in Canada.

On November 5, 2000, Goetz and I drove to Wittholz's home in London, Ontario. Wittholz had not yet agreed to anything except to meet us. We figured that alone was a good sign. Driving along the 401 to London, Goetz filled me in on another incredible development: Schreiber had begun talking to him. The conversations were on the phone, and since the RCMP presumably was listening in, he was not saying too much. But I was thrilled. Schreiber was still suing me and the CBC for a total of $37 million, but this was an interesting twist. Technically, Goetz was a freelancer who lived in Berlin. Still, Schreiber knew that Goetz was also working with *the fifth estate*. Goetz told me he planned to visit Schreiber back in Toronto later in the week.

I was reminded, again, how much our work interfered with our personal lives when Goetz mentioned, in passing, that it was his birthday. He really should have been in Berlin with his new girlfriend; instead, he was spending his birthday with me.

We pulled in to a Tim Hortons. "Happy birthday," I said as I handed him a coffee.

Two hours after leaving Toronto we pulled up to a middle-class house on a tree-lined street; Wittholz greeted us at the door. A neatly trimmed beard framed a pleasant face. Wittholz introduced us to his wife, who served us homemade apple streusel with whipped cream and coffee—another good sign. Goetz and I smiled at each other.

Then it was just the three of us.

Wittholz seemed to be in more of a mood to talk than before. He didn't say so but I suspected his change in attitude had to do with a phone call he told us he'd received since I last spoke to him. A former MBB colleague had told him that Eurocopter's law firm, Blake Cassels, wanted to speak with him.

But Wittholz *had* agreed to speak with us.

He repeated much of the story he had told me earlier, but in greater detail. He explained that he was told the money used to help dump Joe Clark as head of the Conservative Party in Canada had come through the Hanns Seidel Stiftung—a political organization connected to the right-wing Bavarian party, the CSU.

Wittholz had understood the significance of a story alleging foreign influence in a political process. When he first heard it in the mid-1980s, he was a German citizen working in Canada, but now, sixteen years later, he had another perspective: he had loved Canada so much he had become a Canadian citizen. He had raised his family here. He felt it distasteful that a foreign company might be involved in efforts to change the leadership of a Canadian political party—all the more so because *he* was the former president of MBB's Canadian subsidiary, MBB Canada Limited. By the fall of 2000, he also wondered why no one in Canada seemed to be paying attention to the story when it was making huge headlines in Germany.

And so, for a variety of reasons, he made a decision to help us out.

He walked into his study, then came back with copies of the documents I had been hoping to read back in February—and the very documents I believed were under seal in the Eurocopter hearing in Toronto that I had been allowed to monitor but not attend. Wittholz cautioned us: we could make notes, but he could not let us copy the documents. He left us mostly alone in the study as we began writing, popping in now and then to help us if we had questions.

The documents revealed a spectacular paper trail that Wittholz and others had created as concerns mounted through MBB Canada after it learned that its parent company would be paying secret commissions on the sale of helicopters to the Canadian Coast Guard. It all reminded me of the fear that had swept through the North American offices of Airbus when sales agents there realized Airbus was paying secret commissions on the Air Canada sale. The first document we examined was the $27 million contract that MBB Canada had itself signed with the Canadian Coast Guard. The government had included a clause—a "No bribe" clause—making MBB confirm—in writing—that it was not paying any "commissions."

Other documents detailed a growing debate in the company over rumours of secret commissions that had been paid. Wittholz had flown to Germany to confront his bosses, Heinz Pluckthun and Kurt Pfleiderer, about the rumours. He wrote a memo stating he believed that the IAL contract with Schreiber was "illegal and unnecessary."

Wittholz was not the only employee with concerns. Jim Grant had been MBB's permanent consultant in Ottawa for several years and was still officially in that position when MBB had installed Frank Moores as its Ottawa lobbyist. Grant referred to Schreiber as "that slimy little bugger." Grant and Wittholz wrote another memo in 1987 expressing concern about their "consultants" and the fact they had a "friend of [the] PM's on [the] board of directors." They were referring to Robert Shea, an old university friend of Mulroney's. They had met as young students at St. Francis Xavier University, and the Boston businessman had recently been appointed to MBB Canada's board of directors. Wittholz explained that Moores had "whispered" in Kurt Pfleiderer's ear that Shea should be on the board if they were hoping to get more contracts from the Canadian government.

On February 24, 1987, another Wittholz and Grant memo stated that "[changes] in the political climate initiated by a series of scandals published daily by the news media over the last few months make it imperative to review the representation of MBB in Canada in the future." The memo outlined a series of scandals that had rocked the Mulroney government in its first term in office, including allegations of fraudulent tendering, pandering to Quebec and a patronage trail leading straight into Mulroney's office. In their memo, Wittholz and Grant explained that new lobbyist registration legislation could mean that the news media could figure out who was really representing MBB. The memo got to the point: "The areas that are most dangerous at this particular time are: associations with patronage friends of the Prime Minister; retention of the friends of the Prime Minister on boards of directors; any indication of foreign involvement; any indication of foreign money that goes into party funds, directly or indirectly."

As far back as 1987 Wittholz was concerned about foreign money influencing Canadian politics.

We realized we had spent more than three hours at Wittholz's house. He had been generous with his time, and with his documents. But the best was yet to come: he was willing, he said, to appear on-camera.

Goetz and I jumped back in our rental car and raced to Toronto. The streets were dark, the evening chilly. Winter was just around the corner. Six winters had come and gone since I first began working on the story. Thanks to Helge Wittholz, Goetz and I felt as if we had one more shot at the Airbus story. There comes a time in any *fifth estate* project when the bosses decide that the story is either dead and it's time to cut their losses, or that the story is still alive and ready to move into the filming phase. Now that Wittholz had given us the documents and had agreed to an on-camera interview, we knew the answer was all but certain.

We would be producing one final Airbus documentary.

We figured there was no point in putting off the phone call to Kurt Pflei-derer. Goetz had called Pfleiderer once, four years ago, and still had his phone number; so he called him in Germany from his hotel room in Toronto. Pfleiderer categorically dismissed all the allegations.

MBB Helicopter, he claimed, had "the lowest commission rate in the en-tire helicopter business." He said he was proud of his role in setting up the Canadian subsidiary in the early 1980s. "That was the most solid work that I did in my entire life," he told Goetz, and criticized Wittholz—who had been hired to run the company—as a "beginner."

"He [Wittholz] became a Canadian far too quickly and forgot that he worked for MBB," he said.

Pfleiderer was aware of the scandal that had engulfed Mulroney in 1995 and echoed an argument that many others had already made—that the current RCMP investigation was "revenge" against Mulroney because he "won the earlier case."

As for the dump-Clark movement, Pfleiderer insisted he had no idea who Joe Clark was. Pfleiderer also insisted he'd never heard a rumour that the Hanns Seidel Stiftung had ever given money to the Canadian Conser-vative Party or any of its politicians. This answer contradicted what Wit-tholz told us—that it was Pfleiderer himself who had educated Wittholz on the dump-Clark movement and how money from Bavaria had helped dump the leader of the party in favour of Brian Mulroney. Indeed, Wit-tholz had copied down parts of his conversation with Pfleiderer. We had to consider the possibility that Wittholz had faked the notes. But why? What possible motivation would he, and his colleague James Grant, have for concocting such an elaborate story?

Pfleiderer said Schreiber bragged about his connections in Ottawa, but that he was not as close to the politicians as he would have one believe; he said Schreiber failed to get him a signed photo of Prime Minister Mul-roney. "One meeting got made into a close friendship," Pfleiderer said. "Schreiber was less important than one thinks." It appeared Pfleiderer had not kept up to date on recent developments. Indeed, Prime Minister Mul-roney had had *several* meetings with Schreiber.

Two days later, on November 7, 2000, millions of Americans—and Canadians—were glued to their televisions awaiting election results as to who would be the next US president, George W. Bush or Al Gore. As it turned out, they would have to wait several more weeks; it became one of the most controversial election results in American history. John Goetz was staying at the Sutton Place Hotel on University Avenue, and a bunch of us had met in his hotel room to watch the returns. Goetz had to leave partway through the evening.

Schreiber had agreed to meet with him.

I was thrilled. And envious. It had been clear for some time that under no circumstances would Schreiber meet with me. I watched the election coverage but was preoccupied. How was the conversation going? Would Schreiber open up? How much would he say? Schreiber had of course been speaking with other journalists, including Phil Mathias at the *National Post*, George Wolff at CTV News, and Bob Fife, also by then at the *National Post*. But Schreiber had deliberately avoided me, making good on his written promise to me in 1995 that he would never talk with me. His having agreed to meet Goetz was about as close as I would ever get to Karlheinz.

Schreiber had never given an on-camera interview to any Canadian television journalist. In fact, he had hardly been quoted in any of Phil Mathias's print pieces. By now Schreiber had given German-language interviews to practically every television station, had been quoted frequently in all the major German daily newspapers. (One cartoon I took from a German magazine showed a picture of Schreiber in Canada loading shells into a cannon, then blasting them into Germany.) But it seemed his strategy in Canada had been to stay quiet, at least for now.

Those of us who remained in the Sutton Place hotel room waited for hours for the election results to come in—and for John Goetz to come back from his meeting with Schreiber. Finally, well after midnight, Goetz returned. The room was still full of my *fifth estate* colleagues, and a little noisy, so

Goetz took me out onto the balcony. He had news about the dump Joe Clark allegations.

"Schreiber confirmed it all," he said. "He confirmed it all."

Goetz told me that Schreiber laughed about how "we" organized delegates from Quebec to come to Winnipeg, how "we" put them up in a hotel for three nights in Winnipeg, how "we" paid for their flights, how "we" gave them a little shopping money. "And that is how we won!" Schreiber told him.

"There's more," said Goetz.

"It was all done 'in *auftrag*'—on the orders of Franz Josef Strauss. Schreiber told me '*Strauss war voll mitdrin, er wußte alles*'—Strauss was completely involved, he knew everything."

In the fall of 2000, Jean Chrétien called a snap election. He returned to power with another majority, benefiting as always from a right-wing vote split by the Conservatives and the Canadian Alliance. Chrétien had been in power for seven years. In just one more year he'd be tied for longevity in office with Mulroney.

On November 27, Karlheinz Schreiber and Eddie Greenspan were back in court, continuing their battle against extradition. The international media was still paying some attention and the crowd assembled in Courtroom 4-9 watched Greenspan argue that the new Extradition Act, under which Schreiber had been one of the first to be charged, was unconstitutional. His argument: the extradition judge was allowed to hear some evidence that would not normally be admissible in a Canadian court of law. Why the double standard? I stopped by the courtroom on the way to work. Immediately I had the sense that this wasn't going to be a normal day. Schreiber sat across the courtroom from me, but as I looked over he appeared to give me a friendly glance. Did he just smile at me? Instinctively I smiled back and nodded.

When the court broke for a recess, I rode the escalator down to the coffee shop with the new Agence France-Presse reporter in Toronto. We had no idea Schreiber was riding on the escalator behind us. We turned to take the bend to the second floor, a slight bottleneck had formed and Schreiber, now right beside me, motioned for me to stay behind.

"Are you Mr. Cashore?" he said.

"Yes."

He told me he had met John Goetz, and that my colleague from Germany had spoken highly of me. I thanked him. I would love to chat with him and meet for coffee sometime, I said. He didn't respond directly to my invitation, but told me to watch events in Germany over the next two months. As we approached the ground floor, he seemed to offer a rapprochement.

"I'm not against you, Mr. Cashore."

"And me neither, Mr. Schreiber. I'm not against you."

He smiled, waved goodbye, and so did I. He walked towards Eddie Greenspan, who was waiting nearby.

I went back to my office and wrote up a note of what had just happened. It began: "I talked to Schreiber today for the first time in 5 years."

For much of that fall I had been working on a story about false allegations of pedophilia against Saskatchewan foster families. The documentary "The Scandal of the Century" aired on *the fifth estate* on Wednesday, November 29. Canadians saw for the first time how the police and Crown attorney's office in Saskatoon had let a profound injustice continue for years, in order to cover up their own incompetence. The reaction to our story was almost unprecedented; thousands of emails from shocked viewers, enormous television ratings and demands that the Saskatchewan government finally apologize to the innocent families. Still, I had no idea that there would be another benefit. I would find out that Karlheinz Schreiber had watched the documentary; he, too, had been profoundly moved.

It *was* an exhilarating time to be working on the Airbus story again. Goldenthal, Fowler, Goetz and I would draw up lengthy to-do lists, then split them up, ticking each item off as we finished, eager to get to the next one. Goetz, back in Berlin, was on the phone every day with the rest of the team. The day the "Scandal" documentary aired, Goetz called. He was in a cheerful mood. He had been hunting through the Berlin inquiry material and uncovered new MBB documents that turned out to be the missing pieces of the puzzle. (The documents he had obtained were seized by the police in Germany at both Schreiber's Kaufering compound and MBB's corporate offices in Germany. Now they were popping up at the Berlin inquiry.)

The documents confirmed parts of what Wittholz had been telling us. The first document, written by Kurt Pfleiderer, was dated November 11, 1984—only two months after Mulroney had come to power. It contained the admission that MBB *had been* in touch with Tories close to Mulroney even *before* they came to power: "The working together with members of the new Canadian government was already tight before their election victory and among other things has contributed to the winning of the Canadian helicopter call for tenders," Pfleiderer wrote. He added that MBB had "Mr. KH Schreiber" and "Frank D. Moores" to thank for their efforts.

The Pfleiderer memo stated why Mulroney's friend, Bob Shea, was appointed to the board of directors of MBB Canada Limited. "The Minister [Bob Coates] explained that it was the personal wish of the Prime Minister to engage Mr. Bob Shey [sic] from Boston, an American industrialist. This wish was to be fully met." Finally, Pfleiderer outlined to his colleagues what needed to be done "for further action." The first two items stood out: "1. MBB seals a consulting contract with Alta Nova Associates (Mr. Frank Moores) for c.a. $72,000 Cdn a year with charges for later success fees. 2. MBB orders/engages Mr. Bob Shey [sic] to the supervisory board at MCL."

Another letter dated May 31, 1985, was from Schreiber to a senior MBB executive in Germany: "I would like to bring a very important point to your attention: of course use the contact through GCI (Frank Moores), also for other projects which are connected to the Canadian government . . . The use of this contact not only makes sense but is expected from the other side for many reasons."

Schreiber wrote those words less than a year after Mulroney came to power in September 1984. Now, in 2000, they had surfaced in Germany—and provided valuable information about the middleman and his relationship to the new Conservative government in Ottawa.

I could see a problem looming on my schedule.

My wife's parents had booked an all-expenses-paid week-long vacation for Alisa, the boys and me to join them in Hawaii on March 10. It seemed like a long way off, but was really less than three months. Normally I could not plan to take a week off in the middle of our hectic *fifth estate* season. In fact, I had never taken a week off during *the fifth estate* season since I began in 1991. It was understood that whatever time we booked off for holidays, we would take it between April and September, when the program was off the air. I remember once meeting with a human resources specialist at CBC who remarked that I had never officially claimed any of my holiday time at Christmas. I told her I would have done cartwheels in the halls of *the fifth estate* had I ever been *allowed* to take a week off at Christmas. It had simply never happened. And so I approached David Studer about getting special permission to take that week off in March. He agreed.

I would have to watch the days closely. To make matters worse, another unexpected issue came up at work: an RCMP officer was suing me for alleged defamation after we exposed his role in the wrongful murder conviction of the Nova Scotia industrial arts teacher Clayton Johnson. The lawsuit had sat dormant for a while but now I was needed in Nova Scotia to attend meetings and examinations for discovery. I looked at the days remaining before spring break with some concern. There did not seem to be a lot of days left to work on the latest Schreiber lawsuit, the lawsuit in Nova Scotia, the filming and editing of a recently assigned update on our "Scandal of the Century" story, then finish the research, the filming and editing of our latest Airbus story. I could see only one solution: to work even harder, to get to the finish line on time and to go on that family holiday.

There was a silver lining to the lawsuit in Nova Scotia.

Someone had told me I should get in touch with a certain political insider who was close to former Nova Scotia premier John Buchanan, who had run the province from 1978 to 1990, and whose name had shown up a few times in Schreiber's Daytimers. The insider lived in Halifax, but

I knew from a previous conversation would only agree to talk in person. Now, thanks to the Nova Scotia lawsuit, I could finally have that conversation.

The source began by telling me that he knew for a fact that Schreiber had invited one of Buchanan's political assistants to Kaufering. When Schreiber pulled out his Beretta, the shocked political aide was told, "In Germany, you can't be too careful." Schreiber had told the aide that he had installed a panic button by the bar and that "special police" would come if he pressed it. My source told me that the aide also travelled to Lugano to meet with Pelossi. "I got the impression Karlheinz was a buffoon. Not a class act like Giorgio [Pelossi]," the source said. As for the companies that Schreiber represented, these guys "are bigger than countries." The source said that there was a signed picture of Premier John Buchanan in the basement, "To my good friend, Karlheinz Schreiber."

Schreiber had also mentioned to Buchanan's aide that things had "worked out well on the Airbus [deal]," suggesting things could also work out well on the Bear Head project if it went ahead.

"The whole context of the conversation was [that] it was clear he [Schreiber] made friends. He had friends because of what they could do for him. Otherwise why waste time with the [political aide] to Buchanan?" The source told me that Schreiber's job was to "seal deals," and to "take care" of the "old boys."

My source went on: "It became apparent to me [Schreiber] had money and goods at his disposal. It was his way of doing business. He was smart enough not to have any witnesses around. He would do other favours. Condos in Florida. Trips to Europe. Oh, your son is having trouble getting through university? That is the kind of thing Schreiber did for people."

The source told me he knew for a fact that Schreiber gave cash to the Buchanan election campaign in 1988. "I know it was cash," he said. "It was in a brown paper envelope and was passed from one person to another. I was there. I didn't figure it out until later." The source recalled that the exchange took place outside a church hall somewhere in Nova Scotia. "This is from Karlheinz," one political staffer had said to another.

I asked about the battle for the leadership of the PC Party in the early 1980s.

"I heard that Karlheinz Schreiber put big money into the dump-Clark campaign" the source told me. "It is generally accepted that Karlheinz Schreiber was Mulroney's backer from the start. It was important to bring Mulroney to power."

Later in December I called the former Nova Scotia premier, John Buchanan, who was by then a Tory senator; Mulroney had appointed him in 1990. It went about as well as my phone call with his successor, Don Cameron. I explained I wanted to talk about Karlheinz Schreiber.

"No, I don't want to get involved in any of it," Buchanan said.

I told him that his name had come up in Schreiber's Daytimer and that I was just trying to sort it all out.

"My only involvement," the former premier said, "was that they contacted us years ago, both Bear Head and the Power Corporation. But nothing ever happened. I don't think they ever did a thing about it that I can recall."

I asked about the cash contribution to his election campaign in 1988. Buchanan said he "wouldn't have a clue" if Schreiber donated to his election campaign.

"He never gave you cash or money?" I asked.

"No, no, look, I don't want to talk to you anymore. Goodbye."

Eddie Greenspan continued to find ways to delay Schreiber's extradition hearing, and in December went so far as to suggest the case might soon be over. On December 21, 2000, both the *National Post* and the *Globe and Mail* quoted Greenspan saying that a Munich tax court ruling might have put a halt to Schreiber's extradition case. The court had removed a freeze on Schreiber's assets and, according to Greenspan, ruled "there was little, if any, evidence he committed tax fraud in Germany." Whatever Greenspan's initial thinking, the charges remained and the extradition hearing continued. Still, the case *was* sauntering along lazily through the court system. Justice David Watt had told the newspapers it would resume January 23,

2001, with testimony from a federal official on Canada's extradition system. It had been seventeen months since Schreiber's arrest and the hearing was not even close to being over.

Our story seemed to keep getting better.

Jennifer Fowler and I travelled to London, Ontario, early in the new year for some follow-up questions with Helge Wittholz. We told him we had worked hard on the story, but really needed the actual documents; it was not enough just to read them and make notes. Wittholz relented. How far we had come in eleven months, when, for very good reasons, Wittholz did not want to talk publicly or provide his documents.

Howard Goldenthal was enjoying some success too. Working with CBC's visual researcher, Jim Bertin, he discovered old footage from the 1983 leadership review convention in Winnipeg, showing a controversy over the arrival of a busload of delegates from Quebec. A pro-Mulroney supporter named Jean-Yves Lortie had shown up with a single cheque to pay them en masse. Party organizers would not allow it, prompting the Quebec delegates to wait hours for Lortie to come back with individual cheques. That's when Brian Mulroney showed up on the video, complaining about the poor treatment of those particular Quebec delegates.

I knew I had seen Lortie's name somewhere else, but where? Then I remembered. I had only to look up from my laptop to my crowded bulletin board. Thumbtacked on the wall was a cheque for $107 that Mulroney's legal team had sent me in December 1996, along with a subpoena, to travel to Montreal on a Greyhound bus to be a witness at the former prime minister's libel trial. In his real life, Jean-Yves Lortie was a Montreal bailiff. It was he who had cut me the cheque for the bus trip.

Every once in a while I would call Schreiber. On Saturday, January 13, I tried again.

"Harvey, I am in the middle of a meeting, okay? Try another time."

"Okay, thanks."

On January 20, 2001, I phoned Anthony Lawler, the former Airbus salesman on the Air Canada file back in 1988. My old contact from Airbus, Gary Kincaid, had told me Lawler had left Airbus. He suggested I give Lawler a call again. I had been told by others that Lawler was furious when he learned that Frank Moores was somehow involved in selling the Airbus planes to Air Canada. He was willing to talk, if only for background. First, he confirmed he had met Schreiber in Calgary: "I met him once. He approached me in Calgary. He was keen. He took me to his apartment." Lawler heard enough in that meeting, he told me, to conclude that Schreiber was bad news for Airbus. He wrote a memo to his bosses telling them that Schreiber "could do damage" and that his methods would backfire in a country like Canada. He confirmed to me that he had told his bosses he wouldn't touch Schreiber with "a barge pole." Lawler explained, "I just did not think he would be any good. Air Canada would resent it."

And he told me the story of how he first heard of Frank Moores. A vice-president of Air Canada, who Lawler would not name, had received a phone call from Moores one day. Lawler happened to be in a boardroom with the vice-president, when his secretary came in to say that Frank Moores was on the phone. The vice-president explained that "Frank Moores was calling to ask which Airbus aircraft they were evaluating." Lawler's anecdote seemed to confirm, yet again, that at least one person at Air Canada—if not more—knew about Frank Moores's lobby efforts. But who?

On January 25, 2001, the phone rang in my office. It was Karlheinz Schreiber.

"I know we are on different sides of this story," he said, referring to Airbus, but then told me he had seen the Saskatchewan story and was impressed with how Richard Klassen, the central figure, was brave enough to take on a corrupt law enforcement and justice system. "Mr. Cashore, I think you are a courageous journalist for doing that story," Schreiber told me. "And I would like you to tell Mr. [Linden] MacIntyre that he is also a courageous journalist. I used to be a judge for nine years in Bavaria. I know what this means to have an injustice like this. What you did was a credit to every Canadian."

I had the sense we were going to have a friendly conversation, perhaps even discuss the Britan account and Brian Mulroney. But then he brought the conversation back to reality.

"You know I am suing the CBC?"

"Yes, of course," I said. Had he forgotten he was also suing me personally?

"But I want you to know that I admired your work."

I suggested we meet.

"Yes, we should do that. I am very busy this week, but I know that Goetz is coming to town. The three of us should talk together . . . One day you will see that you have been used. You have been a pawn," he said.

John Goetz was back in Toronto the last week of January, but Schreiber agreed to meet only with him, for dinner one night. That night I worked late. I left the building for a minute to grab a sandwich. When I returned to my office I saw the red message light flashing on my phone.

Goetz had left a message. "Harv, where are you? Schreiber wants you to join us. Where are you? Harv, where are you?"

Then he hung up. *Shit!*

"Where are YOU, John?" I yelled at the phone. He hadn't told me where they were. I had left my office for five minutes for a stupid sandwich and I had missed meeting Schreiber. I called Goetz's cellphone, but it immediately went to his message machine.

An hour later the phone rang. It was Goetz. "Schreiber wants to talk to you."

They were at Le Marche–Movenpick restaurant on Yonge Street. I practically ran the entire way.

Goetz smiled when I arrived, then Schreiber stood up too and shook my hand. He suggested I sit next to him. In front of him Schreiber had a plate of raw oysters and white wine. I was introduced to his new business partners, financiers who were getting involved in his pasta business. We made small talk as Schreiber bragged that the pasta machine he owned the rights to was revolutionary. Then, as everyone was talking around us, Schreiber motioned for me to come even closer to him. He put his hand on my knee. He leaned towards me and whispered. "I gave money to Brian Mulroney." He sat back up in his chair, looked ahead, as if he had said nothing. I formed a question, but he put a silencing finger to his mouth.

I knew Schreiber was still stinging from the Luc Lavoie comments. Fourteen months had gone by since we aired the piece, but Schreiber still did not know for sure whether the comment originated with Lavoie or with Mulroney himself. According to Schreiber, Mulroney's "people" had tried to explain to him that I had gotten Lavoie drunk, secretly taped him, then somehow distorted the quotes. At least this is the story that Schreiber had told Goetz. Goetz responded by telling Schreiber that the "I got Lavoie drunk" story was not close to being true. Lavoie and I were not even in the same room, let alone the same city, when the conversations took place.

Goetz came up with a plan. He knew that all the conversations between Lavoie and me were taped. We could prove to Schreiber that the story was not true simply by letting him hear Lavoie's own words. All we had to do was convince Schreiber to sit down with us and listen to the tapes. He agreed. We acted quickly.

Only days after the Movenpick meeting I found myself in John Goetz's hotel room on the fourteenth floor of the Crown Plaza Hotel on Front Street, waiting for Schreiber to knock on the door. We could hardly believe what was about to happen. Schreiber arrived in a cheerful mood. He breezed into the room as if we were old friends, sitting down in a large armchair as Goetz and I sat on either side of him on office chairs. In between us was a small coffee table, a portable cassette player and the stack of audiotapes of my conversations with Lavoie.

But first some small talk. Or rather, Schreiber made some small talk.

I would finally understand what others meant when they told me you do not so much have a conversation with Schreiber as you listen. Try asking a question and you get a look as if you have interrupted the pope while he was dispensing Communion.

Schreiber seemed to sense our impatience and nervousness. He told us a joke that I would hear more than a few more times in the future. The joke went like this: A mouse runs into a barn and sees a cow. "Please help me," says the mouse. "A cat is chasing me and I need somewhere to hide." The cow tells the mouse to come close so he can cover him in manure. Then the cat comes into the barn and sees the cow and a tiny portion of the mouse's tail sticking out of the manure. The cat walks over to the tail, grabs it by its teeth, pulls the mouse out of the manure and promptly eats the mouse.

"And so what is the moral to the story?" Schreiber asked rhetorically. "Number one, if someone shits on you he is not necessarily your enemy. Number two, if someone gets you out of shit, he is not necessarily your friend. Number three, if you ever find yourself in shit, make sure you hide your tail!"

Schreiber followed the joke with an infectious laugh. This was a strange, new experience for all of us. We had different agendas; there was no doubt about that. Schreiber was using us, that was clear, and we were using him. I inserted the first of the Lavoie tapes into the cassette recorder. The room filled with the voice of Mulroney's spokesperson, as we listened in silence to the conversations I had had with Lavoie in October 1999. More than an hour later, the session was over.

Now it was Schreiber's turn to talk.

He told us the tapes proved that we were telling the truth about what was said and how it was said. Schreiber could see that the story that I had got Lavoie drunk was not true. He said he understood that we would probably expect him to start talking now about his relationship with Mulroney. However, it was not the right time, he said.

"My father was a potato farmer," he explained. "You don't harvest your potatoes in the spring. You wait until the fall."

Goetz encouraged Schreiber to repeat what he had told me about giving money to Mulroney. The suggestion angered Schreiber.

"If you continue like that, I get up and leave," he said. "Remember. Time, place, weapon."

After the meeting, Schreiber and I left Goetz's hotel room, taking the elevators together to the lobby. He offered to drive me to the Bloor subway station. We walked across Front Street and into the parking lot under the Workers Compensation building. I was struck by how ordinary it all seemed. We had to pay for parking and when he got the receipt he gave it to me, even though he paid, in case I wanted to claim it as an expense.

He asked if the heater was working on the seat warmer. There was some idle chatter about my family and his pasta machine.

"Harvey," he said, "if politicians could see us now, there would be heart attacks across the country."

CHAPTER THIRTY-ONE
MOVING ON

Time was ticking away too quickly.

By the first week in February 2001 we still had not begun to film interviews for the MBB Helicopter story, yet the March 7 airdate was only a month away. It was becoming increasingly difficult to juggle my responsibilities at home and at work. There were many evenings when I missed dinner, then came home late, exhausted. On those days my wife, still working full-time as a teacher, had to handle everything, from picking the boys up at daycare, to preparing lunches, to helping with homework. Often there was no discussion about it; I simply told Alisa I had to work late. Believe it or not, I actually thought *I* was the one hard done by, having to work all those extra hours. At the time, I didn't fully understand how my schedule impacted *everyone* around me.

Howard Goldenthal and I had an idea. We knew from a published photo in *Bild Zeitung* back in January 2000 that Schreiber had been at a luncheon with both Brian Mulroney and Helmut Kohl in Bonn on June 13, 1999. We wondered if CBC reporters were there at the time, and if so, perhaps they had video of the event. Goldenthal got in touch with Julia Chandler, who runs the CBC's videotape archives in Ottawa. Chandler did indeed have a tape of the event. She made a copy and sent it to Toronto for us to screen. "You're lucky," Chandler told Goldenthal as they spoke on the phone. The tape was part of a collection due to be bulk erased within a week, as part of a routine purging of unbroadcast tapes.

I was sitting in the CBC atrium having coffee with a colleague when Goldenthal came running up to my table, almost out of breath.

"They're on the tape! They're on the tape!"

"Who?"

"Mulroney, Kohl and Schreiber, they're all together."

"Together?"

"You've got to see it. It's all on the video. We have *video!*"

The footage was better than we could have dreamed of. An alert CBC cameraman had filmed a receiving line as the June 13, 1991, luncheon was about to begin. A master of ceremonies introduced guests who then shook hands with Kohl and Mulroney, standing together facing the camera. One could hear the voice introducing "Herr Schreiber" even before he could be seen. Then, walking across the frame, Schreiber appeared. First he smiled at Kohl, shook his hand, then smiled at Mulroney, who smiled back, and shook Schreiber's hand. Mulroney then turned his head to address Kohl, as if to say something about Schreiber.[1] It was impossible to make out what Mulroney said, but everyone looked pleased. Schreiber was smiling; Mulroney was smiling; and then Kohl was smiling.

That segment was and remains the only known footage ever taken of Mulroney and Schreiber together.

As we were assembling the visuals for the documentary, I came into the office on Sunday, February 11, in order to write a note to the new senior producer of *the fifth estate*, Jim Williamson. I explained my urgency. Unless Jennifer Fowler and Howard Goldenthal were assigned to the MBB story exclusively, "I don't see how we can get this story to air on time." (I was probably more preoccupied with the notion I might miss the preplanned

[1] John Goetz asked Schreiber what Mulroney had said to Kohl. "This is my good friend Karlheinz Schreiber" is what Schreiber remembered Mulroney saying.

family holiday if the story got delayed another week.) Then I updated Williamson on where we stood in our research: John Goetz was travelling to Slovenia where we had tracked down Walter Wolf, whose name had already been linked to the dump-Clark movement, Franz Josef Strauss and many of Mulroney's close friends; Jennifer Fowler was flying to New Brunswick to speak with Dalton Camp, the former Conservative insider who had first raised concerns about offshore money (and who would later confirm that the offshore money he had referred to in 1983 was connected to Walter Wolf); I needed to film re-creations of the RCMP raids on Eurocopter and have Linden MacIntyre interview Helge Wittholz; we needed to travel to Ottawa to film a re-creation inside the Château Laurier where Wittholz had that angry showdown with his German bosses; Gary Akenhead, the editor who had worked on all the Airbus stories, needed to begin the edit as soon as possible; Linden MacIntyre and I needed to travel to Europe to try to interview Kurt Pfleiderer, the MBB executive, and Walter Wolf, if he would agree to an on-camera interview; and we needed to send a letter to Brian Mulroney again, asking for another on-camera interview.

We all took a deep breath. From now until our March 7 airdate no one would think of much else. Alisa asked me to look after the kids one weekend; she needed to do some extra work herself. This posed a problem, since I needed to work on the dump-Clark outline. I found a solution. I brought my work with me to the park. The boys wanted to play on a giant metal ant. I crawled inside and sat down. As they climbed high above me, I scribbled notes.

CBC television reporter Carol Off walked by at that moment, incredulous.

"Harvey, is that you?" she asked.

"I'm multitasking," I answered.

The CBC van cruising along the autobahn from Berlin to Cologne in February was packed to the roof. Hans Vanderzande, the cameraman, was taking turns driving with soundman Larry Kent. Linden MacIntyre and I sat in the two seats behind, reading files I had stuffed into my computer bag and discussing the next interview, and, in the back row, sandwiched between camera equipment, sat Jule Scharf, the German fixer we had hired to help us navigate through Germany.

The idea was that we would save thousands of dollars on airfare by driving across the country, with a rather large detour to Slovenia, where Walter Wolf had agreed to be interviewed, and then back to Berlin for a final series of interviews. Our first stop was Cologne, where we spoke to Herbert Leiduck, the German industrialist who had told us that Schreiber bragged about having Canadian politicians in his pocket. Then we stayed overnight at a roadside hotel, making our way to Munich where we had planned to interview Kurt Pfleiderer, the MBB executive. When MacIntyre and Scharf approached Pfleiderer at his house, however, he was wary.

"Yes?" Pfleiderer asked, looking up to see MacIntyre and Scharf.

"I'm from Canada," MacIntyre explained. With translation assistance from Scharf, he asked for an interview about MBB helicopters, the Coast Guard and the dump-Clark movement. Pfleiderer responded that he was still on the company payroll, and that the company had told him to keep his mouth shut.

"I'm very fond of all Canadians," he said, "because our negotiations with the Canadians were the best I ever had in the world." Then he disappeared into his house. MacIntyre and Scharf jumped back in the van. A video segment of Pfleiderer was enough.

We headed to Maribor, Slovenia, to interview Walter Wolf. He was no longer the flamboyant businessman who once owned a Grand Prix race car and clothing line, but we got the sense he was almost nostalgic about the old days. Before the on-camera interview he took us to an old warehouse that looked slightly decrepit. He unlocked a massive door, then opened it to reveal a special-edition Lamborghini Countach.

"Wow," whistled Vanderzande appreciatively.

Wolf's current business was a little more mundane—helping to build factories in the former Yugoslavia. He took us back to his office, where we set up our cameras. Wolf was giving his first interview ever about the dump-Clark movement but I had the feeling he would have talked years ago. No one, it seemed, had asked. MacIntyre reminded him he was one of many who worked to change the leadership of the Conservative Party.

"I was donating money for that cause," Wolf said. "I wasn't the pioneer. There were people who were working against Mr. Clark at that time, starting from Mulroney down."

Wolf recalled a particular day in 1982, when he met Schreiber and others at a Calgary hotel. He had asked them for their help in the fight to dump the leader of the Progressive Conservative Party. "Why should I be the only one to pay?" Wolf said with a smile, telling us that Schreiber said he would be happy to raise money. "He [said he] would be prepared to help in the campaign, yeah," Wolf told us. He explained that he worked closely with Mulroney's friend Michel Cogger, Frank Moores and Schreiber. "I was the one who introduced Karlheinz Schreiber to Frank Moores," Wolf boasted.

He claimed that he helped Frank Moores out financially in the early 1980s. Moores was, Wolf said, close to bankruptcy at the time. "He was in the problems, and because I had the same interest—and that was called at that time, Joe Clark—he [Moores] was very active in it, protecting, if you want to know, Canada from further disasters."

Wolf told us what we already knew: raising money was crucial for the dump-Clark movement because they needed to fund as many delegates as possible to get to the Winnipeg leadership review convention. Delegates were selected at riding associations from across the country and since Quebec did not have a grassroots Conservative party, it meant that they would try to populate the delegate selection meetings with so-called "instant" Tories who could then vote for the dump-Clark delegate. That was just half the battle. The delegates had to fly from Quebec to Winnipeg. Someone needed to pay for the trip. That's where Walter Wolf and Schreiber came into the picture, according to Wolf (confirming what Schreiber had told Goetz in November).

"Don't forget that the delegation from Quebec, unannounced, shipped into Winnipeg, you know, with two big Boeing from Wardair, okay?" Wolf said.

"And how much did this exercise cost?" MacIntyre asked.

"That I will not tell you," Wolf said with a chuckle.

The interview was a crucial step forward in our story. For the first time Walter Wolf had admitted on-camera that he had funded the dump-Clark movement—and confirmed that Schreiber was also involved. Both men were proteges of Franz Josef Strauss, and both men were deeply committed to penetrating the powerful inner circle around Mulroney in Montreal in the early 1980s.

The next day we drove nine hours from Slovenia back to Berlin. Then Linden MacIntyre and John Goetz snagged the best interview of the documentary.

Goetz told us that one of Schreiber's German lawyers, Jan Olaf Leisner, happened to be in Berlin that morning on an unrelated case. Normally he worked in Munich, so Goetz suggested we seize the opportunity. Perhaps we could get a spontaneous interview with him, on-camera, about the MBB case in Canada. The truth is, Goetz had worked hard to form a friendly relationship with Leisner.

Our first stop was at the Moabit Courthouse. We parked outside and waited for the lawyer to emerge. We were not entirely sure if Schreiber had told Leisner that my relationship with the middleman was beginning to thaw, so I stayed down the street at a coffee shop while MacIntyre and Goetz waited with the camera crew. I waited for more than an hour. Then MacIntyre and Goetz returned to the café with huge grins on their faces.

"He did the interview," Goetz said.

"And?"

"See for yourself."

I put on a pair of headphones and watched the interview through the camera's playback machine. MacIntyre started the interview by simply asking Leisner to explain the case from Schreiber's perspective:

"Mr. Schreiber's position in the tax case," said Leisner, "is that he was a middleman who acted on behalf of decision-makers who received money from German companies who are interested in different investments in, for example, Canada or wherever."

"And that is a fairly conventional process in European business," MacIntyre asked, "that people like Mr. Schreiber facilitate between companies that want to sell and the buyers who want to buy?"

"You can't call it conventional," Leisner responded, "but it's necessary for those people who receive the money because they want to stay unknown."

"The decision-makers?" asked MacIntyre.

"The decision-makers," agreed Leisner.

"And when you use the phrase 'decision-makers,' are we talking about Canadian decision-makers?"

"In the certain MBB deal we were talking about, we are talking about Canadian decision-makers, yeah."

"In German there's a wonderful phrase: *schmiergelder*," MacIntyre said. "Give me the translation."

"The translation is 'lubrication money.'"

"Lubrication money," reflected MacIntyre, "makes the wheels of business go around?"

"Yeah."

"Can you explain, as you know, from Mr. Schreiber's point of view, just what his role was in the MBB deal?"

"Mr. Schreiber's main role was to protect the recipients of the lubrication money."

"People who got the *schmiergelder*?" asked MacIntyre.

"That's correct."

"Explain how he provided that protection."

"Mr. Schreiber protected them by making every payment anonymous."

This was the first time any lawyer employed by Schreiber ever admitted that the middleman had paid greasemoney to "decision-makers" in Canada.

I was pleased. The Leisner and Wolf interviews had more than justified our trip to Europe. We could now return to Toronto and tell the bosses that we got even more than we had expected. But we weren't done yet. In Berlin, the public inquiry into the Schreiber affair was ongoing. We sat down with one of the senior parliamentarians overseeing the inquiry, Frank Hoffman, who reminded us why an inquiry into Schreiber was so important. "When people like Karlheinz Schreiber spend money so that the government acts in a certain way, then democracy is undermined," Hoffman told us. "Then people like Karlheinz Schreiber and their money determine public policy, and no longer the people. And that is not tolerable in a democracy."

We wanted to contrast the German treatment of the Schreiber affair with the Canadian treatment. German parliamentarians had collected tens of thousands of pages of documents, all relating to the scandal. Many were stored in an underground vault. We got permission to film inside (promising not to open any of the binders). Linden MacIntyre spoke to the camera, observing that Germans seemed more interested in knowing what Schreiber had done with his greasemoney.

"Thousands of boxes," said MacIntyre, "tens of thousands of documents carefully stored in vaults like this, will eventually yield answers to important questions that ordinary Germans are asking about the integrity of their political institutions. Ironically, these same boxes could provide answers to similar and equally significant questions about the Canadian system, questions that Canadians haven't even begun to ask."

By February 21 we were back in Canada. I was now looking at the clock as much as the calendar. Our March 7 airdate was only fourteen days away. We had two weeks left to edit, finish filming and get the story to air. My early optimism had vanished. I had a horrible, sinking feeling that we could not pull it off. There were only two more shows in March before the hockey playoffs began; those dates were accounted for. The only available dates were either March 7 or March 14, but the latter date was impossible. I would be with my family on a vacation in Hawaii. Somehow, I had to make it to air by the March 7 deadline.

Despite our focus on the dump-Clark movement and the MBB helicopter deal, I expected we would also mention the infamous Britan account. First mention of it had been made in November 1999, but since Goetz had obtained Schreiber's Daytimer for December 8, 1994, we could now put Mulroney in New York City with Schreiber shortly after cash was withdrawn from the Britan account. I needed to review transcripts of Mulroney's 1996 libel suit testimony in Montreal to find out what exactly he had said about his relationship with Schreiber and what, if anything, he had said about any other meetings he might have had with the middleman (other than a largely unexplained "cup of coffee" at the Queen Elizabeth Hotel). Did he say anything that might have hinted at a meeting in New York? Did he some-how allow for the possibility that he had taken money from Schreiber?

Montreal lawyer Claude Armand-Sheppard had asked the questions on behalf of the federal government. I skimmed through two days of tran-scripts, stopping at a section where Mulroney stated that he knew Schreiber as a businessman from Alberta but could not remember exactly where he had first met the man.

"I cannot be more specific than that, although I certainly am sure that I met him in the years prior to 1984."

"And can you go on to describe your relationship over the years?" Shep-pard asked.

"Well, it was, he lived in Germany and he visited Canada. As I could see, he visited Canada infrequently. He went to Alberta, I think, from time to time to Ottawa, to, as I say, work on this particular project [the pro-posed Thyssen Bear Head factory]."

I found the part where Sheppard asked about their relationship after Mulroney left the Prime Minister's Office.

"Did you maintain contact with Mr. Schreiber after you ceased being prime minister?"

"Well, from time to time, not very often. When he was going through Montreal, he would give me a call. We would have a cup of coffee, I think, once or twice. And he told me that he continued to work on his project [Bear Head], that he was pushing a new government." Mulroney explained Schreiber told him he hoped to work with both the Quebec and federal governments to establish the Bear Head project in the east end of Mon-treal. "He had hired Marc Lalonde to represent his interests before the new Liberal government," Mulroney testified. "I wasn't really surprised be-cause the word in Ottawa is that Mr. Schreiber and Mr. Lalonde had had a long relationship in the past. And so he also expressed dismay with me that my Government had not agreed."

Sheppard wanted more details about the post office visits. He pressed for a more specific answer.

"When he passes through Montreal and visits you, is it at your office or at your home?"

"Well, he doesn't pass through Montreal and visit me. When he's on his way to Montreal, he call[s] me and ask[s] me and I say perhaps once or twice, if I could . . . have a cup of coffee with him at a hotel. I think I had one in the Queen Elizabeth Hotel with him. I had one in the coffee bar of the Queen Elizabeth Hotel."

Sheppard asked Mulroney how many conversations he would have had with Schreiber in the aftermath of learning about the RCMP's Letter of Request in 1995.

"Oh, I couldn't say. We had a number of conversations. As I indicated to you, the extraordinary realization of what had transpired in secret hit me like a ton of bricks." Mulroney tried to steer the discussion to the effect of the RCMP investigation.

"I don't want to interrupt you," said Sheppard, "but that was not my question."

Mulroney continued. "I want to answer your question fairly. And because of that, I sought from the Canadian government some assistance as a Canadian citizen: 'What in the name of God is going on? Who are these secret, anonymous sources in the middle of the night, accusing me of a crime? Would you like to ask me? No one has spoken to me about this, would you like to interrogate me? Would you like to examine my documents? Would you like to examine my bank accounts?' They mentioned a bank account in Switzerland. I haven't got a bank account anywhere in the world, except Montreal, and never have. I would have given them complete answers. I was prepared to let the RCMP look at my bank accounts any time they came to see me,"[2] Mulroney insisted. He never mentioned having done any banking elsewhere, across the border.

Sheppard wanted to know when Mulroney first learned that Schreiber had received Airbus commissions. "Did you, in the course of these conversations in November [1995], discuss with Mr. Schreiber whether or not he had been paid, he or his companies had been paid commissions by Airbus?" asked Sheppard.

---

2 And later the next day, Mulroney repeated the point. "I have one bank account at the CIBC in Montreal that I have had here for twenty-five years. 'And if you have any concerns, if you'd like to take a look at it, please be my guest.' That's what I'd have told him if I could have seen Sergeant [Fraser] Fiegenwald. But I couldn't see him."

"I never knew, first, prior to this, I had never heard. I never knew and I do not know to this day what arrangements, if any, had been made by Mr. Schreiber or anyone else in respect of any commercial transaction," Mulroney responded.

Sheppard tried to get Mulroney to clarify his answer. He rephrased the question.

"And the Canadian government alleges that very substantial sums were paid to Mr. Schreiber by Airbus Industries, and you didn't discuss with Mr. Schreiber whether it was true or not?" Mulroney had testified that Schreiber and he had been on the phone several times in November 1995. It might have seemed normal, Sheppard wondered, that Mulroney would have been curious to know if what had been alleged about Schreiber was true.

Mulroney would have none of it. "Mr. Sheppard," Mulroney began, "the document said, among other things, 'This investigation is of serious concern to the Government of Canada, as it involves criminal activity on the part of a former Prime Minister.' This is not an allegation; this is a statement of fact where the Government of Canada is judge, jury and executioner. And what preoccupied me, inasmuch as I had never heard of the Airbus matter in my life, what preoccupied me were the extraordinary falsehoods and injustices as they involve me. And I wondered with my family and my friends, quite frankly, how in the name of God could this come about? How could this happen in Canada? How can something like this actually take place? And the fact that Mr. Schreiber may or may not have had any business dealings was not my principal, my principal preoccupation. I had never had any dealings with him."

By the end of February it had become abundantly clear we were not going to make our March 7 airdate. The bosses officially switched the date to March 14. I reminded them about my family holiday. There was nothing they could do. I gave my wife the bad news. I would miss the first three days of the holiday, I said; she and the boys would have to go ahead of me.

"You promised this wouldn't happen," Alisa said.

We lined up an interview with Allan Gregg, the former Conservative Party strategist and well-known pollster who reminded us again how close the review vote had been—and how important those Quebec delegates had been in determining the future direction of the party at the Winnipeg convention in 1983.

"Here we are in the dead of winter, in Winnipeg—colder than a well-digger's ass—and into the hall comes all of these Quebec delegates out of buses, no one knows where they've come from. They're bullying through the lines to get registered," Gregg told MacIntyre. "You don't have to be a mathematician to figure it out: if you have 2,000 delegates, and twenty delegates swinging their vote from one way to the other, that's 2 per cent in total, one on each way. So a very small bit of jiggery-pokery could make a huge difference to both that outcome of that particular delegated convention, and, arguably, history."

Karlheinz Schreiber had gone from hot to cold again. I was convinced that, having briefed him on the Lavoie tapes, he might warm to us—to me. But there had been almost no communication. In early March, Goetz met with Schreiber to try to convince him to appear on-camera—to at least talk about the dump-Clark movement and the MBB helicopter deal. Schreiber was noncommittal; he alluded to a big story that was about to break. Goetz reported the conversation back to me.

"Schreiber said that in two or three days some things are going to come out that will be very exciting. He says Mulroney is pissed off at him now. Schreiber called someone who said that Mulroney and his people are in an epileptic fit, jumping up and down."

The "big story" never broke.

On March 11, Karlheinz Schreiber agreed to meet Goetz and me at the Four Seasons in Yorkville. It was a Sunday afternoon. My wife and our boys were already in Hawaii. I was walking west on Bloor Street, my chin tucked firmly into my scarf as gusts of arctic wind blew against my face. I looked forward to getting out of the cold and into the Four Seasons where I would meet Karlheinz Schreiber.

Schreiber began our meeting by pontificating about the strength of his case and the overall ineptitude of the RCMP. Goetz and I sat through the conversation with one goal in mind: convince Schreiber to appear on-camera. Our airdate was only three days away. Schreiber had to make a decision now, we told him. Linden MacIntyre joined us for the conversation. He explained to Schreiber that it was in his interest to give us an interview. People would wonder why he didn't talk to us. Schreiber paused to think. Okay, he said, but he had a condition: he did not want to give us a full-blown, sit-down interview; he would not object, however, if we waited outside the Four Seasons and then approached him with our cameras. Kind of a jump with permission.

Later that evening, Schreiber exited the Four Seasons. He saw MacIntyre and the rest of us standing, half-frozen on the sidewalk.

"What are you doing here?" asked Schreiber. He smiled at MacIntyre. He had the biggest Cheshire grin I had seen in my life. The first question was about whether or not he had been involved in funding the dump-Clark movement.

"Mr. [Walter] Wolf approached me," Schreiber said, "and was collecting money to support the leadership of Mr. Mulroney, hoping that he would win."

"And getting rid of Joe Clark in the process."

"Yes, yes."

MacIntyre asked him what the money was for.

"It's expensive to travel, right? For this is what Walter Wolf collected the money, and then get the people in which worked for you, and you paid their fare, and perhaps he said to you they need some money for their wives, they want to go shopping, or whatever, for the hotels."

Only two months before, Schreiber had told me that he had given money to Mulroney, but the admission had been vague and unexpected. I had no real sense of what it might have meant. He still seemed unwilling to provide specifics.

"A number of important politicians in Germany have come to grief," MacIntyre said next. "You've been a part of the downfall . . . I mean, things you've said, business you've done. How worried are Canadian politicians who may think that they may encounter the same fate?"

"I bribed nobody ever in Canada," Schreiber said flatly.

"But you were generous?" suggested MacIntyre.

"Yes, I was always generous. If you want me to disclose to whom I gave donations, it would become a book like a Bible." Schreiber chuckled at his joke.

"You've given a lot of money to a lot of people?"

"Sure."

"Why are so many people afraid of being identified?"

"Because they see the—I can only guess—they see the mess today, and then they think, okay, when I got a donation from him, I may be in the same mess." The information Schreiber imparted that winter evening was not all that new. Schreiber hinted about "donations" he had given to "politicians" but said nothing more. Perhaps the significance was the act itself: giving an on-camera interview to *the fifth estate*. Maybe he was hoping to send a message to particular viewers, that he could say even more if he wanted to.

By the time our story aired on the evening of March 14, 2001, I had already landed in Hawaii (I managed to get a later flight out and join the holiday in progress). Jennifer Fowler, John Goetz, Howard Goldenthal, Gary Akenhead and I had worked so late on the thirteenth that it had turned into the fourteenth. I only had time to get my bag at home and head for the airport.

For the first time the national media seemed uncritical of *the fifth estate*'s work. Many newspapers wrote favourable reviews of our revelations about foreign influence in the dumping of Joe Clark, albeit in the back pages. Reporters in Ottawa asked Clark for his response to the new revelations; he told everyone to wait for his memoirs (as of April 2010 we are still waiting). The *Globe and Mail* even wrote an editorial calling for tougher political party financing legislation.

For me, however, the whole thing felt anticlimactic.

I had spent years wondering where the Airbus millions had ended up. We never did find out and, besides, I wasn't sure anyone really cared. Now that the last documentary was over, I had to wonder whether the hard work had been worth it. I believed that my family always came ahead of work. But was that really how I had behaved? My travelling took me away from home for weeks at a time. I worked long hours. Sometimes I could not attend important family events. I convinced myself I had no option but to stay at work. In Hawaii, my wife summed it up.

"You are selfish."

The words hit me unexpectedly. I had never looked at it that way. My work demanded that I stay late at the office, work weekends, go on the road, miss family holidays, birthdays, our children's first steps. I was oblivious to the impact on both Alisa and me. What *had* made me think the story was so important? I had believed that whatever family events I missed, I would make up for that lost time when I was back in town, or not so busy. What was I thinking?

As for Airbus, I told myself I had finally had enough. I never, ever, wanted to work on the story again.

Three Years Later

PART IV
THE TRUTH SHOWS UP

CHAPTER THIRTY-TWO
THE PHONE CALL

April 7, 2004. I am in my office when the phone rings. I glance at the call display but do not recognize the number.

"Harvey Cashore," I answer.

"Hi, it's Bill Kaplan. I was hoping I could speak with you."

Bill Kaplan? The last time I talked to Bill Kaplan was in the latter part of 1997 when he and I exchanged angry words as he researched his book, *Presumed Guilty*, a spirited defence of Brian Mulroney. At the time I had hoped I would never hear from him again. That was seven years ago. What did he want now?

It had been three years since my last Airbus documentary. In the interim there had been some significant developments. For starters, Schreiber had dropped the "fucking liar" lawsuit against the CBC and paid our entire legal bill. He pressed ahead with his lawsuit against Luc Lavoie, however. They settled after Greenspan hinted he might bring Brian Mulroney into the lawsuit as a named defendant. Lavoie agreed to apologize to Schreiber and to write him a cheque. While the amount did not come close to the $300,000 Schreiber had been seeking, it was more than enough to cover what Schreiber had previously paid to settle with *the fifth estate*.

Then came September 11, 2001; for a while, nothing else seemed to matter.

The 9/11 attacks would impact all of us, as shock waves of fear, anger and revenge engulfed global politics. I was in the Hotel Vancouver on a *fifth estate* shoot when Howard Goldenthal called my room, telling me to turn on the television. In an instant, the story I was working on about Internet gambling seemed irrelevant. I was due to fly to San Francisco later that day but ended up returning to Toronto a few days later. My son Jeremiah, who was then four, was relieved to see me.

"Thank God you weren't on that plane, Daddy, thank God," he had said.

In the spring of 2002, CBC management asked me to work for a new investigative program, *Disclosure*. I jumped at the chance to try something new. I prepared to leave my job at *the fifth estate*, one that I had held in one capacity or another since 1991.

Once in a while Karlheinz Schreiber would call me, often for the strangest reasons. On one occasion we spoke for an hour about the *fungi porcini*, a special mushroom grown only in Switzerland, he claimed. Combined with fresh basil in butter, it made a great pasta topping. Schreiber sprinkled in references to Airbus as we spoke about the mushroom: "I am not against the Mounties," he said. "What happened to Fiegenwald is a crime, the poor bugger is innocent," he said, referring to the RCMP officer who was charged under the RCMP Act in the aftermath of his looking into the Airbus allegations. "I put more than $14 million in Canadian pockets," Schreiber told me, apropos of nothing. He said he should get a "monument" for all the jobs he helped create in Canada. "I am not interested in putting shit on Canada. This is why many things are pending and I am not moving on certain fields . . . When I go a few steps closer, the explosion comes." Oddly, he reminded me that he was still suing me. (Although Schreiber had dropped the "fucking liar" lawsuit against the CBC, he hadn't dropped the $35 million lawsuit he'd launched in 1995. The lawsuit had sat dormant but still existed on paper.)

I would make notes of his calls, file them away and forget about them.

In June 2002, Gary Ouellet died of a heart attack.

"Known as the producer of the World's Greatest Magic television specials," read the press release. It sounds heartless, but for a minute I was mad at myself: Why had we not pursued him more aggressively when we had the chance? I should have gone to see him in person; maybe then he would have talked. I remembered my old source Tower telling me that Ouellet was deeply involved in Airbus, even more than Frank Moores. Now Ouellet was dead. I wondered whether the stress of the Airbus investigation had weighed on him. He had been forced to declare bankruptcy in the early 1990s. He had lied about his involvement in Airbus. Maybe the Mounties were closing in. I had no idea, but I knew one thing: the story was getting old.

There had been developments in various courts, both in Germany and Canada. In July, a judge in Germany sentenced the two Thyssen executives, Juergen Massmann and Winfried Haastert, to jail terms—five years and two years, respectively—for tax evasion and embezzlement in relations to monies they had allegedly received from Schreiber. The *Toronto Star*'s Tracey Tyler quoted Schreiber as saying he felt sorry for them. "I know that these two gentlemen did not get this money," he insisted.

And in October, Canadian Crown attorneys officially laid charges against Eurocopter and the two German executives, Kurt Pfleiderer and Heinz Pluckthun, for paying those secret commissions in the sale of helicopters to the Canadian Coast Guard. Those charges would lead to a preliminary hearing the following year, which itself would take months to unfold. Everything, it seemed, was plodding slowly through the courts.

In the fall of 2002 I threw myself into my new job at *Disclosure*. I produced a story about body checking in kids' hockey, another about the new prime minister, Paul Martin, and how his company, Canada Steamship Lines, made use of offshore tax havens and "flags of convenience"—foreign countries with lower minimum wages—from which to run his shipping empire. Another story took a look at the role of the World Health Organization (WHO) in the SARS outbreak.

On April 22, 2003, the RCMP officially announced that it had closed down the Airbus investigation, stating there was "no further chance" that Mulroney would be charged with anything. (This despite the fact they could never determine whether or not Mulroney received money from Schreiber, let alone what the money might have been for, had he received it.) What the RCMP told the public was that aside from a single charge laid against Eurocopter over those secret commissions, no more charges on the Airbus investigation would be forthcoming.

The RCMP announcement allowed Mulroney's lawyers to claim a final vindication. All those columnists who had criticized *the fifth estate* and the RCMP for their investigations now seemed gleeful. The *Globe and Mail*'s Hugh Winsor led the charge: "The RCMP brought to an ignominious close one of the most ham-fisted, incompetent, politically charged and unduly prolonged investigations in the force's history, with almost nothing to show for it," he wrote, reminding readers that the RCMP initially dismissed the Airbus story until "CBC's the fifth estate" picked it up. The article went on: "Today, there should be red faces all around: at the RCMP, which fumbled the investigation; at the Department of Justice, which misstated unsubstantiated allegations as conclusions to the Swiss government; at the CBC, and in the Liberal cabinet, which did nothing to mitigate the disaster." Winsor hoped that the announcement would "finally close the saga for Mr. Mulroney" for a "grievous" miscarriage of justice.

Later that month, Elmer MacKay's son, Peter, thirty-seven, won the federal leadership of the Progressive Conservative Party, taking over the reins from Joe Clark, who had stepped aside. In one sympathetic profile of the new leader by CP reporter Bruce Cheadle, Peter MacKay called the Airbus investigation a "profound injustice" to Mulroney, echoing the public comments he had made for years in the House of Commons as he tried to have the RCMP shut down their investigation.

In the spring of 2003 my wife, Alisa, and I decided to separate.

I moved into a rented house in Riverdale. We planned for the boys to live with me one week and Alisa the next, and so on. Once in a while I would look at them as they slept in the bedroom they shared in the basement and tell myself they did not deserve the torture they had endured as their parents split up. It was almost too much to recall the day we told them that Mom and Dad would not be living together. As my son Massey had pointed out, Christmas would no longer be the same.

The summers were our great escape.

The boys and I began to spend the entire month of July out on Cortes Island, British Columbia, where they lived in tents, swam in the ocean with a vast array of cousins and hiked 8 kilometres to Squirrel Cove and back, simply to buy a Freezee, and then explained every detail of what had happened along the way over the evening campfire.

I began building the boys a cabin. I knew practically nothing about construction, but borrowed a textbook from my father and started from the beginning, learning how to pour cement for the foundation, then working my way up to the girders and joists. If the boys could not have a traditional family, I told myself, they could at least have a cabin in the woods. Like so many of my other ambitions, the project took on a life of its own, with me wondering whether I would ever finish it.

By the fall of 2003 Brian Mulroney was enjoying a resurgence in popularity. He had been the keynote speaker at the convention earlier in the year that elected MacKay leader of the Conservative Party, then helped broker a deal between MacKay and Canadian Alliance leader Stephen Harper to unite the right. "Mulroney's fingerprints are all over the MacKay-Harper deal," wrote columnist Larry Zolf on the CBC website, as the right-wing parties celebrated their new Conservative Party in December 2003. Mulroney was enjoying the most significant rebirth of his reputation since he left office in 1993. He had recently signed on with Toronto publisher McClelland & Stewart to write a vast memoir of his life in politics.

In early November 2003, as I was driving east on Front Street after work to pick up the boys from their after-school program, I recognized two men whom I had not seen in a while: Eddie Greenspan and William Kaplan.

They were walking out of St. Lawrence Market and into the evening sun. I wondered what they were up to. I had my answer a couple of days later, when the first in a series of three articles appeared in the *Globe*, under William Kaplan's byline.

"Secret trial revealed," read the headline.

Kaplan and the *Globe and Mail* had begun an exposé of the secret MBB hearing that I had first been blocked from attending in March 2000 and which, by 2003, had morphed into a complicated series of legal appeals by Eurocopter.[1] The *Globe* was actually not the first to report about the secret hearing. That honour belonged to Southam news court reporter Shannon Kari, who got the story after noticing Karlheinz Schreiber, Eddie Greenspan and me walk into a courtroom one day. Kari asked Schreiber if he could tell him what was going on. "Oh my God, no, everybody goes to jail." I got to know Kari well while he worked on that article, and now count him as a good friend.[2] Still, the *Globe* lawyers deserved credit, along with the CBC's Dan Henry, for helping to convince Justice Then to reverse his position and allow the public into his courtroom.

But the next day's story caused me concern.

Its Saturday edition is by far the *Globe*'s largest circulation of the week, so it was significant that was when the paper decided to plaster an enormous picture of Stevie Cameron on its front page, along with the headline "Could this journalist be the secret informant?"

For years various journalists had been accused of being confidential RCMP informants, myself included. Now the *Globe* was suggesting on its front page that that person might be writer Stevie Cameron. Eddie Greenspan and Schreiber had made similar suggestions in court, but this was different. Canada's national newspaper believed the allegation merited front-page attention. The *Globe* quoted Cameron saying allegations

1 By this point, the CBC had been allowed to attend but not to report. CBC lawyer Dan Henry fought throughout this period to have the proceedings open to the public.
2 Years later he provided me with a story idea about how an old man from Coboconk, Ontario, was cheated out of his lottery winnings by an unscrupulous store clerk, who claimed the $250,000 ticket as her own. That story led to our eventual discovery that the Ontario Lottery Corporation knew all about a serious problem in its security measures: far more clerks were "winning" lottery tickets than was statistically possible.

she was the informant were "horseshit." Cameron later explained that she *had* spoken to the RCMP, but she had not given them any confidential documents. "I did not give them any names of my sources or any information that was confidential. Paid police informant? Never. A confidential informant? Are you kidding me? Did they promise to protect me? There was no promise; indeed, police assured me that my interview would come out at trial." The *Globe*'s Kirk Makin called to ask me if I was the confidential informant. I reminded him that I had actually stored our Airbus documents in my aunt's basement in Scarborough back in the spring of 1995, specifically to hide them from the RCMP, should they come looking.

I did not see how the story merited front-page attention in the *Globe*. I thought the paper's treatment of Stevie Cameron was so egregious that I contacted her for the first time in two years, by email. I said I was appalled by the coverage. In November, Cameron and I met for coffee at the Elephant and Castle on King Street. She looked pale and seemed edgy. She told me she could barely sleep, that her family was worried about her health.

Then she said had something to tell me: back in the 1995, when the RCMP was canvassing journalists for help in its investigation, she had complied. Some of the documents she handed over, she said, had come from *the fifth estate*; further, my handwriting was on some of them. I was stunned. She never told me any of this while we worked on our book, *The Last Amigo*, back in 2000. Still, I felt conflicted. As taken aback as I was with this news, I considered it all a sideshow to the real story: Where did the money go? When I got back to my office I felt so concerned about the impact of the controversy on Cameron that I wrote her another email telling her not to worry too much. My moral compass was seriously confused.[3]

Over the next few months details would be forthcoming about Cameron's role as an RCMP informant. In February 2004, for example, she gave an interview to the *Globe and Mail*'s Kirk Makin in which she admitted

---

3 Later, when the documents that Cameron provided to the Mounties were released at the Eurocopter hearing, I realized they did not contain my handwriting after all. For some reason Cameron had mistaken Pelossi's writing for mine. As for *how* Cameron ended up with any of the Pelossi documents at all back in 1995, that was also a mystery to me. Today, I presume that Jock Ferguson—who had obtained them from *der Spiegel* in the first place—had provided Cameron with the copies after *the fifth estate* story went to air.

for the first time that she was indeed the confidential informant referred to in the RCMP files. She now realized, she said, that the RCMP had applied that term to her on their own. She said no way she considered herself an informant. What she had given the RCMP in 1995 she dismissed as "pathetic scraps of information." That month the CBC's Jane Hawtin interviewed Cameron on the morning radio show *The Current*. Cameron insisted she only provided the RCMP "material that was in the public record, the public domain."

Unfortunately, records later released in the Eurocopter hearing painted a far different picture. On May 1, 1995, for example, Sergeant Fraser Fiegenwald had made a notation in an RCMP file: "A call was received this morning from Stevie Cameron indicating that she was in possession of all the documents that the 5th Estate [*sic*] and Der Spiegel had used to research their articles. She is willing to provide us with copies of these documents." Another RCMP document from 1995 stated: "Harvey Cashore and Jock Ferguson have decided to not share the same information with us." The internal RCMP documents detailed how Cameron met the RCMP on May 4, provided them documents, and continued to keep in touch; she contacted the Mounties, according to RCMP files, on November 8, 1995, and stated that she "had come up with a new lead concerning offshore accounts of Frank Moores."[4] Years later the RCMP wanted to know if Cameron wanted to keep her identity secret. One document revealed that Fiegenwald reminded his former colleagues that, "Disclosure [of Cameron's identity] would be devastating to 2948's [her code number] professional life and 2948's information had to be kept in a confidential manner." Fiegenwald stated that Cameron had only agreed to come forward and be identified if Brian Mulroney was charged with a crime. Cameron's lawyer, Peter Jacobsen, wrote a letter to the RCMP on May 8, 2003, reminding the Mounties they had promised to protect her identity a long time ago: "At the time the confidential informant agreement was made, our client understood that it would cover all documents that had been provided to the RCMP." On November 26, 2004, Fiegenwald stated under oath in the Eurocopter preliminary hearing that Cameron was "nervous" about handing over the

4 For a complete account of Stevie Cameron's relationship with the RCMP, see William Kaplan's *A Secret Trial: Brian Mulroney, Stevie Cameron, and the Public Trust.*

Airbus documents back in May 1995, telling the Mounties that "she would be shunned by all her friends in the media and no one would trust her any-more." Fiegenwald said Cameron understood the importance of the ma-terial she was about to hand over: "None of the other journalists would give us the information that we needed to start a criminal investigation. And we were ready to close down the investigation because there just wasn't any information to support it. We didn't have the name of the informant that had the banking documents." Documents filed in the Eurocopter hearing show that Cameron had provided the RCMP with several Airbus documents, including the Airbus/IAL contracts, adding up to more than 101 pages.[5] Far from providing "pathetic scraps of information," Cameron had actually been the first to provide the RCMP with some of the most impor-tant documentation ever to surface in the Airbus affair.

The most important of Kaplan's three stories about the Schreiber/Mulroney relationship came out last, on Monday, November 10, 2003. The headline was in large type, above the fold, and on page one: "Schreiber hired Mulroney."

I knew from the chronology of events that *the fifth estate*'s broadcast of the "fucking liar" clip in November 1999 had damaged the relationship between Schreiber and Mulroney, but could never figure out why Schreiber had teased me with specific revelations (as in, "I gave money to Mulroney") without providing details, or even outlining how it happened. I now deduced that Schreiber had gone to Phil Mathias, which made sense. Ever since the scandal broke in 1995, Mathias had written dozens of stories in favour of Karlheinz Schreiber. But what a strange turn of events it must have been for Mathias, who had already reported that Schreiber and Mulroney had said no money had changed hands, and who had writ-ten emphatically that there was "no tainted" money to trace. And what about the *National Post*'s editorial claiming that *the fifth estate*'s putative allegations that Schreiber paid Mulroney $300,000 through the Britan account was "preposterous" and "false"? The *National Post* had done noth-ing yet to correct the record.

5 Justice Then, July 2007, written decision, page 45.

To his enormous credit, Kaplan revealed that Mathias had wanted to report the story, even quoting the first paragraph of the story that the *National Post* refused to publish: "Brian Mulroney was paid $300,000 in cash by German businessman Karlheinz Schreiber, the man at the centre of the Airbus affair, over an 18-month period beginning soon after Mulroney stepped down as prime minister in 1993."

Phil Mathias had worked on the story "for months," Kaplan wrote, and submitted it to his bosses at the *National Post* in January 2001, not long before his retirement.

But the story never came out. Mathias even wrote a letter to Conrad Black and the Asper family—the co-owners of the paper—to tell them the *Post*'s reputation might be damaged if it ever became known they refused to publish the story. Ken Whyte, the editor-in-chief, then suggested Mathias get in touch with William Kaplan for a comment. The author of *Presumed Guilty* was shocked to learn what Mathias told him.

Still, the *National Post* simply refused to report any version of his story, and Mathias eventually gave up. Wrote Kaplan: "The environment for its publication was just not right. In fact, the atmosphere was downright hostile, and so a newsworthy story was relegated to electronic purgatory on the *Post*'s hard drive . . . [Mathias] had uncovered one of the biggest scoops of his career and, instead of getting the front-page treatment the story deserved, it was suppressed and he was treated as though he had a communicable disease. A long career in investigative journalism ended in disgust, and the *Post* continued its campaign of bemoaning the so-called victimization of Mulroney by the RCMP and others on the one hand, while puffing him [up] on the other, particularly when doing so cast the current Prime Minister in a less positive light."

Perhaps it *was* one of the biggest scoops of Mathias's career, but I knew it was spun to him as a reaction to our broadcast of the "fucking liar" clip. Mathias also knew that *the fifth estate* had already reported the cash withdrawals out of the Britan account. Had he wanted the story to get published, he knew he could have approached *the fifth estate*.

In his article, Kaplan explained it was then up to him to report the story: "If all this were true, my book clearly required a sequel," he explained. And he was in a good position to do it. He still had good relations with Mulroney and could get an audience with the former prime minister in ways that *the fifth estate* could only dream of. And indeed, Kaplan got a partial answer straight from Mulroney, as he outlined: "Eventually [Mulroney] explained that Schreiber had paid him the money—though he disputes the amount—for his assistance in promoting a fresh-cooked pasta business Schreiber had started in Canada as well as his international interests." Kaplan explained that Mulroney had a side business apart from his work at the law firm Ogilvy Renault that allowed him to do consulting work. Kaplan quoted Mulroney as saying that all monies were reflected in the books of his company.

Kaplan also quoted Luc Lavoie, who stated that the cash was "to assist Schreiber with his pasta business and to arrange a number of introductions and meetings with international business executives . . . It was straight-forward from the get-go."

In his *Globe* article, Kaplan reported what Mulroney had said in his examination for discovery in 1996. Mulroney had described having that "coffee" at the Queen Elizabeth Hotel but had failed to mention getting money from Schreiber. "Was it perjury?" asked Kaplan. "No. Had he misled the Canadian people? Probably yes. Should he have seized the opportunity to set out the entire story? Absolutely.

"You have to admire Mulroney's bravado," Kaplan wrote, "suing the government for $50-million to refute a claim that he had been bribed by Schreiber when the two had done business together. Balls of steel. Had the government lawyers learned about it, they might never have settled. It was a very close call."

Kaplan quoted Mulroney, sounding nothing like he did in September 2001 in his television interview with Brian Stewart, when he suggested Schreiber should be considered innocent and that he [Schreiber], too, had a family: "If you accumulated all the sorrow over all my life, it does not compare to the agony and anguish I have gone through since I met Schreiber," Mulroney had told Kaplan. "I should never have been introduced to him because the people who introduced me to him didn't know him."

Kaplan ended his article with a quote from the former prime minister about what might happen if anyone wrote anything about the cash from Schreiber.

"Anyone who says anything about that," he threatened, "will be in one fuck of a fight."

The *Globe* deserved huge credit for publishing the story. There was, however, a hole in its coverage. In 1999, *the fifth estate* had reported that a total of $300,000 had been withdrawn from the Britan account in 1993 and 1994. We noted the money had come from the secret commission accounts in Liechtenstein. The *Globe* failed to mention any of this in its coverage. In criticizing the *National Post* for not doing the story about the money, the *Globe* itself had left out important information. Instead, its headline seemed to suggest that Mulroney had performed real work for the money: "Schreiber hired Mulroney." But how did they know? So far, no one had produced any evidence that specific work was actually performed. Neither Schreiber nor Mulroney.

The *Globe and Mail*'s editorials on the Airbus affair would later seem at odds with William Kaplan's revelations. An editorial on February 26, 2004, for example, contained the following question: "Why did the (RCMP) continue when it had little more than dark innuendoes from . . . conspiracy theorists . . . Just as important, if this was an investigation with a political motive, who directed the force to continue with its probe when it was apparent the case had no factual basis?"

When Kaplan called in April 2004, I suspected it might be about Airbus.

"I'd like your help," he said.

He was writing another book about Mulroney, he told me, and wondered if I could take a look at the manuscript. Suddenly I was brought back to a story that I had successfully avoided for more than three years.

CHAPTER THIRTY-THREE
COUNTERSPIN

I took the weekend and pored over every page, grateful that Kaplan trusted me for my comments. From that day forward, I gained a new admiration for him. Today I am pleased to call him a friend. In his book, he described a meeting between Mulroney and Schreiber at the prime minister's summer residence at Harrington Lake in late June 1993. He also wrote about three later meetings after Mulroney stepped down as prime minister—including that coffee at the Queen Elizabeth—where $300,000 allegedly changed hands.

Schreiber had provided Kaplan an interview, but details were still sketchy. Where did the money come from? What specifically did Mulroney do for the money? For now, Schreiber was remaining silent.

Meanwhile, the book was schedule for publication in the fall of 2004.

Incredibly, in the spring of 2004, Karlheinz Schreiber's extradition hearing under Justice Watt was still plodding along: three years old, and counting.

Finally, on May 18, 2004, it ended.

Schreiber lost the case. He was committed for extradition to Germany on all but one of the alleged offences. Schreiber and Greenspan would now begin a complicated series of appeals, all the way to the Supreme

Court if necessary, they vowed, which meant Schreiber would likely still be in Canada for a long time.

There was a question mark: Would Schreiber get bail again?

A few days later, Schreiber received good news: he could remain free on bail pending his appeal. He and his wife would continue to divide their time between their town home in Rockliffe Park, just outside Ottawa, and their luxury apartment in Toronto's Yorkville district.

On March 20, 2004, Stephen Harper was elected leader of the newly formed Conservative Party, a merger between the Canadian Alliance and the Progressive Conservative Party. For the first time in years, the right wing was no longer divided. Paul Martin, the new Liberal leader, took Jean Chrétien's comfortable majority and turned it into a shaky minority in the June 28 election that year, due in part to the fact that the right wing had finally united, but also because of what became known as the sponsorship scandal, which revealed that advertising firms close to the Liberal Party in Quebec had falsified invoices to the federal government while claiming to promote Canada to Quebec. Martin had had nothing to do with the scandal; he had, in fact, called for a full-scale public inquiry. But it all ended up backfiring. Witnesses testified to receiving envelopes stuffed with cash, prompting headlines across the country (and further confusing me about why Mulroney's cash-stuffed envelopes had not received the same attention). The cumulative evidence cast the Liberals as a party that had become far too arrogant for its own good.

For the first time since Mulroney left office in 1993, it seemed as if the Conservative Party was on the verge of reclaiming power. Mulroney could take some credit. As a young disaffected Tory, Stephen Harper had publicly criticized Mulroney, leaving the party in disgust with Mulroney's economic policies and his government's ethical lapses. Now, a decade later, Mulroney could count himself as one of Harper's advisers. Mulroney was discreet about the relationship at first, but his transformation from tainted PM to respected elder statesman was close to complete.

For Schreiber, the changing political landscape would prove significant. Under the Extradition Act, the minister of justice makes the final decision about surrendering a fugitive. For Schreiber, that person would be a Conservative.

In the summer of 2004, my sons and I went to Cortes Island, as we always did, for the month of July. I had still not finished the cabin. What had begun as a simple idea to construct a modest building had morphed into one with a second floor. That year I learned to build a Duroid shingle roof, thanks to my mother, who did some research at Home Depot about how to build the proper scaffolding. My father helped, standing below me and handing me the tiles as I hung on to the roof. The boys pitched in too. I would have to tell them at the end of the summer that no, the cabin would not be finished this year. I was sure we'd get it done next summer.

I returned to Toronto to learn that the long arm of the law had caught up with Germany's former undersecretary of defence, Holger Pfahls. For five years, Pfahls had been on the run from charges he took cash payments from Schreiber. Police tracked him down in Paris as he left his apartment, where he had been living under an assumed name. He was immediately extradited to Germany to face charges.

Then, in September 2004, with a renewed interest in all things Airbus, I took a plane to Ottawa, to the courthouse on Elgin Street. Karlheinz Schreiber was about to be called as a witness in the Eurocopter preliminary hearing. I looked around the courtroom and realized that, apparently, the story was of interest only to me. We were a five-minute walk from Parliament Hill, but no other journalist was present.

Schreiber himself was not charged. Prosecutors believed he was a witness to the secret commissions that MBB Helicopter had paid to the Liechtenstein shell company IAL. I had not talked with Schreiber in a while but found him in good spirits. I sat next to him in the courtroom and told him that I had an idea to do another documentary—and to take him to Montreal and film him in the hotel rooms where the cash had changed hands. Schreiber smiled, noncommittal, telling me he would think about it.

I had hoped to hear details about the cash transaction between Mulroney and Schreiber, but it became clear that Eurocopter's lawyer, Paul

Schabas, was going to object to almost every question about Mulroney, which made it nearly impossible for Crown prosecutor Michael Bernstein to pursue his line of questioning. Schabas even objected to seemingly innocuous questions from Bernstein like, "When did you meet Mr. Mulroney?" Schabas said the questions about Mulroney were mostly irrelevant: "There's not a shred of evidence that Mr. Mulroney is implicated in anything."

Eventually the judge allowed some limited questions about the Schreiber/Mulroney relationship.

Schreiber, however, underplayed his relationship with Mulroney, saying very little of substance. Schreiber had not spoken with me in several months and I wondered if he had adopted a new strategy. Maybe he wanted to get back on Mulroney's good side. In his testimony, Schreiber agreed that he had met Mulroney in the early 1980s and that he had donated money to help Walter Wolf dump Joe Clark in favour of Mulroney. But Schreiber's answers were vague. "I recall I met him at the Ritz Carlton for one or two or three times when I was in Montreal. That's it." His vagueness persisted as he was asked questions about his relationship to Mulroney as leader. "I think I saw him once when he was in Opposition. At least, as much as I recall." Schreiber had a razor-sharp mind; I believed the "as much as I recall" really meant "as much as I want to say." As for their relationship when Mulroney was prime minister, Schreiber was dismissive; he did volunteer that he had attended a "breakfast meeting" with Elmer MacKay and Mulroney over the Bear Head project. He testified he saw Mulroney "once in the lobby from the House or in his office, with the same matter," referring again to Bear Head but mentioning nothing about the numerous letters and other meetings that both men had had on the topic over the years.

There would occur, however, an eye-opening exchange between him and the Crown prosecutor, when Schreiber decided to educate the court on the meaning of "useful expenses"—as mentioned earlier, what Germans called "NAS"—and how they were allowed to deduct these payments from their taxes.

"Were NAS deductible?" asked Bernstein.

"Sure!"

"Was *schmiergeld* deductible?" Bernstein asked, using the singular of the word *schmiergelder* [greasemoney].

"Yes. This is what I saw. This is the law in Germany. It was the law."

Schreiber explained this is what International Aircraft Leasing was designed to facilitate.

"Okay, and IAL is a Liechtenstein company?" Bernstein asked.

"Yes," Schreiber replied.

Bernstein continued. "Then one of the reasons for incorporating in Liechtenstein is for having anonymous—"

"Yes!" Schreiber said, answering before Bernstein finished the question.

"Who would be anonymous?"

"Whoever it would be. This could be—take all the nations around the world, or the governments, or private people. There is no restriction or limit," Schreiber said.

Bernstein wanted to back up a little. "I just want, sir, to ask a question or two about these terms—a few terms. First of all, *schmiergelder*. All right? Which is greasemoney?"

The judge interjected. "Spell that for me again, please?"

The interpreter helped out. "S-C-H-M-I-E-R-G-E-L-D."

The judge: "Sorry. S-C-H-M . . . ?"

The interpreter: "M-I-E-R-G-E-L-D."

"Let me explain what it is and—it's easy to understand," suggested Schreiber. "You have an engine, and to make the engine running smooth, you put oil or fat or grease in it, so it goes smooth."

Finally the court had some clarity.

When asked about his relationship with Mulroney after he was prime minister, Schreiber seemed in no mood to provide the same clarity. Prosecutor Michael Bernstein carefully parsed his words. It was an elaborate dance designed to elicit detail but evade objections from defence attorney Schabas. Schreiber suddenly reacted with impatience.

"I wonder why don't you simply say whether Brian Mulroney was engaged and hired by me after he was the prime minister of Canada? The whole world knows it. Why do you go around? Just simply ask straight-forward questions and I'll give it [an answer] to you."

"He won't let me," Bernstein replied, referring to Schabas.

"I have no problems with that. The whole world knows that," Schreiber repeated.

"So tell me," Bernstein said. "Tell us. Tell us how this came about."

"Number one," said Schreiber, "what has it to do with MBB and the hel-icopters? Number two, this is a fishing trip [sic], in my opinion, based on the whole thing around was Mulroney bribed by Schreiber, or whatever, and did he ever get money? And the whole world knows, yes, he received funds from me."

Schreiber insisted he did not ever bribe Mulroney. Bernstein wanted to know when exactly Schreiber first hired Mulroney.

"Oh, I think it was close to December or even—maybe even '94," Schreiber said. "And he [Mulroney] dealt with his position, to make it very simple for you, Mr. Bernstein, as a member of the board from Midland Archer Daniels [sic]. It's a huge American company dealing with food and agriculture products."

Schreiber appeared to be saying that the money he gave Mulroney re-lated to his work as a director of Archers Daniels Midland. But what ex-actly? Schreiber's answer was unclear.

Bernstein asked if there had been any discussions about hiring Mul-roney before 1994.

"No, and, yeah, in '93, perhaps. But I'm not too convinced whether that was—this particular case, you asked me whether I did—I had many things in mind, and I told you, I wanted to hire Mr. Mulroney for Thyssen to be doing the same thing he's doing now, and it would have been a nice thing to have a previous Canadian prime minister on a peacekeeping track for Thyssen products. Again, as this government wanted the German com-panies to do. I would have been very happy if he would have done this. Un-fortunately, we had no chance for that, but yes, and they told—I was involved in the pasta business and enriched Durham semolina products and this is the moment when I spoke to him [Mulroney] about Archer Daniels. And he provided me with some material on it."

I sat there in the courtroom not understanding a word.

Mulroney gave Schreiber "some material" about the pasta business? But what exactly? And for what purpose? And what was this earlier comment about "I had many things in mind"? What did that mean?

"All right," Bernstein continued, sounding exasperated, "I just want to understand—"

Schreiber cut him off. "But it has nothing to do with MBB."

Bernstein told the judge he wanted to better understand when exactly Schreiber decided to do business with Mulroney. It was like pinning jelly to a wall.

"These thoughts or this idea that you had, this plan, what time are we talking about?" asked Bernstein.

"After Mr. Mulroney has left government," Schreiber replied.

"After he had stepped down as the prime minister?" Bernstein said.

"Yes," Schreiber replied.

But what plan exactly was Schreiber talking about? And what precisely did Mulroney do for Thyssen? And exactly what did he do for the pasta business? The Crown prosecutor had been stymied, was not allowed to ask more than simple, basic questions, and yet the answers that we got were incomplete and confusing.

It was yet another missed opportunity. I wanted to shout, *Would somebody, one day, just tell us one thing that Mulroney actually did to earn the money?*

William Kaplan's book came out that fall. I was wrong about the book's reception.

Nothing happened.

It promptly fell off the radar, just as all the other exposés had in the past: the original *fifth estate* story in 1995; the program's Britan-account revelations in 1999; its dump-Clark revelations in the spring of 2001; *The Last Amigo* later that spring; the *Globe* story in the fall of 2003; and now Kaplan's book, *A Secret Trial*, in the fall of 2004. The only time it seemed the Airbus story got any real attention was when someone launched a lawsuit (perhaps partly because journalists cannot be sued for reporting on court proceedings). Columnist Andrew Coyne would later sum up the paltry coverage of Kaplan's book this way: "The book of the year is also the least noticed. In any other country, William Kaplan's *A Secret Trial: Brian Mulroney, Stevie Cameron, and the Public Trust*, would be a sensation. Parliament would be in an uproar. Public inquiries would be ordered. The implications would be thrashed out in every newspaper, on every talk show. We would be sick to death of it by now."

I was as confused as Coyne. How *could* such revelations fall with such silence on the political landscape in Canada? I decided I had to focus my attention not only on covering the story, but on promoting it as well. The spin doctors had done a good job of keeping the story out of the public eye. Now I was determined to spin back. For the truth to come out, we had to counterspin. We had to go on the offensive ourselves.

The question was, how?

Not long after the release of his book, Kaplan invited me to the Senator, an old-style breakfast café in downtown Toronto.

"I need to tell you something," he confided. "There's more to the story than you realize." Mulroney had taken steps to ensure that Canadians would never find out about the cash from Schreiber, Kaplan said. Rumours were circulating that someone may have even considered soliciting a statement from Schreiber stating that he had never given money to Mulroney.

"That's not all," said Kaplan. "Mulroney filed incomplete tax returns."

Kaplan said Mulroney had not immediately declared the $300,000 he received from Schreiber. (It was only several years later, when news of the Britan account had come to light, that Mulroney instructed his lawyers to approach the Canada Revenue Agency. He made use of the Voluntary Disclosure Program, the amnesty program that invited people to come forward without fear of being charged with tax evasion. Frank Moores himself used the program in the fall of 1995 to report the income from his Swiss accounts—the ones the RCMP were beginning to probe.)

I asked Kaplan to provide more details, but that's as far as he would go.

"You're going to have to find out on your own," he said, without really explaining why he couldn't tell me more himself.

I had a slight problem.

I had left *the fifth estate* in June 2002. By the fall of 2004, nearly two and a half years later, I badly wanted to do another Airbus story. *The fifth estate* owned the story. David Studer had supported it for several years, when other bosses might have told me to move on. I knew I had to talk with Studer, to convince him to hire me back—and to commit to another Airbus story.

Studer and I had not really talked all that much since I left *the fifth estate*. I knocked on his door, hoping he would say yes to both me and the story. I went through all the reasons, gave him a list of all the new evidence, including the alleged cover-up, and explained that even though Schreiber had not agreed to an interview, and I doubted he would, we could craft an hour of television around William Kaplan. I proposed that we examine how the media itself had handled the story from the beginning, how Luc Lavoie's spin machine had been so successful that the real story had been suppressed.

I waited for Studer to make up his mind. I glanced over at the couch, the same one on which I had slept the night before we broadcast the "fucking liar" clip in November 1999. Had it really been five years? He had framed a copy of the cheque for $55,361.61 that Schreiber paid us in 2001, to pay for our legal costs after he dropped the lawsuit against us. We had been through a lot together. I hoped he would see, as I did, that we had the chance to finish it.

Then he smiled.

"Welcome back."

There were, in theory, a lot of people who might know about those two leads Kaplan had given me: first, that Mulroney had allegedly solicited a statement from Schreiber; and, second, that he had filed a voluntary disclosure with the Canada Revenue Agency. I made a list of all the lawyers, government officials and RCMP officers who might know something. Many of the names were long shots, but I would try everyone. Someone would confirm the story.

As usual, I got lucky. It had appeared that both Mulroney's request of Schreiber and his voluntary disclosure had been triggered by my fax to Mulroney on October 8, 1999. I wondered if the letter I sent Mulroney stating that *the fifth estate* had "new information" had panicked the former prime minister. Luc Lavoie called me at the time, of course, to deny that Mulroney had received any money from Schreiber. Now I was told that Mulroney himself called Schreiber's Edmonton lawyer on October 17, 1999, to ask for a letter from Schreiber saying that Mulroney had never received any money from the middleman. I was also told that Mulroney's Montreal lawyer, Gérald Tremblay, called Eddie Greenspan on the same matter. Mulroney wanted the letter in his back pocket, as he contemplated ways to shut down the CBC's broadcast. On the advice of Greenspan, Schreiber did not provide the statement. Greenspan was so concerned about what he had heard, I learned, that he demanded that Robert Hladun write him a note about what exactly Mulroney had said to him on the phone. Hladun complied. I tried to get a copy of that letter, but was unsuccessful.

According to my sources, Mulroney's inability to get the letter from Schreiber prompted another decision: Mulroney had no option but to make a voluntary declaration to the Canada Revenue Agency. He asked a lawyer at his firm to approach the CRA on behalf of an unnamed client who needed to declare a substantial amount of cash he had received way back in 1993 and 1994.

One day in late December 2004, Linden MacIntyre and I met with William Kaplan at his home in Toronto's South Hill neighbourhood to conduct the first on-camera interview for our next Airbus story. The last time MacIntyre and I worked together was nearly four years ago, in early 2001, when we interviewed Schreiber outside the Four Seasons Hotel.

Kaplan explained why he had changed his mind about Mulroney. He reminded us that in his testimony in Montreal in 1996, Mulroney had stated he "had never had" any dealings with Schreiber. "The guy's testifying under oath. He's a former prime minister of the country, he's a lawyer, he's an officer of the court. The only conclusion a fair-minded, reasonable, objective person can draw is that he had never had any dealings with him [Schreiber]. And if he had never had any dealings with him, he'd never taken any money from him."

Kaplan explained how Mulroney tried to suppress the story, even as Kaplan confronted him with the new evidence. "He says to me, look, all I can tell you is that the important thing is that all the taxes were paid and this was completely lawful and if you get into this, it's going to be a complete diversion about what the Liberals were up to, trying to destroy me and my place in history."

Kaplan had a different interpretation. "Everyone knows if you're a former prime minister, you don't meet with someone you'd recently dealt with in an official capacity and take cash. And if you do, and if there is a legitimate reason for it, well, come forward and tell us what it is. Tell us what you took the money for, tell us when you got it, tell us what you did with the cash, tell us when you remitted the GST, and tell us when you declared the income."

MacIntyre asked Kaplan why he thought nobody seemed to want to reopen that can of worms.

"Don't forget, everyone—*everybody*—who has been involved in this story has been burned one way or another. There's me, who, having been led down the garden path, was burned in my first book [*Presumed Guilty*]. The Department of Justice has been hurt. Every single person who has been associated with this story has been hurt by it."

Towards the end, Kaplan described his relationship with Mulroney as it deteriorated in the fall of 2003. Kaplan had asked Mulroney directly why he had described his relationship with Schreiber as "peripheral."

"He says to me, 'I'm sorry for any inconvenience that I may have caused you.' And, well, *inconvenience*? I took time off from my [law] practice writing this first book. I toured the country. I believed him. And unfortunately all the evidence was consistent with his story." Kaplan was unburdening himself in his living room with our cameras rolling. "But now he says to me, 'I'm sorry for any inconvenience that I may have caused you.' And I'm really upset at this point. And I say to him, 'Well, that's not good enough. That's just not good enough.' And he says, 'I'm sorry.' And that's the last time we talked."

More than anything, we were curious about how the media covered the story back in the 1990s, how it had collectively failed to ask important questions. We had some important questions for two of Canada's national newspapers, and two of the most powerful men in Canadian media at the time, the *National Post*'s former editor-in-chief, Ken Whyte, and the *Globe and Mail*'s former editor-in-chief, William Thorsell. Both men helped shape the way the Airbus story was covered in Canada.

Patti-Ann Finlay, a talented associate producer who was brought onto our team, called Ken Whyte, who, according to Kaplan, had personally killed Phil Mathias's story that Schreiber gave cash to Mulroney. Prior to his job at the *National Post*, Whyte was the editor of *Saturday Night* magazine, where he had commissioned an Airbus story highly critical of *the fifth estate* and our pursuit of the money.

In his interview with Finlay, Whyte insisted Kaplan was "entirely wrong" for suggesting that the *National Post* had sat on the story. "Mostly I just ignore these things," Whyte told her, "but it's getting out of hand, so I think I should address it."

It was true, Whyte explained, that Mathias confirmed the $300,000 payment from Schreiber to Mulroney, but he, Whyte, did not feel comfortable reporting it because in his story Mathias had tied the payment to Airbus. "And we had nothing at all connecting the payment to the Airbus affair."

Whyte continued. "All that we had was that Mulroney had received a fee for a piece of work—the fee was not out of line for the piece of work that he is said to have done. We had no way of knowing whether he had or hadn't done the work or whether there was anything untoward about it at all."

If Mulroney refused to provide the *National Post* with any evidence about what the work was for, then why could the *National Post* not simply report what it knew to be true—that Mulroney *had received* cash from Schreiber? If they wanted, they could also have said that the former prime minister would not answer questions about what he did to earn the money.

Instead, Whyte and his editorial team apparently asked Mathias to go back to see if he could find a more direct connection between the payment to Mulroney and Airbus. "He failed to get one," Whyte insisted.

Whyte would have been happy to report a story about the cash only, but "Phil didn't want to go with that because he felt it was somehow connected to the Airbus affair and he was determined to demonstrate the link." Whyte said he did not want to contribute to the "overly aggressive" reporting on the topic and said anything that involves a prime minister— in office or out—"you have to be careful about alleging improprieties. My point is that we gave Phil every opportunity to work on it to land it, but he just didn't have the story."[1]

Actually Mathias *had* the story, at least part of it. Ken Whyte refused to publish it.

Finlay asked Whyte if the *Post* was perhaps influenced by their earlier coverage in the Airbus saga. The paper had called allegations that Schreiber gave money to Mulroney "preposterous" and "false"; it had ridiculed *the fifth estate* for making the suggestion that the Britan account might have been for Mulroney. The *Post* had also claimed there was "no tainted" money to trace. Over the years the paper had consistently ridiculed reporters who had tried to advance the story, and came to the defence of Frank Moores, Brian Mulroney and Karlheinz Schreiber on several occasions. In his interview with Finlay, Whyte downplayed suggestions of bias: "None of us had really been involved in the Mulroney stuff to any great extent." Not even Phil Mathias and the numerous stories he had written on the topic, including one in the inaugural edition of the *National Post*?

"It was a story that needed to be investigated," Whyte said. "Journalists weren't wrong about that. But it is increasingly looking like a dry well. There are still legitimate questions to ask. There are still things to be answered. But when you compare [the evidence] now and 1995 and what was being alleged at the time, it hasn't amounted to much. But it's [the Airbus affair] certainly not resolved."

---

1 I do not believe it is accurate to suggest that Mathias was determined to demonstrate a link to Airbus. I believe that Mathias felt a duty to report the story about the cash changing hands, wherever the cash may have come from. He deserves credit for trying to convince his paper to do so.

It was a story that needed to be investigated. It was something, at least.

And, no, Whyte told us afterwards; he would definitely *not* sit down with Linden MacIntyre for an on-camera interview.

Howard Goldenthal had the job of speaking with William Thorsell, who had written his share of pro-Mulroney, anti-RCMP and anti–*fifth estate* columns. Thorsell had long since left the *Globe* and was then chief executive officer of the Royal Ontario Museum, which is where Goldenthal reached him by phone.

Thorsell recalled that he had spoken to Mulroney as far back as 1995, when the Letter of Request was first leaked to Phil Mathias. "I think it would be fair to say Mulroney was in shock. It was an incredible thing to come out in a newspaper," Thorsell told Goldenthal. And did Mulroney tell him at that time that he had known Schreiber? "No," replied Thorsell.

Then they talked about Kaplan's revelations that Mulroney had taken cash from Schreiber.

"That was a complete surprise," Thorsell said. "When I read the story and saw the context of it, I could sort of see what had happened there. But it was a complete surprise. You might call it highly inconvenient for Mr. Mulroney, that's for sure. That was real news."

Goldenthal knew that Thorsell and Mulroney were friendly, if not friends, and asked if he had spoken to Mulroney after the revelations in the *Globe and Mail*.

"I have, yes."

Had Mulroney told Thorsell what the money was for? Thorsell recalled it had something to do with Schreiber's pasta business. "Apparently it was a very good pasta machine," he said. "There was something else to do with his business in China." Thorsell recalled another conversation with Mulroney. "He wasn't well acquainted with Mr. Schreiber. He had barely met him when he was prime minister. That's what he told me. He said this is all it was. When he [Mulroney] was getting started out there he was doing a lot of travelling to different countries on behalf of clients of all kinds."

Goldenthal asked Thorsell if he had asked Mulroney about the former prime minister's testimony in which he said he "had never had" any dealings with Schreiber.

"I haven't really talked to him about that," Thorsell said. "I think he said people parsed that testimony very carefully, looking back on it. I didn't read the testimony itself. I think he has enough wiggle room in the way that question was asked to be able to get away—just—with the answer he gave."

Goldenthal asked Thorsell if he ever asked Mulroney about the Britan account.

"I don't remember the Britan account. What was that?"

"This was a rubrik inside of an account in Switzerland called Britan—$300,000 came out of it."

"I just lost that in my memory," Thorsell confessed.

And, no, Thorsell later told us, he would also not speak to Linden MacIntyre on-camera.

It was my job to call Phil Mathias.

Phil and I had stopped talking to each other after the summer of 2001, but by the early part of 2005 we had begun to speak on the phone, on occasion. Still, I needed to ask him something in person. We met in the afternoon at the Imperial Pub in downtown Toronto for a drink. The place was nearly deserted.

We talked for a long time, me trying to explain why I wanted him to appear on-camera, as William Kaplan had already done, to explore how the media covered the Airbus story, how it changed and why, and to examine what lessons might be learned. Mathias told me he needed time to think about the proposal.

"I was wrong about Britan." He was staring into his drink. At the time, he said, he believed *the fifth estate* was being reckless, that it could not possibly be true that the Britan account was for Mulroney.

"I was wrong. You were right. I had tunnel vision," he admitted. "I apologize."

Phil Mathias declined to appear on-camera.

CHAPTER THIRTY-FOUR
GUNS LOADED

Early in the new year I travelled with a camera crew to Ottawa, to re-create the limousine drive that Schreiber had taken to Harrington Lake in June 1993 to meet Brian Mulroney, just before all that cash started flowing out of the Britan account later that summer. The conditions were not ideal. There we were on one of the coldest days in January, re-creating a drive to the country that had occurred in the summer. So we improvised. We filmed coniferous trees only from a low angle up towards the sunshine, whizzing by as we drove up the gravel roads; we filmed the yellow lines on the parts of the road where there was no snow;and scenes across the bridge over the Ottawa River were filmed so tightly you could not see the white landscape. We set up a tripod outside Schreiber's place in Rockliffe, to film the beginning part of the trip, then drove as far as the gravel road would take us to Harrington Lake, where there were cameras watching the area in front of a locked gate. Somehow we pulled it off. That sequence we filmed in the dead of winter would open our documentary and appear to be a warm summer drive in June.

Aside from not knowing what the cash payment from Schreiber to Mulroney was for, or what work, if any, was done for the money, there was a lot more we did not know about it: How exactly had the meetings between Schreiber and Mulroney been arranged? Who else might have attended? What denominations was the cash in? What did Mulroney do with the cash?

I knew by now that if I wrote to Mulroney he would simply have Luc Lavoie call me back. So I called Lavoie directly. I was hoping to meet with him and go over the new evidence. We had not spoken since the fall of 1999; a lot had happened since then.

Lavoie called back early in the new year. "I am not sure where this is all heading," he said. But he agreed to meet. On January 19, 2005, I flew to Montreal, and took a cab straight to Lavoie's exclusive men's club, 357C.

A concierge greeted me, and then took me to a small but elegant room. Lavoie was already seated, smoking a cigarette. A couple sat at the next table; otherwise the room was empty. It would be the familiar game: Lavoie was going to try to find out what I knew; I would try to find out what Mulroney knew.

Lavoie was by then a vice-president of Quebecor, the Canadian media giant (but still acting on the side as Mulroney's public relations person).

"Hi, Harvey, long time no see," he said. "Sit down. Have a drink." I had forgotten his voice was nearly as deep as Mulroney's.

I was about to learn he had not got over our infamous broadcast. The broadcast of those quotes had marked the beginning of the disintegration of the friendship between Mulroney and Schreiber. I could understand his resentment. I was just not sure why he was blaming me; I was not the one who broke the confidentiality agreement.

Lavoie, however, held me responsible for all that had happened. "You fucked me," he said. "Why did you fuck me?" He called the broadcast of the "fucking liar" clip the worst day of his life.

"Just admit it, Harvey. You hate Mulroney. You hate him."

Lavoie had used the same argument years ago. I did not hate Mulroney and I suspect he knew it. Perhaps he hoped I would say yes now, given all that Mulroney had put us through. Obviously if I said I hated Mulroney, he would have cause to demand that the CBC take me off the Airbus story.

"I can prove I don't hate Mulroney," I told Lavoie.

"Yeah, how?"

"Let's go visit him right now. Call him on your cell and tell him we're coming over."

"That's not going to happen."

Lavoie tried another approach. "Why are you so obsessed with this?" he asked. "How much of your time has been spent on this story?"

We spoke for hours. And the more we spoke, the more the animosity dissipated. We began to talk about the story in personal terms. I told Lavoie how I first heard about the Airbus story, from that source at Fokker Aircraft in 1994, more than a decade ago. He told me he first heard that Mulroney's name was attached to the letter after getting a call from the former prime minister in the fall of 1995, telling Lavoie that he was the unnamed Canadian politician referred to in the media the week the story broke. We went through the chronology of events, from both of our perspectives, gaining new insights into how we both worked.

Lavoie told me an interesting story about that footage we obtained of Schreiber, Mulroney and Kohl at the luncheon in Bonn. Lavoie said that he was on that trip, as he worked for the Prime Minister's Office at the time. Lavoie recalled that Mulroney himself asked him if he could find a spot at the table for Schreiber, who was not on the official guest list. Unable to find an empty seat, Lavoie gave up his own so Schreiber could sit at the table.

Lavoie told me that he "hated" Schreiber, found him to be "disgusting and despicable," the kind of person he met a lot of times in Ottawa "hanging around and trying to scam deals here and there." Lavoie agreed I was not such a bad person after all. "If we were not adversaries on this story, I think we could have been friends," he suggested.

Later, when it seemed as if I had asked all my questions, and after I had put away my notepad, Lavoie asked me what was going to be in the new documentary. I told him I had asked every question I could think of, but it was clear from his answers that he had no information to help me.

"Well, be specific, maybe I can help you," he said.

I decided to tell him about the story I had heard, that Mulroney had asked his lawyer, Gérald Tremblay, to get in touch with Eddie Greenspan, to try to obtain a letter from Schreiber that he had never given any money to Mulroney.

Lavoie stopped me. He needed to correct a detail. "The request from Tremblay was not about wanting a denial of money changing hands," he said, "but rather Mulroney simply wanting Schreiber to say their business dealings were 'legitimate.'"

I said this explanation made no sense. Mulroney's request for a letter from Schreiber happened at exactly the same time that Lavoie was telling me back in 1999 that no money ever changed hands between Mulroney and Schreiber. ("There never was any money," Lavoie had said.) And so it only made sense that at the same time Mulroney told Lavoie to deny to me that any money changed hands, he also wanted a letter from Schreiber saying the same thing. Besides, I asked Lavoie, why did Mulroney call Schreiber's Edmonton lawyer, Robert Hladun, at the same time? What was the reason for that phone call?

Lavoie seemed to be taken by surprise. I told him Hladun had even written a memo to file about Mulroney's call, stating Mulroney had asked for a statement from Schreiber that no money had changed hands. Lavoie asked me if I could give him a copy of Hladun's memo to file. I admitted I did not yet have a copy.

We moved on to Mulroney's problems with the taxman. I told Lavoie what I had heard about Mulroney's voluntary disclosure to the Canada Revenue Agency.

"Yeah, so?" Lavoie replied. "It is all perfectly legal."

I took this response as confirmation Lavoie knew about the disclosure. I told Lavoie that it was my job to report what was in the public interest, illegal or not. Lavoie countered that it was a private matter between Mulroney and the taxman.

"Would you want to talk about *your* tax situation?" he asked.

Then we turned to the subject of the RCMP and its decision to shut down the Airbus investigation.

Lavoie said the Mounties had approached Mulroney's lawyers in 2003 with a request to interview the former prime minister about the alleged cash payments from Schreiber. Through his lawyers, Mulroney declined to speak with the Mounties. In the past, Mulroney had repeatedly complained that the Mounties had not come to see him. But now Lavoie was saying that when they finally did ask for an interview, Mulroney refused.

It was a strange evening. The conversation fluctuated between civilized discourse and outright hostility, like when he asked about my family.

"Your brother is a professor at Yale University, right?" he asked.

"Yes."

"And your father used to be a cabinet minister in the British Columbia government?"

"What's your point, Luc?"

As a representative of a former prime minister of Canada, Lavoie was an influential man well connected to powerful interests in Canada and abroad. If they wanted to go after me, they had the means to do it.

"It would be a great idea if you left family out of this," I suggested.

It was past midnight and Lavoie had decided he'd had enough. He wanted to go home. He left me at the table, offering one last "You fucked me," before he left and disappeared.

The letter from Mulroney's law firm came two weeks later.

David Studer called me into his office to tell me.

"Not again," I said, recalling the letter that Tremblay had sent the CBC president in 1999, also attacking my colleagues and me.

The letter read: "We represent the Right Honourable Brian Mulroney . . . Given the hostility and malice displayed by its producer, Mr. Harvey Cashore . . . over many years to Mulroney and his family we put you on notice that any new attempt by innuendo, tendentious re-enactment or otherwise to discredit our client or suggest wrongdoing of any kind will result in swift and substantial claims in damages."

It was signed by Yves Fortier, the chairman of Ogilvy Renault, and a former Canadian ambassador to the United Nations. Fortier addressed his letter to Carol Taylor, chair of the Canadian Broadcasting Corporation and Robert Rabinovitch, president and chief executive officer, and included the disclaimer "without prejudice" as he launched a detailed assault against *the fifth estate* and me, in particular.

Yves Fortier was a highly respected lawyer and diplomat, a man of unsurpassed integrity. Now he was launching a stunning attack against me. Naturally the letter would make the rounds in the upper echelons of the CBC. It arrived on Robert Rabinovitch's desk on Wednesday, February 2, but I did not hear about it until two days later, the letter having passed from one senior officer to another, including Pierre Nollet, vice-president of Legal for the CBC.

The letter went on to detail how the Mounties had apologized to Mulroney in 1997, how the RCMP stated any conclusions of wrongdoing were and are unjustified, how a "world class political fraud had been perpetrated on the Canadian people by the RCMP and the Government of Canada," how Justice Alan B. Gold in Montreal had awarded damages to Mulroney at $2.1 million based on the "grievous" wrong that Mulroney had suffered, how Mulroney had been labelled an "innocent person" in the Eurocopter hearing, how in April 2003 RCMP commissioner Giuliano Zaccardelli wrote to Mulroney to state that "no charges will be laid" against him, and how therefore Mulroney had been "fully exonerated."

"Notwithstanding these repeated findings of Mr. Mulroney's innocence," the letter went on, "Mr. Cashore is unpersuaded. He is determined to find wrongdoing by our client and his zeal is boundless. After all, his fruitless decade-long pursuit of Mr. Mulroney was fully funded by the taxpayers of Canada."

The letter contained a section justifying Schreiber's trip to Harrington Lake as not being out of the ordinary: "Any attempt by the 5th Estate [*sic*] to portray, through contrived re-enactment or otherwise, Mr. Schreiber's visit as clandestine and the subject matter as improper or illegal, would be completely false and willfully malicious and will be exposed in court as a blatant fabrication."

The part about the "contrived re-enactment" caught my attention. We had recently filmed the re-enactment of the limousine drive to Harrington Lake. Is this what Fortier was referring to? But how did *he* know? The footage had not yet been broadcast. Had his people been following us?

"Mr. Cashore's career is replete with examples of anti-Mulroney bias," Fortier alleged, "ranging from his work as an opposition political and journalistic researcher to his time at the CBC and his collaboration with Ms.

[Stevie] Cameron on an Airbus book." (I presumed Fortier had mistaken me for my twin brother, Ben Cashore, who worked full-time for NDP leader Audrey McLaughlin as a policy adviser back in the early 1990s.)

Fortier continued: "It would be impossible to find" someone "less qualified to bring fair judgment and objective analysis to bear on this matter."

Fortier ended his letter with this: "We have every reason to believe that Canada's public broadcaster is preparing to televise a program containing material that is demonstrably false, malicious and libellous. Please be advised that if you proceed in such a manner, we shall hold you, your directors and principals jointly and severally responsible for any egregiously spurious allegations that reflect the mindset of a group of prominent anti Mulroney media guerrillas seeking to continue a long-standing personal vendetta against our client and his family."

The letter was brutal and blunt and highly effective.

"What do we do now?" I asked Studer.

We talked again about how to deal with another threatening letter, and I felt myself wavering, wondering whether I really needed to go through the stress of another Airbus documentary which would probably not get that much attention anyway. But that wasn't the only thing on my mind. I wondered more about Lavoie's threats that he could investigate me and my family. I recalled his comments about my brother and my father. I also was not clear what position CBC's senior management team was taking on the issue. Had Fortier's letter had the desired effect? Had it raised enough doubts about my integrity that senior officers in the corporation were now concerned about what I was up to? Aside from having sent Studer the Fortier letter, there seemed to be no indication whether or not they valued the work we were doing.[1] Rightly or wrongly, I came to feel we were all alone again, pursuing a story that would only cause us grief.

"I can't do it anymore," I said. "Let's drop the story."

"Are you sure?"

Studer understood that I was serious. He also would have known the toll it had taken on me, and him, over the years, and perhaps he felt exactly

---

[1] In retrospect, the silence from senior management was probably appropriate. They would have realized that any comments would have jeopardized the editorial independence CBC had created to avoid political influence in the newsroom.

as I did. He had always been discreet about his conversations with management, but I suspected he got a lot more grief than he ever let on. After I told Studer that I could not go through it again, I suggested I start working on one of the other stories I had begun to develop. He made a simple suggestion.

"Why don't you take the weekend to think about it."

I had the boys that weekend. For the first time in a long time I did not bring any work home. I felt refreshed, like an enormous weight had been lifted off my shoulders. I took the boys to their Saturday hockey games, cheering along with all the other parents. In the evening we ordered in pizza and watched a movie. Massey had just turned eleven; Jeremiah would be eight in only a few months.

Late at night, with the kids in bed, I had nothing to think about but my decision to walk away from the Airbus story. I had made that decision, I thought, so that my family and I would not have to go through those tumultuous times all over again. But then I gave further thought to the issue.

What would I tell my sons when they grew up about my work on the Airbus story? How would I explain to them that I had given up, right at the time when it looked as if—finally—the truth might come out? And now my decision did not feel so right after all. For the same reasons I wanted to give up the story, I was now considering sticking with it.

I walked into Studer's office Monday morning.

"Well?" he asked.

"I can't stop now, David," I said. "We've come too far."

Studer probably knew that I was going to change my mind. He seemed pleased, and told me I made a tough but worthwhile decision. Then I got up to leave.

"Harvey," he said as I was almost at the door. "Don't ever look back."

And I didn't. Strangely I had that feeling again, like a huge weight had been lifted off my shoulders. Not because I had given up the story; rather, because I hadn't.

Howard Goldenthal was making his own progress on the story, thanks, again, to William Kaplan. Kaplan had agreed to let us access his research notes from his two books, deposited at the University of Toronto archives. Then, one day, he barged into my office.

"You won't believe what I found."

He had a memo that Luc Lavoie had written to Brian Mulroney on August 15, 1996—the summer prior to the out-of-court settlement. The note was cc'd to Jacques Jeansonne and Roger Tassé, two of Mulroney's lawyers. It covered Justice Minister Allan Rock's media campaign that summer.

In the memo, Lavoie explained he had obtained a copy of an internal briefing note at CTV News. It was written by reporter George Wolff and sent to CTV president John Cassaday, and vice-president of public affairs Eric Morrison. (Lavoie noted that he and Morrison had been friends for close to twenty years.)

The note itself was three pages long and contained revealing details about how CTV was covering the story. Wolff described the pressure tactics he was facing from Rock's political aide, Cyrus Reporter, and other Justice Department officials for his coverage of Rock, which, he wrote, were "unprecedented" in his twenty-six years in journalism.

In his fax to Mulroney, Lavoie did not explain how he obtained the CTV briefing note. Still, CTV had accused journalists like me of working too closely with the RCMP, falsely implying I had given documents to the Mounties. Now we were learning that someone at CTV had decided it was okay to share journalistic work product with Mulroney and his team. It seemed to us like a contradiction.

I only knew of Wolff from his reporting on CTV News. When we found him in St. Petersburg, Florida, he immediately agreed to be interviewed on-camera.

Wolff told us he was deeply concerned to learn that his briefing memos had ended up in Luc Lavoie's hands. He seemed to assume that the documents were intentionally leaked. "So whoever leaked this private correspondence, there's where the sin is," Wolff told us.

Wolff had a lot more he wanted to get off his chest. First, he told us that he believed the media coverage had been manipulated by Schreiber and Mulroney, including his own station. He focused particular attention on the Phil Mathias story in which Mulroney was named for the first time, which had launched the controversy in the fall of 1995, and which allowed Mulroney to go on the offensive and sue the federal government.

Wolff told us that Schreiber had claimed responsibility for the leak. "[Schreiber] spoke to me often of how he had selected Philip Mathias," Wolff told Linden MacIntyre as they talked underneath a palm tree in the bright Florida sunshine. "So here's Schreiber admitting, you know, I picked a journalist, which is the next thing to say, I planted that story, I placed that story."[2]

No one seemed to know at the time just how carefully planned the spin campaign had become, MacIntyre suggested. "What it seemed to substantiate," he said, "was that there was a politically driven campaign [by the Liberals] to slander and possibly ruin Brian Mulroney."

Wolff agreed. "That was the spin on it and at the time I believed it too, that it was—that it was all politics. I no longer believe that." Wolff sensed what was coming: "If you're asking did Brian Mulroney set up his own libel suit? If that's where this is going, the answer is, I don't know."

He told us that Schreiber continued to call, even after Wolff left CTV News. In one particular call in 2000, Schreiber had been upset with Mulroney about the "fucking liar" quote and explained to Wolff that he had, in fact, given a lot of money to Brian Mulroney. Wolff told us what Schreiber had told him. "And [Schreiber] knew that Mulroney better behave because he had this bomb buried in his pocket." Schreiber told Wolff he referred to the $300,000 as a loan, and *not* as income as was being now reported. "And eventually Schreiber's telling me Mulroney doesn't know what he's playing with. 'I've got all of this cash that I gave him. He's in trouble if he doesn't start playing ball with me.' And ultimately he [Schreiber] dropped the hammer."

---

2   Phil Mathias refuses to say who leaked him the document. Schreiber himself later told us he had his "ideas" about who leaked the document to Mathias, but refused to elaborate.

Meanwhile, Howard Goldenthal continued poring over William Kaplan's archival material, including the interviews with Mulroney that had taken place over a one-year period between 1997 and 1998.

Mulroney had made several intriguing comments.

On December 2, 1997, he spoke to Kaplan about Marc Lalonde, the former Liberal cabinet minister who would later put up bail for Schreiber. "All I know is that Marc Lalonde was the lobbyist for Airbus. He was a lobbyist in 1988. We were going to ask him how he got to be the lobbyist, who he lobbied, and how much he got paid." But Lalonde had always denied being a lobbyist for Airbus. Mulroney clearly thought otherwise. Who told him that Lalonde had lobbied for Airbus? Only someone with inside knowledge of the Airbus sale.

On March 9, 1998, Mulroney complained to Kaplan about the RCMP. The Mounties "never interviewed" David Angus, a friend of Mulroney's and a director of Air Canada. "I appointed Angus to the board of directors of Air Canada." Had the RCMP talked to him, he said, Angus would have vouched for the former prime minister. "He told me the other day that I never discussed Air Canada with him at all. Obviously, if I was going to discuss Air Canada with any of the directors, I would have discussed it with him." (In his 1996 testimony Mulroney adamantly told government lawyer Claude-Armand Sheppard that the minister of transport had made the appointments to the board of directors, and not the prime minister.) Later in the same interview, Mulroney raised concerns that the RCMP was looking into his records. "I recently learned from a very reliable source that the RCMP has been poking around in my prime ministerial records. I immediately phoned [the Clerk of the Privy Council] and subsequently wrote her a letter saying that if this were true, I expected it to be stopped. This is my private property and if they [the Mounties] want to poke around in it they need a search warrant. She told me that she would look into and stop it if it was going on."

On May 13, 1998, Mulroney talked to Kaplan about Stevie Cameron and the book she was writing on Bruce Verchere, the Montreal tax lawyer who had committed suicide in 1993, and who had been on the board of the Swiss Bank Corporation. Mulroney told Kaplan that while Verchere did not ever work for him, he later learned that Verchere worked for Frank Moores. "One of the things about Bruce, and I didn't know this until later, is that he also acted on behalf of Frank Moores. One time he called me and asked if I could get together with Frank and him for lunch. I said no. I told Bruce that I chucked Frank out. Bruce asked me why. I just didn't want to see him anymore. At that point, he told me that he had done some legal work for Frank and wanted to mediate our dispute. I said no way."

Mulroney seemed concerned about the possibility that Verchere might have set up an offshore account for him: "I think he did a lot of work in Switzerland. When this whole thing broke, I was worried that he might have set up an account in Switzerland without me knowing. However, after having considered the matter further, I decided this couldn't be possible because he would have had to tell me that I was a beneficiary. Otherwise, how would I have known that there was an account set up on my behalf? Bruce was a principled and honourable man, and if he had done something like this it would have been well intentioned. But I don't think he ever did." (In his testimony under oath in 1996, Mulroney bristled at the idea that he would ever set up an offshore account. But now, contemplating the possibility one of his friends might have set one up on his behalf, he suggested it would have been "well-intentioned," coming from a "principled" man.)

On June 4, 1998, Mulroney talked again about the upcoming book Stevie Cameron was writing about Bruce Verchere. "Apparently, Lynn Verchere [his wife] had a number of telephone conversations with Arthur Hailey, which she later learned Hailey secretly recorded. So did Bruce do anything on my behalf to help me out without letting me know? I have no idea. He has been dead for five years and I have never received any advice about the existence of any fund." Then Mulroney referred to the other "fund" that former senator Guy Charbonneau had wanted to set up for his friend as he left office. "I can tell you that there was no fund set up by Charbonneau. Once I told Charbonneau that I didn't want it, that was it," Mulroney said. "Another interesting thing you should know is that a business friend of mine in Toronto decided to [raise money]. I heard that he was calling around asking for money. I called him and said no. And I can tell you that I needed the money. When I first started out, I needed the money quite badly."

Mulroney had declined to let his friends set up a "fund" for him after he left office, but we now knew that he had accepted envelopes stuffed with cash from Schreiber. Goldenthal and I wondered, Wouldn't the former have been better than the latter?

In an interview on July 29, 1998, Mulroney criticized the Liberals for appointing Roger Simmons, a defeated Liberal MP and convicted tax evader, to the post of consul general in Seattle. "The *Globe* didn't mention the fact that he [Simmons] was a convicted tax felon. He had been convicted of tax fraud. He had a record. He was ripping off Canadians. The headline should have been 'convicted tax felon dispatched to represent Canada.' But that's not what happened, instead there wasn't a single mention of it anywhere. As far as I know, there was no editorial about it anywhere."

At the time Mulroney made those comments to Kaplan, he had not declared for tax purposes the cash he had received from Schreiber, for which he would later file a voluntary disclosure to the Canada Revenue Agency.

Kaplan's notes, sitting in dusty boex at the archives, were a gold mine.

There were also detailed notes of conversations with Luc Lavoie.

In one interview, Lavoie admitted to Kaplan that he had a source on the other side of the lawsuit—the government side—passing him information to be used by the Mulroney team. "Of particular interest," wrote Kaplan, "Lavoie told me that they in fact had someone within the Chrétien camp who was supplying them with information. They were therefore able to anticipate various moves that the Chrétien camp was about to make, both legal and otherwise, and respond to them. This in part explains their success in both the public relations and legal campaigns. While Mulroney had agreed to give me full access to documents, records, et cetera, Lavoie expressed some concern about this given that he had made undertakings to various third parties not to reveal their identity."

Goldenthal found a copy of an email Kaplan had received from Mulroney's university friend, Pat MacAdam. MacAdam had given us that interview in 1999 claiming that Schreiber and Max Strauss visited Mulroney in Ottawa while he was Opposition leader. Now MacAdam was trying to explain to Kaplan what the money was for.

"Karlheinz hired Mulroney to sell Bear Head armoured vehicles to China," wrote MacAdam. "The vehicles were/are top of the line." And as well as selling military hardware to the Chinese, Mulroney was also working on his pasta business. "Schreiber also engaged Mulroney to explore the sale of [Schreiber's] pasta machines," wrote MacAdam. "The machines required a special kind of wheat and Schreiber thought that this would be right up the alley of Archers Daniels Midland. Mulroney was a consultant to ADM."

He disputed the suggestion that Mulroney received $300,000 in cash. The total, he said, was actually $225,000.

Howard Goldenthal had been speaking with Claude-Armand Sheppard, the Montreal lawyer who had examined Mulroney under oath. Sheppard was as intrigued as we were about the new evidence of the cash payments, and agreed to be interviewed for the Airbus story. We flew to Montreal and set up our cameras. We reminded Sheppard that Mulroney had said he hardly knew Schreiber.

"This answer—'I had never had any dealings with him'—" Linden MacIntyre asked Sheppard. "How could you characterize an answer like that?"

"It leaves no doubt that he had no dealings," replied Sheppard. "Whatever relationship existed was not a business relationship of any sort. That's what I would deduce from that answer. He made the statement he had no dealings with Mr. Schreiber. The statement is on the record. And, I moved on."

On that same trip to Montreal we filmed re-creations inside the very courtroom where Mulroney had given his testimony. Then we went to the Queen Elizabeth Hotel, where that "cup of coffee" had taken place. We filmed a re-enactment of two men in suits, one giving the other an envelope of cash.

I wrote a detailed letter to Mulroney about our upcoming story on February 22, 2005. In reality, the letter was written as much by CBC lawyer Daniel Henry as me; Henry was yet again backing up the journalists at *the fifth estate*, even as he was facing numerous questions from his bosses in the Mother Corp.'s Legal Department. The letter suggested it would be "invaluable" to interview him about our story on Airbus, ten years after it all began. We were specific:

> For example, you were Prime Minister of Canada when Air Canada, a Crown Corporation at the time, decided to purchase Airbus planes. That purchase led to over $20 million in secret Airbus commissions going into Karlheinz Schreiber's bank accounts in Switzerland. We would be interested in your reflection on the significance of these commissions, and your thoughts as to how Canadians ought to react to them. We would also be interested in your response to the statement by Mr. Schreiber's German lawyer [Jan Olaf Leisner] that some of the secret commission money was given to Mr. Schreiber to use as 'Schmiergelder' for Canadian 'decision makers'.

The next day Luc Lavoie called Linden MacIntyre. MacIntyre later explained that Lavoie was still furious with me, stating that I had "fucked" him by using the "fucking liar" quote. "Harvey has become the focus of the conspiracy theories that sustain Messrs. Lavoie and Mulroney," remarked MacIntyre in a memo to *the fifth estate*'s Airbus team.

Lavoie said his call to MacIntyre was a "gentle warning" to day that it would be "stupid" if the CBC ran with our story. Lavoie explained that they would not be answering our questions and that their strategy instead was to "sit back, not respond, and wait . . . Then we'll see you in a courtroom in Montreal."

"Our guns are loaded," Lavoie told MacIntyre.

CHAPTER THIRTY-FIVE
MONEY, TRUTH AND SPIN

We never did broadcast a documentary about Airbus in March 2005 as planned. We decided to put it off for the fall. The postponement meant we could do more work over the summer, and perhaps lead off the new season with the documentary. The decision to delay had an unintended benefit: a development that would change the thrust of the documentary and finally, we hoped, catapult the story onto the national stage.

We had begun to believe that Schreiber was courting the Mulroney camp in the spring of 2005. How otherwise could we explain an email that Schreiber wrote to me on March 10? "Do not misinform Canadians. I was not asked to write a letter that would have involved me in not telling the truth." Then, on March 17, 2005, his Edmonton lawyer, Robert Hladun, wrote a letter to Dan Henry, saying almost the same thing:

"I have learned that the CBC has referenced that they have evidence that the writer was asked to have Mr. Schreiber provide a letter to Mr. Mulroney that 'at no time did Mr. Mulroney solicit or receive compensation of any kind from Mr. Karlheinz Schreiber.' First off, to my mind, there is no such evidence because I never had a conversation with Brian Mulroney about compensation."

The denial was intriguing. We were confident, based on the information we were given, that Mulroney had requested such a statement from Robert Hladun. So why were Schreiber and his lawyer both denying it? It seemed like a cover-up of a cover-up. We concluded Schreiber was trying to get back in Mulroney's good books.

It was also during this period that Sam Wakim, Mulroney's old friend from St. Francis Xavier University and now a lawyer at WeirFoulds in Toronto, also got involved. He met with Linden MacIntyre, denied the story, and then invited him out to a baseball game.

"No, thanks," MacIntyre said, politely refusing.

In the middle of March 2005 Mulroney fell gravely ill.

He was taken to a Montreal hospital to have a benign lesion removed from his lung. While recovering he developed pancreatitis, an inflammation which, if left untreated, could be fatal. Mulroney stayed in the hospital for weeks, as doctors treated his condition. He was released on April 21, only to have to return again for another long stay. "Ask anybody what pancreatitis does to you," Sam Wakim told the *Globe and Mail* in early May. "It just kicks the living crap out of you . . . you're on your back with tubes shoved up your nose. Your muscular mass deteriorates. You stare into space."

By mid-May, Mulroney was back at home, recuperating but still not taking visitors. He did, however, take a phone call from Peter MacKay, who told him that his girlfriend, Belinda Stronach, had bolted the Tories to take a cabinet seat in Paul Martin's government. She had left him, too. While Stronach's agreeing to cross the floor allowed Martin to cling to power for a while longer, it seemed like a cynical political move on the part of a prime minister who was losing his reins on power.

In June I was still working on the documentary. I filmed an interview with Andrew Coyne who analyzed ten years of Airbus media coverage. Later I flew to Berlin where I interviewed both a German parliamentarian and John Goetz about how Germans perceived the Schreiber affair. The parliamentarian we spoke to explained how the Germans had to rewrite their legislation so their statute of limitations laws did not run out in the Schreiber case. The new law stopped the clock ticking on the statute of limitations in the event someone was evading extradition to Germany. Everyone called it the "Schreiber law."

Back in Toronto, the CBC team continued to speak to as many journalists as we could, to see who could shed more light on what happened during the 1990s spin campaigns, and who else would appear on-camera. I corresponded with one reporter from CBC's *The National*, to ask if he would help us out. "I have to tell you," he cautioned me, "having been through litigation to the extent that I have in my career, I will be guarded. I fully expect Mulroney will sue you guys if you go with that piece. I am familiar with his letter to [Robert] Rabinovitch. And since it is not a privileged conversation, I or you might end up being quizzed about it under oath, which is a most uncomfortable situation to be in." I understood the reporter's concern. Still, I responded that I was trying hard not to let the threat of a lawsuit affect me. "From my perspective, I have tried never to let the threat of litigation influence the stories I cover. As we know, people can threaten lawsuits for all kinds of reasons. What I care most about is being fair, accurate and thorough," I replied. "I am sorry you think Mulroney will sue. I don't see how anyone can decide to sue someone before they have actually seen the piece that is produced. It sounds to me like you are suggesting Mulroney will sue no matter what we say. That doesn't sound fair to me."

"I agree with some of what you say," the reporter responded. "Obviously, mere threat of litigation should constitute no barrier at all to pursuing a story. And such threats are routine. But threat of litigation from someone who is able to hold up several favourable rulings from judges, plus a federal government climbdown/apology, coupled with deep pockets, and an even deeper sense of aggrievement, would certainly make me ultracautious. Will he sue? I think he's itching to. Is it fair that he might sue no matter what you air? Beside the point. Lawsuits are a bare-knuckle business with no regard for niceties or fairness. And from grim experience, I know that the discovery process vacuums up every note, every discussion, every scrap of paper and email. And that the most innocuous comment or exchange can be held up and used to further claims of malice or intent. So, those are my reservations. I find your determination to exhaust every source of information about Brian Mulroney admirable, and you have quite a reputation. But I am not the one pursuing the story, and for the reasons I just stated, I am leery."

I was struck by the reporter's reluctance. He once pursued the Airbus story himself, back in the 1990s. Now he had left it behind, worried about lawsuits and threats. Clearly he wanted nothing more to do with it, even if it meant refusing to speak to another colleague in the media about the topic.

Schreiber called in late June, just before I left on holiday to Cortes Island.

He said he wanted to meet, to tell me more about why he wrote the email denying he was asked not to tell the truth. He wanted me to know what was really going on behind the scenes. A conversation with Schreiber is almost always exhausting. He always dictates the terms and direction. Asking a question, as the reader has no doubt seen earlier, or attempting to provoke a direct answer to a direct question, is an exercise in futility.

Frequently in our conversations Schreiber subjected me to elaborate theories about how the RCMP and Allan Rock had conspired to attack him and Mulroney; how he had been unfairly arrested in Toronto because the Mounties were in cahoots with the Germans; how the case against him in Germany was falling apart rapidly, including the allegations of fraud against the Saudis, the bribery allegations against Holger Pfahls and so on.

We met, as we had in the past, at the Lobby Bar at the Four Seasons in Yorkville. I brought up the issue of Hladun's memo to file about the call from Brian Mulroney. Schreiber tried to explain what prompted his earlier, apparent denial. "Harvey, you have to understand. The memos Hladun wrote were to Eddie Greenspan and not to me." Schreiber seemed to suggest that he did not have the right to make the document public. "Can you imagine if I pissed off Eddie Greenspan? That is something I don't want to do."

Schreiber told me he would have "paid $20 million" to Mulroney if he asked for it, because of what he did for German reunification.

On July 11, 2005, Frank Moores died of lung cancer in Perth, Ontario. He had given interviews to friendly media that spring, denying to his death that he had ever received any money from Airbus or that he had ever tried to sell A320 jets to Air Canada. While feeling bad for Moores, I found myself again lamenting that had there been a public inquiry into Airbus—as there had been in Germany—both Gary Ouellet and Frank Moores would have been compelled to testify under oath about what really happened.

In the summer of 2005, on Cortes Island, I finally finished the cabin I was building for the boys, sort of. It still needed windows, and a door, but that summer we celebrated as we took down the tent we had been living in for the last three summers and moved our sleeping bags to the second-floor loft. That night I read the boys a chapter from *Charlie and The Chocolate Factory*. Then, after they had gone to sleep, I noticed someone was shining a light in the window opening. I went to investigate only to realize the light came from the moon. I admitted to myself what I already knew: I had built that cabin as much for myself as for the boys. I needed to rebuild my foundation. The cabin was a start.

I had only been back at work for a short time when, on August 15, CBC management locked its unionized employees out of the building. This marked the beginning of a work dispute that would last until October 9. During that time we marched around the building, worrying about making our mortgage payments, but many of us also felt strangely relaxed. For the first time in my life I had no work to do (though Howard Goldenthal and I continued to make Access to Information requests on the Airbus story, wanting to know more about why the RCMP shut down its Airbus investigation).

Mulroney was back in the news in September, thanks to a new book by Peter C. Newman, *The Secret Mulroney Tapes*, in which countless hours of transcribed interviews with Mulroney were laid bare for all to see. They showed a profane and insecure side of Mulroney and created enormous media controversy, with the former prime minister insisting that his old friend had broken an agreement that the interviews would be off the record. Luc Lavoie put all the blame on Newman. "For a man like this [Newman], to tape him [Mulroney] without his knowledge and use it this way is nothing short of betrayal."

The *Globe and Mail* came squarely down on the side of Mulroney, with the headline "Why hate Mulroney so?" As support, it listed his record of accomplishments as prime minister. "On top of all this came," the article then claimed, "the most serious charge of all: that Mr. Mulroney and his government were corrupt—the most corrupt in Canadian history, according to one well-known journalist. In fact, no proof was ever advanced that Mr. Mulroney was 'on the take' (though he has yet to explain adequately why he received $300,000 from German-Canadian businessman Karlheinz Schreiber after leaving office). When he was accused of graft in the Airbus affair, he sued the government and won."

Stephen Kimber, the independent-minded columnist out East, summed up the Peter Newman/Mulroney controversy this way: "Mulroney assumed—on the reasonable basis of a career's worth of deference from a lap-dog press corps in Ottawa—that Newman would know enough not to quote his profane and paranoid pontifications directly." Kimber cited the recent coverage of the cash payments to Mulroney as an example. "The truth is that, for most of his career, the national press gave Mulroney a free pass. Even after he left office, Mulroney has enjoyed the benefits of a quiescent press. Consider just one recent example: Mulroney has never been pressed to account for the $300,000 he accepted from Karlheinz Schreiber, the German businessman caught up in the Airbus scandal, soon after he returned to the private sector, ostensibly to lobby on behalf of another Schreiber enterprise. The *Globe and Mail*, which—to its credit—broke the original story [two] years ago, seemed almost embarrassed by it, and has never done any serious follow up. Neither did any other mainstream media outlet."

The fifth estate hoped to change all that.

On October 9, the CBC labour dispute was settled and we returned to work. As I look back, I am thankful for the stoppage, as it prevented our story from going to air too soon. By the middle of October, Karlheinz Schreiber was in a far different mood than he was the previous spring. He was talking to us—again—more openly than before. There was a possibility, however remote, that he might finally give us a proper on-camera interview.

He suggested we meet at the Four Seasons on October 14. He remarked that he had several important new things he wanted to say.

First, he gave me the names of two former public officials who were allegedly given bribes. When I asked for more details, he simply whistled and pretended not to hear. "Gary Ouellet was the centre of everything," he told me. "He set up a company in Liechtenstein and the money went through there." Because Ouellet handed out the greasemoney, Schreiber told me he could not prove himself where it went.

He spoke evasively of "someone" who had asked him to put money into a bank account in Switzerland for Mulroney, in the early 1990s while Mulroney was still prime minister. Schreiber said he did not do this. He did not bribe Mulroney, he repeated. Mulroney had had "nothing" to do with Air Canada. Schreiber did tell me that Marc Lalonde was involved on the Air Canada sale, echoing what Mulroney had already told William Kaplan. The association did not last long, according to Schreiber. Lalonde discovered that his law firm was also acting for Air Canada. This put the firm in a direct conflict of interest. Lalonde had to return to Airbus all the monies he had received.

Schreiber also told me the RCMP and the Justice Department had approached him to do "a deal"—in other words, would he provide the Mounties evidence that might allow them to prosecute someone else? He and Greenspan considered, he said, but realizing they would not take his extradition off the table, refused.

We talked further about Mulroney's request for a letter from Schreiber in 1999. Schreiber said that Eddie Greenspan was "pissed at Mulroney" and his lawyers because they put him in a situation of being a possible witness. Schreiber would not elaborate.

Later in the evening Bärbel joined us, opening up in ways that Schreiber had not. She told me it had been a tough ten years. It was October 2005; they had not travelled anywhere since April. "We just live in that small apartment in Yorkville and that's our life." Bärbel was fiercely loyal to

Schreiber. We joked about the time we tried to jump him in 1995, and how Trish Wood got caught inside the garage door as Bärbel helped to make sure *the fifth estate* host did not hit her head. And we talked about the time Schreiber called me at the hotel in Zurich, pretending to be the Swiss banker "Emil," claiming he would hand over Mulroney's bank accounts, for a fee. Schreiber told me Robert Hladun had been involved in that subterfuge and that they were all "laughing silly" when they made the call. Schreiber said he got the number for my hotel room from Max Strauss after I had left him a message.

I waited all evening to ask Schreiber if he would appear on-camera. Towards the end of the evening I told him the documentary was going ahead with or without him, that it would be far better if he contributed something to it. He would think about it, he told me. His only reservation, he said, was out of concern for his friendship with Elmer MacKay, the former Mulroney cabinet minister, and concerns that it might negatively affect Peter MacKay, who was a rising star in the Conservative Party.

If he did do the interview, he said, John Goetz would have to be there. Schreiber had known Goetz for several years, and admired him. In Schreiber's eyes, the freelancer was an "independent businessman." Schreiber also admired that Goetz was an American who learned to speak German while visiting Berlin, then actually stayed there permanently to earn a living. Schreiber could identify with all that, making a career out of nothing but one's own determination.

We met up at Rodney's Oyster Bar in Toronto on November 9. Goetz and I remarked that it had been five years, almost to the day, that we drove to meet Helge Wittholz and celebrated John's birthday at Tim Hortons. And for me, it had been eleven years since I had first begun work on the Airbus story.

Schreiber took us back to the night in 1995 when Mulroney talked to him on the phone about the RCMP's Letter of Request. He told us that Mulroney said he was "suicidal." Schreiber was so bothered by this that he asked to get Mila Mulroney on the phone, telling her that if Mulroney really felt that way he should just use a "lead pipe" and get it over with.

Then Schreiber moved on to the so-called "false" statement that Mulroney wanted him to sign. He confirmed that Robert Hladun prepared a memo to file for Greenspan about that conversation. Schreiber also told us that lawyer Gérald Tremblay invited Greenspan to a meeting in Montreal. A week or two after that, for whatever reason, they told Greenspan about Mulroney's voluntary tax declaration.

Schreiber reached into a brown envelope and fished out some pictures. The first was of Mulroney and Schreiber meeting in the prime minister's office, with Fred Doucet and a political aide; the second, Schreiber and Mulroney standing together, smiling at the camera; the third, Schreiber, Elmer MacKay and Mulroney looking at each other, with the inscription "Karlheinz, with best personal regards, Brian Mulroney"; the fourth, Frank Moores, Schreiber and Mulroney, in the foyer of the House of Commons; and the fifth, a black-and-white photo of Mulroney, inscribed "For my friend, Karlheinz, with gratitude and best personal regards, Brian Mulroney."

Then, Schreiber told us he had made up his mind: "I will do the interview."

We didn't waste any time.

The next day we rented a room at the Crowne Plaza across the street from the CBC building. By the time Schreiber arrived, everyone was ready: John Goetz, Howard Goldenthal, cameraman Hans Vanderzande, sound recordist Larry Kent, me and host Linden MacIntyre. We were tense, excited.

The interview began. I kept staring at the list of questions we had to cover and then back at the monitor and then, during a particularly important answer, I would look at Goetz and Goldenthal and nod quietly. Finally, Schreiber was talking.

We started from the beginning.

Schreiber talked about his early days in Alberta, how he came to Montreal to get to know people close to Mulroney involved in dumping Joe Clark as leader of the Conservative Party, and how he met Mulroney, when Mulroney was the president of the Iron Ore Company of Canada. Schreiber described how he felt when he heard the news Mulroney had been elected prime minister: "I was in Saint Tropez, in my home. I got a phone call from a friend of mine, from one of my companies, and he called and said, 'Karlheinz, imagine, Mulroney made it.' I said it's wonderful, it's great."

"After Mulroney became the prime minister, how difficult was it for you to gain access? To become his friend?" MacIntyre asked.

"Not at all, not at all, it was very simple."

MacIntyre asked Schreiber to explain exactly what it was that he did as he facilitated deals between European companies and the Canadian government. As he had done at the Eurocopter preliminary hearing two years prior, he boldly admitted that he paid *schmiergelder* to make the deals happen. He insisted that because German law allowed these kinds of payments that the Germany government was "a participant in the whole thing." Not only the German government, but also Airbus Industrie, MBB, and Thyssen Industrie. They all agreed to give greasemoney to Schreiber, who would then act as intermediary in the doling out of the money. This way the German government, and the companies, could always argue they were not directly involved.

As for Mulroney, Schreiber tried to put some perspective on their relationship. "Well, I've never been to his home. He has never been to my home. We met in his office, at a building—at a restaurant or in a club or what, when he was with others."

MacIntyre asked Schreiber to describe the 1995 phone call when he informed Mulroney about the Letter of Request from the RCMP.

"You see," Schreiber said, "when you are on the telephone, and somebody says, 'Oh my God, Jesus Christ, what is this all about—send me immediate translation,' what more can you say there?" He left out the reference to suicide.

MacIntyre wanted to know more about who leaked the letter to Phil Mathias at the *Financial Post*, which had caused Mulroney to sue the federal government.

"Mulroney was right to sue them when they said he was bribed on Airbus," Schreiber insisted.

"But he launched a very aggressive lawsuit and that only became possible when this letter became public," MacIntyre responded.

"Yes."

"How did that letter become public?"

"I have—I have my—I have my thoughts about this. But I don't want to talk about this."

As for providing any more information about that "false" letter that Mulroney had requested of Schreiber in 1999, Schreiber refused to discuss it.

"Through intermediaries, in a roundabout way, you're asked to create a statement that you never gave him any money," MacIntyre suggested.

"I don't want to comment on this. We had this before. Because that would upset my lawyer very much," Schreiber said.

It was time for MacIntyre to ask about the Lavoie clips, which Schreiber would have heard for the first time on October 20, 1999, when we aired our documentary. He was not shy about characterizing his reaction. He was still extremely upset.

"I could not—my friends, my family said, 'Well, is he sick?' But I never received the proper, a proper apology from the boss [of] Mr. Luc Lavoie. You know what I mean . . . Or do you think I would have allowed him [Lavoie] to say such a mess or shit or whatever you want to say to a friend of mine?"

If the point had not been made enough before, it was being hammered home now. Almost all of Schreiber's anger towards Mulroney boiled down to a simple question of respect. He wanted a phone call from Mulroney apologizing for what was said, yet it never came. He probably wanted his old friendship back too, and that never came either. I was beginning to think this explained, more than anything, why Schreiber was talking with us. He was stung by what he perceived as Mulroney's disloyalty. In Schreiber's world, that made perfect sense. Without friendships, and connections, there really was not much else.

Then we got to the money. According to Schreiber, he got a call from Fred Doucet, Mulroney's closest friend, asking if he could meet Mulroney and help him with the transition from public life into the private sector. Mulroney needed money.

"And it really happened through . . . through Fred Doucet, who told me, 'Karlheinz, Brian is now leaving, has to go to private sector and he has really financial problems . . .' And there was one element which was very important for me, reunification of Germany. Schreiber told us that while Francois Mitterand, the president of France, and Margaret Thatcher, the prime minister of England, were against German reunification, Mulroney "heavily" supported it.

According to Schreiber, then, the money was, in part, a thank you—and a way of helping a friend in need. "It was a thought that he would get money from us," Schreiber said, "from our side to buy a big home, survive at the moment, and get organized, get back to his law firm and start your business or whatsoever."

Schreiber also said that he thought the former prime minister would help him lobby Kim Campbell, the current prime minister, in his efforts to establish the Bear Head project in a new location—Montreal.

Schreiber told us that the first meeting was at the Mirabel Airport hotel, north of Montreal. Fred Doucet told him where to meet Mulroney: "And I was told to see him at the airport hotel, so he was there and he had a suite. So now this was the first meeting where I really brought the first 100,000 to him," Schreiber explained. And then he described the second meeting, at the Queen Elizabeth Hotel in Montreal, which took place later that year, in 1993. "I was there at the gold key section. So he came there to say hello to me and I brought him the other money." And finally he described the meeting at the Pierre Hotel, on December 8, 1994, where the third and final cash transfer took place.

Schreiber explained that he was actually in New York for other reasons. "I was at the Pierre because I had an event there at the Metropolitan Club. And while I was there, I met with other friends, they just had married, him and his wife." (The friend was Elmer MacKay.) Schreiber explained that Mulroney and long-time friend Fred Doucet had come to his hotel to get the money.

"And so Brian came with Fred Doucet, and this is when I brought him the third [instalment of] money."

The interview dragged on for hours, with Schreiber veering off into every direction and MacIntyre trying to bring him back to the chronology of the story. During tape changes we would grab some water, or take bathroom breaks. MacIntyre was about to ask what the money was for, but Schreiber returned to the theme that had dominated the conversation: Why had Mulroney treated him so badly?

Schreiber told us he could never understand why Mulroney did not admit he got the money, back when *the fifth estate* began asking pesky questions in the fall of 1999. Mulroney could have said simply, "Everybody knows I was not rich when I left government, I was short of money and I was very grateful that Mr. Schreiber gave me a deposit, a loan or whatever, for the future, to work with."

"He didn't do that though," replied MacIntyre.

"No," observed Schreiber. "What he did instead of that was to say it was one of his worst days when he got to know me and that I'm the greatest fucking liar on earth. What I never understood why to make a miracle out of all these things by denying it. And finally you find out two things. Either it's very simple or very stupid. Nothing special."

"And which do you think it is?" asked MacIntyre.

"And this case is both," Schreiber replied.

"Simple and stupid?"

"Very simple and very stupid. Simple is that I gave him $300,000. Stupid is that he denied it, simple like that."

We got to the question that had been on all of our minds for years. No one had been able to provide any evidence to demonstrate that Mulroney actually did any work for the money. Now it was our turn to ask the person who so far had declined to explain himself. It began with a question about why Schreiber paid Mulroney in cash—in thousand-dollar bills—why not simply ask Mulroney for an invoice and give him a cheque?

"Well, number one was that we had cash. Number two was to bill for what?"

"So what did he do to earn $300,000?" MacIntyre asked.

Schreiber tilted his head back and sideways, and began to cackle. "So what you are asking me now is—"

"Very simple, what did he do for the money?" MacIntyre repeated.

"What had he done for the money? Ummm . . ." Schreiber laughed again. "Well, I learned to my great surprise that he worked with me on spaghetti!"

Schreiber had already testified at the MBB preliminary hearing that Mulroney had helped him with the pasta business. But he never said what it was Mulroney had actually done. Now he had an answer. Schreiber, it seemed, was about to tell us that Mulroney worked for him in his capacity as director for the U.S. wheat processing company Archers Daniels Midland.

"From Archer Daniel [*sic*]. That's true," Schreiber said. "He [Mulroney] sent me a brochure from Archer Daniel [*sic*]. That's it."

And then, with a mischievous smile, Schreiber added, "Maybe it's a pretty expensive brochure."

One by one we were ticking off the questions that had not been asked, getting important answers on-camera, captured now forever on digital videotape. And then we came to one of the most important questions: Where did the money come from?

The fact is, I already knew.

The fifth estate had long ago seen the Britan account document, along with all the other rubriks from Schreiber's banking records at the Swiss Bank Corporation in Zurich. We knew, from tracing the money flow backwards, that greasemoney from Airbus was deposited into the Britan account.[1] While we had made that discovery in 1999, the revelation garnered little attention. We believed that rebroadcasting the same information in 2006 might make it seem new again. In some ways it *was* new information. By now we had obtained a photocopy of the Britan account document. Back in 1999 we only had handwritten notes.

The Britan bank document told a simple story. In the middle of the page it said, "Rubrik Britan." Just above that, and to the right, the parent account was listed, 18679 "IAL." You did not need to be a forensic accountant to know that the Britan account therefore got money from International Aircraft Leasing. We knew from the documents that Giorgio Pelossi had given us back in 1994 that IAL received Airbus, Thyssen and MBB money, the bulk of which came from Airbus.

Still, although we knew that the evidence was overwhelming that Mulroney received the money out of the Britan account—the Pierre Hotel

---

1   More specifically, the Britan money came from the Frankfurt rubrik, which received money from both Thyssen and Airbus. A forensic accounting firm would later confirm the money into Britan came from Airbus.

meeting and the notes in Schreiber's Daytimer seemed to be a slam dunk—we did not know what Schreiber himself was going to say. He had never before spoken publicly about the cash transaction. When MacIntyre got to the questions about where the money had come from, we all paid close attention.

"There had been speculation about a special account called Britan and that money was withdrawn from that account," MacIntyre said.

"Correct," Schreiber admitted. "There were 500,000 [dollars] sitting, and from there he got 300."

It was that simple. Schreiber had confirmed Mulroney got the cash from Britan.

Schreiber told MacIntyre that he believed there should now be a public inquiry, though he had observed that no one else seemed to want it anymore. He hinted Canadian politicians did not want to unravel the mysteries of the Airbus deal.

"What they try is to get me out of the country or put me in jail or whatever. To shut me up," Schreiber claimed.

"So what you're saying is that this entire controversy, at which you are in the centre, exposes something about our political culture," MacIntyre opined.

"Absolutely."

"That people in that culture do not want to talk about?"

"Absolutely," replied Schreiber. "But I know one thing too. Sooner or later, the truth shows up, whether you like it or not. You have just to wait."

CHAPTER THIRTY-SIX
RETURN TO POWER

On November 25, 2005, Justice Paul Belanger, who had presided over MBB Canada's preliminary hearing, ruled that there was no evidence that the Canadian helicopter subsidiary knew about the secret contract that its parent company, MBB, had signed with International Aircraft Leasing in Liechtenstein until *after* it had signed the deal with the Coast Guard. Belanger concluded that MBB may have acted "sharply or somewhat less than ethically," but pointed out "the criminal law does not exist to redress bad bargains or sharp conduct falling short of fraud." MBB Helicopter Canada, or Eurocopter as it was now known, was off the hook. There would be no trial.

The RCMP had nothing whatsoever to show for its decade-long Airbus investigation.

Two days later—and two weeks after our on-camera interview with Schreiber—Prime Minister Paul Martin's government fell on a vote of non-confidence. An election was set for January 23, which meant that our documentary on Schreiber and Mulroney would be coming out right in the middle of the campaign. We knew that Harper had been courting Mulroney, and vice versa, and wondered what impact our story might have, if any, on the election. Certainly it seemed possible that the Liberals might want to use the new information as a means of deflecting attention from their own ethical lapses in the preceding decade.

Initially it looked as if the Liberals would win.

The Gomery Report had been released at the beginning of the month, criticizing the Liberals for a "culture of entitlement." As he was not personally involved in the sponsorship scandal, Martin had escaped personal criticism. As the election campaign began, polls predicted he would end up with another minority government.

But that all changed on December 27, 2005, when RCMP commissioner Giuliano Zaccardelli issued a press release stating that the Mounties were investigating allegations that Liberal finance minister Ralph Goodale's office had engaged in insider trading prior to a public announcement of changes in the taxation of income trusts. The RCMP stated at the time that they had no evidence of criminal wrongdoing on the part of anyone—including Goodale—but the story captured the headlines for several days. Just the mention of Goodale's name was enough. News of the probe prompted Harper's Tories to attack the Liberals all over again on their weakest issue, allegations they had run a corrupt regime for more than a decade. The allegations would become the watershed moment in the campaign. Shortly after the RCMP's press release, the Tories took the lead in the polls, never to relinquish it, even taking second place in Quebec from the Liberals.

Zaccardelli's decision to announce the investigation in the middle of an election campaign seemed so peculiar that the commissioner for public complaints against the RCMP later conducted an investigation into what prompted the news release. Zaccardelli had waded into the political spotlight only two years before, having written Mulroney a letter stating he was no longer under investigation. Now, two years later, it looked as if Zaccardelli was treating the Liberals differently. The RCMP commissioner was seen exonerating a former prime minister (who still refused to explain the large sums of cash he had received from Karlheinz Schreiber), yet was now publicly announcing a criminal investigation into the Liberals during the politically charged environment of an election campaign.[1]

CBC News editor-in-chief Tony Burman decided to delay the broadcast of the Schreiber documentary until after the election. Our documentary, he explained, had nothing to do with the election campaign and he did not want to make it look as if we were suggesting otherwise. The decision was controversial. For years, the CBC had been accused of anti-Tory bias, and I presumed Burman did not want to add any fuel to that fire. Still, by delaying broadcast we decided that Canadians should not know what we knew until *after* the election. I was not sure how the documentary would have affected voting patterns, if at all. But I was not so sure we made the right call. If voters changed their minds after seeing our documentary, shouldn't that be their decision, not ours?

Paul Martin lost.

The January 23 election saw the Tories go from 99 seats to 124 in Parliament, and increase their popular vote from 29 per cent to 36 per cent. The Liberals went down to 103 seats from 135. Paul Martin announced he would step down.

On February 8, 2006, we broadcast our *fifth estate* story "Money, Truth and Spin." Viewers saw our re-creations of the meetings where cash changed hands: at the Mirabel Airport hotel, the Queen Elizabeth Hotel in Montreal and the Pierre Hotel in Manhattan. Thousand-dollar bills had been taken out of circulation by the time we did our filming, so we borrowed one from Scotiabank. We put a microscopic lens on our camera and filmed the bill so closely you could see details not usually visible to the naked eye. I believe those re-creations of the thousand-dollar bills, along with showing the actual

---

1　Zaccardelli was no longer commissioner when, two years later, the probe into his decision-making was released. Paul Kennedy, the chair of the Complaints Commission, called the decision to issue the news release "inappropriate," adding that Zaccardelli himself refused to be interviewed, as did other senior Mounties. "The police officers who hold a public function and are accountable to the public ought to be accountable for articulating why they did or didn't do something," Kennedy told reporters. Kennedy also revealed that the RCMP's media relations team had drafted two different press releases, one mentioning Liberal finance minister Goodale's name and one not. Zaccardelli chose to issue the one with Goodale's name. "I don't know what the thinking was, one can only speculate," Kennedy would later say. For the record, no Liberal was ever charged, let alone convicted, for the alleged insider trade. The only charge laid was against a civil servant.

Britan account onscreen, impacted viewers the most. Everyone could see the facts for themselves onscreen. Mulroney got cash from the Britan account. The Britan account was connected to IAL. IAL was the shell company into which Airbus deposited its secret commissions. It was not hard to connect the dots.

This time, several newspapers covered the story.

"Mulroney's $300,000 traced to key Swiss account," said the headline in the *Globe and Mail*. Greg McArthur's story read: "The $300,000 that Karlheinz Schreiber paid to former Prime Minister Brian Mulroney came from a Swiss bank account connected to the Airbus affair, according to the CBC's fifth estate."

Andrew Coyne's column, "His Troubling Conduct," appeared in the *National Post* three days later, on February 11. "It is possible," wrote Coyne, "there is an innocent explanation for Brian Mulroney's decision, not long after stepping down as Prime Minister, to accept payments totalling $300,000, in cash, from Karlheinz Schreiber, the notorious international arms merchant and prolific dispenser, by his own account, of *schmiergelder*: bribes, in English. After this week's *fifth estate* broadcast, it is now incumbent on Mr. Mulroney to offer it . . . As a citizen he has the right to be presumed innocent. As a former prime minister of Canada, he has the obligation to dispel growing doubts about his conduct, even in private life, that threaten to tarnish the office he once held."

Coyne stated that the RCMP investigation "should be reopened" and given Mulroney's "misleading testimony in the lawsuit, it may even be considered whether the government ought not to sue to recover the damages it agreed to pay. That is not to say that Mr. Mulroney is guilty of anything. But it is unlikely that the government would have agreed to settle had it known of Mr. Mulroney's dealings with Mr. Schreiber, whose existence he not only neglected to mention in court, but appeared expressly to deny."

Coyne argued it did not matter if the events in question happened years ago. "Is it worth revisiting a matter that is now more than a decade old? Mr. Mulroney is 66 years of age. Four prime ministers have occupied the office since his departure. Is anything to be achieved by turning over this old soil? Yes. For one thing, Mr. Mulroney remains highly influential in Conservative party circles, not least with the current Prime Minister. . . . More broadly, the citizens of Canada have a right to know that the people who govern them are acting in their best interests."

Montreal *Gazette* reporter Elizabeth Thompson called the RCMP to see if they were going to reopen their investigation. An RCMP spokesperson was quoted as saying the force had a policy of not publicly confirming investigations. Three years prior, the Mounties had said Mulroney would never be charged; their position appeared to have changed. In Thompson's article, NDP MP Joe Comartin publicly called on the RCMP to officially "reopen" the Airbus investigation. "Yesterday, Comartin said he will discuss with his caucus whether to formally write to the RCMP and ask them to examine the information collected by the Fifth Estate."

The *Gazette*'s editorial page stated, "Mulroney should speak up." The paper cautioned that no one should jump to conclusions, "but Schreiber's appearance on the CBC's *the fifth estate* this week ripped the scab off a mysterious and ugly wound. Both Mulroney and the federal government have good reason to help us all expand our understanding." They had some advice for the new prime minister: "As for Stephen Harper and his government, we should bear in mind that the government does not tell the RCMP what to investigate. But a government elected on an anti-corruption platform might be expected to have some interest in the Airbus affair, no matter where it may lead."

I had long ago given up believing there would be the kind of blanket political coverage I thought the Airbus story warranted. Now, I was pleasantly surprised. No, the story did not lead the national newscasts. No, there was not a story in every newspaper. But it *was* beginning to resonate. One week there would be another story calling for the RCMP to act. Another week another columnist would weigh in.[2] Instead of fading away like the other *fifth estate* stories, this one seemed only to gain more attention as time went on. I felt as if we were almost there. If we continued to push, sooner or later the story would get the attention it deserved.

I had a new ally: the *Globe and Mail*'s Greg McArthur. He and I first bumped into each other while interviewing Schreiber in January, just before

---

2 Norman Spector, once Brian Mulroney's chief of staff and now a *Globe* columnist, played a significant role as he criticized his former boss over the cash payments.

our broadcast. He told me the *Globe*'s editor-in-chief had assigned him to work on the file. I had once lamented the lack of media interest; now I worried McArthur could scoop us. He felt the same about my involvement. We solved the problem by agreeing to team up. We shared documents, compared interview notes and decided to coordinate any future *fifth estate* broadcast with future *Globe* stories.

At twenty-seven, McArthur clearly had more energy than me. A whiz kid, as well, he had worked his way from the *Kingston Whig Standard* to the *Ottawa Citizen* to the *Globe and Mail* in a few short years, already winning awards for his investigative stories.

Schreiber told me he loved the latest *fifth estate* documentary—at first.

"Bärbel says it was the best interview I ever did," he told me the night of the broadcast.

But something happened to change his mind. Perhaps it had to do with the new political landscape, and his extradition battle, which was coming to an end.

A few weeks after our broadcast, the Ontario Court of Appeal announced it was about to make its ruling on Schreiber's extradition appeal. As part of his bail conditions, Schreiber surrendered himself to the Metro West Detention Centre. The next day he learned he had lost his appeal. His only recourse was to hope the Supreme Court of Canada would hear his case. That decision would also take some time. Seven days later Schreiber was released on bail, pending the high court's decision.

Schreiber and I spoke briefly after his release, but as the weeks wore on he became increasingly angry. He blamed me for not reporting about an RCMP sting operation against him.[3] He fretted that no one cared about the

---

3 Documents from the MBB Helicopter case revealed that the RCMP used an undercover agent, Vahe Minasian, to ingratiate himself with Schreiber. Schreiber only knew Minasian as an extravagant businessman who always bought him gifts—Veuve Clicquot, Pinot Grigio and Russian caviar. Schreiber told McArthur and me that former Tory senator Michel Cogger had even provided a reference for Minasian. Still the Minasian story had become too convoluted for the documentary and we saved most of the details for the front page of our website: www.cbc.ca/fifth/moneytruthandspin. Cogger refused to talk about his relationship with Minasian, or whether he knew him as an RCMP agent or simply as a businessman.

revelations that he gave cash to Brian Mulroney. His goal, after all, had been to avoid extradition to Germany; but it looked as if the new Tory government was not paying attention. I did not know what was going on exactly, but a few months after the February 2006 broadcast of "Money, Truth and Spin," Schreiber stopped talking with me altogether.

Shortly after Stephen Harper came to power, the *Hill Times*, the newspaper for Ottawa's political junkies, pointed out the similarities between Mulroney's old Conservative government and Harper's newest version.

"Look around Ottawa these days and Mr. Mulroney's imprint can be found all over Prime Minister Stephen Harper's minority government," wrote *Hill Times* reporter Christopher Guly. Guly recalled that Elmer MacKay's son, Peter, was the new foreign affairs minister; Senator Marjory LeBreton, who had worked in Mulroney's PMO and was close to his family, was appointed by Harper as government leader in the Senate; Derek Burney, once Mulroney's chief of staff, had organized the Harper Tories' transition into government; Hugh Segal, another former Mulroney chief of staff, helped to "tone down" Harper's public image; Michael Fortier, the public works minister, was a former law partner at Mulroney's law firm, Ogilvy Renault; Marie-Josée Lapointe had been Mulroney's deputy press secretary, now she was a spokesperson for the Harper team; Jean-Pierre Blackburn, the new minister of labour, had been parliamentary secretary to Mulroney's minister of defence; Paul Terrien, who had written speeches for Mulroney, had been responsible for Harper's Quebec "strategic communication." It seemed as if Mulroney's reintegration into the Conservative Party was a metaphor for the entire party. Once badly split, now, back in power, the party reappeared happy and united.

On March 8, William Kaplan met with Luc Lavoie. They discussed the most recent *fifth estate* broadcast, and me in particular. Kaplan called me the next day.

"Luc Lavoie called your ex-wife!" Kaplan told me that Lavoie told him that he had cold-called Alisa to get information, and that he had convinced her to talk. Lavoie gave Kaplan the details.

"Lavoie says she booted you out of the house not because you worked hard and were dedicated but because you were an asshole."

On March 16, 2006, Howard Goldenthal and I made an Access to Information request to the Department of Justice, wanting to know what the reaction was inside the federal Department of Justice to "Money, Truth and Spin." We mailed off our request for any records that might mention Karlheinz Schreiber and/or payments to Brian Mulroney, even though we knew that most access requests take months to complete, if not years. Also in March 2006, Linda Guerriero and I began a major investigation into possible lottery fraud at the Ontario Lottery and Gaming Corporation. I had heard that story about the pensioner from Coboconk, Ontario, Bob Edmonds, who claimed a clerk had stolen his winning $250,000 lottery ticket. Soon *fifth estate* host Gillian Findlay got involved in the story as well.

Then, in the middle of April I heard from my colleague Louise Elliott, who works for CBC Radio at the parliamentary bureau in Ottawa. She is a determined journalist who politely, but persistently, demands straight answers from politicians. She'd called to tell me she would be attending a ceremony for Brian Mulroney. He was receiving an award after being voted Canada's "greenest" prime minister. The event was taking place at the Château Laurier, down the street from Parliament Hill, and would include an introductory speech by Prime Minister Stephen Harper. Elliott and I wondered whether this might be the chance to finally ask Mulroney the question about the money.

The evening of April 20 reporters took their positions behind a cordoned-off area where they were allowed to film Mulroney arriving. Elliott had staked out her position early. Mulroney appeared through an entranceway with Mila, his wife, by his side. They were flanked by Quebec premier Jean Charest and his wife, Michele, and Stephen Harper and his wife, Laureen. Cameras flashed as all six of them smiled and stared for a photo op. Then a reporter shouted a question in French about the money. Mulroney, Harper and Charest smiled silently, as if they had not heard the question.

"*Bonjour, madame,*" Mulroney eventually replied.

Louise Elliott jumped in. "In English, Mr. Mulroney, what was the money from Mr. Schreiber for? Can you answer that?"

More uncomfortable stares.

"Stay tuned," Mulroney finally said. Then the three couples turned away and walked into the ceremony room, where hundreds of people were waiting to see Brian Mulroney make his first public appearance in Ottawa in several years.

The room was packed full of politicians and celebrities. Fred Doucet was there too, the man who had helped arrange the meetings between Mulroney and Schreiber where the cash changed hands. Old Liberal opponents like Sheila Copps attended. Everyone recognized Mulroney's son Ben, the host of CTV's *e-Talk Daily* and *Canadian Idol*. Comedian Rick Mercer was in the audience as well. Mulroney was not so much receiving the greenest-PM award, as he was being welcomed back into the a united Conservative family. The new prime minister, Stephen Harper, spoke first:

"When Mr. Mulroney left public office in 1993, few would have predicted, if you read the quotations from the era—dare I say not a soul in this room would have predicted—that all these years later Mr. Mulroney would be honoured by the environmental movement, at a head table with Sheila Copps and introduced by the former lieutenant of the Reform Party," Harper joked. "But what all of this shows, I believe, is that history will be kind to Brian Mulroney." Harper spoke of his recent friendship with Mulroney. "Although we first met many, many years ago, I've only come to know Brian Mulroney personally over the past three years. In our relationship Brian Mulroney has proven generous with his time and frank with his advice."

Then Harper introduced Mulroney to the audience.

"Ladies and gentlemen, Canada's greenest prime minister!"

Mulroney rose to the podium and shook Harper's hand.

"Thank you very much."

"Welcome back," Harper replied.

On June 13, 2006, the *Gazette* republished an editorial critical of Mulroney's silence after our story aired. "We will re-print it," the article said, "from time to time until Brian Mulroney—or someone—sheds more light on this subject."

In question period that day, Liberal MP David McGuinty asked, "Mr. Speaker, this morning we read for a second time an editorial in the Montreal *Gazette* about former prime minister Mulroney and his relationship with Karlheinz Schreiber. In light of this powerful editorial, is the prime minister prepared to call a public inquiry into this matter?"

Harper delegated cabinet heavyweight John Baird to respond. "Mr. Speaker, the last time a Liberal spoke to this issue, there had to be a million-dollar-plus settlement, which cost taxpayers literally hundreds of thousands, well in excess of a million dollars!"

In his blog for *Maclean's* magazine that day, political affairs reporter Paul Wells stated, "Why does a government obsessed with accountability not find these interesting questions? Why was Louise Elliott[4] of the CBC the only reporter who bothered to put these questions to Mulroney, the last time he appeared before a roomful of reporters in Ottawa? Why has he not received more criticism for brushing off her question with a non-answer?"

I sent DVDs of "Money, Truth and Spin" to both Liberal MP McGuinty and Conservative minister Baird. Then I called their offices to let them know. As part of *my* counterspin, I continued to send DVDs that year to anyone who asked, and even some to those who didn't.

In the early part of September, as we were putting together our lottery documentary on Bob Edmonds, I got a call from one of my sources. He told me that the past summer Mulroney had spent the weekend at Harrington Lake with Stephen Harper and his family. Somehow Schreiber had heard about the visit before it happened. Schreiber hoped Mulroney would put in a good word for him with the current prime minister. He supposedly apologized to Mulroney for appearing on-camera on *the fifth estate*.

"Schreiber sent Mulroney a letter begging forgiveness," the source told me.

Now I knew why Schreiber was not returning my calls.

4   Another journalist had shouted a question as well, in French.

On October 12, 2006, Howard Goldenthal and I received our Access to Information documents in the mail from the Justice Department (one of the speediest responses I've had to a request to the federal government for information). Still, we were both so busy on other stories, we did not get a chance to read them until early January 2007.

We had wanted to know if officials in the federal Department of Justice discussed our February 2006 Airbus story—where we showed the Britan account and interviewed Schreiber.

They certainly had. Dozens of documents, mostly internal correspondence, profiled exchanges between senior officials who had watched our program or the news stories on *The National* and who had read the investigative pieces in the *Globe and Mail*.

An email on February 8, 2006, from Assistant Deputy Minister William McDowell, to John Simms, the deputy minister of justice, reminded him when to watch: "Airbus, Schreiber, Mulroney etc—9:00 PM tonight on CBC TV." McDowell wrote Simms another email the next day: "Watch 'The National' if you can," referring to a news story about the Britan account and Mulroney's cash. Among the documents was a handwritten note someone apparently made while watching *the fifth estate*. "The account was opened after Mulroney left office but the money came from the IAL account. Cbc.ca/fifth." It appeared they had visited our website.[5]

From our review, Justice Department bureaucrats seemed surprised to learn that Mulroney had taken cash from Schreiber. (Those facts in particular had been published long ago—but with so little fanfare or coverage that even key Ottawa bureaucrats did not hear about it.) Now that they had noticed, however, Justice Department officials seemed eager to act.

Within days, the Department of Justice was looking into whether it was legally feasible to attempt to get the government's 1997 $2.1 million court settlement back from Brian Mulroney. We found a Memorandum for the Minister entitled "CBC report on payments made by Mr. Schreiber to Mr. Mulroney." The briefing note began, "This is to provide you with an update on a recent CBC report on cash payments made by Mr. Schreiber to Mr. Mulroney." The memo included excerpts from Mulroney's 1996 testimony,

5   Go to www.cbc.ca/fifth/moneytruthandspin or www.cbc.ca/fifth/airbusaffair.

which were then compared with the new evidence, and ended with the official's "considerations" for the minister:

"The Government's settlement with Mr. Mulroney is governed by Quebec law which provides that a settlement is a contract that may be set aside on the same grounds as any other contract. One such ground where one party to the contract committed fraud on the other so as [to] vitiate the consent to contract of the latter party. To date, [the] Justice [Department] has not been asked to consider whether an attempt should be made to set aside the settlement."

The bureaucrats were concerned about the matter being raised in question period. What would the minister say to a question about the $2.1 million settlement in light of the new evidence? One bureaucrat proposed that the new justice minister, Vic Toews, say simply, "My officials are reviewing the matter in light of the *Fifth Estate* report and will be providing me with advice in due course. You will appreciate that this is a matter that will require some degree of inquiry as it relates to a settlement negotiated just under ten years ago. I will not speculate as to the possible result of that review."

Then the paper trail simply stopped.

There was no information about whether any "review" had actually taken place. There was also no information about why the Justice Department had apparently decided not to attempt to get the money back. PR officials at the Department of Justice told us that the minister never got any of the proposed briefing notes. Someone had put a halt to the planned review. Who? No one would tell us.

We believed we had enough information, however, to tell a story on CBC News. The fact that bureaucrats had even looked into the idea at all was newsworthy. My colleague Scott Anderson began calling as many people as he could to shore up the research. He prepared an exhaustive background briefing note for Linden MacIntyre. On January 23, 2007, we were ready to go to air with a four-minute news item. Just as we were about to go home for the day, word got out that Tony Burman, editor-in-chief of CBC News, had killed the story. The story never went to air.

I was confused about the decision. Maybe Burman had a good reason; I just had no idea what it might be. The following week, David Studer and

I met with him. We did not know enough about what happened, Burman explained. We needed to find out if the minister himself quashed the decision to review the settlement. He urged me to do another Airbus story, but he wanted it to be more significant.

"Your next story has to hit the ball out of the park," he said.

I listened to all his arguments, but respectfully disagreed. One could contend that there was never a single home run in any of our Airbus coverage—just a series of base hits. Each new development had inched the story closer towards a greater understanding of the truth. I believed these Justice Department documents did just that. The information was released by the government under the Access to Information Act. Even if they contained more questions than answers, why should we be the only ones to read them? Shouldn't the public get them as well?

The *Globe and Mail*'s Greg McArthur and I had been working together on the Justice Department story. We were planning to time a *Globe* story with a CBC broadcast. I had to call him with the bad news: CBC was not doing the story after all. The *Globe* went ahead anyway. "Ottawa explored revoking Mulroney settlement," read the headline on the front page.

I had spent more than a decade criticizing our competitors in the media. Now I had to rethink my judgments. CBC itself had killed an Airbus story that I thought was squarely in the public interest. Obviously, journalistic decision-making was far more complicated than I had understood.

CHAPTER THIRTY-SEVEN

THE TRUTH SHOWS UP

Greg McArthur and I had not heard from Schreiber for several months when he called us to a meeting on March 14, 2007, at Vaticano, an Italian restaurant in Yorkville. I got to the posh Toronto neighbourhood early and spotted Schreiber at the corner of Bellair and Cumberland. He shook my hand, smiled a broad grin.

"Harvey, it's good to see you."

We walked up the street together to the restaurant. There was a point to the meeting and after McArthur arrived, we pulled out our notepads.

Schreiber was all business. He had several new things to tell us.

First, the meeting he had with Mulroney at Harrington Lake was on June 23, 1993, two days *before* Mulroney had stepped down as prime minister. We had opened our 2006 documentary, "Money, Truth and Spin," with a re-creation of the drive to Harrington Lake and stated the meeting happened just after Mulroney had left office. Now we were learning Schreiber and Mulroney met just days before Mulroney ceased being prime minister. (I was not sure the difference amounted to that much. The more important issue was what exactly was discussed at that meeting, and why.)

Next, Schreiber told us he met Mulroney in Zurich in 1998. Now he had our attention. We knew that by 1998 Schreiber was a fugitive from German justice. He had moved permanently to Switzerland. We also knew that Mulroney had testified in 1996 that he hardly knew Schreiber. In 1997, he received a formal apology and a $2.1 million settlement from the RCMP. So why would Mulroney risk a meeting with Schreiber in Zurich in 1998? Wouldn't the former prime minister now want to keep as far from the Airbus middleman as he could?

Schreiber explained. It was Mulroney who arranged the meeting on February 2 at the Savoy Hotel. Mulroney rented a suite and entertained him with a lunch of smoked salmon and pumpernickel. Schreiber told us he and Mulroney had a friendly conversation and caught up on their families. Then the former prime minister got to the point. "Mulroney was worried," Schreiber told us. He claimed that Mulroney wanted to know if there was any evidence in those Swiss banking documents that he, Mulroney, had received any money. Schreiber told Mulroney not to worry; there was no evidence. Besides, he would never betray a friend. Mulroney left the meeting feeling far better, Schreiber said.

We asked Schreiber if he could prove any of this.

He reached into his Louis Vuitton bag and pulled out an invoice from the hotel. It showed that Brian Mulroney had paid for lunch with his Visa card. The bill came to 2,106.05 Swiss francs (approximately $2,063 CAN). He also told us that Mulroney's assistant, identified as Paul Terry, was waiting outside the room. Terry could confirm the meeting too.

(Later, when I inserted the Zurich lunch into my chronology of events, I discovered that the meeting happened soon after Mulroney had spoken with author William Kaplan and journalist Bob Fife about how he had been falsely linked to the Airbus money.)

Then Schreiber showed us a letter that Mila Mulroney wrote to his wife, Bärbel, dated January 24, 2001. McArthur and I knew that timeline well—it was just after *the fifth estate*'s October 20, 1999, broadcast featuring revelations of the Britan account and Luc Lavoie's inflammatory statement about Schreiber. The letter was handwritten on stationery with "Mila P. Mulroney" stamped across the top.

Dear Barbel [*sic*],
I had wanted to put pen to paper sooner but at times like this words do not seem adequate. I know what you are going through. It never is easy when

our husbands have difficulties. Rest assured that it will pass. Things will get better, you have an excellent lawyer and the truth is certainly the best weapon. With this note I send my best wishes to you and your family.

Most sincerely,

Mila Mulroney

Schreiber ended our meeting with a reminder that the Tories had once called for a public inquiry into the Airbus affair. All those voices had now fallen silent, he remarked. "Maybe they are afraid," he said.

Or maybe Schreiber was afraid.

On the surface you could never really tell what Schreiber was feeling, as he always looked confident, in control, even buoyant. "Schreiber is actually looking very good for a man who is almost certain to be sent back to Germany soon," I wrote in a memo later that day. But what was he really feeling? He had been fighting extradition to Germany for eight years; he had spent millions in legal fees doing it. At times it seemed as if he had not a care in the world. He had put on a few more pounds since he first arrived in Toronto in 1999, but he had seemed almost relaxed as he aged into his seventies. In the early spring of 2007, however, I would come to know another Karlheinz Schreiber, one who was as ruthless as he was calculating. But he also betrayed a fear that for so long he had been able to mask. The clock was ticking down rapidly on his extradition to Germany and now, backed into a corner, he played his next chess moves quickly and mercilessly.

On March 22, 2007, Toronto lawyer Richard Anka launched a lawsuit on behalf of Karlheinz Schreiber against Brian Mulroney in an effort to recover the $300,000, plus interest. In his Statement of Claim, Schreiber alleged that the defendant, Brian Mulroney, "has failed to provide any services" for the money. News of the latest lawsuit flashed across the country. I was intrigued by the timing of the suit. Why was Schreiber making the claim *now*, thirteen years after the fact? To someone of Schreiber's apparent means, the amount of money he was suing for seemed trivial. Why go public and in such a confrontational manner? Certainly the action would prove embarrassing—even humiliating—to Mulroney. It would broadcast to the public yet another reminder that the former prime minister had failed to provide any details showing what he did to earn the money. It could also force Mulroney to testify under oath about that very issue.

Still, many lawsuits take years to get to trial. It seemed unlikely that the suit would be resolved before Schreiber was extradited to Germany.

McArthur and I realized we had to go to our bosses to formalize our partnership once again.

Schreiber was beginning to reveal a lot more information and we suspected there might be enough for a new *fifth estate* documentary to be timed with a *Globe* investigative report. The bosses agreed.

Brian Mulroney must have wondered how much longer he had to endure the Schreiber/Airbus story. If he had to do things over again, he probably would have been better served to have simply admitted back in 1995 that he had taken cash from Schreiber. He would have been criticized, for sure, and his confession would have been controversial, no doubt. But had he been the one to reveal the cash transaction, I am convinced it would have muted the reaction. Had he simply apologized for the error in judgment back then, it would have been doubtful that a decade later anyone would even be thinking about it. Instead, Mulroney's aggressive lawsuit, his misleading testimony and the $2.1 million settlement only served to cement his denials, making any apology virtually impossible. Instead of being able to admit to it, the cover-up just got worse and worse.

By the spring of 2007 he and Mila had a house in Montreal, another in Florida and an apartment in New York City. He was sixty-eight years old, a Companion of the Order of Canada and a proud father and grandfather. So far he *had* weathered the Schreiber storm. In mid-March he appeared on CBC's *The Hour with George Stroumboulopoulos* to promote his role in the new reality show *Canada's Next Greatest Prime Minister*.

Mulroney was also putting the finishing touches on his memoirs, which would be published that fall. McArthur and I wondered how much Mulroney would talk about the Airbus affair. Perhaps he would save a full explanation for the cash payments for the book? We knew one thing, however: by publishing his book that fall, Mulroney himself was putting his political life back on the national agenda. That meant that any stories we might broadcast on Schreiber and Mulroney would have additional relevance. We waited to see what Mulroney might say about former friends like Frank Moores, Gary Ouellet and Karlheinz Schreiber.

McArthur and I decided we had to meet Schreiber again. He and Bärbel were back in Rockliffe, where Schreiber's wife most enjoyed her time. On April 9, we flew to Ottawa and met with Schreiber at the Westin Hotel, just off Rideau Canal.

Over the next day and a half we peppered Schreiber with as many questions as we could get in. This time he actually answered many of them. We had not really spoken in depth to Schreiber for nearly a year. Much had changed; Schreiber appeared a bit less confident than his usual self. A bit more anxious.

He brought us up to date on what had been going on in his life. Schreiber had been trying to get Mulroney to help him fight extradition, he said. He knew Mulroney would be meeting with Prime Minister Stephen Harper at Harrington Lake in 2006. He figured he needed to apologize to Mulroney in advance of this meeting. He hoped Mulroney would help convince Harper to quash the extradition. He pulled two documents out of his bag. The first was an email, dated June 25, 2006, from Elmer MacKay (sent from his wife's email account) to Schreiber outlining proposed wording for the apology.

> Dear Brian,
>
> I wish to tender my profuse apologies to you for the misleading, erroneous and unfair characterization of your business relationship with me as depicted on the CBC program, "The Fifth Estate." Without excusing my part, it is fair to say that I was misled by the producers that the programme would deal with my complaints about the "sting" operation mounted against me by the RCMP. May I state, for the record, that my testimony under oath in prior legal proceedings is the only correct description of our business arrangement, that is to say, you, after returning to private life, at my request, agreed to advise and consult with me in certain business affairs.

You were the best advocate I could ever have retained, and I am grateful for your efforts.

Next, Schreiber showed us the letter he actually sent to Mulroney. Dated July 20, 2006, it contained some of Elmer MacKay's suggestions, and included a few more personal additions from Schreiber:

> Despite the fact I was very angry about the statements made by Norman Spector, Luc Lavoie and Bill Kaplan, I regret deeply that the people from CBC's Fifth Estate [sic] were able to entrap me, just as they did with so many others before me. This was possible with the help of an American journalist, whom I have trusted for a long time. He was misled, as was I.

Schreiber went on to apologize exactly as MacKay had suggested, then added,

> I still believe that my statements in the book, "The Secret Trial," together with my testimony under oath at the Eurocopter trial and my statements to Bob Fife, have made it crystal clear what my position is. There is no "Airbus Affair" involving Brian Mulroney and furthermore there is nothing to hide. The discussion and financial arrangements between you and me about future industrial projects have been correct, private and nobody's business. You were the best advocate I could have retained.

Suddenly, however, the tone turns. Schreiber sounds more like a spurned lover than a sometime business partner.

> It is far too long since we had lunch together. I think it is wrong not to speak to each other. Too many people talk too much. I have not changed. I have always been your friend, even though I was irritated for some time, which I regret. For the sake of objectivity and fairness, I ask you to accept my apology. I am happy that your health is fine again: so let us clear the air and bring peace to our families and ourselves.
>   Yours sincerely,
>   Karlheinz Schreiber.

Schreiber wanted his friend back.

Schreiber said he had been led to believe that the apology worked. He had had assurances, he claimed, that Mulroney would put in a good word for him with Harper. As I have said, the final decision to extradite under Canadian law is a political one; the minister of Justice must always approve the court's decision. Schreiber said he believed that Mulroney even brought along a letter Schreiber had written to Harper, to hand deliver to the current prime minister. The purpose, said Schreiber, was "to get the mess"—his extradition—"out of my hair."

In fact, the tactic had not worked. Now, eight months later, Schreiber said he felt duped. In December—when Conservative justice minister Vic Toews upheld his Liberal predecessor's decision to extradite Schreiber to Germany—Schreiber realized he'd been had. Mulroney had not helped. He said he now believed that Mulroney did not even give Harper the letter. The entire thing had been a set-up to extract an apology from him—Schreiber—for the benefit of Mulroney. By keeping the email from Elmer MacKay, Schreiber said, he could prove that he was "pressured" into making the apology in order to get a deal to stay in Canada. (It sounded to us that Schreiber was doing the pressuring, not the reverse.)

Schreiber showed us letters to Mulroney—filled with glowing praise—that he had written in the summer of 2004 (coincidentally, the same period Schreiber had stopped talking to us). "I like the man Brian Mulroney even more than the Prime Minister Brian Mulroney," he gushes before asking Mulroney if he would help him market his fresh-pasta machine.

Schreiber then showed us copies of letters he had written Mulroney after realizing the "apology" had failed to work. The first, dated February 20, 2007, demanded Mulroney pay back the $300,000, with interest, for a total of $485,000.00. "Unfortunately, nothing came of our plans as discussed during our meetings in 1993 and 1994. Meanwhile, events have unfolded that brought us considerable public embarrassment, media attention and court battles, some settled, others still pending." Schreiber had last seen Mulroney after both attended the same Toronto dinner in 2000; now he was being reminded of the conversation: "When we last spoke on the occasion of the dinner in honour of Mr. Peter Munk on May 23, 2000, we agreed that we would meet again after your return from Florida. But we never met. To date, the only messages I received were underhanded comments as early as 1999 from Luc Lavoie." Schreiber reminded Mulroney that he did not even reply to his cordial letters in 2006 asking him for help with the pasta business. He underlined the next sentence: "The fact is you did nothing. You even ignored my letters and refused to meet with Elmer and Mike to discuss the pasta obesity fighting programme for children."

Mulroney was not the only one on the receiving end of increasingly bitter letters from Schreiber. Stephen Harper was another. Schreiber's letters to Harper were convoluted and confusing, crowded with underlining and bolding for emphasis. Schreiber demanded an inquiry into his maltreatment by the RCMP over the Airbus scandal. He wanted the Liberals to be investigated.

Schreiber produced a document we had wanted to see for more than two years: Robert Hladun's memo to file about the phone call from Brian Mulroney in October 1999. The memo itself was written on January 26, 2000, and addressed to Eddie Greenspan. It explained how Hladun had first received a telephone message from Mulroney's lawyer Gérald Tremblay on October 17, 1999, "who advised that he needed a letter from Mr. Schreiber to keep on file and not to disseminate [*sic*] anyone in order to be able to send out a letter to CBC. The letter he would send to CBC, would in his opinion, "shut down the airing of the CBC Fifth Estate story on the 'AIRBUS'—October 20th." Hladun wrote he received a call from Mulroney the same day—October 17, 1999—who stated there would be "terrible consequences" if *the fifth estate* linked him to the Airbus allegations. Mulroney told Hladun that his lawyer, Gérald Tremblay, was about to write a letter to *the fifth estate*, "but first [Mulroney] wanted an assurance or comfort in writing from Mr. Schreiber saying that he would confirm what he had said publicly on many occasions, that at no time did Brian Mulroney solicit or receive compensation of any kind from Schreiber." Mulroney suggested the letter "should stop the whole Fifth Estate programme from being aired."

We knew Schreiber had not provided the proposed letter to Mulroney. What we did not know was that a few months later—in December 1999—Schreiber would meet with Fred Doucet, who would also want Schreiber to endorse yet another proposed letter for Mulroney.

The meeting happened over the Christmas holidays in late 1999 (and just as Mulroney was about to file his voluntary disclosure with the Canada Revenue Agency). Schreiber and Bärbel visited the Doucet home and as the wives visited upstairs, Doucet and Schreiber went downstairs to discuss what to do about the growing concerns that the cash payment to Mulroney might be revealed. The discussions continued into the new year, as the two men met again at the Royal York Hotel in Toronto. Schreiber said that was when Doucet pulled out the agreement he had prepared for him to sign.

He showed us a document with the word "Mandate" printed at the top. It purported to describe a business relationship between Schreiber and Mulroney:

> To provide a watching brief to develop economic opportunities for our companies . . . Including traveling abroad to meet with government and private sector leaders to assist in opening new markets for our products and to report regularly to us in this regard. In this context, priority should be given to opportunities relating to Canadian based manufacturing of peace keeping and/or peace making military equipment in view of Canada's prominence in this area. The mandate will be for a period of three years. The fee to cover services and expenses is set at _____[1] for the period.

The document was unsigned and undated. McArthur and I remarked on the fact that it was written in the present tense. Of course, Schreiber agreed. It was deliberately written to appear as if the memorandum had been drawn up *before* Mulroney received those cash-stuffed envelopes from Schreiber.

Fred Doucet gave him the memo to sign and date, he said.

Schreiber hesitated. Instead of signing, he took it away and gave it to his lawyer, Eddie Greenspan, who put it away for safekeeping.[2]

---

1 This part was left blank in the proposed "Mandate" agreement.
2 Fred Doucet would later provide another version of this agreement, one on which Schreiber had made handwritten notes, including the name of one of Schreiber's Alberta companies. This version also remained unsigned.

We had spent so much of our time looking at the attempted cover-up of cash payments to Mulroney that we had neglected the original story: Airbus. The documents that Schreiber would show us took us all the way back to the beginning.

First, Schreiber provided us letters that proved—yet again—that Frank Moores had lied about his role on Airbus. He showed us a letter from Moores to Franz Josef Strauss, dated February 3, 1988, right in the middle of Airbus negotiations with Air Canada. At the time, Strauss was the Bavarian premier and chairman of Airbus Industrie. "I would like to bring to your attention," the letter begins, "a situation that has developed regarding the sale of aircraft to Air Canada." Air Canada wanted a "deficiency" guarantee from Airbus, which, in plain language, means that the manufacturer guarantees the future resale value of the airplanes.[3] In Strauss's response, dated March 29, 1988, he assured Moores that Airbus would do all it could to help with the financing of the planes. Strauss's timing could not have been better. The next day the Air Canada board of directors held a special meeting to approve the $1.8 billion purchase of thirty-four Airbus aircraft (though the decision was not publicly announced until later that summer).

I remember thinking, *Shit, this is so unfair!* I had worked for more than a decade trying to piece together tidbits of information, like some gigantic puzzle, into a coherent picture of what had really happened when Air Canada purchased those Airbus aircraft. Schreiber had had the whole picture all the time—all of it in the documents he was pulling out of his bag. It almost seemed too easy. How I wished I had had these back in 1995!

Schreiber showed us a congratulatory telegram from Brian Mulroney, dated February 23, 1982, soon after he had become a Canadian citizen. "Dear Karlheinze [*sic*], Congratulations and best wishes on this important and first day of your new relationship with our country. It is a pleasure to welcome you to Canada. Brian Mulroney."

3   In his press conference later that summer explaining why Air Canada chose the Airbus A320s, Pierre Jeanniot mentioned Airbus's "deficiency guarantee" as a deciding factor.

Lobbyists Frank Moores, Gary Ouellet and Gerry Doucet, Schreiber said, knew long before the Tories were elected that the four were going to form a lobbying group in Ottawa when and if Mulroney came to power. That lobbying group would turn out to be GCI. Schreiber hinted at a direction we might pursue with regard to the Airbus story: "The secret of the whole thing is where went the money from GCI."

Schreiber also showed us a letter he received from Mulroney on September 18, 1989, thanking Schreiber for his letter of August 28, 1989, in which he reminded the prime minister about the telegram he had sent Schreiber back in 1982 when he became a Canadian citizen.

"You can be proud of your contribution to helping to ensure the continued growth and future prosperity of your new home, Canada," wrote Mulroney.

It had been a long and exhausting day and we still had not managed to get through our list of questions. McArthur and I decided we would stay overnight. Schreiber and Bärbel invited us to dinner at Stella Osteria, a restaurant in Ottawa's ByWard Market.

As we had learned, Schreiber was a master of self-control and discipline. But this evening would prove the most dramatic exception.

Bärbel looked anxious.

Normally she remained silent and smiling on the sidelines and let Schreiber command the conversation; tonight she spoke openly and bluntly about what their lives had really been like in Canada. She and Schreiber lived in constant fear, she said. I must have looked skeptical. They both worried that they might get blown up starting their car one day, she said. Gary Ouellet, she believed, possibly had been murdered.

The conversation was surreal. I wasn't sure if we were the victims of some preposterously elaborate joke or if they were serious.

Karlheinz was getting depressed, she worried. Schreiber listened, silently.

They talked about old friends, like Elmer MacKay. He had put up bail money for Schreiber in 1999, but had recently withdrawn his support. He told Schreiber that the optics did not seem right since his son, Peter, was now a cabinet minister. I sensed MacKay's decision had been a body blow to Schreiber. Another old acquaintance, they said, Michael Cochrane, had contemplated stepping in but had since declined. Schreiber said he learned that Cochrane had been promised a government job. Schreiber was told that Cochrane worried being seen to be publicly supporting Schreiber might jeopardize that prospect.[4]

Whatever his faults, Schreiber was a proud man. The fact that former friends were abandoning him in his hour of need seemed to deepen his gloom.

He was reminded that Peter MacKay had stopped defending him in the House of Commons. Schreiber shrugged; he no longer cared about the political fortunes of Elmer's son. Schreiber said he had once invited Peter MacKay to his house in Rockliffe. He claimed he told MacKay about the $300,000 cash he gave Mulroney.

After that meeting, a furious Elmer MacKay called Schreiber. It would have been better, he said, if young MacKay were kept in the dark.

At one point during dinner, Schreiber lowered his voice to an almost incomprehensible whisper. We had to lean forward to hear him.

"Fred Doucet knew all about the Airbus commissions," he told us.

Up to now, Mulroney had distanced himself from any splatter over allegations that Frank Moores had received Airbus commissions by insisting that he and Moores had had a major falling-out. Fred Doucet, however, had been, and remained, one of Mulroney's closest friends. Doucet had worked both in the Prime Minister's Office and as an Ottawa lobbyist; he had arranged the meetings in New York and Montreal, where Schreiber had given the cash to Mulroney. Doucet and Mulroney were confidants.

Schreiber explained. Back in the early 1990s, both Frank Moores and Fred Doucet were "constantly" fighting over the Airbus commissions. He told us he even had correspondence from both of them as they fought each other over the money. Schreiber said he was keeping the correspondence in a secret location in Europe.

---

4 Michael Cochrane has always refused to speak with me. I do not know his side of the story, nor do I know how the former Air Canada executive first met Schreiber or what their relationship is or was.

Sometime in the early 1990s, he said, when Mulroney was still prime minister, Doucet wanted Schreiber to put money in a bank account in Switzerland for Mulroney. (I recalled that Schreiber had told me the same story two years before, but without mentioning Doucet by name.) Schreiber told us that Doucet even gave him the name of the Geneva lawyer to whom he should have given the money. So far, Schreiber had been unable to locate the note. He said he never did give the money to the Geneva lawyer. He quoted Doucet: "You do know that Brian was involved in Airbus?"[5]

A week after McArthur and I spent those two days in April 2007 with Schreiber at the Westin Hotel in Ottawa, Brian Mulroney was back in the nation's capital for yet another tribute and another glowing speech from the current prime minister, Stephen Harper. Mulroney was being awarded the Order of King Yaroslav the Wise at a Ukrainian dinner at the Château Laurier. Again, Harper sang Mulroney's praises. "That's the way it is with real, effective leaders. While in office, they set clear goals. Then they remain true to these objectives, and they see them through against attacks motivated by misunderstanding, misinformation or just plain old political opportunism. And, in due time, they are recognized and rewarded. So it is with Brian Mulroney."

Mulroney seemed to feel the same way about Harper. "Thank you, Prime Minister, for your very generous and kind remarks and I appreciate them greatly," he said. "As I, along with growing numbers of Canadians, appreciate your strong, vigorous and visionary leadership." Mulroney reminded the audience of the previous gala they had attended. "A year ago, almost to the day, the PM and I were with Laureen and Mila together as the PM has said in similar circumstances at an event in another ballroom of this hotel, where I had been named by a panel of environmentalists perhaps to their own surprise and mine as, maybe you recall, Canada's greenest PM. Looking at our wives then, and again tonight, I thought that Stephen Harper and I had one very important thing in common. We both

5   While Schreiber would later repeat this story under oath, he has not provided proof for this allegation. Fred Doucet vehemently denies that he ever said any such thing.

married up," Mulroney said. The audience laughed appreciatively. "Not only that, Laureen is for Stephen, as Mila was for me, the best campaigner in the family and the best adviser that the PM has." Mulroney was fully back in the Conservative Party.

On June 13, 2007, Greg McArthur and I were walking up Parliament Hill with Karlheinz Schreiber. We were escorting him to a private room in the press gallery where we had set up our cameras for another sit-down interview. Bob Fife, now the bureau chief for CTV News, spotted us. He told his camera crew to film us as we walked along the road just in front of the Senate Chambers. It turned out CTV was in the middle of filming a special feature on Mulroney, timed to coincide with the release of the former prime minister's memoirs.

Linden MacIntyre showed up a short time later and would conduct the interview. We had last formally interviewed Schreiber in the fall of 2005. By now we realized he had held back a lot of important information. McArthur and I took our spots behind the cameras.

Why was Schreiber deciding to speak again, this time? MacIntyre asked him.

Schreiber was ready: "There comes somehow a moment from my family and from my friends, especially from my wife, where we say enough is enough. And Canadians should get to know what really happened. Because I came to Canada, I fall in love with the country. And what I faced then on lies and betrayal is incredible. And I keep my mouth shut. But now I have enough, I have simply enough."

Schreiber started from the beginning; he reminded MacIntyre of his entry into Canadian politics via the dump Joe Clark campaign—helping others who would then want to help him. "So that is the secret more or less of my personality. That I made all these friends before and we helped them. And when you come with money and when you help them and when you are friendly, it's easy to make friends. And it's easy to have relations and then it's easy to do business."

Schreiber spoke of happier times, when Moores and he realized Air Canada was about to purchase the Airbus aircraft. "Oh, he was happy.

We were all very happy." He told MacIntyre that before long everyone became somewhat unhappy, with everyone wanting more of the Airbus commissions than they had received. "Look, this is very simple. When it goes with money I have never seen in this—in this circumstances that people say oh this is too much please take it back. It's always not enough."

In particular there were three new revelations we needed to cover with Schreiber: the meeting in Zurich; Mulroney's request for the alleged false statement; and his decision to file the voluntary disclosure with the Canada Revenue Agency.

We began with the meeting at the Savoy Hotel on February 2, 1998.

"In 1998 then there was a series of telephone calls," Schreiber explained. "Then he [Mulroney] came to see me in Switzerland. And I thought it was nice. It was a beautiful hotel, Hotel Savoy, in the centre of Zurich at the Paradaplatz. Where all the nice banks are around and everything. And so Brian Mulroney rented a suite there for lunch with me."

Schreiber told MacIntyre about the reason for the meeting. "I found a very nervous, very nervous Brian Mulroney, and the reason for his, for his visit was more or less to find out whether there would be any evidence that he received any money." Schreiber told MacIntyre he could not understand why Mulroney was so worried. "If he would have said 'I never received from him 300,000 . . . I don't even know what he [Schreiber] is talking about,' I would have had no way to prove that he got 300,000 from me. So when he left I thought he was somehow in good shape."

MacIntyre asked about Brian Mulroney's call in October 1999 to Robert Hladun, Schreiber's Edmonton lawyer.

Schreiber recalled what Hladun had told him. "'Mulroney wants some kind of declaration or affidavit that he never received any money from you.' I was not prepared to do that because it was a clear request for, towards me to commit perjury. And why would I do that?" Schreiber gave some of the credit to his Toronto lawyer, Eddie Greenspan. "He only said to me if you ever sign any affidavits or any documents or whatever without my permission, as long as I'm your lawyer, I cut your hands off or you look for a new lawyer. He's a very humorous guy. When I asked him that there was a request that I should give such a declaration, he said under no circumstances. End of story."

MacIntyre asked Schreiber about the tax declaration to Canada Revenue Agency.

"How do you know about the voluntary tax declaration?" MacIntyre asked.

"I learned this from my lawyer."

Schreiber did not explain how Greenspan would know but, in effect, Schreiber was saying: Don't believe me; believe Eddie Greenspan. (Greenspan would neither confirm nor deny what Schreiber had told us.)

MacIntyre asked Schreiber about the prospect of finally having to leave Canada.

"It's not my intention to leave the country, under no circumstances," he said, understanding he would immediately be incarcerated on reaching Germany.

"I'm finished. I'm eight years in custody. This would be lifetime sentence. It would finish me off, therefore that's not going to happen."

The interview ended and we packed up the cameras. MacIntyre had to get back to Toronto, but as Schreiber seemed to be in a talkative mood, McArthur and I decided to take advantage of it. We continued a conversation that dragged on for hours. Once again we found ourselves, later that evening, at a restaurant with Schreiber and Bärbel.

And once again the two seemed uncharacteristically downcast and despondent. This time, the dour topic was their belief that they would "never" return to Germany.

The comment made no sense. There was a very good chance Canada would soon order Schreiber back to Germany for trial—not an ideal reunion with his homeland. But what could the "never" have meant? Were they thinking of fleeing? How did they expect to get away with that?

"We are going to commit suicide," said Bärbel.

Schreiber agreed. "We are going to commit suicide."

McArthur and I just sat there, stunned. We didn't know what to say, or do. Again, we wondered: Are they joking? Also, we were journalists looking into a story. If what they said was true, we were veering into dangerous ethical territory. Should we tell someone?

"No, you're not," was all we could say.

"Yes, we are," they insisted. From the surreal to the bizarre: Schreiber had one more thing he wanted to say. Something which—under the circumstances—came at us from deep left field.

"Pelossi was right. The Devon account was set up for Brian Mulroney."

Devon was the coded bank account set up by Frank Moores and Giorgio Pelossi in 1986 at the Swiss Bank Corporation. It would turn out that no deposits have even been made to the account, but no credible explanation had ever been made for the reason it had been set up in the first place. Schreiber had always steadfastly denied allegations that it had been created for Brian Mulroney. He had claimed, instead, that a disgruntled Giorgio Pelossi made up the allegation to get back at Schreiber following their falling-out. Now Schreiber was admitting the discredited allegation was true: the Devon account had indeed been set up for Mulroney.

We had been so focused on the Britan account that the Devon account had fallen off the radar. Now it was back. I had long ago come to the conclusion that Pelossi was probably telling the truth. To be sure, Schreiber's statement proved nothing. Even if it was true that the account was set up for Mulroney, it is absolutely possible that Mulroney had no knowledge of the plan. We decided the most direct way of finding out might be to get Schreiber to agree to repeat his allegation on-camera and then see where that might lead. Schreiber agreed. The next day we set up our cameras—exactly as we had the day before—and I would ask the questions this time. Only one problem: sometime between then and now Schreiber had changed his mind. He refused to comment on the Devon account. Period.

"I may express my thoughts on things, but this is nothing you can use. You have lawsuits on your neck left and right and centre because you can prove nothing."

McArthur could not contain his frustration. "That's not what you said last night."

There was no point. Schreiber would not budge. Once again we were left wondering, Why?

Later that summer, Schreiber showed us another letter he had written Mulroney. Dated the previous May, Schreiber told Mulroney—in bluntly intimidating tones—that he wanted his extradition problems solved, or else:

> The time has come that you bring the whole battle with me to a peaceful and satisfying end. This is my last warning. I am prepared to disclose: that you received payments from GCI, Frank Moores, Fred Doucet, Gary Ouellet; that I was asked by Fred Doucet to transfer funds to your Lawyer in Geneva (Airbus); what the reason was for your trip to Zurich in 1998; that you asked me through my lawyers to commit perjury to protect you; that you supported fraud related to the Thyssen project and more . . . It is in your hands what is going to happen. My patience comes to an end.[6]

Mulroney would later call it the "blackmail" letter. He certainly had a point.

In July 2007, Justice Edward Then finally issued his ruling on whether the RCMP had cause to identify Stevie Cameron as a "confidential informant." Cameron had strenuously denied she was an informant. But Justice Then reminded the court he was not making a ruling, either way, on whether Cameron *was*, in fact, a confidential informant, but rather on whether the RCMP *was justified* in making the claim. Indeed, they had been, he ruled. "Superintendent Mathews has conducted himself with exemplary fairness to Ms. Cameron and more particularly has conducted himself in good faith with respect to his duties to the administration of justice."

I read the ruling and hoped we could all put that issue to rest. Cameron had been through enough. I believe that her secret relationship with the Mounties had been exploited most by those who did not want Canadians to get at the truth. It was time to stop dwelling on that sideshow.

That summer, Greg McArthur, Howard Goldenthal and I made a series of calls to Air Canada executives about the new information that connected

6 This letter was later tabled as an exhibit at a Parliamentary committee.

Moores to Airbus. We spoke to dozens of executives, airline economists and former lobbyists, concluding, again, that certain people at Air Canada knew far more about the secret commissions than they had let on. Clearly, Moores had had a contact at the airline. Otherwise, how did he know so much about what was going on? We still could not determine for sure who it might have been, though we had some ideas. Goldenthal and McArthur also spoke to a source in the United States who provided them with an anonymous report written in 1988, outlining serious concerns about possible corruption inside the Air Canada/Airbus deal. It was titled, "CANADA: An Airbus Strategic Objective" and contained a detailed analysis of how Airbus sought to conquer the North American market. The memo also described a "council of war" meeting held in November 1986 in Ottawa, as senior political staffers met to try to convince Wardair to purchase Airbuses:

"The key attendees at the November meeting were Frank Moores, Gary Ouellet, and Gerry Doucet of GCI, Fred Doucet, senior advisor to Mulroney and Gerry's brother; Lucien Bouchard, the Canadian ambassador to France; plus representatives of Airbus North America."

It also named Liberal Marc Lalonde as having been involved: "Marc Lalonde, a key Quebec Liberal, close associate of Pierre Trudeau, and another lawyer at Stikeman Elliott, also came into the picture. Lalonde has had close ties with Pierre Jeanniot for many years. . . . Up until the beginning of 1988, Lalonde was on a personal retainer from Frank Moores, a relationship he now may have severed due to the possible political fallout." The report also noted that Pierre Jeanniot had put a new vice-president of finance in place just before the decision to replace the fleet of Boeing 727s. The new VP was Dennis Groom, "long time friend of both Frank Moores and John Crosbie," the report stated.

McArthur and I decided to track down the "Paul Terry" who had apparently accompanied Mulroney on his trip to Zurich in 1998 to meet Schreiber. Eventually we realized that Paul Terry was actually Paul Terrien, the former Mulroney speechwriter now working for the Harper Tories. McArthur gave him a call. "I'm an innocent bystander," Terrien joked.

"The meeting did happen but I forget how it was set up." Terrien confirmed that he did wait outside the room at the Savoy Hotel where Schreiber and Mulroney met. "I have no idea what they talked about."

Believe it or not, Luc Lavoie agreed to meet with Greg McArthur and me in August 2007, at 357C, the same club where I met him in February 2005. The weather was warmer this time, but Lavoie had not thawed one bit—at least, not towards me and what he mocked as my Airbus-and-Mulroney "obsession." He wondered what else new we were going to say in my "fifty-third" documentary on the topic.

We asked Lavoie if he had any new details about what work Mulroney had done for Schreiber's $300,000.

"A lot," he said. We asked for examples. First, Lavoie said, "the pasta business." When we pressed for details, he said that Mulroney had helped Schreiber in his efforts to have Toronto's George Brown College use his pasta machine in their cooking school. Mulroney also did work in his capacity as a director for Archers Daniels Midland, but could provide no additional specifics. Again we pressed for details. Finally, he seemed to give up. "So what if Mulroney did nothing for the money? Lots of people get retainers and do nothing for them."

McArthur reminded Lavoie about the events in the fall of 1999. We wondered why Mulroney did not just call Schreiber directly instead of asking for a letter through Robert Hladun. "It's because Schreiber was talking to people like this asshole," Lavoie said, pointing to me. This reminded me, again, that Lavoie and Mulroney had come to the mistaken belief that Schreiber was talking to us back in 1999—a belief that likely led to the decision to call Schreiber a liar and which, in turn, led to the falling-out between Mulroney and Schreiber and the revelations of the money.

Lavoie admitted that it was a "mistake" for Mulroney to take the money in cash. This was the first time we had heard such an acknowledgment from Mulroney—even indirectly through his spokesperson.

McArthur and I left our meeting with Lavoie in a good mood. For a reason that I still can't fully explain, I felt better after the conversation.

Lavoie had played rough and dirty over the years, but his theatrics no longer bothered me. I saw him now for what he was: Mulroney's employee. He was, after all, only doing what he was paid to do.

On September 2, I was standing outside the Savoy Hotel in Zurich, Switzerland, with a handheld camera in my hand. The very suspicious hotel manager came out to ask us what we were doing there. Standing next to me was Isabella Kempf, a German journalist who worked for John Goetz in Berlin and who had flown to Zurich to help with additional research and to translate. There was Timothy Sawa, who had been brought onto the project as co-producer. There was Joe Passaretti, who is technically our sound recordist, but is involved in every aspect of the documentary, from developing the editing style, to picking music, to filming sequences and, his true passion, taking still photographs of the team as we worked. We were all there to film a scene for our upcoming documentary, which we planned to call "Mulroney: The Unauthorized Chapter." The reference, of course, was to his recently released memoirs—in which any discussion of Airbus had been conspicuously ignored. Our idea was to film lots of feet moving, doors closing, cars driving by, as if to re-create the drive that Mulroney and Terrien took as they arrived at the Savoy Hotel in 1998 to meet Schreiber. Still we had one problem: we needed to know which room.

"Do you know Karlheinz Schreiber?" I asked the hotel manager.

His eyes lit up. "Of course!"

We were Canadians filming a documentary about Schreiber and what had happened to him, I explained.

The manager told me how unfair it all was. "Everyone pays commissions, it happens all the time," he said. He took me into his office, wrote a brief note on the back of his business card and asked me to give it to Schreiber. Then I asked him for a favour. I said we were going to describe an important meeting that took place at his hotel between former prime minister Brian Mulroney and Karlheinz Schreiber. Did he know in which room that meeting took place? The manager walked around to the hotel's computer, punched a few buttons, then confirmed to me that

Mulroney was at the hotel on February 2, 1998, and that he stayed in room 209.

"Here's the key," he said. "Film what you want."

We trooped up to the room and went in. I must admit the scene was plenty eerie. It was hard to convince myself that in this very room where I was now standing—back in 1998—Brian Mulroney had met Karlheinz Schreiber, by then a fugitive from German justice. If only the walls could talk.

Later that evening we set up our cameras on a bridge over the Limmat Canal and waited for the sun to go down so we could film the city lights reflecting off the river. We decided to use this backdrop for Linden MacIntyre's opening sequence. When the light was just right, MacIntyre spoke directly into the camera.

Good evening and welcome to *the fifth estate*. I'm Linden MacIntyre in Zurich, Switzerland. Tonight, Brian Mulroney, once one of Canada's most reviled prime ministers, enjoys redemption in a book he wrote himself and a television portrait partly crafted by his image-makers. But an old political associate who helped finance his rise to power and its awkward monetary aftermath faces a more uncertain future—extradition followed by imprisonment in a land he left behind a decade ago. Tonight . . . an unauthorized and still unwritten chapter in the political biography of Brian Mulroney.

We packed away the disc of MacIntyre's stand-up, then readied ourselves for next day's assignment: a trip to Lugano—and a trip back in time for me to where the story had begun so many years ago.

We met Giorgio Pelossi at a park on the north edge of Lake Lugano. He had aged gracefully, looking not much older than when we had first met in 1995. He smiled and shook my hand, still as polite and soft-spoken as always.

"Harvey, it's been a long time. You have grey hair."

"I know."

Without Giorgio Pelossi there would have been no Letter of Request. There would have been no German party spending scandal. There would have been no Airbus affair in Canada. No one would have known about the briefcase of cash Schreiber handed to the treasurer of the Christian Democrats. Or about the cash he gave to the two Thyssen managers, Juergen Massmann and Winfried Haastert. Nor would Holger Pfahls, a respected civil servant in Germany, have fled the country ahead of an arrest warrant. Helmut Kohl would not have had his reputation tarnished either. In Canada, no one would have ever learned about the Britan account, or the cash that Mulroney ended up taking from Karlheinz Schreiber in hotel rooms in Montreal and New York City. The former prime minister would, without a doubt, have led a happy and comfortable life out of politics, travelling the world as a businessman and elder statesman. All of that political, and personal, turmoil could be traced back to one ordinary man, a semi-retired grandfather, living out his life in serenity, near the shores of Lake Lugano.

We wanted to ask him if he had any regrets about blowing the whistle on his former friend and partner, Karlheinz Schreiber.

"I thought we would find an arrangement," Pelossi reflected, explaining that he never thought his dispute with Schreiber would get so serious. He still admitted that, yes, he had taken money out of the IAL accounts without telling Schreiber. "I helped him all this time, then when the money came and he had to share he didn't want to share."

Pelossi said he would have never gone to the police in Germany and Canada but that he had no option after Schreiber gave him no choice. "He forced me, you see. He made a criminal charge against me."

"So were you concerned in any way that when you did start to talk about this, it was going to create a huge political scandal in Canada?" asked MacIntyre.

"Possibly," Pelossi acknowledged.

MacIntyre noted that Schreiber would likely be coming back to Germany soon, and heading straight to jail. "Do you feel sorry for him?"

"No, because it's his fault, not my fault. He did everything wrong."

We drove back to Zurich that night. Isabella Kempf, Timothy Sawa, Linden MacIntyre and I went out for dinner at a café near the canal. MacIntyre had something on his mind.

"Do you see this ring on my finger?" he said.

I had seen it many times, a black X mounted on a gold base. It was his 1964 graduation ring from St. Francis Xavier University in Antigonish, Nova Scotia. Every graduate, he told us, received the same ring. MacIntyre reflected that the motto of the university was *quaecumque sunt vera*—whatsoever things are true. St. FX—as it was affectionately called by alumni—was the same university attended by Brian Mulroney and many of his pals, like Fred Doucet, who would form part of his inner circle.

MacIntyre fingered the ring. I knew he had come from a working-class family in Cape Breton and had worked hard to get that education, which got him his first job at a local newspaper, and eventually, through a long and remarkable path in journalism, to *the fifth estate* and the table we now all shared at the restaurant.

"Mulroney wore this same ring," MacIntyre reflected. It was hard for him to understand what had happened. I wondered if MacIntyre felt betrayed by a fellow St. FX grad.

"It's time that Canadians find out exactly what happened," he said.

On Wednesday, October 3, Karlheinz Schreiber surrendered himself into custody—not for the first time—at the Metro West Detention Centre in Toronto. The Supreme Court would be ruling on whether or not it had agreed to hear Schreiber's appeal on extradition. If yes, he would be spending at least several more months in Canada; if not, he could be on a plane to Germany the following morning.

Detention centre guards informed Schreiber that RCMP officers were waiting outside to take him to court. Schreiber said he had worried immediately that the Mounties were there to take him to the airport. He was led to the discharge section of the jail. At exactly 9:45 a.m., the Supreme Court dismissed Schreiber's leave to appeal. Schreiber's lawyers immediately flew into damage-control mode. Paperwork was prepared and arguments made for yet more appeals. Schreiber sat in the discharge section for hours awaiting the verdict; finally, the guards came in. He was told to get back into his jailhouse clothes. The RCMP would not be taking him to the airport. He would not be on a plane to Germany. Not yet, anyway. Later, Schreiber would refer to this event as the "attempted kid-napping."

Schreiber would remain in custody several more weeks; it was his longest stretch of incarnation in the eight years he had been fighting extradition. Over the years, Eddie Greenspan—in his legal battle with the Canadian justice system—had pulled every rabbit imaginable out of his hat.

And it wasn't over yet.

The *Globe and Mail* and the CBC timed the latest Airbus revelations to come out on October 31. That morning readers saw the story on the front page: "Brian Mulroney: the payments and the taxman." Wrote Greg McArthur: "Former prime minister Brian Mulroney, who received $300,000 in cash from German-Canadian deal maker Karlheinz Schreiber in 1993 and 1994, did not pay taxes on the payments in the years he received the money. The former prime minister filed a voluntary tax disclosure some time later, The Globe and Mail and CBC's *the fifth estate* have learned, an option that the Canada Revenue Agency offers for people who have previously filed in-accurate returns and subsequently decide to correct the record." The CBC.ca story quoted Schreiber: "Mulroney tried to cover up cash payments he received in hotel rooms." Alison Crawford reported the story for CBC Radio, Paul Hunter and Rosemary Barton for *The National*. Viewers heard all the details about the prime minister's voluntary tax disclosure to the Canada Revenue Agency and the attempts to cover up the cash payments, still as yet unexplained.

That day the Airbus snowball turned into an avalanche.

Liberal MP Robert Thibault raised the first question on the floor of the House of Commons. He reminded Parliament that Canadians paid $2.1 million to Mulroney for his lawsuit before anyone knew he had received cash from Schreiber. "Therefore, the previous settlement now appears unjustified. What steps has the prime minister taken to recover the $2 million?" Thibault demanded to know. Opposition MPs began demanding a public inquiry. In a scrum outside the House, NDP leader Jack Layton said he believed a "judicial inquiry" was in order. "Someone has to get to the bottom of what's been going on."

That night *Globe and Mail* staffers and CBCers met at a pub in Toronto's Annex neighbourhood to watch the hour-long broadcast on *the fifth estate*. Afterwards, Greg McArthur, Timothy Sawa and I joined some of the others for a night of karaoke at a basement pub on Bloor Street. Our rendition of Journey's classic song "Don't Stop Believin'" may not have been the best, but no one could fault us for lack of enthusiasm.

The next day the demands for an inquiry became a chorus. Liberal leader Stéphane Dion led the charge. "Mr. Speaker, new and disturbing information has come to light about a former prime minister of this country. This information damages the integrity of the office of the prime minister, a key component of our democracy . . . Faced with this information about Mr. Mulroney, will the prime minister call a public inquiry?" The government repeated the now-familiar party line: there was no evidence of wrongdoing. This time the Opposition roared back: "Mr. Mulroney is a personal friend and confidant of the prime minister," Robert Thibault stated. "However, these new allegations concerning Mr. Mulroney and cash payments of $300,000 he received demand immediate action on the part of the government. Why is the government not doing anything? What is it afraid of? Will it call a public inquiry?" Harper seemed flabbergasted when the press asked him for his perspective on an inquiry into Mulroney. "This call by the Liberal Party is really extraordinarily dangerous. Do they really want to say that I as prime minister should have a free hand to launch inquiries into my predecessors?"

But the calls for an inquiry did not stop.

For the first time since 1995, the story was being covered in every newspaper and on every television station. Columnists were weighing in daily and demands increased from all quarters that Mulroney finally break his silence. Cartoonists began lampooning Mulroney, showing him with a fistful of dollars in his suit pockets. The Airbus affair was becoming a liability for Stephen Harper and he would have to find a way of containing it; doing nothing no longer seemed like an option. For the first time, the media, and Parliament, were approaching the topic in ways I had always imagined—my phone rang every minute, emails poured in on my Black-Berry. Everyone wanted me to explain the meaning of the word *schmiergelder*, and to be reminded when and where the cash transactions had happened. I was a frequent guest on *Newsworld*, where I explained what Mulroney had said under oath about the cup of coffee with Schreiber, while neglecting to mention the thousand-dollar bills.

It had taken thirteen years to get there, but finally the real Airbus story was on the national agenda. I had been an energetic, if naïve, young reporter in 1994, eager to get to work every morning to tackle the story. In the ensuing years I had become disillusioned with the way power and money controlled so many of our democratic institutions, including the media. The story had fundamentally changed the way I thought about the world: it proved to me that deception, lies and bullying really did work. Sometimes the truth did not always prevail. Now, in the first week of November in 2007, I was starting to feel just a little more optimistic. It looked as if Parliament was functioning the way it should, as it demanded answers to important public policy questions. It remained to be seen what the Department of Justice might do, or if the RCMP would rethink its decision to close down the Airbus investigation. But I could not complain. It seemed everything had changed, and almost overnight. One reporter from *The National* sent me a private email. He apologized for the approach he had once taken. I now believed that most of us in the media were working in the same direction, wanting to follow the facts, wherever they took us. And Canadians were talking about the controversy in workplaces around the country. They were able to make their own judgments about what it meant to them. Finally ordinary citizens were beginning to learn what happened. At least, as much as we knew so far. Now, more than ever, it was time to get back to work, to unravel the unanswered threads in the story.

For me, there was just one problem: my boys, Massey and Jeremiah, and I were planning to leave on a holiday to Puerto Vallarta on Sunday, just as the country was finally paying attention to the story. How could I leave now? I was a little older and, hopefully, wiser now than I was in 2001 when I missed part of the family's spring vacation to finish an Airbus documentary. If I had thought about all the work I had done on the story since 1994 I would have concluded this was the *one* week that I simply had to stay in Canada. I should have cancelled the holiday, and rescheduled for later.

But that's not at all what I was thinking. Massey and Jeremiah had been looking forward to this holiday with their father and grandparents for months. We could smell the salt water already. That Sunday, November 4, 2007, with the country riveted by revelations of serious political misconduct, the boys and I packed our bags, put on our sunglasses and baseball caps, and drove to the airport for our flight to Mexico.

That ranks as one of the best decisions I ever made on the Airbus story.

CHAPTER THIRTY-EIGHT
COVER-UP II

At first, it really did look as if parliamentarians were going to get to the bottom of the Airbus affair.

On Friday, November 9, the week that I was away, the Prime Minister's Office told reporters that Harper would be holding an impromptu press conference. The day before, Schreiber—from jail—had produced an affidavit with fresh allegations. Among them, Schreiber was claiming Fred Doucet had asked him to send Airbus money to Prime Minister Mulroney's lawyer in Geneva, and that Mulroney had promised Schreiber he would raise his extradition problems with Harper at their Harrington Lake visit in 2006.

Harper had apparently heard enough. He told reporters: "Under these circumstances I am announcing today that I will be appointing an independent and impartial third party to review what course of actions may be appropriate given Mr. Schreiber's new sworn allegations." And then, "I think it will be incumbent upon myself and also upon members of the government not to have dealings with Mr. Mulroney until this issue is resolved."[1]

---

[1] This meant people like Senator Marjory LeBreton, a close friend of Mulroney and his family, would cease all communication with him.

Mulroney had worked hard rebuilding his relationship with Harper. Yet that relationship seemed to have crumbled in an instant. That weekend the former prime minister gave a speech in Toronto, organized by his former alma mater, St. Francis Xavier University. Mulroney put on a brave face. He even upped the ante by demanding a "full-fledged Royal Commission of Inquiry." Before a packed audience, Mulroney was unequivocal:

"I want to tell you here tonight that I, Martin Brian Mulroney, eighteenth prime minister of Canada, will be there before the Royal Commission with bells on because I've done nothing wrong, and I have absolutely nothing to hide."

On November 13, 2007, Prime Minister Stephen Harper announced a full public inquiry, and appointed University of Waterloo president David Johnston to prepare "terms of reference." Karlheinz Schreiber was still behind bars in Toronto awaiting what appeared to be his imminent extradition. In fact, two days later, Schreiber lost what looked like his final appeal. Were he to be extradited, Schreiber threatened, he would not co-operate with any inquiry. It did not take an Einstein to realize that if Schreiber were shipped back to Germany, any inquiry would lose its key witness and collapse. Still, the Harper government seemed disinclined to take any steps to delay Karlheinz's departure. The House of Commons Ethics Committee intervened. It was controlled by opposition party members who convinced speaker Peter Milliken to seize on an arcane instrument known as a Speaker's Warrant to allow Parliament itself to retain Schreiber.

NDP MP Pat Martin later explained: "We were running against the clock. If the Conservatives ragged the puck anymore, Karlheinz Schreiber would be on an airplane back to Germany and we would lose our last faint hope of ever getting to the bottom of this [affair]." The chair of the Ethics Committee was Liberal MP Paul Szabo. "We had to fight the minister of justice to keep him [Schreiber] here," Szabo told us. "We had to get a Speaker's Warrant. We had to get the unanimous consent of the House to allow him to stay and put him into the protective custody of the Parliament of Canada. It's extraordinary. It only happened once before in our history." (Back in 1913 the Speaker of the House of Commons used the same powers to temporarily detain a witness, R.C. Miller, for failing to appear at a public accounts committee.)

The Ethics Committee decided to hold its own mini-inquiry as a prelude to the official inquiry Harper had requested. On November 29, 2007, Karlheinz Schreiber, technically a prisoner of Parliament, arrived on Parliament Hill from Toronto for his first day of testimony. He emerged from the back of an RCMP cruiser in handcuffs. Reporters shouted questions and camerapersons jostled for a better angle before Schreiber disappeared into a back entrance. A short time later he emerged into a packed committee room.

The Ethics Committee may have expected full and complete disclosure. What they got instead was vintage Karlheinz Schreiber. Schreiber, on the advice of his lawyer, refused to answer any questions until he had time to properly consult his documents.

Pat Martin, one of the MPs who had fought hard to keep Schreiber in Canada, could not hide his frustration at Schreiber's evasiveness.

"Did the cash payments that you gave to Mr. Mulroney come from the account of the secret commissions on the Airbus sale?" Martin asked.

"I rest on my statement," Schreiber said.

"Well, surely that's a very straightforward question," Martin fired back. "You must remember where the money came from, Mr. Schreiber."

"I am not prepared to answer that," Schreiber said.

"Surely," Martin complained to no one in particular, "he [Schreiber] has some personal memory if at some point from 1980 to now he bribed somebody, somewhere, sometime. Surely he can remember that without checking all of his notes."

Despite his endless parrying and dipping and ducking, Schreiber was pressed for details anyway. The MPs were turning surly—even hostile. Schreiber explained he had every intention of testifying more fully; he just needed more time. It was a familiar Schreiber pantomime. Bloc Québécois MP Carole Lavallée posed an interesting hypothetical question that seemed to pique Schreiber's interest.

"If I asked for $300,000 because I've trouble making ends meet, would you give it to me?" she asked.

Schreiber smiled. "Under the circumstances, yes." Everyone laughed. Schreiber, ever the charmer, once again had brought down the house.

Schreiber would make two additional appearances before the Ethics

Committee in early December. He told the committee that the $300,000 had not been paid to Mulroney for work *he had done* but for work he *would do* after he left the Prime Minister's Office. He told the committee that he had also been grateful to Mulroney for his support on German reunification. His testimony was generally confusing and contradictory. He preferred to answer direct questions in a one-step-forward-two-step-back, often sideways manner. He inferred potentially incriminating details but consistently failed or refused to provide corroboration. He took forever to get to the point. What had begun as a serious inquiry degenerated into a media circus. Committee protocol contributed to the circus atmosphere. Members were restricted to only ten minutes to question a witness. Moreover, partisan bickering threatened constantly to derail the inquiry.

Schreiber's decision to stonewall the Ethics Committee was partly an end move to delay his extradition. He was banking on the probability of being called as a key witness in a full inquiry sometime in the future. He would tell all, he teasingly reminded the committee, *at some later date.*

It was a clever—but not foolproof—strategy.

Committee chair Paul Szabo—not wishing to delay what he all but assumed would be the full-scale inquiry everyone had been demanding—had decided not to invoke subpoena powers that might have prolonged the start of the main event. However, Schreiber's frustratingly vague testimony—and his theatrics—actually undermined his credibility in the eyes of some, and moved them to wonder if a full-scale inquiry was really needed after all.

"The case for a public inquiry has melted away," Margaret Wente wrote in the *Globe and Mail.* Columnist Lysiane Gagnon, who had concluded in 1995 that there was nothing untoward about Air Canada's decision to purchase Airbus aircraft, came to the baffling conclusion that corruption allegations against Airbus stemmed from a "latent prejudice widely held in English-speaking North America" that somehow a "partly French-made aircraft couldn't be as good as an American one." The tone from the Tory camp seemed to be redirected from calls for a full inquiry to attacks on Schreiber's integrity and character. On November 30, 2007, Canadian Press quoted Peter MacKay saying he was "leery" of Schreiber and told his father [Elmer] not to associate with him. "I don't really talk to my father in depth about his friendships," MacKay told reporters. "But I can tell you this: It was my opinion for a number of years that he should not associate with Mr. Schreiber, and I voiced that opinion." The implication was clear: Schreiber—and anything he had to say—could not be trusted. It was a remarkable new position for MacKay; after all, it had not been that long ago that he had risen in the House of Commons several times in noisy defence of Karlheinz Schreiber. Pundits complained about what a full inquiry would cost the taxpayer and questioned why anyone should trust Schreiber in the first place.

The *Toronto Star*, however, made the pro-inquiry case. Inquiries are sometimes needed, the paper declared, to repair our institutions: "And yes the inquiry will cost money. But keeping our democracy healthy is not something that can be had for free . . . public inquiries are needed at times to consider whether or not politicians and bureaucrats have abused their power." Andrew Coyne would later put it this way: "Mostly, we need to send a message—not just to those who may have been taking Schreiber's money then, but those who might be contemplating similar actions now: that however well you cover your tracks, however far you run, however long you stall, we will get you. Or shall we wait to find out twenty years from now about things we might have prevented today?"

Meanwhile, anticipation was peaking at the prospect of Brian Mulroney's testimony at the ethics hearing in mid-December. The former prime minister had refused to comment at all about his testimony before that date. He did announce, however, that he had hired a new public spokesperson to replace Luc Lavoie: Robin Sears, former NDP party strategist.

For us at *the fifth estate*, it was a stunning appointment. As mentioned earlier, Robin Sears is the brother of Kit Melamed. Melamed was among the first to investigate the Airbus allegations for *the fifth estate* back in 1988 and we had worked together on the story many times since then. Was it possible Mulroney had no idea of the family relationship? Certainly. But it struck me as odd that of all the suitable candidates he would choose the brother of a *fifth estate* employee who just happened to have worked on the Airbus story.

The circus had arrived in town: Brian Mulroney testified before the Ethics Committee on December 13, 2007.

Cameras followed him and his family into the committee room on Parliament Hill. I sat in the audience, watching as Mila and children Caroline, Ben, Mark and Nicholas sat in their seats just across the aisle from the reporters and me. Mulroney appeared angry but unbent—the undersized but determined boxer facing a hulking opponent. He made an opening statement:

"Twelve years and one month ago, my family and I were hit by the biggest calamity of my life. The government of Canada stated formally to a foreign government that I was a criminal from the time I took office. I was completely devastated by these totally false allegations. They had [the] capacity to destroy my reputation and to destroy my family. Only a person who has gone through such an ordeal can fathom its impact. It was like a near death experience." Mulroney wanted everyone to know he'd had nothing to do with the Airbus sale. "I never received a cent from anyone for services rendered to anyone in connection with the purchase by Air Canada from Airbus of thirty-four aircrafts in 1988."

In private, Mulroney had previously told others he regretted meeting Schreiber, but now he was doing it live, on television, as hundreds of thousands of viewers watched. "My second-biggest mistake in life, for which I have no one to blame but myself, is having accepted payments in cash from Karlheinz Schreiber for a mandate he gave me after I left office. I will tell you today how that came about. My biggest mistake in life, by far, was ever agreeing to be introduced to Karlheinz Schreiber in the first place."

Interesting, I thought, that Mulroney would suggest he had "no one to blame but himself," but then seemed to blame his downfall entirely on Schreiber—as if having met Schreiber was the same thing as accepting large amounts of cash from him.

In his testimony, Mulroney attempted to address questions about the money. Yes, it was true he received $75,000 in cash from Schreiber on each of the three meetings, he said—but not $100,000 as Schreiber claimed. He confirmed that the denominations were in thousand-dollar bills. He said he took the money received from the two meetings in Quebec (one at the Queen Elizabeth Hotel in Montreal and the other near Mirabel Airport) and put it in a safe in his house in Westmount. He claimed that the cash he received from Schreiber at the Pierre Hotel in New York City was put in a safe deposit box at a nearby Chase Manhattan Bank. That had struck Liberal MP Robert Thibault as curious. "In your deposition on the lawsuit against the Government of Canada," he asked Mulroney, "you stated, 'I haven't got a bank account anywhere in the world except Montreal, and I never have.' How can you explain that statement?"

"It was a safety-deposit box,"[2] replied Mulroney.

The money, he said, was payment for lobbying on behalf of Thyssen. Mulroney told the committee he lobbied Russian president Boris Yeltsin, among others. "But obviously this was the kind of consultation I was doing around the world with [French] President Mitterand, with the Chinese leadership, with leaders of the United States government, trying to promote the international dimension of the mandate that I had been given." Mulroney insisted he had briefed Schreiber on his activities at their meeting at the Pierre Hotel. "I reported, for example, in great detail for almost an hour in the presence of another person [Fred Doucet] to Mr. Schreiber in New York City in the Pierre Hotel at the end of 1994 about my visits to China, Russia and France, for example."

Mulroney said he once had notes of his reports, but that was fourteen years ago. He no longer had them.

A memorable exchange occurred when NDP MP Pat Martin asked Mulroney if he had had any qualms about the settlement money he received after his lawsuit.

"Are you willing to give that $2.1 million back to the people of Canada? Now that we know that you did take money from Schreiber?"

"No, I took compensation from Schreiber for serious work done on his behalf around the world. And I have also indicated—"

"Then why did you deny even having any dealings with the man?"

2 There are still many unanswered questions about Mulroney's Manhattan safe deposit box. We do not know, for example, what else, if anything, he might have kept in it. Mulroney later stated it was opened after he left office but we do not know the exact date it was opened.

"That's completely false."

"By omission you led us to believe you had virtually no dealings with the man under sworn testimony."

"I did not omit anything. I explained to you that in the province of Quebec, the manner in which, and I think—"

Martin cut him off. "Well, you're splitting hairs, sir."

"I'm not splitting hairs."

"You're splitting hairs, sir, and the country isn't buying it. I'm not calling you a liar, Mr. Mulroney, but I don't want anybody here to think I believe you. Let's put it that way."

Mulroney had almost finished his testimony when Conservative MP Mike Wallace provided Mulroney an opportunity to shift the focus back on Schreiber and issues of his character and honesty. Fretting aloud about his (and presumably fellow Tory party members') doubts about the proposed judicial inquiry, Wallace asked Mulroney why he wanted one. He seemed incredulous. "Mr. Schreiber wants one," Wallace said, "you want one. I'm not sure I want one. But what are your expectations from the public inquiry and why are you asking for it?"

"Well, let's put that perhaps in a different tense. I asked for a Royal Commission of Inquiry into this. But when you look at what has happened now, the evidence that you have, I think it's now clear that we've got an entirely different situation on our hands."

In fact, Mulroney claimed to have been victimized by some on the committee, which he compared to nothing so much as a witch hunt. He had his lawyers submit a letter to Chairman Szabo bitterly complaining about his treatment. Mulroney refused to co-operate any further. When Szabo, asked Mulroney to testify again, the former prime minister declined the invitation.

On January 10, 2008, CTV's Bob Fife broke the story that there would not be a full-scale inquiry after all:

"Prime Minister Stephen Harper is expected to establish a limited public inquiry into the Mulroney-Schreiber saga after receiving a report from an independent third party, CTV News has learned. Johnston rejected a full-scale inquiry that would re-examine allegations of possible kickbacks in the 1988 sale of Airbus jets to Air Canada, arguing the matter has already been thoroughly investigated by the RCMP.

"Johnston," wrote Fife, "also left open the door for the prime minister to avoid setting up a public inquiry if he is satisfied with the work of the Commons [Ethics] committee, according to sources. But a senior insider said Harper has no choice but to immediately set up a public inquiry, otherwise the 'opposition will scratch out our eyes.'"

Johnston characterized the RCMP's investigation into the Airbus matter as "well tilled ground." He said, "My view would be different if there existed significant evidence that had only now come to light."

First, the Airbus matter was *not* well-tilled ground. The principal players all had steadfastly refused to talk to the RCMP. Millions of dollars in secret commissions remained unaccounted for. To my mind there were too many important questions that remained unanswered. Second, why would Johnston's views be different if he had learned of "new" evidence? Wasn't that one of the purposes of a public inquiry—to produce the facts? Isn't that why witnesses are compelled to testify under oath?

Johnston's interim report confirmed for me that Harper and the Tories had cooled to the prospect of a full-scale public inquiry. But why? What could have happened those many years ago that could pose any threat to them today?

My only consolation was that this was an "interim" report. Johnston's final report would come out after the Ethics Committee had finished its work.

In January 2008, Greg McArthur suggested we take a closer look at Mulroney's explanations for what he did to earn the cash he received from Schreiber. Among other things, Mulroney had said he lobbied officials in China, Russia and France on behalf of Thyssen—the manufacturer of light armoured vehicles. We set about looking for anyone who could verify his claims. The *Globe* hired German journalist Isabella Kempf to help out. At the CBC, reporter Paul Hunter and I tackled the story. Surely someone would be willing to back up Mulroney's story.

Kempf located Winfried Haastert, the former Thyssen executive who had worked closely with Schreiber, and asked him about Mulroney's lobbying efforts.

"He never worked for Thyssen," said Haastert. "Maybe Mr. Mulroney had also tried to get interest in China or Russia but not on our intention, not on our charge and we never had known about it." When told of Mulroney's testimony, Haastert was incredulous. "I cannot imagine how he could expect to sell something like this [light armoured vehicles] to Russia or even to China. It's absolute nonsense. Maybe he tried to support us. I don't know." Kempf also spoke with Anja Gerber, a spokeswoman for ThyssenKrupp. Mulroney had "no official business with Thyssen," she said.

Greg McArthur summarized the findings in the *Globe and Mail*: "None of the experts interviewed said they have evidence to contradict Mr. Mulroney's testimony. However, they described the work he says he did as implausible and in violation of trade sanctions Mr. Mulroney imposed while he was prime minister." Christopher Foss, from *Jane's Defence Weekly*, told McArthur, "To me, it just doesn't stand up." McArthur had also tracked down Fred Bild, Canada's ambassador to China at the time Mulroney said he lobbied officials there. Bild recalled meeting Mr. Mulroney, but told McArthur there was no mention of Thyssen light armoured vehicles. Bild said he was "doubtful" that such lobbying took place. "I would have got wind of it," he said. "As a recently retired prime minister who has imposed sanctions on China, I can't see myself . . . going to China, making representations to break those very sanctions which are still in effect. I can't see that,"[3] Bild said.

The House of Commons Ethics Committee called several more witnesses, including three key players on February 12: Fred Doucet, Marc Lalonde and Greg Alford, the former GCI staff member and later vice-president of Bear Head.

---

3 Mulroney would later clarify that he was lobbying those countries to support a UN initiative; that he was not trying to sell tanks to China. There is still no independent verification for any of his putative lobbying efforts from anyone, anywhere, in the world.

One by one, each testified that he knew nothing about Airbus.

"What can you tell us, sir, about the involvement of GCI in the Airbus purchase by Air Canada?" Liberal MP Sukh Dhaliwal asked Alford.

"GCI had no involvement," he answered. "Airbus was not a client of GCI."

Liberal MP Charles Hubbard was stunned. "Maybe I missed what you said, but you seemed to indicate, or at least what I heard, is that GCI was not involved with the Airbus deal. Did I hear correctly? GCI was not?"

"That's right," Alford said.

Marc Lalonde testified that "Neither Mr. Schreiber nor any of his businesses hired me to represent them regarding the Airbus affair. Nor GCI."

Finally it was Fred Doucet's turn to appear before the committee. In his testimony, Schreiber had claimed that Doucet told him he should give Airbus money to Mulroney. Doucet denied it.

"I want to say I have no knowledge at all about anything involving Airbus," Doucet told the committee.

As Mulroney had again refused to co-operate, the Ethics Committee, in late February, brought its inquiry to a stunningly inconclusive and even inconsequential end. On April 4, in his final report, David Johnston recommended against a broad inquiry. There had been, he decided, an "exhaustive" RCMP investigation into the Airbus matter, so any further inquiry would be "inappropriate." The inquiry—officially the Commission of Inquiry into Certain Allegations Respecting Business and Financial Dealings Between Karlheinz Schreiber and the Right Honourable Brian Mulroney—would limit itself to a postage-stamp-sized patch of real estate in what had been—and still was—a huge story.

I was stunned.

The headline over Andrew Coyne's column said it all: "It's Official: the Last Chance for the Truth is Gone."

Late in 2008, Bärbel Schreiber flew to Switzerland—ostensibly to visit her mother—but actually her visit had a more practical purpose: she returned to Canada with a suitcase full of incriminating documents, including Schreiber's Daytimers covering a vast expanse of time from the early 1980s to the present; records from his Swiss bank accounts; correspondence from Frank Moores, Fred Doucet and Greg Alford—and all about Airbus.

Schreiber, who was now living in Rockliffe, free on bail again pending his testimony at the upcoming inquiry, called McArthur and me. He told us he had something new for us to look at. We flew to Ottawa and met him at the Marriott Hotel on Kent Street.

I was like a kid in a candy store. He showed us a document dated June 10, 1987. It was a memo from Greg Alford at GCI—"re: Airbus" and "to Karlheinz Schreiber."

"I have spoken today with [Transport] Minister Crosbie's office regarding his visit to the Paris Air show," Alford wrote. What followed was a detailed description of members of Crosbie's staff with recommendations on whom to lobby for best results. If Schreiber ends up talking directly to Crosbie, Alford reminds him "not to make any reference to your recent contact with Maz."[4] [Don Mazankowski was the deputy prime minister at the time.] Alford reminds Schreiber that Crosbie's "Air policy adviser" Karen Mosher would be at the Paris Air Show. "I have asked her to look for you and have told her of your association with FJS [Franz Josef Strauss], whom she admires."[5]

Schreiber showed us a second document that brought to mind the recent testimony of Marc Lalonde and raised some interesting questions about the integrity of his recollection. It was labelled "Memorandum" and had been sent to Frank Moores, Gerry Doucet, Gary Ouellet, Greg Alford and Karlheinz Schreiber. It originated with James MacEachern, a GCI lobbyist·who had previously worked in the Prime Minister's Office. He wrote, "SUBJECT: AIRBUS." And then: "I met with Marc Lalonde on Thursday, November 26, 1987. He had just met with Pierre Jeanniot. Jeanniot had just returned from Seattle and a meeting with Boeing." It later confirms details about GCI's efforts to get Air Canada to purchase Airbuses. "With respect to Airbus," MacEachern wrote, "Jeanniot advised that the financing was very important . . . Furthermore Jeanniot advised that there would be a

---

4 Underlining in original document.
5 I remembered I had spoken to Karen Mosher back in 1995. At that time, she told me that she had no idea Schreiber worked on Airbus. When I called her back thirteen years later, she refused to talk to me, and would not discuss the Alford memo.

board meeting of Air Canada on December 18 where the issue of replacement aircraft would be raised."

The memo appeared to contradict Lalonde's testimony to the Ethics Committee; it also seemed at odds with what he had told me in 2000, when he had insisted he had not lobbied for Airbus.

Schreiber shared with us some documents that bore directly on Frank Moores and Fred Doucet and suggested that both men were aware of secret commissions involving Airbus.

The first was a handwritten note from Frank Moores dated March 1, 1992, in which he breaks down the commission received for that year and commissions to be paid in 1993 and 1994, for a total of $1,257,000 "to be divided."

Shortly thereafter, on March 24, 1992, Fred Doucet contacted Schreiber in Germany. "I do not want to bother you with the matter of the Birds [the Airbus planes]," he wrote, "but since you insisted when we last spoke that I raise this matter with you by March 15, I decided to drop you a note on it. As you recall you felt that by now I would have heard from F.M. [Frank Moores] and that, if not, I should let you know. I have not heard from him."

Doucet wrote again on August 27, 1993. The date was significant. It was on this day that Mulroney received his first cash payment from Karlheinz Schreiber at the hotel near Mirabel Airport in Montreal: "Dear Karlheinz, Mr. Biro has confirmed that thirty-four Airbus have been purchased and delivered to Air Canada according to the enclosed schedule. I sincerely hope that this evidence, many times stated before, is emphatically and categorically relayed to F.M." Enclosed was a letter of confirmation from Air Canada to Fred Doucet. Sent to Doucet by "Denis A. Biro, Manager, Investor Relations," it was a complete list of Airbus 320 airplanes delivered for each calendar year beginning in 1990:

"1990 – 7; 1991 – 12; 1992 – 12; 1993 – 3; Total 34."

Doucet again wrote to Schreiber—this time in Ottawa—on April 28, 1994.

I have now been able to carry out (once again) my assignment to find out accurately how many A320s were bought and fully paid by Air Canada directly from the Airbus company. The answer today is the same provided to me the last time I sought this information. The answer is 34 and this number is two more than what was originally contracted.... For me settling this matter is so very important for reasons I will tell you about in person.

Thanks very much.

Yours sincerely, J A Doucet.

P.S. I did not ask anything about the recent order for the large Airbus by Air Canada.

We asked Schreiber what Doucet was referring to when he said "settling" the matter was important and that he would tell him in person. Schreiber told us he "could not remember" what that reason was. Was his "could not remember" an "I *do* remember but I won't tell you"? It seemed obvious he was withholding something. He consistently refused to properly explain exactly how Doucet first got involved in the Airbus file. Had Doucet been interested in the commission for himself, or on behalf of someone else? Was it a complete coincidence that on the same day Doucet had arranged for Schreiber to meet Mulroney in Montreal he received a fax from Air Canada confirming delivery of the A320s to Air Canada? Schreiber could not say. More likely, he *would not* say.

What McArthur and I knew for a fact was this: Fred Doucet was one of Mulroney's closest friends and trusted confidants. Doucet had stood by Mulroney loyally throughout the 1980s and into the 1990s, both in office and out. The obvious question was: Did Fred Doucet ever tell Mulroney about his relationship with Schreiber with regard to the Airbus commissions?

I called Doucet one more time. I explained that I had come into possession of documents that seemed to contradict his sworn testimony at the Ethics Committee inquiry.

"So be it," he said and hung up.

Marc Lalonde told me in 2000 that he had never worked for Airbus. Further, he claimed never to have heard of Stuart Iddles, at the time vice-president of Airbus.

I called him back. His memory for details had improved.

"I got a phone call from Schreiber one day," he told me. "I didn't know him at all, frankly I had never heard of him, asking me whether I would be willing to consider a mandate from Airbus. I said sure, I was looking forward as a new lawyer back in practice since the end of '84, and he introduced me to [Jean] Pierson, who was the president of Airbus at the time. And I met with Pierson in Bourget, in Paris, at the exhibition at the air show."

He did not work for Schreiber, Lalonde told me, but was hired directly by Airbus, a contract, "signed by Stuart Iddles, who was the vice-president that Mr. Pierson said I would be dealing with." To me, Lalonde's admissions now—in December 2008—were inconsistent both with my earlier interview in 2000 and with his testimony before the Ethics Committee. I wondered, *Why?*

In early January 2009, Schreiber let us take a look through his Daytimers for the calendar years 1992 and 1993.[6] McArthur and I wanted to know if there were any notations that might add to our understanding of the dispute between Doucet and Moores. We met Schreiber again at a Marriott Hotel on Kent Street in Ottawa. McArthur and I looked on as Schreiber began flipping through the pages of his Daytimers. It seemed that Schreiber himself had not gone through them in some time. We had to keep asking him to slow down. We would notice familiar names—Frank, Fred, Marc, Brian, Elmer, Gary—and have him stop to explain or go back.

There was a notation for September 9, 1992, that piqued our interest.

Frank Moores
Bruce Verchere
Benet Jones Verchere
514-871-8193

---

6 The German authorities had seized Schreiber's 1991 and 1994 Daytimers back in 1995 but Schreiber had managed to hold on to all the other years. He would not let us look through the entire collection, but he agreed we could look at these two additional years.

This was the same Bruce Verchere who would commit suicide a year later, in 1993, and who would be the subject of Stevie Cameron's book *Blue Trust*. Schreiber said Verchere was the Geneva lawyer to whom Fred Doucet had suggested he give the Airbus money. Verchere had been a Montreal-based tax lawyer who sat on the board of the Swiss Bank Corporation. Perhaps that explained the Geneva connection, I mused. In any event, Schreiber told us that he never did make the call to Bruce Verchere. There was also a notation about lunch with Fred and a reminder to call Fred and Elmer. Did he remember any details about that lunch or phone call? No, Schreiber said.

He turned a few pages, and McArthur and I read as quickly as we could. On the page for December 18, 1992, I spotted the entry "460 PM."

"Stop there, Karlheinz. Turn back."

"Who is PM, Karlheinz?" I asked.

He stopped and stared, completely silent. He seemed to be thinking. "This PM is so confusing because I never, to say it bluntly, I don't recall that I ever used for Brian Mulroney, PM."

He was telling us he had never referred to Brian Mulroney as PM. Which was odd, as he had used PM for Brian Mulroney on other occasions in other entries in his Daytimers. I reminded him of the fact. He shook his head.

"It's difficult, it's really difficult."[7]

There was actually more in the entry than 460 PM. In the margins Schreiber had written FDM 230: 5 = 460 PM. Underneath that he had written *"bis no.23,"* German for "up to no.23." Schreiber would not elaborate. He continued to suggest he had no recall of what the entries might mean. McArthur and I speculated that FDM was a reference to Frank Duff Moores. The notations could be shorthand for how Schreiber had divided up

---

7   Schreiber would later testify that PM meant "per Machine"—as in *per plane*—suggesting that he was simply computing the average commission on five airplanes and not divvying up the Airbus commissions between five potential recipients. This could be possible. If so, however, it would also mean it was a coincidence that the amount he divided by five—$2.3 million—was also equal to the amount one would get by multiplying "up to" twenty-three planes by $100,000. That's because multiplying $100,000 by twenty-three planes and then dividing by five does not get you an average amount per plane. In any event, even if Schreiber was designating the money for certain recipients, it does not mean that those people knew he was doing this.

portions of the Airbus commissions up to the twenty-third plane delivered. He appeared to have assigned a commission value of $100,000 per plane. He looked to have multiplied that by twenty-three to arrive at $2.3 million. Then he divided that by five to come up with $460,000.

There were four names written below that entry: Marc, Giorgio, Fred and Garry. Marc Lalonde, Giorgio Pelossi, Fred Doucet and probably Gary [Garry] Ouellet.

And, above those names, a fifth entry: 460 PM.

We decided to do another Airbus documentary.

Building on Schreiber's latest revelations, I decided to go back to where the story began: Air Canada's decision to purchase Airbus planes back in 1988. Joining me for what I now know is the last Airbus documentary I would ever produce was associate producer Andreas Wesley.

On March 5, 2009, I was working at home and googled "Brian Mulroney" and "Air Canada" under their "Books" category. I came across a reference in a 1995 academic textbook called *The Political Economy of Privatization*. I knew that the Mulroney government had sold off many crown corporations. Mulroney had even appointed a minister responsible for privatization. But this book suggested that Mulroney had been reluctant to privatize the airline, even though Air Canada's management seemed to be in favour. "The momentum towards privatization halted in January 1985 when Prime Minister Brian Mulroney, emerging from a meeting with Louis Laberge of the Quebec Federation of Labour (FTQ), declared that Air Canada was not for sale," wrote authors Thomas Clarke and Christos Pitelis. If I had heard before about Mulroney making this statement I must have forgotten. Why would Mulroney declare Air Canada not for sale when his government was committed, philosophically, to privatization of Crown corporations? Curious, I read on: "Air Canada set up an internal task force on privatization in 1987 and moved a key manager with Treasury Board experience from Montreal to Ottawa to work closely with government officials. Months of preparation ended in summer 1987 when the federal Cabinet shied away from the go-ahead on privatization." I was more intrigued. Not only did Mulroney say Air Canada was not for sale in 1985, his cabinet also "shied away" from privatization as late as 1987? I wondered why.

I needed to find out more. Did anyone ever find out why Mulroney had seemed so reluctant at first to privatize the airline? I asked the CBC reference library if they could give me all the articles written on the topic of Air Canada's privatization in the 1980s. There were many. On March 1986, the *Globe and Mail*'s Christopher Waddell wrote an article stating that as early as 1984 the transport minister, Don Mazankowski, had begun discussing the possibility of privatizing Air Canada with Michael Cochrane, the airline's former vice-president. But it never happened. Waddell suggested Mulroney might have been influenced by public opinion which was opposed to privatization of the airline. In December 1986, the Economic Council of Canada had publicly urged Mulroney's government to "privatize" Air Canada. Then on January 13, 1987, Air Canada's chairman, Claude Taylor, stated publicly that Ottawa "must" act swiftly to cut Air Canada loose from state ownership. "There are no longer any public policy reasons justifying Air Canada being retained as a Crown corporation," Taylor told a business luncheon in Toronto. The *Globe and Mail* pointed out that Air Canada management was soon going to be replacing its aging McDonnell Douglas DC-9 jet and would be better off doing it as a private corporation.[8] By the summer of 1987 privatization looked like a sure thing. On June 12, Canadian Press reported that Air Canada was "on the verge" of being sold. On July 8, the *Globe and Mail* weighed in. "A sale of Air Canada shares to its employees and to the public awaits only the approval of Prime Minister Brian Mulroney. The announcement could come as early as this week, in conjunction with a meeting of the inner Cabinet, the priorities and planning committee, in Edmonton tomorrow and Friday."

I wondered what happened at that meeting. My colleague Andreas Wesley, who had been working on the Airbus file for several months, took over. Working closely with our visual archivist, Leslie Morrison, he wanted to know if CBC had any footage of the event in Edmonton. We did. Wesley and Morrison ordered the footage from our Edmonton bureau. We watched together when it arrived. On the tape, Mulroney is questioned by reporters about why he did not approve of the plan by Barbara McDougall,

---

8 That plan changed. Air Canada chose not to sell off the older DC-9s after all but rather its Boeing 727s. Some have suggested that Airbus did not have a suitable replacement for the DC-9s.

the privatization minister, to finally sell off the airline. Reporters, after all, had seen Barbara McDougall enter the cabinet meeting.

"I can tell you that it [Air Canada privatization] was not discussed," Mulroney told reporters.

"In any way?" asked a female reporter.

"I can just tell you what I just said, Ms. McDougall was not there today," Mulroney said.

"We saw Ms. McDougall go into the private elevator to the fourth floor today," another reporter protested.

"I didn't say she didn't go in the building."

"Did she meet with you at all?"

"No, she did not."

The *Globe and Mail* would later report that it was Mulroney himself who had "aborted" the privatization of Air Canada at the last minute. "The Crown-owned airline had gone as far as preparing 25,000 brochures explaining to employees a federal Government decision to sell all of Air Canada's shares to the public. A series of television commercials was also in the works as part of a public relations blitz. But privatization was not announced and appears unlikely to be in the near future. A few of the eight-page brochures are circulating underground, but Air Canada had to scrub the commercials, which invited the public to 'share in our future.'"

So why did Mulroney consistently stop efforts, some from within his party, to privatize Air Canada? It is possible he was concerned about public opinion, which continued to be against it. But on April 12, 1988, Mulroney had changed his mind. The Mulroney government finally approved the privatization of Air Canada. The announcement was made at the press gallery in Ottawa, attended by Transport Minister Benoît Bouchard, Deputy Minister Don Mazankowski, Air Canada president Pierre Jeanniot and Chairman Claude Taylor, who seemed the proudest.

"For me personally it is a giant step towards the realization of a dream I have cherished for a long time," said Taylor.

What the public did not know at the time was that on March 30, 1988—less than two weeks before the privatization announcement—the Air Canada board of directors had met in private to approve the sale of Airbus jets to Air Canada. The decision to purchase the Airbus jets paved the way for Karlheinz Schreiber and Frank Moores to earn millions in secret commissions. Now I really wondered. Was it a coincidence that Mulroney changed his mind about the privatization of Air Canada only days after the Crown airline committed to the Airbus purchase?

Our story, which we called "The Elephant in the Room," aired in mid-April. We explored the latest evidence around the Airbus sale to Air Canada, including the revelation that Moores had written a telex to Schreiber in advance of the Tories coming to power in 1984 mentioning Air Canada and "political donations." We reminded viewers that the largest and most controversial sale in which Schreiber was involved in Canada—Airbus—was likely to remain off the table at the Oliphant Inquiry.

The Commission of Inquiry into Certain Allegations Respecting Business and Financial Dealings between Karlheinz Schreiber and the Right Honourable Brian Mulroney (or otherwise known as the Oliphant inquiry) commenced in the spring of 2009. Presided over by former Manitoba associate chief justice Jeffrey Oliphant, the inquiry would limit itself to business matters between Karlheinz Schreiber and Brian Mulroney. Schreiber testified in April but, because of the limitations imposed by the inquiry, he was asked mostly about the Bear Head project. Schreiber was asked, again, about the cash transactions, but Airbus questions were off limits. Almost every other witness that testified, from Marc Lalonde to former Tory cabinet ministers Bill McKnight and Perrin Beatty, were asked excruciatingly detailed questions about Thyssen's proposed light armoured vehicle factory.

Still, commission counsel had made public several additional pages from Schreiber's Daytimer. I went hunting through them and noticed an intriguing reference to Airbus, and in an entry for May 25, 1988: Kohl—ABI—Brian.

This had been a crucial time. The Air Canada board of directors had just approved the Airbus purchase, but the Mulroney cabinet had not yet provided its approval. Indeed, the proposed sales agreement would be scrutinized by several government departments, from Treasury Board to Transport, and eventually make its way up to the Mulroney cabinet for final approval, in the summer of 1988. "Kohl" referred to German chancellor Helmut Kohl. "ABI" meant Airbus Industrie. "Brian," I presumed, meant Brian Mulroney. This was the first evidence I had seen that linked Mulroney to Airbus.

We broadcast the story on *The National.*

Mystifyingly, Schreiber would never be questioned about the reference. Or any other question that had any link to Airbus. Oliphant said the question the commission needed to address was this: "What payments were made, when and how and why?" How answering this question could be done without also exploring the Airbus matter baffled me and McArthur.

Still, when Fred Doucet came to testify on April 27, I naïvely hoped that the Oliphant Commission might show some flexibility in the direction of truth.[9] After all, Doucet had been the author of numerous letters to Schreiber about Airbus—including one the very day Mulroney received his first cash payment on August 27, 1993. If the commission actually was looking for the truth behind Mulroney's relationship with Schreiber, didn't this seem like a promising path to explore?

We thought it just might happen when commission counsel Richard Wolson received special permission to table the letters Fred Doucet wrote to Schreiber. However, just as quickly, Judge Oliphant reiterated the narrow guidelines for the inquiry: "It is most certainly not my intention, because I have no authority to do so—not my intention to turn this inquiry into an investigation of Airbus."

Doucet was asked if he remembered any of the letters.

He said he did not. A number of them were read out to him in an effort to jog his memory. No, he repeated. None of it sounds familiar.

That seemed to be it. Doucet apparently did not remember a thing, so Wolson let the matter drop. It seemed not to have occurred to anyone to subpoena the Air Canada official who wrote the fax to Doucet. No one suggested the commission call any of the former Air Canada executives involved in the purchase to find out what they might remember about Frank Moores or Fred Doucet or Karlheinz Schreiber or Marc Lalonde. No one suggested hearing testimony from Pierre Jeanniot, the former Air Canada

---

9   Oliphant had ruled earlier that Doucet would be compensated for all of his legal fees. His lawyer was present for almost all of the testimony.

president, or Claude Taylor, the former chairman. Or Dennis Groom, the former Air Canada vice-president of finance who had already told McArthur and me that Frank Moores lobbied him on Airbus. No one suggested calling Stuart Iddles, the former Airbus vice-president, to testify. Nor apparently did anyone think to call Jean Pierson, the former Airbus president who is mentioned prominently in Schreiber's Daytimer. Any one of these witnesses might have shed some light on what Doucet claimed he could not remember: details that would have gone a long way towards clarifying the Airbus story and perhaps, also, Mulroney's relationship with Schreiber.

Over the years I have come to realize that there is the truth, and then there is the Truth. And the Truth was slipping away.

On May 13, 2008, I was back in Ottawa for Brian Mulroney's testimony before the Oliphant Commission. He would be facing numerous embarrassing questions about the cash he received from Schreiber and the putative taxes he paid on it. There is a new revelation: Mulroney is alleged to have received a special deal from the Canada Revenue Agency to pay only half the taxes he would have paid had he declared the income in the years he actually received it.

For the first few days Mulroney was examined by his own lawyer. It's wonderful theatre. The strategy was, clearly, to preempt damaging revelations from the commission council by revealing it yourself. *Mea culpa*. But first, a bit of personal history. In one sensitive moment, Mulroney breathes deep and talks about his son Nicolas, and what it was like to tell him his father was under investigation by the RCMP back in 1995. It was devastating, he told us. No one can imagine how devastating. Mulroney's eyes mist over. He chokes up. Mulroney is a proud man and a patriot who has served his country well. And how has his country repaid him? By dragging him down into the gutter and sullying his good name.

Has he made mistakes? Sure. But who hasn't? But he never did anything wrong. He has always told the truth. Sure, he should have reported the cash for tax purposes right away. But eventually he did report the income.

I think about the truth. And the Truth.

During a break a few minutes later I heard from my colleagues that Robin Sears, Mulroney's new spokesman, was saying that McArthur and I were laughing at Mulroney's testimony. That is the reason Mulroney cried. He can't be serious. That's the story, they say.

Then Sears approached me in person. "You made Mulroney cry."

It is *opéra bouffe* at its most comically surreal. Sears marched off and immediately input the story on Mulroney's website. Suddenly I am the story. I did not laugh at Mulroney's testimony. Reporters who had been seated around McArthur and me came to our defence: they did not see or hear us laugh either. Sears was livid; he refused to believe us or anyone else who actually was there to witness it. A few minutes later a CTV camera crew approached me for a quote. I say it never happened.

"What did you do then?" yells the cameraman. "You must have done something."

Sears tells others that he tried to take pictures of me laughing but just missed getting the moment of "giggle." *Jesus Christ*, I think, *This is insane. He has got to be kidding.* I am actually beginning to miss Luc Lavoie.

What this scene accomplished, of course, was to portray Brian Mulroney once again as the victim. First it was Schreiber and his baseless accusations. Now it was two reporters "giggling" at Mulroney's sullied name.

The next day, Stephen Maher, the Ottawa bureau chief for the Halifax *Chronicle Herald*, wrote a column about the incident. Mulroney had spent a good part of the day, Maher wrote, and the past fifteen years, claiming he was the "innocent victim of a media vendetta" that had destroyed the good name of his father. That claim, Maher, said, "is under increasing strain."

Schreiber had once denied any involvement in the Airbus affair, Maher wrote. As had Frank Moores, Marc Lalonde, Greg Alford, Gary Ouellet and Fred Doucet. "One by one all of them have been decisively linked to it." Still Mulroney played the victimized innocent.

It wouldn't wash. Not anymore. Maher reminded readers that reporters and the Mounties had had good reasons for looking into the Airbus deal. Twenty million dollars had been skimmed on the deal and deposited into a shell company in Liechtenstein where the cash was divided up for distribution. Were there legitimate reasons to wonder if any of that money had fallen into the hands of the former prime minister? Yes there was. Journalists, Maher wrote, have a right to ask important questions when it comes to public money and public institutions. He reminded readers that when some of us had tried to do just that back in the nineties, a powerful spin campaign was directed against us in an effort to destroy *our* reputations.

But Mulroney was still complaining about *his* damaged reputation?

Wrote Maher: "Those reporters and police officers should be congratulated for doing their jobs, and we should treat with suspicion any attack on the good names of their fathers."

Then I sent Maher's column to *my* father.

I have a pretty good idea who is laughing now.

Certainly not Karlheinz Schreiber, who spent much of his twilight years fighting extradition to his homeland. And not Mulroney, whose life has been irreparably harmed by his relationship with Schreiber. And not RCMP sergeant Fraser Fiegenwald, who was nothing but an honest cop, yet left the service as a "disgraced" police officer. And not Allan Rock, who saw his prime ministerial ambitions go up in smoke. Fred Doucet has been embarrassed and humiliated too. There is a long list of many others in Canada, and elsewhere, who wish they never met the middleman. Back in the 1980s, Schreiber had come to Ottawa promising to enrich the lives of both his German and Canadian friends; but, in the end, delivered nothing but grief for so many, including himself. Canadian taxpayers were the biggest losers. Countless federal dollars have been spent on court costs for extradition hearings, lawsuits, preliminary hearings, RCMP investigations, secret trials, settlement costs, and yes, for the Oliphant Commission too.[10] And for what?

The answer to that brings us to the one party that surely remains very happy with how things worked out.

Airbus Industrie.

Back in the 1980s Airbus was on the brink of bankruptcy. It could not crack the lucrative North American market and so began an ambitious

---

10 The Harper government paid Mulroney's entire legal bill for the Oliphant Commission.

plan to save their ailing industry. They used Karlheinz Schreiber as their middleman, paying him more than $20 million to pay whoever he needed in order to make the deal happen. And if that meant corrupting Canadian politics in the process, so be it. Their strategy worked. Airbus not only survived, it has rivalled Boeing as the world's top aircraft manufacturer. Yet not once through the fifteen years of crisis and scandal had they ever been made to account for their actions. Jean Pierson, the president, who dealt directly with Schreiber, is now retired and refusing calls. Stuart Iddles, Airbus's former vice-president of marketing, who was allegedly designated the code name "Stewardess" in Schreiber's bank records, continues to split his time between Mexico and Spain. In the 1980s Iddles worked closely with Frank Moores, Schreiber, Marc Lalonde and Pierre Jeanniot to make sure the Airbus sale happened. In one way or another, all of those men have faced serious scrutiny in the aftermath of the Airbus sale. Yet Iddles and his colleagues at Airbus had never faced the same serious scrutiny.

Which brings me to the last time I ever saw Karlheinz Schreiber, at Vaticano restaurant in Yorkville on June 24, 2009. We all suspected that Schreiber's extradition, having been delayed another two years so he could testify at the Oliphant Commission, was probably imminent. But we didn't talk much about that. Schreiber wanted to show me a copy of an email he had recently received from Stuart Iddles, who had seen our last Airbus documentary, "The Elephant in the Room." Iddles had wanted to tell Schreiber he quite liked it. But it's how he ended his email that struck me most, as if oblivious to Karlheinz Schreiber's impending doom, and yet a reflection of how well life had gone for him, and for Airbus, since they first signed that agreement with International Aircraft Leasing in 1985. Iddles had written, simply:

"Keep smiling!"

I would be smiling too, if I were Stuart Iddles.

Epilogue

It is Sunday August 3, 2009, and I am in Kitzingen, Germany. It is a picturesque town on the edge of the Main River in Franconia. A small bridge takes you into the heart of the town, with cobblestone streets and pedestrian walkways. My wife, Isabella, grew up here; we are visiting her family.[1] I am typing on my laptop on the patio, just outside the front door. Her father, Reinhard Kempf, passes me a plate of freshly picked tomatoes. I met Isabella in Zurich while filming "Mulroney: The Unauthorized Chapter." Our daughter, Madison, now thirteen months old, is playing inside. It is nearly 2 p.m. I have to make a phone call. Karlheinz Schreiber is still in Canada, but for how long? He has been told to surrender to the Metro West Detention Centre by 5 p.m. that day, Toronto time. I reach him at his house in Rockliffe Park.

"You are up early, Harvey," Schreiber remarks. I tell him I am in Germany, so it is actually the early afternoon. "Oh, you are with Isabella!" he says.

After a little more small talk, he tells me Eddie Greenspan will try to launch another emergency appeal on Sunday. He tells me he will drive to Toronto later that morning but says Bärbel will stay behind at their town

---

[1] Isabella and I were married in Janurary 2009.

home in Rockliffe. His lawyer does, in fact, manage to get an Ontario court judge to hold an emergency session on the Sunday of a long weekend. But it doesn't work. That night RCMP officers come to the detention centre to collect him. This time there is no rabbit that Schreiber can pull out of a hat. The Mounties drive him to the airport and put him on the evening Air Canada flight to Munich. When the plane lands the following morning, German authorities will take their prisoner to Augsburg, forty-five minutes outside of Munich.

The German prosecutors had filed for Schreiber's extradition from Canada in 1999. Ten years later he is on his way home. But not to a home-coming.

"How far is it to Augsburg from Kitzingen?" I ask Isabella.

"Less than two hours."

The next day I am driving down the autobahn at 170 kilometres an hour. I turn on the radio. I can't speak much German but I keep hearing the name "Karlheinz Schreiber." I make my way to a press conference where the chief prosecutor, Reinhard Nemetz, will be speaking. The room is crowded. There must be sixty journalists and camerapersons in the room. Schreiber's arrival in Germany is front-page news in every paper. He's on all the TV stations. The entire press conference is in German. I can't understand a thing.

I shout a question in English.

"What do you say about how long it took?"

Nemetz looks up. Does he remember me from when I spoke to him ten years ago?

"Too long," he says. "Too long."

"Why do you think it took so long?" I asked.

"Ask your Canadian officials, please."

When it is all over I get back in my rental and type the address of the prison into the car's GPS device. I end up in a downtown street. I see the high, concrete walls, the barbed wire and the surveillance cameras. Schreiber, I know, is on the other side of the wall. I can't get in to see him; only two visitors are allowed per month.

The next morning I go back to the courthouse, where Schreiber will be charged with bribery, fraud and tax evasion. Reporters are not allowed into the courtroom; we do not even get a glimpse of him through the glass doors.

I get back in the rental car and head to Kitzingen where Madison and Isabella are waiting. In a few weeks we will be back in Toronto with the boys, Massey and Jeremiah.

The Airbus story has been part of my life since 1994.

But this time, I believe, it really is over.

Postscript

On Monday, January 18, 2010, Karlheinz Schreiber's trial began in a courtroom Augsburg, Germany. His lawyer, Jan Olaf Leisner, argued that his client was not guilty on all charges of tax evasion, breach of trust, and accessory to fraud. (There was still some debate about whether the bribery charge would remain: no one seemed to know for sure if the statute of limitations had taken effect.) Reports out of Germany suggested that, if convicted on all charges, Schreiber could face up to ten years in prison.

Schreiber came out swinging; his lawyer argued that the German government had, a long time ago, been involved in the very deals for which Schreiber was now on trial. "The tone was set by high-ranking politicians," Leisner said, as if to suggest that Germany itself had condoned Schreiber's past conduct. He had a point. Schreiber was, after all, only a middleman. The German government had indeed installed Schreiber as a secretive go-between to facilitate the flow of *schmiergelder*.

Schreiber's trial had been expected to last until the end of May and would hear testimony from dozens of witnesses who were, back in the 1980s, powerful men from the business community and politics. The opening days of the trial generated some colourful headlines but, even in Germany it was appearing that the story was becoming old. It was possible Schreiber—the consummate poker player—would have an ace up his sleeve—a startling revelation sensational and important enough to bring the story back to center stage. Maybe. But probably only for a moment.

Less and less the image of the rich and powerful player, Schreiber now appeared tired and beaten. His story less a shocking expose than a small—perhaps soon to be forgotten—footnote to history.

While Schreiber awaited his fate in a German courtroom in the spring of 2010, former prime minister Brian Mulroney was *still* waiting for the Oliphant Commission to issue its final report. In November 2009, Canadians were told that the commission would not make its December 31 deadline. The delay, according to commission spokesperson Barry McLoughlin, was due largely to "extensive analysis" of the more than 150,000 pages of documents filed with the commission. It was promised the report probing the business relationship between the former prime minister and the middleman would be released on May 31, 2010—just about the time the Schreiber trial was expected to wrap up.

Perhaps it was fitting that the story would come to a close at roughly the same time in both Germany and Canada. And perhaps, at the end of the day, there will be some important lessons learned in both countries about how to improve the strength of their democratic institutions.

Or, perhaps not.

Acknowledgments

In the winter of 2009 my daughter and wife and I were out for a walk along Danforth Avenue in Toronto's Greek district when we bumped into Phil Mathias, a former writer for the *National Post*, who you will have met in these pages. There had been some friction between Phil and I over the years, but that was all in the past.

I told him that I was planning to write a book about my investigation into former prime minister Brian Mulroney, middleman Karlheinz Schreiber and Airbus.

"Do you think anyone will read it?" he asked.

I sure hoped so.

"I know one thing," I said. "I have to write it."

It was true. For many reasons, I *had* to write this story: for history, yes, but also for my children, and, perhaps most of all, for me. Writing the book was cathartic. Occasionally, as I reread old notes and documented what happened—and with a perspective that only time can bring—I learned some uncomfortable truths about myself. Most of all I believe I have charted uncomfortable truths about the way the media, politics and power works in this country.

Or perhaps how power *worked* in this country. In late December 2009, the Supreme Court of Canada made a ruling that provided the media with what is being called the defence of "responsible communication" in libel and defamation lawsuits. As long as journalists are being responsible, and fair, they should not be expected to know the complete story at the time of their first publication or first broadcast, the court decided. Reporters should be allowed to discuss controversial topics in the public interest— as a means to an end of arriving at the truth. I point this out because so much of the powerful, sometimes institutional, bullying that you have read about in this book happened in an environment of extreme "libel chill." Reporters and media outlets were, in many instances, afraid to report on the story for fear of joining the group of us who had already been sued for tens of millions. It remains to be seen how the ruling will work in practice, but it seems as if the high court has come down squarely on the side of the public's right to know.

It has been a long journey from the day I began looking into the Airbus story in the fall of 1994, but the journey was not a solitary one, nor was it exclusively my journey. There are many people responsible for making the story happen and I must start with many of my colleagues at CBC's *the fifth estate*. They are: Alex Powell, Suzanna Mayer, Susan Teskey, Sally Reardon, Jock Ferguson, Kit Melamed, Jennifer Fowler, Sheila Pin, Howard Goldenthal, Colin Allison, Declan Hill, Virginia Smart, Brigitte Thompson, Liz Roche, Gary Akenhead, Avi Lev, Joe Passaretti, Timothy Sawa, Paul Seeler, Hans Vanderzande, John Griffin, Jim Williamson, John Badcock, Diana Redegeld, Eleanor Besly, Anita Mielewczyk, Oleh Rumak, Deborah Carter, Leslie Morrison, Jim Bertin, Alister Bell, Mike Savoie, Tim Kindrachuk, Scott Anderson, David Kaufman, Trish Wood and the late Eric Malling. Linden MacIntyre, who was always able to raise our investigative documentariess to something far more than the sum of its parts, deserves special mention, as does David Studer, our executive producer, who demonstrated true courage as he fought off our detractors and allowed us to keep at the story.

At CBC News I thank Sheila Mandel, Neil Macdonald, John Gushue, Tyana Grundig, Cecil Rosner, Paul Hunter, Rosemary Barton, Don Newman, Brian Stewart, Jamie Purdon and Peter Mansbridge. In CBC management I thank a succession of people: Sig Gerber, Bob Culbert, Jim Byrd, Tony Burman, John Cruickshank and Jennifer McGuire. I cannot say enough about CBC's legal counsel Daniel Henry, who helped us find a way of getting our stories to air when other lawyers might have buckled.

In Germany, I owe my gratitude to Mathias von Blumencron, Conny Neumann, Hans Leyendecker, Michael Stiller and my investigative partner of many years, John Goetz. A small group of people read some of my initial drafts and provided the right mix of helpful comments and positive feedback: Wayne Chong, Jack Campbell, and my brother, Ben Cashore, who kept telling me that if this was a book about American politics "you would be a millionaire." Ben was an inspiration, if also an exaggerator. Nathan Crocker organized my files, did extra research, smiling cheerfully the entire time. Thanks to another inspiration, Randy Katz.

My colleagues outside the CBC deserve special mention too: David Walmsley, Eddie Greenspon, Rick Salutin, Linda McQuaig, Norman Spector and Andrew Coyne, who helped keep the story alive during the lean years. William Kaplan brought me back into the story at a time when I thought I had left it behind. For that, I remain eternally indebted. I thank him also for his advice and friendship. I must single out Greg McArthur as a brilliant investigative journalist who had already accomplished more in his twenties than others might in a lifetime.

My 6 a.m. running partners, Danny Loucaides and David Harriss-Smith, deserve thanks for me keeping fit and sane during the process. In Germany I thank my new extended family, for making meals, the fresh tomatoes, and otherwise helping out while I typed at patios and cafés while supposedly on holiday in Franconia: Reinhard Kempf, Hilde Kohl, Joachim and Silja Rieger. Thanks also to my parents, John and Sharon Cashore.

Thanks to my agent, Ashton Westwood, at Creative Artists. Key Porter Books took on this project when no one else would; I hope their decision pays dividends. I thank copy editor Liba Berry for her attention to detail, and for her colourful comments that popped up in a yellow bubble on my computer screen as I read her corrections. Executive Editor Jonathan Schmidt deserves a medal for taking a deep breath after receiving a rather lengthy first manuscript then patiently telling me how and where to cut. For his editorial judgments I will be eternally grateful. The manuscript is far better off thanks to his efforts.

My immediate family has taught me that family matters most. To my children, Massey, Jeremiah and Madison: you have brought me more joy than a parent could ask. To my wife Isabella, I thank you for coming into my life—and for putting up with the last year as I wrote the book. I know it hasn't been easy. In the immortal words of the Weakerthans, "I know you might roll your eyes at this, but I'm so glad that you exist."

Index